DEADLY MONOPOLIES

Also by Harriet A. Washington

Medical Apartheid: The Dark History of Medical Experimentation on Black Americans from Colonial Times to the Present

Living Healthy with Hepatitis C: Natural and Conventional Approaches to Recovering Your Quality of Life

DEADLY MONOPOLIES

**The Shocking Corporate Takeover
of Life Itself—and the Consequences
for Your Health and Our Medical Future**

HARRIET A. WASHINGTON

DOUBLEDAY

New York London Toronto

Sydney Auckland

All rights reserved. Published in the United States by Doubleday,
a division of Random House, Inc., New York, and in Canada
by Random House of Canada Limited, Toronto.

www.doubleday.com

DOUBLEDAY and the portrayal of an anchor with a dolphin
are registered trademarks of Random House, Inc.

Jacket design by Emily Mahon
Jacket illustration © Thomas Collins / Getty Images

Library of Congress Cataloging-in-Publication Data
Washington, Harriet A.
Deadly monopolies : the shocking corporate takeover
of life itself—and the consequences for your health and
our medical future. / Harriet A. Washington.—1st ed.
p. cm.
Includes bibliographical references and index.
Summary: "An in-depth exploration of the way the pharmaceutical
industry is manipulating us and our world"—Provided by publisher.
1. Drugs—Marketing—Moral and ethical aspects.
2. Pharmaceutical industry—Economic aspects.   I. Title.
[DNLM: 1. Drug Industry—ethics.   2. Patents as Topic—
ethics.   3. Drug Industry—economics. QV 736]
HD9665.5.W37 2011
338.4'76151—dc23
2011013033

ISBN 978-0-385-52892-4

PRINTED IN THE UNITED STATES OF AMERICA

10 9 8 7 6 5 4 3 2 1

First Edition

For Corene Marie Washington and
Percy Cecil Washington Sr., my parents

This is the patent-age of new inventions
For killing bodies, and for saving souls,
All propagated with the best intentions.

—LORD BYRON, *Don Juan*

CONTENTS

DEADLY MONOPOLIES

INTRODUCTION
Patents, Profits, and the High Cost of Living

The past is a foreign country: they do things differently there.

—L. P. HARTLEY, *THE GO-BETWEEN*

In the wee small hours of a perfect May night, I made my way home from the high-school graduation party of a close friend's granddaughter. Then, blissfully wilted from a night of champagne, dancing, and laughter, I sprawled in the backseat of the cab to check my BlackBerry and was rewarded by a flurry of congratulatory messages from my writers' group, all directed at Katherine Russell Rich, whose riveting book *Dreaming in Hindi* had just been published to worshipful reviews and radiant profiles in the *New York Times*, auguring certain literary success. This would have been a thrilling achievement for anyone, but it is an especially joyous triumph for Kathy, who, just a few years earlier, had cheated death via a harrowing bone-marrow transplant.

As I exited the cab, I mused that thriving, not just surviving, after breast cancer is a modern miracle. For that matter, so is living long enough to watch your grandchildren grow up. We are living lives that have been extended and transformed by medical research.

But, as pharmaceutical companies constantly remind us, these modern miracles are also modern luxuries, and they have not come cheap. Drug companies miss no opportunity to remind us that ours is money well spent, pointing out that by quelling major killers, by controlling infectious disease, and by providing the eternal vigilance of monitoring tests, modern biotechnological research has bestowed upon us more than decades of healthy life—it has also changed those lives.

Illnesses like polio, mumps, measles, diphtheria, and whooping cough used to fill parents with dread and carry off our children with regularity, but today even doctors have forgotten what they look like. We have swept polio and smallpox from the medical landscape, at least in Western industrialized nations. We have tamed, if not conquered, tuberculosis and syphilis while developing treatments that save the lives of most who suffer from childhood leukemia and testicular cancer. The discovery and refinement of insulin has transformed diabetes from a fatal mystery into an utterly controllable disorder. Drugs have tempered HIV from a feared scourge into a controlled virus, at least in the affluent West, and have reduced a constellation of other ailments from killers to annoyances.

Aging has been transformed as well. New knees, new hips, new hearts, newly sculpted eyes, and bodies and bones shored up by osteoporosis prophylaxis have enabled vigorous new adventures and careers that begin at sixty, an age most of us didn't even reach a century ago. Before 1900, U.S. life expectancy was only 49.2 years.

Pharmaceutical companies take credit for these advances by claiming a single-minded pursuit of human health and happiness. "Life is our life's work," Pfizer declared for years, before replacing this with "Pfizer. Working for a healthier world." Sanofi-Aventis exists "Because health matters." GlaxoSmithKline's mission? "Do more, feel better, live longer." Merck is "Where patients come first," and Germany's Schering declares that it is "Making medicine work," while Poland's Polpharma consists of "People helping people." Seemingly, these companies have no thought except for our better health and greater happiness.

The Great Leap Forward

But their research laboratories forge their miracles at great costs, which separate many of us in the United States and abroad from the medicines and medical care that we need. The price we pay is not only economic but also cultural: as *Deadly Monopolies* will reveal, medical culture itself has been transformed in the upheaval of the last thirty-plus years, as the university has been made into a partner of, or even an arm of, for-profit corporate entities. Unaffordable medications are merely the tip of this iceberg.

To understand what these costs are and why they have burgeoned, this book begins by revisiting the pivotal year 1980, when the Government Patent Policy Act, commonly known as the Bayh-Dole Act, catalyzed a proliferation of arrangements between universities, researchers, and private U.S. biotechnology companies. Now universities sell and license patents developed with taxpayer dollars to privately held firms, including biotechnology and pharmaceutical companies, which underwrite the cost of drug research and development.[1]

Another paradigm-shifting legal decision fed the proliferation of these biotechnology firms and pharmaceutical companies. In June 1980, the Supreme Court decided, in a 5–4 vote, to officially permit the patenting of living things, ruling in *Diamond v. Chakrabarty* that Dr. Ananda M. Chakrabarty's "oil-eating" bacterium was not a product of nature, but rather a man-made invention that deserved patent protection.[2] Life joined university patents on the auction block, and living entities were now viewed as patentable commodities.

What resulted from this newly cozy relationship between the university and industry, and from the newfound ability to patent living tissues, animals, bacteria, viruses, and even—especially—genes? As we will see, there were many and varied consequences, some of them unintended. We'll examine the case of the surveyor John Moore, who discovered that his doctor had patented the unusual products of his oversized spleen, built a lab to commercially exploit them in partnership with Sandoz, and then concealed these acts from him. Moore was first in a long line of people who have lost control of their own tissues and body parts as the courts consistently ruled against them and for university and corporate patent holders.

Deadly Monopolies lays out the malign consequences of these developments in detail. Researchers who had habitually valued collaboration and sharing of data found that such collegial warmth threatened the exclusivity upon which the patent applications were based. Now such behavior is considered risky or worse: researchers have even been jailed on suspicion of sharing information with the wrong scientists. In an attempt to maximize patent profits, a zeal for devising derivative "copycat" or "me too" drugs instead of truly novel medications has come to dominate the medical-research landscape. The processes of medical research and publication have been distorted by the corporate agenda as pharmaceutical companies instruct researchers to withhold damaging data from studies and hire ghostwriters to package their marketing messages as scientific studies. With their eye on the bottom line, pharmaceutical companies even fund and oversee studies whose goal is to directly increase sales rather than to generate reliable scientific data.

Drug prices have soared as for-profit companies have assumed the direction of much medical research and have tended to place patent protection and profits above patient welfare. Companies and their university partners have even thwarted the work of some medical researchers, who have been forced to stop studies of needed medications because companies feared they would not be profitable enough or become the next billion-dollar blockbuster.

As profit potential has come to rule the research agenda, medications for common but relatively trivial ailments such as gastric distress and erectile dysfunction continue apace, but the killers that decimate poor developing nations—such as tuberculosis, cholera, and malaria—go largely ignored. As we'll learn, pharmaceutical makers slight the medical issues of the Third World, even as its populations constitute huge pools of laboratory subjects who save the corporate-university research consortium a great deal of money and time. U.S. medical research is exported to poor developing nations in India, Africa, and even Eastern Europe, where research is completed far more rapidly and cheaply than it could be in the United States, amid practices and risks that American citizens are not asked to accept.

Corporations, notably pharmaceutical companies, now work closely with universities and their researchers in order to stimulate research, innovation, and profitability. But we'll examine the deep inequalities of this alliance, with corporations holding the purse strings after a patentable entity has been developed, often with federal funds. The company that pays for R&D chooses which university's and scientists' candidate treatments to support, which to ignore, and which to abandon. Thus the legislative movement of the 1980s has created a medical-industrial complex that eventually robbed universities of their independence and seized control of medication design, costs, and even its evaluation in medical journals. This marriage, coupled with an American penchant for patenting an ever-wider range of living things, has not encouraged the production of important new cures, but rather has stymied it. The easy maximization of patent profits, not the arduous production of new drugs, has become the new corporate focus.

We'll also examine the cultural revolution in medical research. Before the sea change of 1980, most twentieth-century medical researchers tended not to work for corporations but for universities or sometimes for private research organizations, including their own. Thus scientists were insulated from the commercial zeal of corporations. Scientists did seek recognition for their work, but their energies were more focused on reaping the honors of fame, influence, and academic advancement, along with the glowing satisfactions of altruism and being hailed as benefactors.

In the thirty years since Bayh-Dole, however, medical-research culture has been rendered unrecognizable to those raised in an earlier, less venal culture. The laws that fostered corporate-university partnerships in 1980 blurred the line between the two, and now the university has lost pivotal values that protected the public's interests because they interfere with the profitability at the core of corporate missions.[3]

The Cost of Innovation

Valuable patents have been granted for living organisms, genes, biological processes, medically important animals, and even for human embryos. We'll see how this expansion of patentability was sold to the American public as a strategy to stimulate creativity, to reward ingenuity, and to spark the development of important new therapies. Some hail this post-1980 medical-research paradigm shift as an unquestioned success, pointing to the more than five thousand biotechnology and other companies, based on university research, that have generated more than 2,500 patents since 1980.

But we'll also see how, from the perspective of the medical consumer, medical innovation based on widely commercialized patents has raised prices, limited access to medicines, catalyzed the conscription of tissues, and has been associated with harmful effects of expensive new medications, many of which are withdrawn from the markets within a few years of FDA approval. By quelling competition, our monopolistic research models retard the development of important new diagnostic tests and medicines.

The medicines that do emerge from laboratories are expensive, and the pharmaceutical industry is quick to justify the sticker shock. For each experimental modality that reaches drugstore shelves, we are told, many others fall by the wayside after years of very expensive research and tests. As a result, the firms say, research and development today causes the cost of each new medication to soar from $800 million to as high as *two billion dollars*—and beyond. This stratospheric cost, the industry assures us, explains why medications are so expensive: the companies must recoup the costs of R&D while they cover the costs of the many experimental treatments that fail to attain perfection and approval. To paraphrase a quote often attributed to the late Senator Everett Dirksen, "$800 million here, $800 million there, pretty soon you're talking about real money." During the twenty years that a patent gives a company to profit from exclusive sales of the medication it developed, the industry claims, it must charge a price high enough to support the wider expense of saving our health.

Glaring inaccuracies cripple these arguments, most notably that the $800 million to $2 billion estimate for each new medication is wildly inflated, as I explain in Chapter 2. The high prices reflect not a need to recoup R&D costs, but the drive to shore up mammoth wealth for the $310 billion pharmaceutical industry, which was until 2006 the most profitable industry on the globe. (It has since slipped to the number-three spot, behind network and other communications equipment, and internet services and retailing.)[4]

Deadly Monopolies explains why most expensive "new" drugs touted by the pharmaceutical manufacturers and approved by a cooperative FDA are not new at all, but "copycat" versions of older drugs that are often not only cheaper but also safer. The industry has been getting away with a staggeringly high markup on today's duplicates of yesterday's medical miracles.

Cui Bono?

Experts in intellectual-property law disagree about the degree to which patents stymie innovation, raise prices, and discourage the production of new cures. These experts also disagree about what should be done. Should life and medication patents be done away with in some arenas? Should they be more strictly regulated, less strictly regulated, or should we adopt some new, more equitable model for rewarding drug innovation? I am indebted to a number of intellectual-property experts on every side of the issue for generously helping me illuminate these problems, as I survey the effects of patent laws and policies on everyday people and ask, *cui bono*—who benefits?

Do current laws and policies on treatment and research benefit only pharmaceutical firms at the expense of the everyday people who serve as consumers and research subjects? Are governments and agencies such as the FDA also responsible for such inequities, and to what extent? This book examines everything from the testing of patients without informed consent to the shadowy appropriation and marketing of Americans' tissues to the biocolonialism that governs the appropriation of everything from seeds and plants to genes from poor people in the developing world. Many of these issues have lurked below the ethical and media radar or are not usually considered in the light of pharmaceutical economics.

Pharmaceutical companies have always been faced with the perhaps insurmountable challenge of serving both medicine and Mammon—an inevitable tension in a capitalist economy. But the marriage of corporations and academia subjected the university medical centers, publicly supported and with a very different agenda, to the same pressures. Within these pages, I explore what happens when formerly public institutions and advocates become minions of Big Pharma. I do so through the personal experiences of patients, research subjects, and even of researchers whose tugs-of-war over patents have landed them in jail, or who may have spent decades on a promising drug only to have a pharmaceutical company pull the plug over fears of market competition.

I detail how unwitting tissue "donors" such as Henrietta Lacks and John Moore lost control of their bodies when their tissues were appropriated and exploited for profit by the physician-researchers to whom they entrusted their medical care. Their betrayal has been compounded by a string of rulings in which the U.S. courts proved unsympathetic to Americans' claims to their own body parts—but honored the claims of medical researchers to these same tissues. What role does the patent rush and the post-1980 university-corporation partnerships that catalyzed it play in today's transformed research landscape? Almost none of us possess the unusually valuable and unique tissue of Lacks and Moore, but as we'll see, value today lies in harvesting large numbers of healthy normal tissues, so we are all at risk of the type of nonconsensual appropriation that befell them. For example, at some hospitals, surgery patients are routinely asked and sometimes required to surrender the right to their excised cells, blood, and tissues before undergoing the procedures they need.

Global Concerns, Heightened Risks

The devastation that medical monopolies have visited upon Westerners has a face, and that face does not differ much from you the reader: it cuts a swath across nationality, economic status, race, gender, and sometimes even class.

But most people in the developing world lack the health-care infrastructure and drug availability that we enjoy, so they experience medical damages at a heightened level. New cures are often generated from biologicals found among poor native peoples and are often tested in Third World clinics. But once perfected, these medications tend to be priced out of the reach of the communities that made them possible.

We shall see how often sick, medically desperate people of the Third World are used as the laboratory subjects of the West as pharmaceutical companies impose on them all the risks of medical research but withhold the benefits of the approved medications. I'll describe how the children of Kano, Nigeria, were victimized when Pfizer descended in the midst of a meningitis epidemic to test its newly patented but unapproved remedy—without, by many doctors' accounts, informed consent. Pfizer left in its wake dead and injured children, lost records, outraged local physicians, and mourning parents who stormed courts on two continents to seek justice for their children who were sacrificed on the altar of an unapproved drug.

And why are tuberculosis, smallpox, and polio conquered only in the affluent West? In poor developing nations, these scourges are still untamed because their people lack money for vaccines and medications. Why are important diseases that strike poor people abroad (and sometimes here as well) so devoid of attention and resources that they are called "orphan diseases"? Because it is well known that no pharmaceutical company will take them on. Most of these diseases, such as malaria and African sleeping sickness, predominantly strike the developing world. The biological and pharmaceutical patents did not create this situation, but their wide deployment and other forms of medical monopolies have escalated it dramatically. In *Deadly Monopolies*, I describe how this escalation has come about.

Leaving aside for the moment the moral unacceptability of withholding medicine from poor people in order to maximize profits for one of the world's most profitable industries, we must consider the global extent of drug makers' control over our medical fates.

Most discussions treat Third World medical-access issues as if they were completely separate from those of developed nations, but I will argue that we in the United States share with them a common vulnerability at the hands of drug makers. I would not trivialize the suffering of the Third World by suggesting that our problems in the West are comparable to theirs in degree: this is why I devote separate chapters to their medical treatment at the hands of the pharmaceutical industry. But our medical interdependence has a common cause that may share common solutions.

E. Richard Gold, a professor of intellectual property at McGill University, validated this view when he commented on "Toward a New Era of Intellectual Property: From Confrontation to Negotiation," a report published by his International Expert Group: "We found the same stumbling blocks in the traditional communities of Brazil as we did in the boardroom of a corporation that holds the patent to a gene that can determine the chance a woman will develop breast cancer."[5]

The Pending Reformation

Many economists, activists, patient-consumers, and scientists have decided that our monopolistic medical model is doing more harm than good. Already the first successful shot across the bow has been fired, by a coalition whose lawsuit effected the repeal of seven patents on the BRCA1 and BRCA2 breast cancer genes held by Myriad Genetics. Their patents made genetic testing painfully expensive and blocked access to other tests. In January 2005, the European Patent Office had also rejected the essential points of BRCA1 gene patents. In July 2011, as this book went to press, the U.S. Court of Appeals for the Federal Circuit restored most of these patents on appeal,[6] but future appeals will probably reach the Supreme Court. Which culture's model will triumph? That of the patent-hungry United States or of the relatively parent-wary Europe? As we will see, the U.S. courts may be adopting a more European point of view because both the Obama administration and thousands of geneticists and other scientists support this lawsuit to bring down gene patents.

Breast cancer is only one of the many diseases with a prominent genetic component whose detection, treatment, and cure may be stymied, not abetted, by the drug industry's myopic focus on protecting their patent profits. *Deadly Monopolies* explores ethical and therapeutic questions as it traces the growing dissent from the corporate "ownership" of human genes.

Gene patents are only the beginning. Increasingly, legal experts, medical leaders, lawmakers, and outraged citizens are calling for patent restraint in all quarters. Outright rebellions against life patents in the form of editorials, proposed laws, lawsuits, and political lobbying have begun to emanate from around the globe as scientists and advocates realize that monopolies on life threaten rather than serve public health, human freedom, and dignity.

Medical researchers, economists, and philanthropists have also joined to create imaginative models that provide wider access to drugs and preserve patent profits without exploitation. They dream of a world where access to medical miracles is not limited by accidents of birth, money, or land of origin: not a world devoid of corporate profits, but a world no longer in thrall to them. A world where lives depend not upon a patent but upon a passion for healing.

My friend Kathy shares this global vision in *Dreaming in Hindi*, her poignant memoir of traveling in India with stage IV breast cancer. Her wrenching realization that poor women in remote Indian villages have no access to mammography or standard chemotherapy, to say nothing of $3,400 gene tests or $25,000 bone-marrow transplants, forces her—and us—to confront the naked truth about medical monopolies, the profit motive, and the merciless geography of survival reflected in the eyes of a lone dying woman.

At a time when unemployment, the lack of adequate insurance, and a simple inability to afford medications are common burdens, even in the affluent United States, that woman could be any of us. This may be the best argument for restoring the patient, not the patent, to the center of the medical-research universe.

CHAPTER 1

A NEW LEASE ON LIFE

The Patent in American Medical Culture

How does it feel to be patented? There was a sense of betrayal. I mean, they owned a part of me that I could never recover. I certainly have no objection to scientific research . . . but it was like a rape. In a sense, you've been violated, for dollars. My genetic essence is held captive.

—JOHN MOORE, THE SUBJECT OF U.S. PATENT NO. 4,438,032

In 1982, the mother of Japanese biotechnology scientist Dr. Heideaki Hagiwara was suffering from cervical cancer.[1] When he learned that Dr. Ivor Royston at the University of California at San Diego was developing cell lines to treat cancer, he asked to join the laboratory and, once there, convinced Royston to use tumor cells from Hagiwara's mother's lymphatic system to create a therapeutic cell line.

A cell line is a community of cells, usually animal or human, that grows continuously in the laboratory, proliferating indefinitely under glass in precise, artificially maintained conditions, where it is used in research. In a warm living body, with its genius for homeostasis, every cell receives ample oxygen and nutrients in a dynamic environment tailored to its needs. But cells exiled to the cold, sterile prisons of unresponsive glassware tend to die quickly without the most assiduous coddling, although cancer cells live somewhat longer. Cell culture is the meticulous process by which optimal temperature, gas concentrations, and nutrients, which vary with the type of cell being cultured, are maintained, often with great difficulty.

Carefully tended cell cultures boost medical research by providing living human material for risk-free testing of the effectiveness and safety of drugs. But cell cultures can also host viruses and other pathogens, permitting them to be prepared in quantity for the manufacture of vaccines. Polio, measles, mumps, rubella, and chickenpox viruses are currently produced in cell cultures. In the early twentieth century, Ross Granville Harrison of Johns Hopkins University established the technique of maintaining cells in vitro and dubbed it tissue culture.[2] Because cancer cell lines are somewhat more long-lived than those of "normal" human cells, many extant cell lines are derived from cancers. By the mid-1900s, cell cultures were commonly used in laboratories.[3]

Some cell lines retain the characteristics of and produce substances that are peculiar to their cells of origin. Royston was working on a cell line that he hoped would treat cancers by producing antibodies that attack cancer cells. Hagiwara suggested that he use lymph cells from his sick mother, and Royston did so, fusing Hagiwara's mother's cells to the line. UCSD researchers soon agreed that this particular cell line possessed unique cancer-fighting properties, so Royston patented the promising cells. Hagiwara then returned to Japan, surreptitiously taking with him a sample of the cell line, which he used to treat his mother, who rallied but ultimately succumbed to her cancer.

Months later, Hagiwara gave the cell line to his father, Dr. Yoshide Hagiwara, who was also a biomedical researcher, for use in the family firm, the Hagiwara Institute of Health in Osaka. He claimed patent rights to the cell line and the antibodies it produced because it emanated from his mother's body, entitling his family, he said, to a financial interest in the cell lines. The U.S. Office of Technology Assessment disagreed and sued Hagiwara fils for taking the patented cells without permission.[4] Hagiwara argued that despite the UCSD patent, the fact that the cell line had originated with his mother's tissues gave his family rights to the cells as well.

Hagiwara won these rights in a 1983 settlement with the university that gave the Hagiwaras the sole license to the patent throughout Asia.[5] Patented entities can be licensed in an exclusive or a nonexclusive manner, and they can be licensed for specific geographic regions, and even for specific uses.[6] In this case, the Hagiwaras' agreement with UCSD permitted them to use the line in research, but not to license it commercially elsewhere.

Twenty years later, another family affair was handled quite differently when FBI agents tracked down, arrested, and jailed Dr. Jiangyu Zhu, thirty, of China and Dr. Kayoko Kimbara, thirty-two, of Japan on June 19, 2002, in La Jolla, California.

The married couple were former fellows of Harvard Medical School who had resigned to pursue new research positions. But their time at Harvard had been very fruitful: from November 1998 through September 1999, Kimbara identified two genes that block the action of calcineurin, an enzyme that signals the immune system to reject transplanted organs. This was a potentially lucrative discovery that could transform organ transplantation by leading to immunosuppressive drugs, medicines that drastically lower the risks of organ rejection. It also was a potential treatment for several diseases that affect the cardiovascular, immune, and nervous systems, which multiplied its commercial potential. Then, on October 22, 1999, Harvard filed a provisional patent on the two genes and their products.

On December 13, 1999, Zhu and Kimbara accepted university research positions at the Institute of Biotechnology at the University of Texas, San Antonio, and when they left Harvard, they took some materials and notes with them, as researchers are wont to do. They were to begin on January 15, and by early January 2000 they shipped some additional materials from Harvard to their new lab.

But the university's complaint says that in direct violation of the participation agreement signed by both Zhu and Kimbara, Zhu emailed Medical and Biological Laboratories of Nagoya, a biochemical company in Japan,[7] indicating that he intended to collaborate with a researcher there to commercialize the antibodies suggested by his Harvard gene research after he left Boston. Harvard says that Zhu also sent three other genes to Japan without its knowledge.

Harvard officials angrily accused Zhu and Kimbara of violating the terms of their agreement by sneaking into the lab in the wee hours to remove contested material, and of lying about having done so. The duo denied this, and the facts were never established in court. But according to the university's complaint, the Japanese company did succeed in producing antibodies against two of the three genes and then shipped them to Zhu at the University of Texas, where he now ran his own lab.

Removing materials is not a crime and is certainly not prosecuted unless the materials are alleged to be the property of the university, not the researcher. Even removing university property is acceptable if the amounts are not excessive and the researcher has appropriate permission. If the accusations of having lied about the removal of large quantities of university property are true, the couple become less sympathetic.

But it is important to evaluate such actions in the context of research culture: researchers typically remove materials from their laboratories when they leave for other institutions and sometimes do not ask permission to do so. There is no question that Heideaki Hagiwara, for example, had violated the spirit and the letter of the agreements he signed, yet he and UCSD were able to come to an amicable arrangement that recognized his contribution and shared the rights in the contested cell line. Therefore, many in the research community felt that Harvard overreacted when the university decided to play hardball.

Moreover, given that they were sued by Harvard, an academic behemoth of sterling reputation, it is also easy to overlook that Zhu and Kimbara steadfastly denied having taken disputed materials with them and that Harvard's very public accusations of theft were never publicly backed up with copies of agreements or evidence of wrongdoing.

The school brought criminal charges, and the two were charged with conspiracy, theft, theft of trade secrets, and (since they had left Texas and were now ensconced in new labs in San Diego) interstate transportation of stolen property.[8] The case was investigated by the Federal Bureau of Investigation in New England.

The Department of Justice press release, titled "Pair Charged with Theft of Trade Secrets from Harvard Medical School," focused on the fear of corporate competition, speculating that the two shared an "intention of profiting from such information by collaborating with a Japanese company in the creation and sale of related and derivative products."

Because any attempt to develop drugs from the pair's Harvard discovery threatened Harvard's own ability to patent calcineurin and sell the rights to a biotechnology company or corporation, this was a turf battle between Harvard and Medical and Biological Laboratories as well as between it and its erstwhile fellows. Unlike UCSD, Harvard did not seem inclined to share patent rights with the Japanese firm. The school and the FBI's public statements, however, focused on Zhu and Kimbara.

"Prosecuting people who steal the intellectual property of individuals and institutions is a very high priority for the Department of Justice," declared U.S. attorney Michael J. Sullivan. "Congress has enacted a series of laws to assure that innovators get credit for their inventions and if people steal the ideas that belong to someone else and try to use those ideas for their own economic benefit, they will be prosecuted. Protecting cutting-edge ideas is crucial to the creation of new products and our economy as a whole."

Discovering the genes was Kimbara's achievement, but the patent "ownership" was governed by her signed agreement with the school, which was never made public. As a research fellow at Harvard Medical School myself, I was required to sign an agreement ceding patent rights for any discovery to the "President and Fellows of Harvard College," but this was years after the Zhu-Kimbara incident and may not reflect agreements they made. I can't help reflecting that the oft-voiced virtue of the patent as a means of protecting the rights of "innovators" sounds ironic considering that Kimbara, who discovered the gene, was being assailed for exercising her rights to it.

In fact, the only rights that immediately accrued to the duo were the Miranda rights read to them while being taken into custody in La Jolla. Sitting in the La Jolla jail, the researchers learned that they faced up to twenty-five years in prison and at least $750,000 in fines.[9]

In the subsequent hearing, the FBI and Harvard made a highly unusual request for a six-month delay. Then Harvard announced that Medical and Biological Laboratories, the Japanese company, had cooperated fully and returned all research data and products to Harvard Medical School.

After Zhu and Kimbara made bail, they were indicted by a grand jury, but there was no trial. Following a July 11 arraignment,[10] all charges were dropped, prompting their lawyers to respond: "The indictment returned today abandons any claim that our clients stole trade secrets or attempted to commercialize them, recognition that there was never any truth to those charges."

As the pair left the courthouse, they were mobbed by Japanese reporters, whose intensive coverage of their case came not only because Kimbara was a Japanese national and a Japanese firm was involved, but also because the life patent was then foreign to Japanese scientific culture. Japan, unlike the United States, had refused to patent life-forms or to bolster a U.S.-style university-corporate symbiosis.

The Japanese bewilderment over bitter patent litigation that spilled over into criminal courts continued. In May 2001, the Cleveland Clinic similarly prosecuted researchers over monopolistic patent rights and Japanese journalists thronged its courtrooms as well, to convey the bizarre spectacle of scientists on trial over corporate property rights based on a patent. Today Japan is a major center of drug and biological design and treasures scientific innovation, but, in the words of *Science* magazine, "The Japanese are ill equipped to deal with stricter US laws on intellectual property."[11]

A Medical Sea Change

By contrast, Americans seemed unfazed by the interstate pursuit of medical research scientists on charges of the sort normally reserved for Ponzi scammers and mafiosi. For many of us, used as we are to acrimonious turf battles over intellectual property, the salient question turns on whether the Zhu-Kimbara team was guilty, not whether they should have been legally pursued.

But for the purposes of our present discussion, this event is important for a different reason: it dramatizes how the landscape of university medical research has changed in the United States. Medical-research culture has been transformed from a milieu of collegial public-goods resources devoted to the health of the community to a product governed by patents and other monopolies. Once a collaborative haven for independent inquiry and pure research, the university medical-research center is today just another arena of commercial corporate endeavor that takes competition seriously enough to deal harshly with disloyalty and raiding, to the point of seeking to send former colleagues to prison.

How did we get here, and what does the change augur for patients, medical consumers, and other everyday Americans? This acerbic exchange between Harvard and its former researchers was triggered by the potential loss of a lucrative patent that would enable someone— Harvard and its corporate partners, or another institution—to profit from the couple's research. It illustrates a face of the patent at odds with the very American values of ingenuity and independence upon which medical research has always relied.

However, the contentious climate of the patent gold rush has led to far more than mere turf squabbles, and these issues are the subject of this book. Biological patents, or "life patents," are those obtained for monopolies on living things such as pathogens, plants, animals, or portions of our own bodies, including, but hardly limited to, our genes. The requirement that U.S. patents be issued only on truly novel substances would seem to preclude U.S. biological patents on things that are commonly found in nature. So might the prohibition against patents on "laws of nature" or naturally occurring material. But the U.S. Patent Office has often issued patents on naturally occurring living things, as long as researchers have "purified," "isolated," or otherwise "transformed" the patented version into a new entity that, they argue, is not found in nature. Life patents, patents on products of nature, and related pharmaceutical patents on medications are now rife, highly profitable, and the frequent subjects of legal tugs-of-war between corporations.

Patents on human genes provide an excellent example. In 2000, thirty-four thousand new patent applications listing at least one gene or sequence (and usually more than one) were filed each month. By the end of 2000, five hundred thousand naturally occurring genes and DNA sequences (portions of genes) were patented or had patents pending. Corporations, academic institutions, and the U.S. Department of Health emerged as the major holders of these life patents and pharmaceutical patents.

The latter patents are also key to maintaining and improving human health, through the promulgation of medications, the regulation of drug prices, and the mining of animal and human tissues for medically active substances. Until the 1980s, all this was the province of the academic research center, but today it takes place largely in corporate settings and is largely funded and supervised by for-profit corporations.

To explain how all this came about, we must trace the history of the patent as a shaper of contemporary U.S. medical research in order to understand its medical consequences for good and ill today.

Laying the Patent Bare

What does the possession of a patent mean? The word "patent" derives from the Latin verb *patere,* meaning "to lay bare" or "to open up." This concept undergirds the granting of a patent: the period of monopoly during which the holder enjoys the exclusive ability to profit from the invention is a privilege granted to an inventor or his assignee as a reward for eventually "laying open" his invention—for divulging the nature and operation of a technology, invention, or process and placing it in the public domain so that, after the patent holder's period of monopoly ends, everyone may exploit and profit from it.

There are many types of patents besides the biological and pharmaceutical patents addressed in this book, including business method patents, chemical patents, and software patents. Patents on new and useful entities such as medications or computer chips fall into the broad class called utility patents. Industrial design rights or "design patents" protect the visual design of objects that have aesthetic as well as practical value; plant breeders' rights are often called "plant patents," and some plant patents, because they govern living things with medical utility, are discussed in this book as well. Each has its own regulations and history.

None imparts literal ownership. For a time, though, a patent confers something just as profitable, giving its holder at least twenty years of legal monopoly over the possession, distribution, manipulation, and use of the patented entity. A patentee can prevent others from using, manufacturing, selling, advertising, or importing his invention. However, holding a patent does not automatically confer the right to manufacture or sell the invention; for this, the patentee may have to submit to other legislation or licensing criteria. For example, the inventor (or his assignee) of a medication or medically valuable molecule may patent it, but cannot offer it for sale without obtaining Office for Human Research Protections or Food and Drug Administration approval. Similarly, the designer of a better mousetrap may have to secure rights from the patent holder of any patented component that it incorporates; in the same way, some drug patents require prior access to other patented molecules or even patented research tools. One can use such patented entities only with the permission of the patent holder and, typically, after paying a licensing price.

The period of unfettered profitability is meant to reward an inventor's ingenuity by protecting his ability to profit without competition throughout the life of the patent. But after these few decades, he must "open up" the patented item and share it to encourage future innovation so that all can benefit from his invention. Thus patents are meant to encourage open communication and sharing of the expertise and creativity of the sort that propels medical advances, a laudable goal.

Image Versus Reality

Where did the concept of patents arise? The granting of monopolies that closely resemble our patents was recorded in Greece as early as 500 B.C., when its wealthy southern Italian colony Sybaris held gastronomic competitions, with the top chef winning the exclusive rights to his favored dish for one year: after this, anyone could prepare and sell it. In the third century A.D., the Greek-Egyptian writer Athenaeus described this decree: "Encouragement was held out to all who should discover any new refinement in luxury, the profits arising from which were secured to the inventor by patent for the space of a year."[12] The victorious dish was oysters stuffed with honey, which passed deliciously—at least according to the tastes of the ancient Greeks—into the public domain after a year of exclusivity.[13]

By the thirteenth century, several patents were documented for boat-lowering devices in Venice,[14] and the Venetian Statute of 1474 provided legal remedies for inventions' "legal protection against potential infringers."[15] In the sixteenth century, Queen Elizabeth I made royal grants of monopolies which were long to be royal prerogatives in England.[16] In 1594, Galileo was granted a patent for a horse-drawn water pump. Over time, patents or closely related monopolies became a pervasive feature of Western laws and culture, a well as in China and Japan.

Conventional wisdom holds that patents reward individual vision and the patent awardee's personal investment of time, effort, and brainpower. This belief is buttressed by the widespread myth that patents have always been treasured as emblematic of American ingenuity and as a testament to our nation's pioneer spirit. However, our forebears, including prominent inventors such as Benjamin Franklin, Thomas Jefferson, and George Washington Carver, were deeply suspicious of patents.

Because the United States won its independence just after England embarked on the Industrial Revolution, questions of technology and enterprise loomed large for the new nation's economic survival and political prestige, including the question of whether to grant patents and under what circumstances.

During the U.S. colonial era and throughout the early days of our republic, patents represented hated royal monopolies through which Britain rigidly controlled commerce, fattening itself on the fruits of American industry. In seventeenth-century England the crown could bestow "letters patent" that granted monopolies over entire key industries, such as salt. England eventually granted so many monopolies that they caused widespread resentment throughout the American colonies.[17]

These coercive monopolies could be held and granted only by the British colonizers. They exploited and crippled the nascent American economic system in a manner that led our forebears to resent and distrust patents as emblematic of British tyranny, even as the crown bestowed land on favored individuals and companies through a "land patent" system. Even colonial patents, such as those first granted by the Massachusetts Bay Colony of 1624, tended to mimic the English Statute of Monopolies.

Thus it is ironic that the names of Thomas Jefferson and Benjamin Franklin are so often invoked when defending the "American" virtues of patents, because although both were eager and prolific inventors, they long shared a strong aversion to patents.

Benjamin Franklin, the inventor of bifocals, the lightning rod, the Franklin stove, and, less famously, a flexible urinary catheter, shunned patents. He declined the offer of a patent for his famous Franklin stove with "As we enjoy great advantages from the invention of others, we should be glad of an opportunity to serve others by any invention of ours and we should do so freely and generously."[18]

The year that Jefferson became U.S. secretary of state he also became the first director of the Patent Office, established under the United States Patent Act of 1790, "An Act to promote the progress of useful Arts."[19] The act established the Patent Commission of the United States. Jefferson shared the Patent Board duties with Secretary of War Henry Knox and Attorney General Edmund Jennings Randolph. As the trio met to consider each invention, Jefferson himself read the application, and he sometimes even laboratory-tested the candidate's inventions.

Jefferson was a natural in this role. In the finest patrician tradition of his time, he was also an amateur scientist who conducted experimental vaccinations and was an American Mendel who bred four hundred varieties of fruits and vegetables at Monticello. Jefferson's catalog as an inventor included a plow, a horse-drawn buggy, several types of specialized chairs, and a pedometer. However, although he was avidly pro-innovation and "agreed that inventors should have full rights to their inventions," he worried about the constitutionality and economic wisdom of patents.

The right to exclusive profits from an invention is one we take for granted, but it was not a guaranteed feature of the colonial economy, in which the crown could stipulate exclusive commercial rights for a product to whomever it wished. Jefferson believed that inventors should reap the fruits of their inventions by being able to sell or otherwise profit by them, but he was opposed to giving inventors an exclusive right to do so. As he saw it, his role was to encourage invention, not to protect monopolies. He believed in granting patents sparingly so that all could enjoy access to new technologies.[20]

In fact, Jefferson castigated patents as "embarrassments to the public," in the sense that they provided hindrances to trade. He spoke often of patents' potential for exploitation and of his fears that they would delay the public's access to new inventions. He did not apply for patents on any of his own inventions and expressed his hope that "the new nation would abolish . . . monopolies in all cases . . . the abuse of frivolous patents is likely to cause more inconvenience than is countervail[ed] by those really useful."[21]

Throughout his two-year tenure at the Patent Office, Jefferson was miserly with his approval, granting only forty-nine applications,[22] among them one for Eli Whitney's famed cotton gin. Jefferson's negative attitude toward patents eventually softened, and he may have been swayed by James Madison's insistence that, although "nuisances," patents were an appropriate reward for revealing the secrets of construction and invention.

Eventually American attitudes like Jefferson's were tempered. Between independence and the adoption of the federal Constitution, including Article I, Section 8, which established patent guidelines, the initial animosity toward patents yielded to acceptance, and most states generated their own patent laws. Patents grew economically and politically important to the United States, sometimes at a moral or political cost. Eli Whitney's cotton gin, for example, had encouraged the growth of both the nondiversified Southern agrarian economy and slavery.

In 1793, the new Patent Act incorporated Jefferson's definition: "Any new and useful art, machine, manufacture or composition of matter and any new and useful improvement on any art, machine, manufacture or composition of matter." It also stipulated that patents could be awarded only to citizens of the United States; this criterion validated intellectual-property theft by cheating enslaved inventors of credit for, to say nothing of profit from, their creations. Many masters had long taken credit for slaves' inventions anyway, but the act provided a legal rationale and discouraged those who had been inclined to reward their ingenuity. Despite a wealth of inventions by slaves, not until around 1834 did Henry Blair become the first African American to receive a U.S. patent, for a seed planter. In 1858, U.S. attorney general Jeremiah Sullivan Black further reinforced the practice of withholding recognition and awards from the enslaved when he specifically ruled that an enslaved man could receive no U.S. patents because he was not a citizen of any country and could not take the required oath of citizenship.

The United States Patent Office was formally created in 1802 and granted hundreds of thousands of patents over the next two centuries.[23] In 1859, Abraham Lincoln famously declared, "The Patent System added the fuel of interest to the fire of genius."[24] Mark Twain subsequently pronounced patents necessary for continued American progress, writing, "A country without a patent office and good patent laws was just a crab, and couldn't travel any way but sideways or backways." By the end of the nineteenth century, the patent was well ensconced in U.S. economics, and Jefferson's protestations were all but forgotten.[25]

Yet pockets of resistance persisted. *Atlantic Works v. Brady*,[26] an 1882 Supreme Court decision, waxed poetic in its belief that undeserved patents were being awarded for trivial steps in the discovery process. The case dealt with the bid to patent the use of tanks on a propeller dredge boat for the removal of sand and mud at the mouth of the Mississippi River. The boat used tanks that were filled to settle the boat evenly in the water, keeping it level until it reached the bottom; afterward, the tanks were emptied via powerful pumps in order to raise the boat again. But tanks had long been used to maintain the balance of other watercraft as they were lowered, and such use in New Orleans had been specifically noted in print in 1859. The court found that the invention was not novel and thus not patentable.[27]

But it went further: the Court questioned the wisdom of granting patents indiscriminately to each step in "the process of development ... which the skill of ordinary head-workmen and engineers is generally adequate to devise and which indeed [is] the natural and proper outgrowth of such development." It advocated for reserving a patent for "substantial discovery or invention":

> It was never the object of those [patent] laws to grant a monopoly for every trifling device, every shadow of a shade of an idea, which would naturally and spontaneously occur to any skilled mechanic or operator in the ordinary progress of manufactures. Such an indiscriminate creation of exclusive privileges tends rather to obstruct than to stimulate invention.
>
> It creates a class of competitive schemers who make it their business to watch the advancing wave of improvement, and gather its foam in the form of patented monopolies, which enable them to lay a heavy tax upon the industry of the country, without contributing anything to the real advancement of the arts. It embarrasses the honest pursuit of business with fears and apprehensions of concealed liens and unknown liabilities, lawsuits and vexatious accountings for profits made in good faith.

Chief among historical patent dissenters is that great American inventor George Washington Carver, celebrated by *Time* magazine in 1941 as "The Black Leonardo," and more than a half century later named by *People* magazine as the most beloved American scientist. Carver turned down a million-dollar industrial salary in order to serve the needy at Tuskegee Institute and dismissed suggestions that he patent his hundreds of scientific and medical inventions, with the words "God gave them to me. How can I sell them to someone else?"[28]

Enshrining "The Hand of Man"

For most of our nation's history, the subjects of American patents were technological devices and inventions such as farm implements, telephones, stoplights, and scientific and medical instruments. Patentable American ingenuity was by common consent restricted to inanimate objects.

But in the early twentieth century, U.S. plant breeders lobbied to profit from the advantages of patenting new cultivation techniques and varieties of plants. There were precedents at home and abroad: Finland had granted the first known patent on a living organism in 1843, and Louis Pasteur had obtained a U.S. patent for a pathogen-free yeast in 1873.

To determine the patentability of plants, the patent office had to reconsider the question "What determines patentability?" The legal criteria for granting a patent have been fluid, changing over time and specific to the kind of patent being sought.

Generally, two types predominate: *product* patents (or "utility patents") for inventions, and *process* patents for methods, acts, and operations that are performed to produce a physical result (such as a particular "shopping bag" feature of an internet sales site). There are other more specific types as noted above, but most pertinent to the plant breeders were plant patents, granted for inventors who manipulated the asexual reproduction—such as cuttings and grafting—of plants.[29]

Patents and their criteria differ widely and finely in the details, making patent law breathtakingly complex. However, some requirements for patenting have remained fairly consistent. Only the inventor may be granted a patent. Patent eligibility requires that the idea must be a *novel*—a truly new—idea. A patent must be *non-obvious*, something that would not be immediately apparent to a person who is skilled in the art required. Also the patent must be *useful*—it must have a practical purpose or a marketable use. And finally, the patent application must describe it fully and accurately enough to be interpreted by a person skilled in the field in which it will be used. Illustrations are often a key component of these descriptions. But because of the requirement for novelty, if the patent application describes information that is already available to the public, it is said to be "prior art" and ineligible for patenting.

In one sense, Pasteur's ability to patent the strain of yeast is puzzling: as a naturally occurring organism, yeast was not a patentable "invention," but rather a discovery. However, Pasteur successfully used an argument that persists in the procuring of life-related patents today. He argued that he had purified the yeast from the environs in which it grew, producing a sample that was free of germs and thus would not cause disease. It was therefore considered "an article of manufacture," and eligible for a patent despite its living status through a "hand of man" argument, which insisted that human ingenuity, not nature, had devised the pure yeast, transforming the nature of the yeast.

The hormone adrenaline was patented under the same rationale in 1911 by Japanese scientist Jokichi Takamine, whose influence spanned two continents. Takamine was born in 1854 in the city of Takaoka to a long line of physicians, and he traveled extensively in Europe before visiting the United States, where he fell in love with both America and Caroline Field Hitch, whom he married in 1884. They settled first in Tokyo, then in New York City, where he established a private laboratory and worked with the pharmaceutical firm Parke, Davis.

Takamine also served as a scientific and cultural ambassador who energetically promoted warm relations between Japan and the United States. If you have ever drunk in the delicate beauty of Washington, D.C.'s cherry blossoms and basked in the camaraderie of its Cherry Blossom Festival, you have Takamine to thank, because he persuaded Japan to donate the trees and promote the event as a goodwill gesture. But he bestowed an even greater gift when he isolated the hormone adrenaline, a neurotransmitter secreted by the adrenal glands that is critical for our "fight-or-flight" reaction and for much subsequent medication. Takamine won a patent for adrenaline, but the patent was challenged in court on the grounds that the hormone was not invented but rather discovered and purified from the adrenal glands.

The courts affirmed the patent's validity: "Takamine was the first to make [adrenaline] available for any use by removing it from the other gland-tissue in which it was found, and, while it is of course possible logically to call this a purification of the principle, it became for every practical purpose *a new thing* [italics added] commercially and therapeutically. That was a good ground for a patent."[30]

Congress responded by passing the Plant Patent Act of 1930, which extended the right to patent certain plants because they are transformed by grafting and budding techniques devised by man. This rationale similarly invoked the "hand of man" argument, arguing that breeders, not nature, had created the newer strains and breeds. No patent rights were extended to plants that are propagated by sexual reproduction, over which the courts still yielded to nature's primacy, so that no patent rights then governed commerce in seeds.

Patents on these living things and hormones allowed someone—typically a company—a lucrative monopoly to license and sell the patented version of the living thing for profit. However, most twentieth-century medical researchers tended not to work for corporations but for universities or, sometimes, for private research organizations, including their own (as Takamine did). Thus they were insulated from the commercial zeal of corporations. Also, much university research was funded by the government, and patents from products of that federally sponsored research could not legally be sold to corporations. Even more significantly, medical-research culture also militated against commercialism, which was deeply frowned upon. For example, in 1923, its inventors agreed to sell the patent for insulin to the University of Toronto—but for only $1.

Because a career in medical research necessitated years of study but was not a lucrative field, people without means—the poor, the lower middle class, the ethnically marginalized—were dramatically underrepresented in medical research, and the field attracted people who sought rewards other than money. Scientists did seek recognition for their work, and the rewards they sought did change over time, but these riches remained principally prestige, fame, honors, academic advancement, scientific and political influence, being revered as a benefactor, and a sense of altruism.

A rich vein of medically themed literature holds a mirror to the era's culture and how it viewed commercial medical research. Most iconic is Sinclair Lewis's 1925 novel, *Arrowsmith*, a masterwork of American realism for which Lewis, who won the Nobel Prize in 1930, also won a Pulitzer.

A passage describes the reaction of fellow scientists when ascetic German immunologist Max Gottlieb, heralded in the novel as "the spirit of science," goes commercial. Gottlieb (a thinly veiled portrait of the researcher Jacques Loeb) has fallen upon hard times after an ill-advised confrontation with the dean of his medical school leads to his termination. Now a pariah within U.S. academe, and desperate to feed his family, Gottlieb sinks to a nadir: he accepts a job with a pharmaceutical company.

In the medical periodicals the Dawson Hunziker Company published full-page advertisements, most starchy and refined in type, announcing that Professor Max Gottlieb, perhaps the most distinguished immunologist in the world, had joined their staff.

In his Chicago clinic, one Dr. Rouncefield chuckled, "That's what becomes of these super-highbrows. Pardon me if I seem to grin." In the laboratories of Ehrlich and Roux, Bordet and Sir David Bruce, sorrowing men wailed, "How could old Max have gone over to that damned pill-peddler? Why didn't he come to us? Oh, well, if he didn't want to—Voilà! He is dead."[31]

When he hears the news, Gottlieb's erstwhile disciple Martin Arrowsmith laments to his wife, "God, Leora, I wish HE hadn't gone wrong!"

Until the last quarter of the twentieth century, medical-research culture retained an animus against patents and profit as moneygrubbing and beneath the dignity of the researcher. Profiting from medical investigation was also regarded as fundamentally wrong, an unworthy motivation that stood in opposition to the scientific mission of the researchers and of the university.[32]

When Selman Waksman of Rutgers developed the antibiotic streptomycin in the 1940s, it became the first effective treatment for tuberculosis and earned Waksman the Nobel Prize and fame as America's most esteemed scientist. Waksman patented streptomycin and licensed it to Merck Research Laboratories in nearby Rahway, New Jersey, but he was so worried about the public's rancor if it learned that a private company was reaping enormous profits from research by a state university that he persuaded Merck to return the license to Rutgers, which enabled streptomycin to be sold generically—and very cheaply.[33]

The disdain for seeking a lucrative monopoly by patenting medical advances is also revealed by the actions of Jonas Salk. When he developed an effective polio vaccine in 1955, neither he nor the March of Dimes, which had helped fund it, chose to patent the vaccine, which was in tremendous demand. When Edward R. Murrow asked him who owned the patent, Salk countered, "The American people, I guess. Could you patent the sun?"[34]

But before there could be a vaccine for polio, there had to be a Henrietta Lacks.

Henrietta Lacks, HeLa, and the Body as Property

In the early 1970s, you could choose your war. True, the War on Poverty had dwindled to a few anemic thrusts and parries and the Vietnam War, once bitterly divisive, languished on life support. However, the Cold War and the War on Cancer held everyone in thrall, and in January 1973, the Russians struck a single blow for both.

With great pomp, Soviet scientists presented the United States with what they described as six tumor-cell samples harboring human cancer viruses, taken from six different Russian patients. The glass cylinders held skeins of whitish human cells spun across translucent lakes of blood-hued nutrients. Many scientists had tried to identify such viruses, but they were elusive, and even if found they were unlikely to survive in culture for long. If the Russian samples indeed harbored viruses that caused human cancers, they could be invaluable because anticancer therapies could be tested on them in the laboratory. No one had yet succeeded in making such cultures, so these medical totems were as important to politics as they might be to medicine. Isolating a human cancer virus was the holy grail of cancer research, and this gift was a step toward détente, an impulse toward political and scientific cooperation with a common medical enemy.

Dr. Walter Nelson-Rees, then curator of the University of California's cell bank,[35] insisted upon extensive tests that would begin by confirming the human source of the cells, declaring, "One must be sure about these things."[36] No one would be more surprised than he had the Soviets managed to produce the elusive human cancer viruses, but he understood that great delicacy would be necessary if his analysis disappointed them.

His analysis shocked them. Every cell had two X chromosomes, a troubling coincidence that meant they were all from women. Moreover, every cell had the same fast-moving A variant of the enzyme glucose-6-phosphate dehydrogenase (G6PD)—a biological marker often, but not exclusively, found in descendants of African peoples. Black people lived in the Soviet Union, of course, but the coincidences were mounting in a troubling manner. In the 1970s, for example, nearly all cell lines were assumed to derive from the bodies of whites because researchers often used cells from their own bodies, or those of their families.

Cell lines from six different black women struck Nelson-Rees as unlikely: it was much more likely that the cells came from one woman. What's more, Nelson-Rees felt sure that he knew her name: Henrietta Lacks.

A Priceless "Gift"

The Russians' tumor cells did not harbor cancer viruses. Instead, they were the progeny of tumor cells that had been taken from Lacks, a Baltimore woman, in 1951, and that have thrived in laboratory glassware ever since. Nelson-Rees theorized that the Russians had been working with Lacks's cells (conventionally named HeLa, from the initial letters of her first and last name) in their laboratories, and that although they may have begun with human cancer cells at some point, the HeLa cells had contaminated and replaced the cancer lines without their realizing it.

It was a scenario that Nelson-Rees had discovered and described many times before, because the Russians were not alone in their confusion. Like 15 to 20 percent of all cultures of the period, the HeLa cells in researchers' laboratories had contaminated other cell lines or been misidentified as other cell lines.[37] Patrick Burke, of American Type Culture Collection, the country's premier cell-line bank, explained in 1994, "HeLa was so widely distributed that a lot of contamination ensued—it would overgrow the other cell lines. . . . People found it pretty traumatic that they were doing research, spending a lot of money, then being told 'This cell line is not what you thought it was.' "[38]

By 1974, fiery accusations and indignant denials engulfed the normally staid world of medical research after an article in *Science* revealed the extent of HeLa's proliferation. Nelson-Rees embarked on a near-messianic campaign to alert scientists around the world to the shocking extent of HeLa contamination, "outing" many labs and making few friends in the process. The popular press gleefully seized upon this scientific embarrassment through headlines that trumpeted, "Dead Woman's Cancer Cells Spreading" and "Researchers' Errors Set War on Cancer Back 20 Years." Within academia, careers faced dissolution as labs backpedaled furiously to trace and prove the integrity of their cultures.

Scientists lost sleep and face, especially because of their penchant for creating cell lines from their own tissues or from those of their children. When "their" cell lines were accused of harboring HeLa's "black" cells, these scientists faced a distasteful dilemma: they could admit to HeLa contamination or, like one Dr. Monroe Vincent, they could lay claim to "remote Negro ancestry."

The global panic finally touched the lives of five ordinary people on Baltimore's New Pittsburgh Street when scientists descended upon the Lacks household to take blood and tissue samples from Henrietta Lacks's children in hopes of helping researchers differentiate the HeLa from the non-HeLa cell lines in their laboratories.

In the zeal to save their livelihood and careers, scientists found it easy to forget that these medically important cells came from an unwitting benefactor whose family had no idea that their mother's cells had become a precious medical commodity—against their will.

Henrietta was born on August 18, 1920, to John and Eliza Pleasant in Clover, outside Roanoke, Virginia. She and David Lacks were married on August 15, 1935, and moved to Baltimore. Sixteen years later, in January 1951, disaster disrupted her church-and-family-centered life as a pinkish vaginal discharge was followed by a ceaseless flow of blood. After a month of heavy bleeding, she and her frightened husband drove to Johns Hopkins Hospital, where she received her diagnosis: cervical cancer.

Even in the 1950s, the Lackses could hope for a cure of this small, localized cancer. On February 9, her gynecologist implanted radium capsules in her uterus to dispense the gamma radiation that was then standard therapy—but not before taking two samples of the tumor tissue for a colleague, Hopkins scientist George Gey.

Gey had taken on the daunting challenge of refining human cell-line culture—keeping cells alive outside the body to be used for research. Cell lines were rare, valuable, and delicate, quickly expiring at the least deviation from optimal temperature, light, or nutrient mix, although lines from cancerous cells were somewhat hardier. A few lived for weeks and the truly rugged survived a month. Gey dreamed of cell lines that would live for months, long enough to finish an experiment or test a vaccine.

A specific vaccine. In 1950, parents lived in fear of polio, and a cell line that would survive long enough to test candidate polio vaccines was urgently needed. Gey's technicians, including his wife, Margaret, constantly swept the hospital, taking cell samples from patients.

"They wanted to take samples and asked if they could take tissue," Henrietta's husband, David Lacks Sr., told me in 1994. "Doctors told me it would probably help someone in the future. But I said 'No.' I wouldn't sign the papers."[39] Lacks's refusal was ignored and the samples were taken anyway.

On February 9, Henrietta Lacks's gynecologist gave Gey a half-inch-square sample of Henrietta's cells. Heartened by HeLa's vigor, Margaret described it as "spreading like crabgrass" and with these hardy cells Gey founded a cell line that ensured his fame.

Meanwhile, in another wing of the hospital, doctors followed Henrietta's radium implants with X-ray therapy. By July, masses of tumors had filled her abdominal cavity, and on September 26, 1951, a doctor ordered all treatment except painkillers stopped. For a week, she drifted in and out of consciousness, and on October 4 she died. She was thirty-one.

After her death, Gey swiftly obtained more tissue samples, but they were normally delicate tissues that soon expired. The only "immortal" samples were those that had been collected earlier, but there were plenty of these: they were doubling in size *every twenty-four hours.*

As her cells overran their petri dishes, her family laid Henrietta Lacks to rest. Henrietta's cells transformed medicine. The first continuous human cell line meant that vaccines could now be tested and lengthy experiments completed that would have been unthinkable a few months earlier.

One advance was immediate and dramatic: after nearly seven years of focused research, the Salk polio vaccine was tested and perfected only a year after Henrietta Lacks died. Dr. Jonas Salk used HeLa as the host cell for calibrating the effectiveness of the vaccine's action as, every week, a laboratory at Tuskegee University that was dedicated to HeLa production dispensed twenty thousand tube cultures.[40]

But HeLa's usefulness did not stop at the polio vaccine. Gey did not patent HeLa, so no financial barriers impeded its global use and dissemination. HeLa became and remains a versatile tool in the laboratory, and many treatments and cures were predicated on its use. In 1995, Victor McKusick, MD, a professor of medicine at Johns Hopkins Medical

Center, verified that "the number of medical advances due to HeLa are too numerous to list. I think, in the aggregate, a tremendous number of advances have relied on the use of HeLa. In lecturing on the history of medical genetics, I point out that the single individual who contributed most to the fields of somatic cell genetics is Henrietta Lacks, not a scientist."

A company named Microbial Associates began selling HeLa widely, and laboratories that were not perfectly scrupulous in their handling of the cells contaminated their other cultures with HeLa, leading to the global identity crisis that threatened the work of so many researchers and laboratories.

The Lacks family remained unaware of the scientific whirlwind driven by their mother's cells' unique properties, because her identity was kept secret. Medical and news accounts variously identified her as Helen Larson and Helen Lane, pseudonyms Gey had employed as a "subterfuge to protect the Lacks family from journalists," according to McKusick.[41]

"I don't know what he thought he was protecting," scoffed David "Sonny" Lacks Jr., her son, as we discussed his mother over Cokes on a steamy day in May 1994, in downtown Baltimore's Old Town Mall. "I think they didn't want people to know that she was a black lady helping the world."

In appropriating the biological treasure of her cells, researchers hid more than Henrietta Lacks's name. A quarter century after her death, waves of worried researchers attempting to separate HeLa from their other cultures appeared at the Lackses' door. "They said they wanted to see if my wife's illness affected any of the children," Mr. Lacks recalled in 1994. And this time, he permitted the taking of periodic blood samples from them "to protect my children." But the story was always the same. "They would promise to get back to us, but we would never see them again. Dr. Gey promised to tell me what he found in my wife's blood. But it's been so long now, he *died*." The samples from the Lacks family allowed researchers to identify the interloping HeLa cells and to regain the purity of their cultures.

Today HeLa cells proliferate with undiminished vigor in laboratories and tissue banks, and no other cell lines have surpassed their longevity. Gey gave HeLa samples away, but HeLa has also been bought and sold around the world for sixty years and is still available from cell banks such as American Type Tissue Collection. In 1989 the ATTC mailed thirty-five thousand specimens throughout the globe, but the company refused to say how many were HeLa.

The true value of HeLa cell lines lies not only in the perfection of the Salk vaccine but also in the many medical advances they have enabled and will enable still, all without patenting or licensing headaches and expense because they were never patented. Yet the scientists who proclaimed HeLa "priceless" shied from affixing a dollar value. In 1995 McKusick called HeLa's value inestimable: "I think you cannot price them."

In their zeal to procure Henrietta Lacks's cells, George Gey and his colleagues ignored the fact that they were morally and legally bound by the need to obtain her or her husband's consent. This requirement had been established by the Nuremburg Code, by a 1947 Atomic Energy Commission ruling, and subsequently by a variety of U.S. professional and hospital guidelines that seem to have been honored more in the breach than the observance, especially where African Americans were concerned.

Interestingly, many medical and journalistic discussions of HeLa cells celebrate not their intrinsic value but the technical expertise of George Gey, who consistently reinforced his image as the "father" of HeLa. He paternalistically referred to HeLa as his "precious baby" and had a penchant for delivering cultures personally to other researchers, keeping the tubes in his breast pocket, where, as he often explained, his body warmth served as their incubator, supplying the optimal temperature for their survival.[42]

Henrietta Lacks's husband complained, "As far as them selling my wife's cells without my knowledge and making a profit—I don't like that at all. They are exploiting both of us. If they've been making a profit they should give me some kind of restitution."[43]

By the time the Lackses learned that medical scientists had appropriated their mother's body for profitable global research, the statute of limitations for any suit they might bring for conversion, or the illegal appropriation of her tissues, had long ago expired. It is questionable whether the courts would have been sympathetic in any case, because they have typically dismissed such claims, ruling that the purloined tissues were "discarded."[44]

Because HeLa was not patented, there was no monopoly hampering its wide distribution. "Because of the culture of the 1950s, no one would have thought of patenting HeLa," McKusick assured me when we spoke by telephone. "HeLa was developed with public funds, but the ethos at that time was that the findings of a researcher remained in the public domain. Neither scientists who made the discovery nor anyone else would think that personal profit would be derived from the affair. It's a very different atmosphere now."

If there is a silver lining of this medical theft, deception, and betrayal, it is the plethora of medical advances that have depended upon the free distribution of an unpatented HeLa. It remained cheap and ubiquitous, a freely available medical blessing, and many people lived and enjoyed restored health as a result of Henrietta Lacks's sacrifice. This perspective cannot excuse the exploitation of the Lacks family in the service of HeLa, but its common use as a medical tool lends a measure of counterweight to the harms done them.

Patents on Humans: The Opening Salvo

By the latter half of the twentieth century, living things and other products of nature continued to receive the occasional U.S. patent. Even in Europe, which was far less patent friendly, some life patents were granted under the terms of regulatory meetings such as the Paris Convention of 1961, the 1967 Treaty of Budapest, and the European Patent Convention of 1973. And in 1975, U.S. plant patents expanded to include a product of sexual reproduction, long barred as a bastion of natural processes: University of Illinois researcher Earl Patterson was granted a utility patent on a new corn hybrid seed in 1975.[45]

However, patents were not sought on most medically important living things, and for a decade after HeLa's discovery, human cell lines were not patented.

This changed when the human cell line named WI-38 (because it originated at Philadelphia's Wistar Institute) was developed in 1962 by University of Pennsylvania microbiologist Leonard Hayflick. Hayflick is best known for identifying the microorganism, a mycoplasma, that causes atypical pneumonia, commonly known as "walking pneumonia" in humans. And, in a finding of great significance for research on aging, he had demolished the myth that human cells are immortal, capable of dividing indefinitely. Instead, he determined that normal human cells have a limited capacity for dividing before they essentially commit suicide: the "Hayflick limit," which equals about fifty divisions.[46]

Hayflick sought to patent cell line WI-38, but the U.S. Patent and Trademark Office initially rejected his application on the basis that patents were not granted on living cells.

The suit was complicated by the fact that Hayflick's work was supported by federal grants and the university had filed its own patent application for the line, though no decision had been made. When the government funds research, it has the right to hold the patent, and profit-making corporations are legally prohibited from buying such patents. The federal funding statutes did, however, allow Hayflick to disseminate his unpatented cell line to companies that manufactured measles and mumps vaccines, and these companies made a handsome profit while Hayflick, who had created WI-38, received nothing.

Hayflick decided not to accept this state of affairs, and in 1972 he founded a start-up company to market WI-38 to manufacturers and entered into a contract with Merck that gave the drug maker options that would entitle it to buy $1 million in cells.

Hayflick was also short-listed for an important position at the National Institute of Aging. As part of his background check, James W. Schriver, head of management survey and review at the National Institutes of Health (NIH), discovered Hayflick's income from the cell line and charged among other things that he was illegally profiting from the sales of WI-38.

The government contended that WI-38 was solely its property and shared detailed documents supporting its views with the national press, exposing Hayflick to nationwide criticism. When Stanford learned of the NIH investigation, it undertook its own, which seemed likely to result in disciplinary action. Instead, Hayflick resigned.

Out of a job, his reputation shadowed by government charges, and his income from WI-38 suspended awaiting the resolution of the NIH investigation, Hayflick found himself standing on the unemployment line for weeks until he obtained a position at Children's Hospital Medical Center in Oakland, California, where he secured grants that allowed him to continue his research.

Then, in 1975, the National Institutes of Health sued him, not over the ethics or hubris of patenting human life, but rather in a squabble over the ownership, patent rights, and potential profits of cell line WI-38.[47] The NIH claimed that even without a patent, WI-38 was the property of the government because federal funds had supported the line's development and dissemination. Hayflick responded with a lawsuit challenging the basis for the NIH's ownership, seeking damages and demanding title to and profits from the sales of WI-38.[48]

WI-38's anonymous "tissue donor" was not party to the suits, and in fact she never knew of them, for the line was developed from the lung cells of an aborted fetus.[49] For years, the wheels of justice ground at a glacial rate, keeping Hayflick, and the case against him, suspended in a legal and professional limbo.

John Moore's Body

Just a year after the NIH sued Hayflick, and a quarter century after the illicit procurement of the HeLa cells, doctors appropriated the body parts of another person without his knowledge. This time, however, the story spun out differently. In the fall of 1976, John Moore, a Seattle surveyor who was working on the Alaska pipeline, learned that he had hairy-cell leukemia, or HCL, a rare and usually fatal cancer of the white blood cells. Moore's father, a doctor, urged him to come back home to Southern California, where he could be treated by UCLA blood specialist David Golde, MD, a specialist in HCL. Golde told Moore that his grossly enlarged spleen had to be removed, and on October 5, 1976, Moore dutifully signed the consent form for the splenectomy. Moore, who was not expected to survive long, recovered, and the surgery was a success. It was a success for Golde as well, because although he did not tell Moore, the twenty-two-pound spleen was producing an unusual volume of blood proteins that had triggered an extraordinarily effective immune response against his cancer.

Golde surreptitiously moved Moore's spleen to a research wing of the hospital, establishing a lab where he used it and other of Moore's tissues to develop a cell line from a key component of Moore's immune system, his T-cell lymphocytes. For several years, Golde insisted that Moore travel at his own expense from Alaska to Los Angeles for frequent follow-up visits, during which Golde extracted blood, cells, tissues, and semen, always explaining that this solicitousness was to ensure against a recurrence. Actually the tissues were used for Golde's anticancer research based on Moore's body parts.

Then, 1980 arrived, a year that saw a confluence of laws that dictated the medical fate of John Moore and many Americans who followed him.

A New Lease on Life

In the 1970s, as Dr. Hayflick began grappling with the NIH and John Moore learned he had a life-threatening blood cancer, Dr. Ananda M. Chakrabarty[50] left academia to join research and development at General Electric Company in Schenectady, New York. He was searching for an intellectual challenge that would yield commercial value, and he hit upon the idea of manipulating a class of bacteria—pseudomonads—that were blessed with "nutritional versatility." That is, they were able to assimilate or "eat" unusual organic compounds such as camphor, naphthalene, and petroleum. They could also convert crude oil into protein-rich biomass, making these pseudomonads a potential gold mine because, as Chakrabarty wrote, "In some parts of the world oil was cheap but protein expensive."[51]

He hoped the bacteria would generate cheap food sources that would provide GE with a profitable way to alleviate world hunger. But each type of bacterium could transform only a few types of oil, as dictated by the DNA contained within genes in each bacterial cell's plasmids, energy-generating organelles. Chakrabarty manipulated a bacterial strain that contained DNA from many plasmids into a single plasmid, which allowed one strain of bacterium to digest many types of oil. This was a prerequisite of transforming the bacteria into protein factories—a great achievement, especially because he accomplished it before contemporary genetic recombination techniques were available. Unfortunately, by the time Chakrabarty perfected this process, oil had risen in price and its use to produce food protein was no longer economically feasible.

However, Chakrabarty and his colleagues reasoned that his custom-designed "oil-eating" microorganisms could profitably be used for cleaning up oil spills. In June 1972, GE decided to patent not only the oil-consuming bacterium itself but also the *process* of constructing these organisms. Otherwise anyone, including GE's competitors, would be able to construct and use the valuable bacteria.

In 1973 the U.S. Patent and Trade Office (USPTO) granted GE and Chakrabarty a patent on the process of engineering the microorganism, the first time such a patent had been given. But it rejected the patent application for the organism itself on the grounds that a microorganism is a product of nature, and as such cannot be patented. Over the following years, recombinant genetic techniques were developed and gained currency, allowing the wholesale manipulation of many organisms, for which some patents were applied. But the USPTO did not grant a patent on the "oil-eating" bacterium. Instead, because these additional patent applications had begun rolling in for living things, the Patent Office turned to the Supreme Court for a ruling on the patentability of living microorganisms.

In June 1980 the Supreme Court decided in a 5–4 vote to permit the patenting of life, ruling in *Chakrabarty v. Diamond* that Chakrabarty's "oil-eating" bacterium in question was not a product of nature but rather a man-made invention that deserved patent protection.[52] In granting the patent on his bacterium, the Court quoted the congressional report leading up to the 1952 Patent Act stipulating that "anything made by man under the sun" should be patentable. Yet the Court's ruling made it clear that the decision was meant narrowly, due to the extensive manipulation and particular circumstances in *Chakrabarty*. The Court did not address the larger questions of patenting higher forms of life.

Yet the USPTO interpreted the decision broadly, and no one professed as much surprise as Chakrabarty himself:

> Even though the Supreme Court based its decision in
> a focused manner centered on a genetically engineered
> bacterium, the USPTO interpreted the decision in a much
> broader manner, granting patents on genetically altered
> plants, animals, human cells and tissues, disease genes, and
> the like . . . an outcome wholly unforeseen but to some extent
> anticipated or feared during the controversy surrounding the
> patenting of the oil-eating pseudomonad.[53]

Chakrabarty v. Diamond was not the only paradigm-shattering patent development of 1980. A report by the U.S. comptroller general posited that innovation was being stifled because universities and corporations did not want to invest in developing technology that they did not own. This included patented discoveries that had been financed by federal funds but lay undeveloped because the government funding placed them in public domain and laws prohibited corporations from owning them. The university could own them but did not have the funds or incentive to develop them.

As a result, American technological innovation was stifled, according to Senator Birch Bayh, an Indiana Democrat, who complained that the vast majority of twenty-eight thousand patented discoveries made in universities with $30 billion in taxpayers' dollars were "lying there, collecting dust": only 5 percent of these patented items were being developed into commercial products with public utility.[54] Kansas Republican Bob Dole agreed, and together in 1980 they sponsored the Government Patent Policy Act of 1980,[55] commonly known as the Bayh-Dole Act, to foster the commercialization of inventions based on university-held patents financed by government grants.

Not everyone approved of this proposed marriage of academia and industry. Dissenters included the influential Admiral Hyman Rickover, "Father of the Nuclear Navy," who voiced his unambiguous, strident, and frequent objections on the grounds that corporate ownership of university innovation would spawn ungovernable monopolies: "In my opinion, government contractors—including small businesses and universities—should not be given title to inventions developed at government expense. That is the gist of my testimony. These inventions are paid for by the public and therefore should be available for any citizen to use or not as he sees fit."[56]

The powerful senator Russell Long of Louisiana, a Democrat, agreed. On September 24, he proclaimed to Congress, "I am adamantly opposed to the House bill. I urge you to join with me in taking whatever steps are necessary to prevent this monopolistic provision from being included in the final form of any patent policy legislation." In private, he railed to Bayh's staff that "this is the worst bill I have seen in my life." The Carter administration agreed, Congress was convinced, and the Bayh-Dole bill died in the regular sessions of the Ninety-sixth Congress.

By December, however, Jimmy Carter was a lame duck, and when Congress was briefly revived for a necessary budgetary session, Bayh wanted the bill slipped in for another vote and another chance at passage. But Bayh had lost the election, too, and so wielded even less political clout than earlier. Long had the power to withhold the bill from consideration during the budgetary session.

However, good ol' boy sentiment trumped congressional fears of renegade monopolies. Russell Long, in a farewell act of respect for the departing Bayh, called him to say, "Birch, take that patent bill, you're entitled to it. You've earned it."[57] Long released the bill for consideration and withdrew his opposition; following his lead, so did the other representatives.

Thus Bayh-Dole became law on December 12, in the last hour of the last congressional session during the waning days of 1980, reversing more than three decades of public policy that reserved to universities the sole right to own inventions that resulted from federally funded research.[58]

Moreover, not only could colleges now sell and license the patents developed with taxpayers' dollars[59] to private companies, they could do so without publicly disclosing the deals. To abet the patenting and development of new and useful inventions, colleges and universities were now actively encouraged to court the very industries with which they formerly had been prohibited from partnering.[60]

The Stevenson-Wydler Technology Innovation Act was yet another piece of 1980 legislation that supported federal funding to pay for university research.[61] This act encourages technological innovation by fostering cooperation among government researchers, universities, large corporations, and small businesses, notably biotechnology start-ups. Bolstered by such laws as the 1981 Economic Recovery Act,[62] Stevenson-Wydler provides incentives in the form of tax credits to companies that contribute research equipment to universities, and a number of amendments have reinforced these laws' aim of establishing intimate government-university-corporate research ties.[63]

What did this newly cozy relationship between the university and industry betoken? Corporations, notably pharmaceutical companies, now work closely with universities and their researchers in order to catalyze research, businesses innovation, and profitability. In the medical arena, the goal is to encourage the production of new drug treatments and to make large profits while doing so. This and subsequent laws encouraged universities and private corporations to form closer ties while allowing them to exploit profits from research and development conducted by universities and paid for with federal funds.

Reversal of Fortune

The laws passed in 1980 also changed the trajectory of Leonard Hayflick's and John Moore's lives. Suddenly, the fact that WI-38 was living no longer presented a bar to Hayflick's patent application. Just as suddenly, Hayflick's stratagem for gleaning corporate profits from taxpayer-funded research was no longer illegal: instead, it was legislatively encouraged.

Accordingly, he and the NIH signed a settlement that ended their legal dispute. Under its terms, all charges against Hayflick were dropped. He kept $90,000 of proceeds from the sale of WI-38 as well as patent rights over some of the cell line, enabling him to sell WI-38, although the government retained patent ownership on most of the line. The settlement merely dictated the terms under which the cells and patent would be shared, but did not answer the larger legal questions of what rights should accrue to scientists whose discoveries are licensed and sold, questions that still bedevil us today.

On January 15, 1982, eighty-five prominent U.S. scientists signed a letter in *Science* applauding what they called Hayflick's exoneration and warning that similar prosecution over the patenting of their inventions could await other researchers in the future. The government largely maintained silence except to deny that its about-face constituted an "exoneration" of Hayflick.

Hayflick went on to become one of the most important and prolific American scientists, winning more than twenty-five major awards in the United States and Europe, and authoring 275 papers that are frequently cited in biochemistry, biophysics, cell biology, enzymology, genetics, and molecular biology. Today he is a professor of anatomy at the University of California at San Francisco.

And John Moore? As we have seen, Golde was taking frequent tissue samples from an unprotesting Moore, but the latter's suspicions were triggered when Golde began pressuring him to sign a new blanket-consent form that would belatedly give Golde absolute rights to Moore's "discarded, worthless" tissue samples. A wary Moore checked and signed the box that read "I do not consent," and an agitated Golde immediately called and wrote him, urging him to rectify his "error." Instead, Moore hired a lawyer, who quickly discovered that the Regents of the University of California had responded to the bounty of corporate-friendly legislation of the 1980s with alacrity: they had applied for a patent on John Moore's "Mo" cell line, made from his spleen and the samples that Golde had been harvesting during Moore's supposedly therapeutic visits. The patent, U.S. Patent No. 4,438,032: "Unique T-Lymphocyte Line and Products Derived Therefrom," was granted the next year.

Moore's lawyer also discovered that UCLA, on the heels of the Stevenson-Wydler Act, had used the patent to sign lucrative contracts with the Genetics Institute, Inc., and Sandoz Pharmaceuticals.[64] Between 1981 and 1983, Golde was showered with seventy-five thousand shares of stock as a token payment and shared $440,000 from Sandoz, Ltd., with his partners. The cell line's estimated worth was then $3 billion. UCLA could not have done this without the *Chakrabarty* decision, Bayh-Dole, and the subsequent rulings that allowed it first to secure a patent on a living entity—John Moore—and second, to transfer the patent to Sandoz.

Moore lost no time in suing the UCLA Medical Center for misappropriating his valuable tissues—for "converting" them (in legal argot), for hiding their lucrative commercial nature, and for deceiving Moore about the true nature of the medical attentions he had received. The California courts denied Moore's claims, but the state court of appeals ruled that a person's tissues are his personal property, opening the way for Moore to lay a claim on the patent and part of the profits of any genetically engineered commercial products developed from them.

Biotechnology companies, pharmaceutical firms, and researchers objected vigorously and scientists complained that this ruling could sabotage biomedical research—and with it, the welfare of future patients. Many research institutions and corporations filed amicus curiae briefs urging that Moore's claims be invalidated in the interests of science. Although the California courts also found that Golde had violated his "fiduciary duty" to warn Moore about his tissues' lucrative nature, they repeatedly upheld Golde's patent and specifically denied that Moore retained any rights in his own tissues.[65] In 1990, the justices of the California Supreme Court, swayed by these arguments, ruled against Moore, expressing their concern that allowing patients to sue for rights to their cells and tissues would set a precedent for a "litigation lottery."

However, the courts also determined that Moore had been deprived of the legally mandated right to informed consent and that patients must be informed of and agree to the use of their tissues for research. The court opined that upholding this right to informed consent was sufficient to protect Moore's interests in his tissues as well.

This aspect of the decision is more than a little hazy: If a patient gives such consent, does it cover everything done with his tissues by researchers in perpetuity? Does it cover abdicating rights to market use and profits? Before being asked to give such consent, how much information should the patient be given about the possible commoditization of his tissues?

For that matter, from whom should the researcher seek informed consent? In the case of Hayflick's cell lines, which came from a fetus, should consent have been elicited from the parents? When you consider that the researchers themselves cannot always know the eventual value and uses of excised tissues, or even their specific origins, the complexity of this issue becomes apparent, and it has only deepened with biotechnological advances.

Finally Moore's appeals reached the U.S. Supreme Court, accompanied by the usual flurry of amicus briefs from research institutions, but the high court also upheld UCLA's patent in 1990, ruling that Moore had no property rights in the cells taken from him, a move that was widely regarded as a triumph for biotechnology companies.[66] Notably, the Supreme Court also expressed concern that extending "property" to include organs would exercise a chilling effect on medical research. This concern seems to have trumped the individual's property rights in his own body.

"My doctors are claiming that my humanity, my genetic essence, is their invention and their property," Moore lamented. "They view me as a mine from which to extract biological material. I was harvested."[67] Throughout his legal battles he remained a tireless and vocal advocate for patients' rights until his death in 1990 as he lost his final battle in the Supreme Court. He was fifty-six and died in a hospital where he was undergoing experimental treatment for his illness.

John Moore's story illustrates how the same courts that grew to welcome patent claims from universities like UCLA, from researchers like David Golde, from biotechnology start-ups like Hayflick's, and from companies like GE and Sandoz have dismissed claims brought by patients themselves and their survivors, the primal sources of those valuable medical innovations.

Since these events, a flood of life patents, or biological patents, has been granted to researchers not only for simpler organisms such as bacteria and yeast but also for medically important higher animals, such as Harvard's cancer-prone "oncomouse."[68] Human genes, cells, tissues, and "products" that include revolting human-animal chimeras have been granted patents. In fact, everything has been patented short of an entire human being. Perhaps to allay fears of such an eventuality, the USPTO in 1987 offered reassurances that it would not allow the patenting of human beings.[69] Although it did not cite case law or explain its legal reasoning, antislavery statutes are thought to preclude such patenting, even though body ownership and body patenting are legally distinct. But pragmatically speaking, the distinction is not that comforting because the courts have tended to treat control over a person's body and body parts as a property issue, and they have repeatedly ruled that in these circumstances, people hold no property rights to their bodies.

Disease genes and parts of genes have been patented, often even before their function was known, which would seem to violate the insistence by the USPTO that a patent application specify the use of the patented entity. Other potentially lucrative technologies have been patented as well, including a human hematopoietic stem cell patented by a Stanford University researcher. Hematopoietic stem cells are medically valuable because they are tabulae rasae, able to develop into many types of tissues, and devoid of compatibility problems. Unlike the unique tissues of John Moore and Henrietta Lacks, such stem cells are ubiquitous, harvestable from embryos and newborns.

These developments mean that the medical-industrial complex takes a fiscal interest not only in patents that ultimately emanated from the extraordinary tissues of John Moore and Henrietta Lacks but also in patents on the tissues of everyday people.

In 1991, the financing structure of the USPTO, which had relied upon tax revenue, was changed so that it became largely funded by fees from those who sought patents. Seventy percent of the USPTO budget comes from such maintenance fees,[70] and in the eyes of many, this reliance upon funds from applicants compromises the office's independence. Some tie the pressure upon patent examiners to approve applications to the desire for fees. Other factors exert pressure upon the patent office to accept rather than to reject patent applications.[71] Some applications filed by pharmaceutical companies are four hundred thousand pages long,[72] and firms often employ fleets of lawyers to fight rejections and patent-office challenges. Patent officials are often simply unable to resist applicants' legal pressure, and discussions on USPTO websites are filled with complaints from examiners who bewail the pressure they feel to approve applications.[73]

Blurring the Lines

As 1991 drew to a close, I was oblivious to these developments. I was working as a newspaper editor and a classical-music announcer, having left the positions as a technician in hospital laboratories where I'd worked a decade earlier, just before the accelerated commercialization of research. Back then, the laboratories I frequented had been staffed by investigators whose ambitions turned toward academic advancement, tenure, fame, and the alleviation of human suffering, not always in that order. No one I knew there entertained dreams of riches. Every day, to enter our lab, I passed a door adorned with a cover from *Travel & Leisure* magazine that featured well-heeled vacationers lounging in luxurious surroundings: the typewritten legend below it read, "If you're looking for leisure, keep traveling."

In 1992, I began two years of study at the Harvard School of Public Health on a journalism fellowship. In my naiveté, I expected classrooms helmed by Martin Arrowsmiths, but I was instead introduced to a transformed medical-research culture. During the traditional first-day-of-class exercises, I internally cringed as we were asked to introduce ourselves and to say a bit about our backgrounds, our work, and what we hoped to take away from the school. As I listened, I learned that impressive scientist-humanists who held MDs, PhDs, or both made up most of our class. Some had spent years rendering care to the poor in developing nations, others had mounted campaigns to care for traditionally underserved patients at home, while still others had already tasted success in the laboratory, conducting research into HIV, tropical disorders, or multidrug-resistant TB. An astonishing number had done all three, and still others were young idealists fresh from schools of medicine. Then, it was my turn.

"I'm a journalist," I muttered, fighting the temptation to slip a bit lower in my seat. A look of disdain from the professor would not have surprised me. Instead, I soon became accustomed to the sudden, galvanized attention my admission tended to draw from professors. Most flew to my seat to give me their cards and to chat about the nature of their work. I was invited to lunch, to visit their labs, and to tour their biotechnology companies. Initially I was flummoxed, but I soon realized that in addition to their work as professors of immunology or toxicology, most of my biomedical science professors were nursing biotech companies. They let me know, subtly or overtly, that they would welcome any press attention I could garner for them in the pages of the *New York Times*, *USA Today*, or even the *Boston Globe*. One fellow, who will remain nameless, eagerly asked, "Can you help me get on *Oprah*?" Positive press attention enhanced their fledgling companies' visibility and could help attract a large pharmaceutical company's financial attention.

The drug industry was not only buying the technology these professors devised but was also acquiring the most promising start-ups themselves. It was a sage bargain because the pharmaceutical corporations did not have to outlay funds to subsidize the research and development: the federal government and the biotech firm had done that. Thanks to the Bayh-Dole Act, large drug companies had only to pay for the patent (or for the company, in which case the patent came with it) and then, after a relatively small investment of their own, to enjoy the profits from licensing the patent or from selling the resulting medication, tests, or other product.

For their part, the universities understood that there was much money to be made even after giving the researcher his cut. Researchers typically sign a contract with their university that stipulates the terms under which a patent based on their work will be assigned to the university. A third to half of the money generated by a discovery is typically assigned to the inventor, with the rest split between his department and the university. Universities benefit from more than the sometimes enormous cash infusions when they sell or license a patent to a corporation.

They can also benefit from payments they receive for conducting clinical trials. Once they have ceded the control of the patent to industry, however, the university no longer dictates the terms of such research, nor can it decide which drugs will be developed and marketed and which will be abandoned.

Unlike researchers and the university, the taxpayers, whose dollars funded the discoveries made and patented in academia and commercialized by drug makers, receive nothing except the presumption that they—we—will benefit down the line from an increased number of medical advances.

Chief among these medical advances were supposed to be new drugs for important diseases. And by the early 1990s, there were plenty of these. HIV disease was still a murkily understood and terrifying plague that had slipped over into pandemic status. Tuberculosis was undergoing a horrible renaissance, recurring in virulent forms that were unchecked by the traditional antibiotic regimens. In fact, antibiotics in general had lost their efficacy from overuse because public-health strategies such as infection control, hospital design, case-finding, and disease surveillance had been abandoned. People were beginning to succumb to old infectious diseases like meningitis that we thought we had conquered, as well as to new terribly virulent ones such as "flesh-eating" necrotizing fasciitis.

We desperately needed new antibiotics. We needed treatments for killers such as heart disease and stroke and a myriad of cancers. Parkinson's, which was increasingly prevalent among people under forty, Alzheimer's disease, sickle-cell disease, an array of cancers, serious psychiatric syndromes, and devastating genetic disorders such as Tay-Sachs and Canavan's cried out for treatments. There was no dearth of medical challenges, and the university–pharmaceutical industry marriage brokered by the government, we were told, would escalate the development of answers and bring those answers to market.

Yet, in a sense, we Westerners had it easy. Malaria, tuberculosis, sleeping sickness, and emerging diseases roiled the developing world, which lacked access to medical care and basic drugs that already existed for long-standing conditions such as cancer. Poor and developing nations were utterly unequipped to treat new ones, such as AIDS and other emerging infectious diseases.

Did the academia-corporation partnerships bring us the drugs and treatments the world needed? Subsequent chapters will discuss this vexing question in detail.

The Medical-Industrial Complex

Medical-research practitioners still work and compete to devise ways to alleviate human suffering and to conquer disease. But the culture has changed. Buying, selling, and the desire to make a profit now are integral goals of academic research, as they have always been goals of corporate research.

Bayh-Dole is widely credited with stimulating significant growth in the university-industry technology transfer and research collaboration. And indeed it did catalyze the $43-billion-per-annum biotechnology industry and enrich scientists as they began to organize their university research to ferret out patentable ideas, schemes, and inventions that they developed with the help of industry.[74]

Colleges and universities obtained only about 260 patents a year before 1980's Bayh-Dole Act: today universities secure approximately three thousand patents a year, according to the Association of University Technology Managers, which represents the employees of university technology transfer offices.[75] (In 2010, the U.S. Patent and Trademark Office approved 220,000 patents of every kind.) These early scientist-entrepreneurs had to figure out their economic strategies and marketing as they went along, but eventually universities chose to dedicate technology-transfer departments to coordinate this lucrative mission. Before Bayh-Dole, only twelve technological powerhouses—including MIT, Stanford, the University of California, Johns Hopkins, and the University of Wisconsin—had set up technology-transfer offices to broker patent and licensing agreements that transformed researchers' findings into patented, marketable commodities for corporations.

But by 1991, the number of patents and licenses obtained by North American colleges, research institutes, and hospitals had leaped more than a hundredfold to nearly 2,800 patents and licenses gleaning $218 million in royalties. Biomedical research was now big business, and small biotechnology start-ups, including those held by instructors and professors who licensed their patents shrewdly or sold their companies to large corporations, could and did become rich. By 2003, North American university researchers had started 374 companies,[76] and academic institutions had completed 4,516 licensing arrangements that earned them more than $1.3 billion.[77] By 2006, technology-transfer offices generated at least $45 billion, largely from licensing fees. Some universities did astonishingly lucrative business: Stanford University made $61 million in 2006, and New York University acquired $157 million.[78]

Technology transfer is an issue for students, too. Students who are inventors can reap 33 to 50 percent of the funds earned by a new product, and the balance of the profits from their discoveries usually goes to the university. The university often also pays the patent fee, which can be prohibitive for a student, reaching $15,000 or more. By contrast, a scientist working in industry usually collects nothing: the corporation takes the patent rights.[79]

A Delicate Balance

Is there a downside to the collaboration that has proven so fruitful for universities and drug companies? In *Science in the Private Interest*, Tufts professor of urban and environmental policy and planning Sheldon Krimsky argues that universities harbor several "personalities" that serve essential public functions. Among them is the Baconian model of the university, named after the English philosopher Francis Bacon, who has been called the "father of empiricism" because he championed the scientific method of induction (discovering general principles from empirical evidence) over theories and mathematical models as a way of understanding the world. For Bacon, the collection and interpretation of facts and data were paramount, and he extolled the value of collaboration between investigators in an institutional setting. In the Baconian model, the university's stores of knowledge are valued for their ability to abet productivity. In this role, the intellectual products of the university contribute to the economic and industrial development of society, and the university itself serves as a wellspring of productivity. The pursuit of knowledge is as valuable as the marketing of products resulting from the university's intellectual property. In the medical sphere, the university spurs the generation of medicines and therapies *because they are needed by the public*, not because they are most likely to be profitable.

However, Krimsky notes that the university has also long been recognized as a unique arena where knowledge is a virtue that is pursued not for the development of intellectual property, but for its own sake. This facet of the university as a collegial haven, marked by the free and open exchange of knowledge and by collaboration, is a cultural resource that should be protected to preserve intellectual vigor. Such unhindered collaboration profits society because if researchers had financial disincentives to collaborate, the rate of discoveries would be much slower.

Collegial sharing of data was never flawless. In his 1968 memoir *The Double Helix*,[80] James Watson related how he, Francis Crick, and Maurice Wilkins raided King's College researcher Rosalind Franklin's xerographic data in the early 1950s in a conspiracy that helped them become the first to determine the structure of DNA and may have cost her the 1962 Nobel Prize that the men shared. Typically for the times, this act was motivated by a lust for scientific glory, not by monetary motives. But the conspiracy was so shocking because it violated the collaborative norm, or at least the ideal. Sharing of data *was* the norm and a virtue, essential to maximizing researchers' chance of success. Collaboration also showed that the results were more important than who discovered them. Today, however, data sharing is more than unexpected, it is viewed as risky behavior and sometimes as criminality, as the Zhu-Kimbara case that opened this chapter illustrates.

But the pure pursuit of knowledge is valuable in its own right because basic science pursuits are a fertile source of important but serendipitous discoveries. Alexander Fleming discovered penicillin when mold destroyed bacteria in a culture whose dishes he had neglected to disinfect; the artificial sweetener aspartame was discovered when chemist James M. Schlatter, who was attempting to produce a medication for ulcers, absentmindedly licked his fingers and was surprised by their sweet taste. Researchers seeking a cancer treatment stumbled upon eflornithine, the best medication devised against African sleeping sickness; Viagra was originally developed as an oral medication for hypertension and angina, but in Phase I trials it did a better job of inducing erections than protecting the cardiovascular system; and lithium carbonate's ability to temper the mood swings of people with bipolar disorder was discovered when guinea pigs, given the drug in an attempt to increase their urine production, became sleepy. The freedom to pursue basic research is important because discoveries often are not tied to specific research plans, but to happy accidents.

The university and its researchers also play a key role in a third important arena: national defense. As with the Manhattan Project, researchers and the university are trusted to maintain confidentiality as the custodians of important scientific information for our national defense. In this role, the university is depended upon to place national interests above its own and that of its faculty members. "In fulfilling this mission," Krimsky reminds us, "universities have accommodated to secrecy in defense contracts."

Finally, there is what Krimsky refers to as the "public-interest model," which casts the university as dedicated to public welfare in a wider sense. For-profit corporations serve the public interest when to do so dovetails with their financial interests, but the university serves a wider and very different public-interest role.

Instead of capitalist self-interest and competition, the university is an oasis of resources and expertise wielded by researchers whose work is underwritten by the federal government. Its work is dedicated to economic, social, and medical problems without being influenced by the market viability or profitability of these approaches. This is a mission hardly to be found elsewhere, and in the medical arena it again casts the university in the unique role of an entity dedicated to the alleviation of human suffering and the betterment of health for their own sake, not for the sake of profit.

A delicate balance characterized the relationship of the various university roles until 1980. But the slew of laws that fostered cozy relationships between corporations and universities in 1980 blurred the line between the for-profit corporation and the university. As a result, the university has lost these pivotal values that protected the public's interests as they interfered with profitability and corporate missions.[81]

As Sheldon Krimsky has observed, "The public ethos of science slowly disappears, to the detriment of the communitarian interests of society."[82]

CHAPTER 2

THE HIGH COST OF LIVING

How Patent-Based Monopolies Inflate
Drug Prices

*Expensive medicines are always good: if not for the patient, at least for
the druggist.*

—RUSSIAN PROVERB

"Could you say that again?" Heather managed to croak weakly.[1] What
she thought she heard had so stunned her that she was surprised she
could produce any sound at all. Robin, the benefits manager, hesitated
a moment before replying. "I said that despite the changes to the insurance plan, your medication costs will continue to be covered. However,
there is a deductible, and you will be responsible for the out-of-pocket
costs of your medication until the deductible is met."

"And the deductible is $2,500?" demanded Heather incredulously.
Not waiting for an answer, she continued, "So I have to pay for my meds
until I have bought $2,500 worth?"

"Yes."

Heather, thirty-five, knew she should be angry. And scared. "But the
truth is, it just didn't sink in for a while. I was in shock. I had walked into
the HR conference room for what I thought would be a routine benefits
meeting and I was going to leave not knowing how I would pay for my
pills. I felt clueless and confused. But I knew I needed my medication."
Her medication is called Mysoline, and Heather needs it to function
because she suffers from epilepsy. She is also a strong, vibrant woman
who runs half-marathons, volunteers at a food bank, and holds down a
high-energy position as a publicist for a small New York City publisher.

But she well remembers being a delicate child beset by allergies and racked by frequent seizures until a doctor finally discovered that Mysoline quelled them without triggering her numerous sensitivities. For twenty-four years she has never missed a pill or a doctor's appointment, and she has been rewarded with a seizure-free life.

Suddenly, Heather felt that she couldn't leave the meeting without pressing her case. "You can't do this to me. Twenty-five hundred dollars—I don't—how many people have that kind of money lying around? I can't afford this. You're putting my health in danger, I cannot function without Mysoline." The benefits manager began to repeat the new policy, but Heather interrupted her. "I understood what you said. Did you hear what I said? Without my pills, I will have seizures. I can't work. I can't function." Swallowing, she fell silent for a moment before pleading, "*Please* don't do this to me." Uncomfortable, Robin stared at the sheaf of papers before her, fingering them as if the answer were written there somewhere. "I am afraid . . ." she began, but didn't finish.

Instead, she looked into Heather's eyes. "Heather, my hands are tied. We have to cut costs, and we don't want to lay anyone off. This is the best we can do. Can't you borrow the money?" Heather looked down and shook her head back and forth, not trusting her voice.

"Does anyone else have questions?" Robin asked the room. "No? Well, feel free to call me for a meeting if you need more information." As the group filed out of the room, Robin turned to Heather, who was still sitting silently. "Let's go to my office. I think we can arrange a loan with liberal terms. I'll do what I can to help you get through this."

After receiving the bad news in January 2008, Heather quickly discovered that area pharmacies sold the 250 mg Mysoline tablets she needs only in a three-month supply, for $1,200, which she had to borrow. After that, she ordered a one-month bottle online. But

Suddenly, I couldn't find the formulation I needed online, or anywhere else. I called a woman at the insurance company, MedCo, and she was great, very helpful. She would find a pharmacy in the New York City area that carried it, call to tell me, and I would drive over and buy up all they had because I was so afraid of running out. Once I drove to Oceanside in Queens to buy it, then to a pharmacy in Howard Beach where they said they had ordered it for me but I had to buy the entire bottle at $700, which I did and finally satisfied the $2,500 deductible. But one day in June I called MedCo and they could not find a pharmacy that carried it anywhere. I called the drug's maker in California and the representative informed me in a casual voice that they had stopped manufacturing it and he didn't know if or when it would be back on the shelves. He said it like he was saying "It's sunny outside." He also said something about it being off-patent or the patent changing hands; I was so nervous, I don't remember. I asked, "What am I supposed to do? I need it," and he said airily, "Oh, there must be a generic." No, he didn't know the name. No, he didn't know where I could get it. No details or advice: that was it.

Now I was really scared. I couldn't take just any anticonvulsant: I'm allergic to Dilantin and can't take phenobarbital. Mysoline allows me to function: without it, I would be seizing. What if there wasn't a generic? If there was one, what if some "inert" ingredient in the generic triggered an allergy?

Mysoline is branded but off-patent. Heather's doctor found that there is a generic version, but warned that she wasn't out of the woods yet. "My doctor is convinced that Mysoline is superior to primidone, the generic version, and he was concerned that the generic could cause me trouble or work less efficiently. He says that generics have quality issues and are not always the same as the branded versions."

Heather's doctor is correct in saying that generics and patented medications can differ. Generic medications can be made and sold without patent protection because the formulation of the generic drug may be patented, but its active ingredient is not, opening the door to equivalent formulations and market competition that usually reduces the U.S. price dramatically, by at least 20 percent. Although generics must be "bioequivalent," with the same active ingredients and exerting the same effects, the "identical" description used by the FDA to describe generic versions of drugs is more a legal label than a scientific one, because generics can diverge from patented drugs in their dosages, administration, and even formulations. In Heather's case, her doctor performed repeated blood tests and found that the generic worked for her, fortunately without triggering any of her allergies.

"Then," Heather recalled, "in the summer of 2009, the company called to tell me that the medication would be back on the shelves in mid-July. I was glad to get it, but I resent the indifference that the drug maker and my employer showed toward my life and health." Although Heather suffered no physical harm from her ordeal, it has changed her outlook. "This wasn't elective; this was a necessity, and I was shaken to think that my medical lifeline could be snatched away just like that. I don't think I'll ever see drug companies the same way again."

Mysoline, Heather's medical lifeline, is not a novel "blockbuster"— usually defined as a drug with annual revenues of over $1 billion. Mysoline is not even very profitable despite its substantial price tag, because relatively few people buy it. It is an unfashionable drug introduced in 1950 by a company that is now known as AstraZeneca, and it is now used by a small minority of people with epilepsy. In the decades since Mysoline's advent, it has been surpassed by many more modern anticonvulsives, although it is less toxic and triggers fewer side effects than most newer drugs. Doctors long ago fell out of the habit of prescribing it, and most who take it are older people who resist changing a medication that works for them or people who, like Heather, cannot tolerate the contemporary drugs.

It went off-patent a long time ago and several drug makers have manufactured and distributed generic forms of the drug that compete with Mysoline for its shrinking market. By 2009, Valeant was making Mysoline in the 250 mg formulation Heather needs; it had vanished from store shelves in 2008 after its previous maker determined that it failed to meet "certain commercial criteria."[2] It simply wasn't profitable enough.

But its sudden, unannounced withdrawal had put Heather and others who depend on it at risk for more than isolated seizures: as its label clearly warns, abruptly discontinuing Mysoline can cause *status epilepticus*, a life-threatening condition in which the person's body is racked by repeated, frequent seizures that can kill.

The Right to Profits

At first blush, one may be tempted to brush aside complaints about profit-driven marketing decisions and argue that a nongovernmental for-profit company has the right to abandon any product that fails to meet its commercial criteria. Ours is an unapologetically capitalist society, and "profit" is not a dirty word. Pharmaceutical corporations are entitled to profit by patents on medications that help us live longer, happier lives—and by other kinds of medications, if they can legally sell them. But Dr. Eva C. Winkler, an oncologist and expert in the organizational ethics of health care, points out that there are ethical and legal limits to profit making in health-care settings. "In a healthcare organization, competence is ensured by setting high standards, promoting continuing professional development, *tying incentives to quality of care rather than to costs alone* [italics mine], and ensuring adequate staffing."[3] Heather's situation dramatizes the toxic economy and ethical morass that sometimes result from exploiting patents that are key to health rather than placing quality of care ahead of profits.

In the absence of sufficient countervailing factors, the weighing of profits over patient welfare has generated a host of such real, not philosophical, American nightmares. They arise partly because the U.S. government allows drug companies to set prices without the regulation and controls employed by some countries, such as Brazil and Canada.

Happily married and with three children aged six to eleven, John Colacci thought of himself as a blessed man. He was supported by an extended family, many friends, and a can-do attitude as he stood before a packed ballroom at a 2001 colorectal-cancer fund-raiser in Toronto. There, he quoted Eleanor Roosevelt: "Yesterday is history; tomorrow is a mystery. Today is the gift: That's why it is called 'the present.'"

The fund-raiser was held to raise money to offset the considerable medical expenses of cancer patients like himself. "None of us knows for sure how long we have to live," he continued, "but we always have a choice how we spend our time in the present moment." In 2004, however, Colacci learned that he was running out of time: the Avastin he had been taking since his cancer recurrence had stopped working, and the statistics gave him just 4.6 months to live.

As he anxiously researched his treatment options, Colacci learned that Erbitux, a last-ditch medication for metastatic colorectal cancer, existed, but not for him. (If Erbitux sounds familiar, this is because it is the drug that led to Martha Stewart's jailing over insider trading in 2004: ImClone, the biotechnology company that developed it, was founded by her friend Sam Waksal.) Erbitux helps many cancer patients who do not respond to other medications,[4] but Bristol-Myers Squibb (BMS) had decided not to launch the drug in Canada because it could not charge a high-enough price there.

In 2004, Erbitux cost $17,000 a month, making it one of the most expensive cancer drugs. Moreover, it treats colorectal cancer, which strikes 106,000 Americans a year. But it was not the costliest cancer drug by a long shot: Zevalin treatments for an unusual type of lymphoma cost $24,000 a month. By contrast, the Avastin that Colacci had been taking was a relative bargain at C$4,000 a month.[5]

BMS decided to shun the Canadian market, which has long been a thorn in the side of the drug industry because it flatly refuses to pay top dollar for the pharmaceuticals it buys to distribute through its governmental health services. Instead, its Patented Medicine Prices Review Board assesses a drug's cost in Germany, France, Italy, Sweden, Switzerland, the United Kingdom, and the United States, then applies a formula to ensure that Canada pays something near the list's median. For many years, this strategy guaranteed that Canadians' medications cost less than those in most other affluent Western nations, including the United States.

Recently, however, drug makers have reacted by playing hardball and refusing to sell their medications in Canada at all—in essence, holding Canadian patients hostage for a higher price. Because Erbitux was protected by patent, no other company could legally offer it for sale without a license from BMS, leaving patients like Colacci without access to the drug.

So Colacci turned to the United States. During the Erbitux standoff, Canada spent $208,125 within a year in order for him to cross the border and undergo weekly treatments with the U.S.-licensed drug at the Roswell Park Cancer Institute in Amherst, New York. Colacci was lucky: some other Canadians had to pay similar sums out of pocket.

Was the drug effective? "I got fabulous results from it," Colacci, forty-three, exulted in 2008. "It literally melted it [the tumor] away."

Bristol-Myers Squibb finally relented and decided to sell Erbitux to Canadians at their government's price—a hefty $56,000 for the average course of therapy—high, but considerably lower than what the Canadian government had paid for Colacci's U.S. drugs, and lower than what we pay in the United States. However, E. Richard Gold, director of McGill University's Centre for Intellectual Property Policy, sees this less as a happy ending than a cautionary tale. "Both the Commissioner of Patents and the Competition Bureau should be prepared to step in to prevent such abusive behavior in the future."

John Colacci died surrounded by his family on Thursday, June 18, 2009, at the age of forty-four. Was the Erbitux worth the astronomical price? Perhaps a better question is, "Why did it cost $208,000?" This is not an isolated case: cancer medications tend to be very expensive, and there are eight such medicines for which Americans pay more than $200,000 annually, as well as three others that cost in excess of $350,000 a year.[6] A slew of other cancer drugs are just as expensive per dose, but they are typically taken for less than a year and so never top the annual price tag of the other medications. Some common but relatively pricey medicines include Lipitor, which lowers blood cholesterol and costs $1,500 a year, and the schizophrenia drug Zyprexa, which costs $7,000 a year.

Why do our medications cost so much—too much—and how can we change this sorry situation?

The Numbers Game

Pharmaceutical companies, principally represented by PhRMA, the Pharmaceutical Research and Manufacturers of America, don't deny that their prices are high: pharmaceutical firms claim that high prices are necessary to recoup their gigantic investments in developing patented medicines. Defending and profiting from their patents, they argue, is also necessary to protect their investment. After the USPTO issues patents for a company's medicines, genes, cell lines, genetically tailored animals, or other medically valuable inventions, the company can realize profits only by exploiting that exclusive patent. Companies also say they depend upon profits to provide funds that underwrite additional research and more medicines, so that research into new cures would grind to a halt if prices were lowered.

The companies add that they need their patents to protect their huge investment in research and development from interloping competitors who, were it not for patents, could simply reverse-engineer, reformulate, and offer the medications for sale on the cheap because they would not be saddled with the considerable expenses involved in research, development, and FDA-required clinical testing.[7]

Thus, drug makers offer rationales for prohibitive pricing, claiming that they need to charge high prices in order to fund the risky, expensive, and lengthy business of bringing medications to market that fight important diseases while extending the lives and alleviating the sufferings of Americans. As PhRMA states on its website:

> It takes about 10–15 years to develop one new medicine from the time it is discovered to when it is available for treating patients. The average cost to research and develop each successful drug is estimated to be *$800 million to $1 billion* [italics mine]. This number includes the cost of the thousands of failures: For every 5,000–10,000 compounds that enter the research and development (R&D) pipeline, ultimately only one receives approval. . . . Success takes immense resources.[8]

The $800 million figure quickly became ubiquitous, cited even in a 2010 entry on the World Records Academy website:

> MOST EXPENSIVE MEDICINE—
> WORLD RECORD SET BY SOLIRIS
> CHESHIRE, CT, USA—Soliris, a drug made by Alexion Pharmaceuticals, which is given intravenously to treat a rare disorder [paroxysmal nocturnal hemoglobinuria] in which the immune system destroys the red blood cells at night, costs $409,500 a year—setting the world record for the most expensive medicine. . . .
>
> Alexion spokesman Irving Adler said the high price of Soliris reflects several factors, "including an $800 million investment to develop the drug," as well as a 15-year investment of time. . . .
>
> Last year Soliris sales were $295 million. Since Alexion started selling Soliris two years ago, its stock price is up 130%.[9]

(Moreover, in 2009 PhRMA agreed with an upward revision of the estimated cost of bringing a new drug to market, to between $1.3 billion and $1.7 billion. The study methodology was very similar to that of the 2001 study and shared its flaws, which are detailed below.)[10]

Pricing Innovation

Does it really cost more than $800 million to create a new drug? In 2001, Joseph A. DiMasi, now director of economic analyses at the Tufts University Center for the Study of Drug Development, partnered with the University of Rochester to calculate the answer: each new drug for the U.S. market takes twelve to fifteen years and costs $802 million,[11] a price that has doubled since 1987.[12]

The Tufts study was based on a survey of ten pharmaceutical companies and on information supplied by PhRMA. The confidential data provided by the companies to Tufts included several categories of research expenditures used to calculate the cost of bringing a single drug to market. These included the costs of research and the profits the drug makers could have realized by investing their money elsewhere than drug design and testing.[13]

PhRMA praised DiMasi's study and verified the accuracy of its findings, constantly citing the $802 million figure—often rounded down to $800 million—in its publications and in interviews that defended high drug prices. But Clay O'Dell, a spokesperson for the Generic Pharmaceutical Association, was less impressed: "The methodology of this study is suspect. It ignores the fact that some of the drug development costs are tax deductible, and that some of the research is subsidized by the government through the National Institutes of Health." In fact, a U.S. government study just the year before had determined that a new drug took from ten to twelve years to come to market, at a cost of $359 million—less than half that alleged by the Tufts study.[14]

From the beginning, independent expert analysts had wished to scrutinize the study's data, but they went unexamined by outsiders for nearly a year because the Tufts analysts did not release the data on which the authors relied. The individual pharmaceutical companies that had supplied data insisted that their numbers were proprietary—industry secrets—and successfully fought their release to these independent evaluators.

Over the next year, the $800 million figure remained unchallenged as analysts unsuccessfully sought to force the release of the proprietary data on which it was based. During this time the report's numbers were widely accepted and had gained currency among the public as well: a surprising number of people can cite the $800 million estimate.

Drug makers certainly can—the gargantuan price tag forms the backbone of their rationale for high prices. The industry complains that R&D is so very risky that only one in a thousand candidate drugs ultimately finds its way to pharmacy shelves and profitability. Because most medications fall by the wayside during research and development, industry earnings must cover the cost of these failed drugs as well as that of the relative few that become profitable.

The DiMasi report also claims that conducting clinical trials, which generate up to 70 percent of the high R&D bill, costs $282 million per new drug.[15] But this figure far exceeds that arrived at by the Congressional Research Service, and it also outstrips the 29 percent figure in PhRMA's own 1999 survey.[16] However, the purportedly high cost of clinical trials not only feeds the purported $800-million-per-drug price tag, it gives the industry a useful basis for lobbying the FDA to ease and speed up the drug-approval process.

The drug companies marry the claims of the hefty price of a new drug to a warning that if they do not earn enough to recoup the staggering price of drug development, the pipeline of needed new drugs for major medical problems will dry up and the American public will face a dearth of the medicines that keep us alive and healthy. Industry analysts argue that because a patent confers a twenty-year monopoly from the date of application and a new medication takes as long as fifteen years to develop, test, and bring to market, the company that holds the medication patent has as little as five years to exploit that patent and recoup these stratospheric costs, to say nothing of earning a profit.

These claims are studded with factual and logical flaws that cause a dramatic overestimation of medications costs. Many of these issues are detailed in financial writer Merrill Goozner's revelatory book *The $800 Million Pill: The Truth Behind the Cost of New Drugs.*

Among the flaws in the Tufts study:

THE TUFTS STUDY CALCULATED THE COSTS OF ATYPICAL DRUGS.

Instead of a broadly representative sampling of drugs, the Tufts study confined itself to pricing a narrow, atypically expensive selection of drugs that it called "self-originated new chemical entities." These are more commonly called "new molecular entities," or NMEs, and they are the rarest type of medication in that they represent a completely novel treatment for disease, rather than a "retread" of existing medications. Over the twelve-year period preceding the Tufts study, only 42 percent of new drugs were NMEs, and only about twenty-six such drugs enter the global market each year.[17]

By contrast, most drugs that appear on the U.S. market today are slightly modified versions of existing drugs, popularly called "me too" or "copycat" drugs. They are created by tweaking the molecular structure of FDA-approved drugs to produce a closely related drug with similar effects. Or the "new" drug is chemically unchanged but released on the market in a different strength, or reformulated as extended-release pills, syrups, or inhalants. Alternatively, medicines are paired with other drugs, as when Claritin was combined with the decongestant pseudoephedrine to create Claritin-D, which does double duty by treating people who suffer from allergies *and* colds. A drug may also be turned to novel uses, as when Prozac was "repurposed" as Sarafem for menstrual symptoms. All win fresh patents for the firm and are sold as expensive "new" drugs.

Such doppelgänger drugs rarely meet a new medical need: they are routes to obtaining new patents or other monopolies on existing drugs, and, unlike NMEs, they are familiar, predictable, and relatively cheap to formulate and test.

But NMEs are much more difficult to discover, formulate, and test than are the "copycat" drugs that have come to flood the market, so they are also the most expensive. This leads us to the next of the study's distortions.

THE TUFTS STUDY CALCULATED THE COSTS OF UNUSUALLY EXPENSIVE DRUGS.

Not only did the Tufts calculation include only the atypical, expensive NMEs, it focused on the rarest, costliest kind—the drugs whose development and testing costs are borne wholly by the pharmaceutical industry. Not one of the sixty-eight drugs in the study was developed with any kind of government financial support, which is very unusual.

Government-funded academic researchers are usually responsible for the discovery and innovation that the pharmaceutical industry has capitalized. The early development costs of most drugs are borne by the government, which subsidizes university and other public research through grants. Biotechnology companies tend to develop the university's government-supported drug discoveries, and then the biotechs partner with or are purchased by large pharmaceutical companies. Thus the drug firms acquire the medication and the patent without paying for the taxpayer-subsidized research.

Dennis Slamon of UCLA discovered Herceptin, which staves off breast cancer recurrence; Craig Jordan of Northwestern University developed tamoxifen, also for breast cancer, and Brian J. Druker of Oregon Health and Science University shepherded kinase inhibitors, which offer tailored, focused attacks on cancer cells rather than the more diffuse attacks that also ravage healthy tissue. One such kinase inhibitor, Gleevec, is the most effective cancer treatment for chronic myeloid leukemia, a surgical strike that was developed in academia. Entire families of essential medications, such as protease inhibitors for HIV/AIDS, were discovered and initially developed in academia, not in corporate laboratories.

During the period of the Tufts study, the U.S. government spent close to $10 billion supporting the academic development of drugs, twice as much as industry did.

THE TUFTS STUDY INFLATED ITS ESTIMATE BY
ADDING A SPURIOUS "OPPORTUNITY COST."

DiMasi found that the average price of developing an atypical NME drug without any government support totaled approximately $400 million. But he then added an additional charge that more than doubled the figure, to $802 million. That charge is the "opportunity cost."

John Stuart Mill introduced the concept of an opportunity cost as the cost of what one surrenders in one direction in order to pursue an investment in another. Investing in one arena, such as drug design, precludes spending those funds elsewhere, so you lose the benefits posed by the other opportunity. If, for example, I use $10 to buy a movie ticket instead of depositing the cash in a savings account, the opportunity cost is the interest I would have earned from the $10. If I wait a few years to apply the opportunity cost, the interest rate will increase its value. If I wait long enough to calculate it, the value of the interest on that $10 in forsworn savings will double it to $20. The fact that I also could have doubled it in an hour by playing bingo cannot enter into the calculations, because although there may be more than one alternative way to spend the funds in question, warns Goozner, the opportunity cost is always the value of one choice, not all of them.

Similarly, if a pharmaceutical company spends, say, $240 million developing a new drug instead of banking the funds, the opportunity cost is the interest it would have earned had it made that deposit. Or the opportunity cost can be the dividends the firm would have earned had it bought stock in Starbucks instead. Or it can be the warm sense of altruism, elevated self-esteem, and glowing corporate image the firm would have basked in had it donated the same funds to global hunger relief, because an opportunity cost needn't be limited to money. But in this case concerning drug-development costs, money is what is at stake.[18]

In their study, the Tufts analysts decided that the opportunity cost was the loss of the investment income that drug makers could earn if they invested their funds instead of dedicating them to the search for new drugs. This cost is usually assessed some time after the research is complete, with interest. Because DiMasi included opportunity costs and added them only some time later, after they had accrued value with interest, the value of the opportunity costs approximately *doubled* his estimate of drug-development costs.

Although the accounting firm Ernst & Young validated this cost for the Tufts team, Goozner points out that applying the opportunity cost contradicts generally accepted accounting practices. For a drug company, drug research is not an investment; it is a business expense. If drug companies invested their resources in Starbucks or in global hunger eradication instead of drug design, they would no longer be drug companies. Expending resources on drug design and marketing is not an option for a drug company; it is a necessity.

This means that, for tax purposes, the expenditure on drug design is a business deduction, not an investment. Opportunity costs simply do not apply, and most independent drug-firm studies recognize this. In fact, only two of the seven studies that the Tufts report references include an opportunity cost. This cost does not properly apply here, and it should not have been part of these calculations, slashing the $802 million price tag roughly in half, to $403 million.

THE TUFTS CALCULATIONS IGNORED DRUG MAKERS' HEFTY TAX BENEFITS.

Pharmaceutical companies receive more tax deductions than any other industry: in fact, after tax benefits are applied, the real expense to the industry of each R&D dollar spent is only $0.66.[19] When these tax breaks are applied to the per-drug cost calculations, the cost is further reduced, from $403 million to $240 million.[20]

THE TUFTS CALCULATIONS OVERESTIMATED THE ACTUAL COSTS OF DRUG TRIALS—AND THEIR NECESSITY.

By DiMasi's own estimates, the cost of conducting clinical trials of drug candidates constitutes 70 percent of the cost of bringing a new drug to market. But this is only because clinical trials conducted by the drug industry carry an unusually high price tag, much higher than comparable ones conducted by the government.[21]

The National Institute of Allergies and Infectious Diseases, or NIAID, for example, spent $1.5 billion to conduct 1,700 clinical trials between 1992 and 2001. The agency had to pay for the studies and also for the treatment, care, and testing of one hundred thousand volunteers. The Government Accounting Office found that the average extra cost of maintaining a patient in their clinical trials of an experimental therapy was only $750 more than maintaining him on standard therapy.

In clinical trials conducted by private industry, however, the average additional cost was $2500. This inflation leads some analysts to cry "foul" and to wonder why drug firms pay so much more for clinical trials.

Moreover, a strange practice inflates the cumulative cost of the drug industry's clinical trials. Pharmaceutical companies claim that they must spend a great deal of money to test candidate drugs for FDA approval, but many of the medications in their clinical trials do not require testing or approval, because they have already been FDA-approved for the indication in question. A CenterWatch study determined that in 2000, the industry spent $1.5 billion on clinical trials of drugs *that had already been approved.*

Why? Because industry's clinical trials include "seeding" trials, in which pharmaceutical sales representatives induce doctors to prescribe a drug to a large number of patients. The resulting data are collected and exhaustively mined by the company for any positive results that can be used in marketing, advertising, and "physician education" about the product.

Similarly, in "switching" trials, large numbers of doctors are induced to change their patients to another medication—that of the company conducting the trial—and the data are scrutinized for any impressive-sounding results. Seeding and switching studies are not conducted for FDA approval, but in order to increase the marketing, visibility, and sales of medications. These clinical trial data are used by sales representatives in persuading doctors to use the drugs, to replace other firms' drugs with the one being studied, or to use the tested drug for a different indication. Such trials often lack a control group, are sloppily designed, or otherwise fail to meet FDA standards, but they are useful for spurring sales.[22]

Bristol-Myers Squibb, for example, like many other major firms, produced an FDA-approved statin drug (also known as an HMG-CoA reductase inhibitor). Statin drugs include Mevacor, Lipitor, Zocor, Pravachol, Lescol, and Crestor, which reduce blood cholesterol, a waxy substance that is associated with heart attacks, stroke, and other cardiovascular diseases.[23] BMS amassed clinical data from seeding and switching trials to convince doctors that its statin drug works better than Merck's, even though the BMS drug lowered cholesterol less. BMS spent tens of millions of dollars and emerged with data that might not have stood up to FDA review but was invaluable for pitches to doctors, public relations, press conferences, marketing—and for inflating the average R&D cost.

Appalled, the editors of thirteen medical journals united to write a *New England Journal of Medicine* editorial that condemned this practice.[24] "Patients participate in clinical trials largely for altruistic reasons, that is, to advance the standard of care," it read. "In the light of that truth, the use of clinical trials primarily for marketing in our view makes a mockery of clinical investigation and is a misuse of a powerful tool."[25]

Such seeding and switching trials should not have been included in the price of bringing a drug to pharmacy shelves.

Thus, Goozner calculates that even when it includes the inflated costs of irrelevant clinical trials and of atypically expensive industry-generated NMEs, the corrected cost of bringing a pill to market, using PhRMA's own data, falls to $240 million—"not chump change, but not $800 million, either."

What did other analysts find when they examined the Tufts study? The Global Alliance for TB Drug Development (TB Alliance), a Swiss-based network dedicated to providing needed drugs to the developing world, estimated the cost of a new drug at $150 million to $240 million—identical to the Goozner-corrected $240 million estimate above.

In December 2001, the Health Research Group of the Ralph Nader–founded Public Citizen made a calculation of drug-development costs that utilized a different methodology. It used PhRMA's data, but added *all* the R&D costs expended by pharmaceutical companies over a similar period in the 1990s and divided it by the number of new drugs that won FDA approval and reached the market during that period. Public Citizen arrived at a figure of $110 million.[26] After tax deductions, this fell to $71 million, although the average R&D costs for NMEs were higher: $150 million. Not only is Public Citizen's $150 million figure within the TB Alliance's $150-million-to-$240-million range, but, observed Goozner, "If the industry-funded academic economists at Tufts had factored out the half of industry research that is more properly categorized as corporate waste, their numbers would have been similar to that of the Global Alliance." (See "Rx Markup," below.)

Rx Markup: Cost to Bring a New Drug to Market

Group	Cost
DiMasi/Tufts/PhRMA	$802 million–$1 billion
Merrill Goozner	$240 million
TB Alliance	$150–$240 million
Public Citizen	$110–$150 million

So the Public Citizen, Merrill Goozner, and TB Alliance account-ings of R&D costs for new drugs brought to market between 1994 and 2000, based on PhRMA's own data, range from $71 million to $150 mil-lion ($240 million for the atypical NMEs).

And the $800 million figure so widely touted by drug companies? "This is just a thinly disguised advertisement for the pharmaceutical industry to justify continued price-gouging," Public Citizen's Dr. Sidney M. Wolfe told the *New York Times*.[27]

The high drug price tags are not just a U.S. problem. In the poor-est regions of developing countries such as India, where two-thirds of the populace earn less than $2 a day, people who need expensive cancer drugs such as Avastin and Erbitux simply die. In fact, most branded Western drugs are out of their reach. A poignant 2009 *New York Times* essay, by my friend and breast cancer survivor Katherine Russell Rich, documents how in poor Indian villages oncologists are all but non-existent.

Rich accompanies a local doctor to visit a woman dying from ovar-ian cancer and is shocked when the doctor urges the indigent woman to take heart from Rich's recovery, which came only after expensive can-cer medications, diligent medical monitoring, and a hellish $250,000 bone-marrow transplant.

> "Look at her [Katherine Rich]. She has had cancer, and she is not crying. She is happy and hale." The woman's eyes widened. I felt my jaw tighten. She pulled herself out of bed. "Thank you," she whispered, bowing gratitude on shaky legs, beaming at our connection, at this solid proof of hope, and it was as if I'd been socked. All this time, I'd thought what I'd had was miraculous luck, but in this plain white room, the knowledge came, inescapable: miracles are limited by place.
>
> "If you smile, you heal faster," Dr. Aggrawal told the patient. Away from her room, he said simply, "If you get cancer here, you die." And her? Too advanced, he said. He brightened. "If you make a patient smile, you make them healthy," he chimed. So cruel, I thought, breathless with anger. Then I saw. That's what he had: words.

Most inhabitants of developing countries have little or no access to the cheaper drugs that Americans take as a matter of course (such as painkillers, vaccines, and antibiotics), so they die of ailments that are routinely avoided or treated in the United States.

These deaths are directly related to patent protection, because were the patent holders willing to allow licensing of low-cost or generic versions of their protected medications, which they do only rarely, more people would live.

In the United States, generic medications can often cheaply substitute for those medicines with expired patents. Generic medications are cheaper bioequivalent drugs that act in the body in substantially the same way as the branded medication, with blood levels close to that produced by the branded medication.[28] The FDA considers that they have the same safety, efficacy, and manner of use and administration. Because the patent has expired, competition is possible, which tends to dramatically lower the price of generics in the United States.

Generic drugs are not the answer for developing countries, however. There are fewer drug manufacturers competing for these markets, and generics are often sold by the same corporation that sells the brand-name medications. This means that when generics are available, they tend not to be as cheap in the developing world as they are in the United States.

India had long been a traditional source of cheap drugs because its industrial tradition is coupled with a patent system that until recently issued monopolies on the various *processes* of making medications but did not recognize patents on the drugs' *components*. So Indian firms reverse-engineered expensive branded drugs, then manufactured and sold them cheaply to the nations of the developing world. But World Trade Organization–brokered agreements have forced India to respect the Western patents it once flouted, and it is now legally blocked from reproducing cheap versions of many medicines.

The patent-mediated pricing crisis in developing countries is far more extensive and dramatic than in industrialized Western nations and Japan—the countries that pharmaceutical companies call home. Medication-access crises in the developing world are fed by complex political and cultural factors, so its struggle for drug access usually is treated as peculiar to the developing world.

However, medications that are priced beyond the ability of the populace to pay can also be viewed on a spectrum that encompasses the developed as well as the developing world. The crisis in the Third World is the same as our own domestic crisis in drug affordability because it shares the same cause: the determination of pharmaceutical manufacturers to maximize profits from their patents, regardless of patients' ability to pay.

In contrast to our nation's policies, some developing nations have not shrunk from their versions of "march-in" solutions. "March-in" or "step-in" powers are those wielded by governments when they intervene to, in effect, overrule a patent. Governments sometimes sweep a patent aside, refusing to recognize the monopoly in order to guarantee their citizens' access to a needed drug. They issue a "compulsory license" that allows a company other than the patent holder to market cheaper versions of the medication, as, for example, Brazil did when it marched in to give its poor citizens with HIV and AIDS free access to lifesaving antiretroviral and other drugs.

Working Without a Net: Vanishing Health Insurance

Despite our much higher annual income, Americans, like citizens of the developing world, are increasingly unable to afford our medications. A 2010 Harvard Medical School study, the largest such ever performed, found that one in five prescriptions are never filled, and "affordability" topped the list of reasons why as given by doctors.[29] Little wonder: according to a report by the University of Minnesota's Stephen Schondelmeyer, PharmD, PhD, drug prices rose 27.6 percent between 2005 and 2009.[30]

Because health insurance is tied to employment in the United States, the recent double-digit gains in unemployment have created a new army of the uninsured. Data show us that a recession leaves people out of the workforce for longer than usual, during which time residual health benefits expire. Some of the unemployed may extend their health insurance through the Consolidated Omnibus Budget Reconciliation Act, or COBRA, but this program requires the newly unemployed to pay at least the entire cost (up to 102 percent) of the premium to their former employer. COBRA is expensive and is likely to be one of the first lingering perquisites of employment to be abandoned in favor of staples such as housing and food. Even for those who can afford to maintain the benefits, it is temporary, expiring after eighteen months. But the recent surge of U.S. unemployment is only the latest challenge: medication prices have been rising beyond the reach of Americans for a long time.

Even those who are still employed have lost the level of health benefits they enjoyed a decade ago. As Heather, whose story opened this chapter, discovered to her dismay, companies with their eyes on the bottom line are forcing employees to shoulder an increasing proportion of their health-care insurance and costs, including medication costs. In 1999, a worker's contribution to health insurance premiums averaged $1,543; by 2000, it had more than doubled, to $3,515.[31] (See "Average Annual Health Insurance Premiums," below.) Health insurers shift the responsibility for expensive care through plans that require employees to pay a large portion of their premiums or higher deductibles or to fund their own care through "health accounts" that are easily emptied by serious illness. (See "Percentage of Covered Workers," p. 72.)

Small businesses constitute 95 percent of U.S. firms and are the

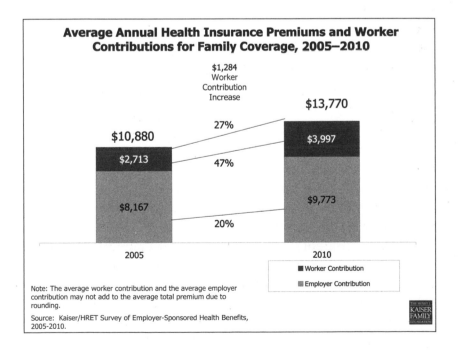

Average Annual Health Insurance Premiums and Worker Contributions for Family Coverage, 2005–2010

$1,284
Worker
Contribution
Increase

$13,770

$10,880

27%

$3,997

$2,713

47%

$8,167

$9,773

20%

2005

2010

■ Worker Contribution
■ Employer Contribution

Note: The average worker contribution and the average employer contribution may not add to the average total premium due to rounding.

Source: Kaiser/HRET Survey of Employer-Sponsored Health Benefits, 2005-2010.

THE HENRY J.
KAISER
FAMILY
FOUNDATION

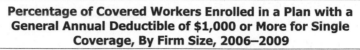

Percentage of Covered Workers Enrolled in a Plan with a General Annual Deductible of $1,000 or More for Single Coverage, By Firm Size, 2006–2009

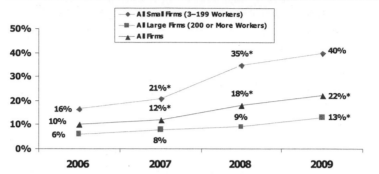

*Estimate is statistically different from estimate for the previous year shown (p<.05).

Note: These estimates include workers enrolled in HDHP/SO and other plan types. Because we do not collect information on the attributes of conventional plans, to be conservative, we assumed that workers in conventional plans do not have a deductible of $1,000 or more. Because of the low enrollment in conventional plans, the impact of this assumption is minimal. Average general annual health plan deductibles for PPOs, POS plans, and HDHP/SOs are for in-network services.

Source: Kaiser/HRET Survey of Employer-Sponsored Health Benefits, 2006–2009.

most likely to offer their employees very limited insurance or none at all. Those who have no health insurance are likely to be the working poor who can least afford to pay for their own maintenance medications for high blood pressure or diabetes. They are unable to shoulder the medication costs associated with catastrophic illnesses such as cancer or stroke. Yet some very small businesses cannot afford to offer health insurance, especially when a single employee's catastrophic illness could bankrupt the company.

As Heather's case illustrates, even those fortunate enough to retain a job with health benefits have no guarantee that they can procure expensive lifesaving medications when they need them.

In 2009, the public "town hall" meetings around President Obama's health-care-reform proposals drew thousands of people who shared horror stories of being financially ruined by medical costs or of being dropped by their insurers on some pretext when they developed a medical need. Such stories have become a commonplace of television and newspaper reports.

PhRMA has addressed the anxiety over drug affordability on its website, which offers a pie graph illustrating that "retail medication costs" represent only 10 percent of all health-care costs, according to an industry-supported report. To determine the significance of this cost estimate, one must know how a "retail medication" is defined, because medication costs are not confined to private expenditures by patients at pharmacies: medications are obtained during hospitalization, in nursing homes, and from in-hospital pharmacies, so perhaps medication accounts for well more than the 10 percent of health-care costs cited here. The site doesn't divulge their roles in the overall figure. What's more, the graph fails to acknowledge that the percentage of health-care costs ascribed to medications is escalating rapidly. In 2000, the $121.8 billion spent on retail medications accounted for only 9.4 percent of total health-care expenditures, but the Centers for Medicare & Medicaid Services calculated that the annual increase of retail medication expenditures is now 15 percent.[32]

Frankly, though, the invocation of such percentages is simply misdirection, just as the magician's flourish draws one's eyes away from the meaningful action. The 10 percent figure means little because health care of all types is far too expensive in the United States, where our total health-care expenditure reaches $1.3 *trillion*: what percentage of this unimaginable sum goes to medications is beside the point. At $130 billion, it is immense, and it is beyond our ability to pay.

We might be tempted to think that we have already expended the funds for these health-care costs, so that we obviously *can* pay for them. But this perspective fails to take into account that funds spent on expensive medication means funds diverted from other essential health services. Moreover, we are no longer able to cover even critical medication costs: despite the massive expenditures we have made, many medication needs are going unmet, even those that are promised by designated government programs. To illustrate this, let's take the example of the federally funded but state-administered AIDS Drug Assistance Program (ADAP), which was established to provide expensive antiretroviral drugs to HIV-positive Americans who need them to live but cannot afford them.

Without reliable access to the medications, which cost an average of $12,000 a year, people with HIV are more likely to develop full-blown AIDS, to transmit the virus to their children or sexual partners, to require much more expensive hospitalizations and treatment, and to die.

But ADAP funds are now depleted with regularity, and we have had to resort to rationing care.

Some states have had to open ADAP waiting lists, for example, to limit the drugs that are provided, or even to close the ADAP program to new enrollees.[33] In September 2009, there were 157 people on the waiting list for ADAP; by September 2010, the waiting lists had ballooned to 3,337 people who were without the HIV medications they needed and could not get them from ADAP.[34]

For underinsured, HIV-infected people, the high prices of anti-retroviral medications and the ADAP waiting lists have created a national crazy quilt of risk, with most HIV-infected people in some states getting the medications they need, while those in other states are more likely to die without treatment—or to require very expensive hospital intervention to treat opportunistic infections that could have been more economically—and humanely—prevented by ADAP meds. The expenditures we make in overpriced medicines mean that we cannot cover other, perhaps more important and efficient ways of protecting health.

Unaffordable Medications—A Common Cause

In the end, what matters is not the percentage of health-care costs that medications represent but the percentage of Americans who cannot afford their out-of-control medication prices. This is not just a problem for the elderly, because according to Washington, D.C.'s nonpartisan Center for Studying Health System Change, 13.9 percent of people under age sixty-five could not afford their prescriptions in 2009—up from 10.3 percent in 2003. This means that costs forced about thirty-six million employment-age adults and their children to go without prescription drugs in 2009, nearly twelve million more than in 2003.[35]

The inability to afford medications challenges the middle class and the poor, the employed and the unemployed, and young and older Americans alike. But older people are especially vulnerable. When Medicare was enacted in 1966, well before passage of the Bayh-Dole Act, medications were inexpensive because private companies could not patent the fruits of government-sponsored university medical research and so could not enforce the monopolies that enable stratospheric drug pricing.

And in those halcyon times, we have seen that some researchers chose not to patent their drug discoveries. No Medicare provision to cover the cheap prescription medications was thought necessary.

Today the medications for the chronic ailments that plague older Americans are quite expensive. The aging are caught between the Scylla of fixed income and the Charybdis of rising health issues that multiply with aging—such as diabetes, osteoporosis, cancers, and prostate disease. Forty-two percent of the elderly take four or more drugs.[36]

Their ability to stave off catastrophic ailments such as heart disease and stroke depends upon their affording prescriptions of hypertension pills, blood glucose, beta-blockers, and other preventative medications. They are not alone: recent studies suggest that the financial need to forgo necessary medications afflicts as many as half of all Americans. About half (49 percent) of the respondents to a July 2009 Kaiser Health Foundation survey cited cost as the reason they had taken risky steps such as skipping pills or letting prescriptions go unfilled.

One of every three said that the inability to afford medications had forced them to "rely on home remedies or over-the-counter drugs instead of seeing a doctor," and one of every five said that cost had kept them from filling a prescription for a medicine. In addition, one of every seven Americans reported skipping a dose of medicine or cutting pills in half to make their medications last longer.[37] No reports tell us how many, out of pride, do not admit to their doctors or to pollsters that they cannot afford to fill their prescriptions and so leave clinics as unprotected against catastrophic illness as when they arrived. (See "Half Put Off Care Due to Cost," p. 76.)

It's not surprising, then, that 94 percent of Americans in a 2009 Harvard/Kaiser Family Foundation poll think that drug costs are unreasonable.[38] However, pharmaceutical corporations do not rely upon the court of public opinion to secure their pricing structures against political assault. Instead, the industry takes its case directly to lawmakers, deploying 1,544 lobbyists. In 2009, pharmaceuticals and health product lobbying totaled $263,377,975,[39] and PhRMA's share alone was $26,150,520.[40] Through the lobbyists, pharmaceutical companies defend the high cost of prescription drugs as essential to recoup and subsidize research expenses and obtain special protections against unwanted controls and price constraints. Even more troubling, fully half of these

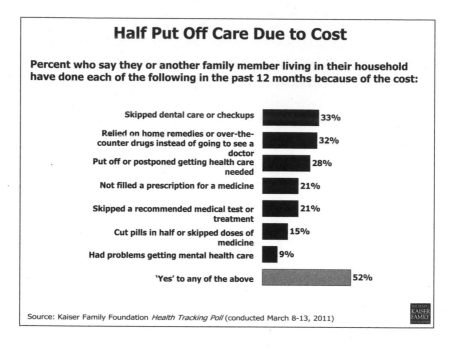

Half Put Off Care Due to Cost

Percent who say they or another family member living in their household have done each of the following in the past 12 months because of the cost:

Skipped dental care or checkups	33%
Relied on home remedies or over-the-counter drugs instead of going to see a doctor	32%
Put off or postponed getting health care needed	28%
Not filled a prescription for a medicine	21%
Skipped a recommended medical test or treatment	21%
Cut pills in half or skipped doses of medicine	15%
Had problems getting mental health care	9%
'Yes' to any of the above	52%

Source: Kaiser Family Foundation *Health Tracking Poll* (conducted March 8-13, 2011)

health-care lobbyists are former government officials, cutting deals with their erstwhile colleagues for the industry's benefits and special protections.

To this end, the drug industry's lobbyists fight against the expansion of generic drug use and against proposals to allow the importation of cheaper drugs from Canada, both of which would help break its monopoly on some expensive drugs. Corporations also lobbied against lawmakers' attempt to ease the plight of the elderly by adding a prescription drug benefit to Medicare.[41] This is a battle that PhRMA would seem to have lost when health-care reform supplemented Medicare with just such a prescription benefit, yet in a surprising turnabout, the industry was a powerful and vocal champion of the Obama administration's health-care reform.

Strange Bedfellows

On March 23, 2010, President Obama signed the historic Patient Protection and Affordable Care Act into law. The Obama administration's brand of health-care reform is a brilliant piece of legislation that demolished several tenacious barriers to health-care access. It also recognizes governmental responsibility by providing access to the health-care system outside the private sector, by uncoupling health insurance from employment, and by providing mandatory coverage for the forty million Americans who currently lack it.

Health-care reform, most key tenets of which take effect in 2014, recognizes Americans' personal responsibility as well, levying fines on people who neglect to obtain health insurance, for example (although this requirement to obtain health insurance may not survive legal challenges that were brought in 2010).

Corporate responsibility is also necessary. One critical step in that direction was achieved in a provision of the bill that eliminates the "pre-existing condition" as a criterion to deny or delay insurance coverage. This move clearly favors the needs of patients over the desire of insurance companies to curtail their costs. The provision extends coverage to higher-risk patients with known diseases that are likely to result in greater health-care expenditures. The law also prohibits lifetime limits on insuring health care, provides for covering children on family plans until age twenty-six, not nineteen, and expands access for low-income patients by subsidizing an additional sixteen million people who are added to the government's Medicaid health insurance program. Coverage of abortion, that perennial political football, is prohibited.

The bill was fought by health insurers and their lobbyists through America's Health Insurance Plans, a national association that represents 1,300 health insurance companies that cover more than two hundred million Americans.

But the pharmaceutical industry, which had similarly fought the Clinton administration tooth and nail when it attempted sweeping reforms in the early 1990s, lavished $100 million in marketing, television advertising, and grassroots organizing to promote the Obama administration's reforms. Why?

. Perhaps because, while President Obama's reforms are sweeping and laudable, they are not perfect, in that they fail to regulate pharmaceutical drugs, eschewing the price controls and tightened federal regulation that the industry feared most.[42] Even though the federal government is the nation's largest purchaser of medications, through Medicaid, that agency consistently fails to use its purchasing clout to negotiate a better price, or even to import cheaper medications from Canada. In fact, Congress passed bewildering legislation in 2007 that expressly forbids Medicaid, the government, private retailers, and even private citizens from buying cheaper supplies of U.S. drugs from foreign sources—a tactic called reimportation.[43]

For example, a U.S. pharmacy may not purchase Canadian Prozac even though the drug costs 53 percent less there and is manufactured in the same plant. Law enforcement often looks the other way when private citizens buy small amounts of their drugs abroad—often capped at ninety days' worth. Yet the rejection of price controls means a windfall for U.S. drug makers.

And it means a lost opportunity for the rest of us, because the Congressional Budget Office estimates that price controls that were proposed in 2003 would have saved the government $19 billion over the following decade, and private citizens would have saved $80 billion more. It is easy to see how; we've already seen why Canadian drugs are much cheaper than our versions, but the trend is global: for example, the same dosage of Nexium, a common heartburn remedy, costs $36 in Spain but $424 in the United States.[44]

Meanwhile, as noted above, the federal government provides subsidies and research-and-development funds to university researchers that allow pharmaceutical firms to produce these very drugs much more cheaply than they otherwise could. Finally, the expansion of medical insurance and access to care for tens of millions of Americans translates into tens of billions of dollars in earnings to drug makers as more people flock to doctors' offices and leave with prescriptions for the industry's products. According to a *Huffington Post* estimate, industry insiders expect health-care reform to boost new pharmaceutical-industry profits by more than $137 billion.[45]

All this makes the pharmaceutical makers, not the American people, the biggest beneficiary of health-care reform, which explains the industry's heavy spending on reform's behalf. Companies such as Johnson & Johnson, Pfizer, and Merck enjoy profits that averaged between $2 billion and $10 billion in 2008, making pharmaceuticals, as we've seen, the nation's third-most-profitable industry, while the health insurance industry ranks a distant twenty-eighth. Yet the latter is heavily controlled by reform, and the former's pricing and other business practices remain largely unregulated.

Pharmaceutical Missions

What do we, the medical consumers, receive for inflated drug prices, untouched by health-care reform? PhRMA's website trumpets the value we are getting for our money, pointing to our longer life expectancy and reminding us that it has leaped more than thirty years since 1900, when the average U.S. life span was forty-seven years. (U.S. life expectancy dipped slightly in 2010, however.) And indeed, within the past century the drug industry has produced medicines that have transformed our lives by taming killers. Diabetes and childhood leukemia have been transfigured from death sentences into survivable illnesses. Better treatments for heart disease have contributed seven years to the average U.S. life span, and cancer treatments have extended it by 2.4 months, according to Roberto Ferrari, president of the European Society of Cardiology.[46]

Medications have freed sufferers of serious mental ailments from institutionalization, allowing them to become happy, stable, and productive members of society. Antirejection medications have permitted the development of surgical transplantation that allows patients to survive with new hearts, livers, and kidneys. The list goes on.

PhRMA reminds us that without pharmaceutical companies' ingenuity and long years of arduous and expensive research, development, and testing, we would still be at the mercy of infectious killers such as tuberculosis, syphilis, and smallpox.[47] This is true. Much of the medical innovation it refers to, however, is quite old and predates the post-1980 commercialization of research. More recent innovation has not addressed the major life span challenges such as producing an HIV vaccine, addressing the problem of drug-resistant antibiotics, or giving us medications that address the consistent health challenges faced by most of the world.

PhRMA does not, for example, discuss the fact that a baby girl born today in Japan, an industrialized nation that is home to 20 percent of the world's fifty largest pharmaceutical companies, can expect eighty-five years of life, but a girl born the same day in Sierra Leone, where the average annual income is $139 and medications are hard to come by, can expect only thirty-six years. Fully ninety cents of every dollar expended on medical research is lavished on conditions that cause only 10 percent of "the global burden of disease."[48]

The industry's stirring commercials feature earnest young researchers who recount how the ailments of family members or cherished patients sent them on a personal mission to save others from a medical killer. Soaring anthems trumpet the company's humanitarian mission of ameliorating human health at home and abroad.

Yet pharmaceutical companies seem driven by motives that they decline to trumpet, for the drug industry does far more than recoup its costs: its annual sales of $400–600 billion speak for themselves, eloquently announcing that pharmaceutical makers are living large. The industry's profits, nearly 10 percent of its gross income, exceeded $65.2 billion in 2008 alone.[49]

For approximately twenty years pharmaceutical companies enjoyed the highest profits of any U.S. industry. In 2002 the combined profits for the ten drug companies in the Fortune 500 ($35.9 billion) exceeded the profits of the other 490 businesses put together ($33.7 billion).[50] (See "Profitability of Pharmaceutical Manufacturers," below.)

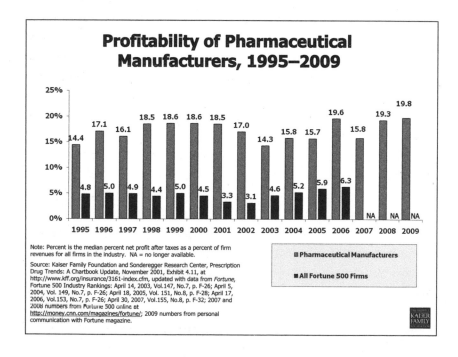

Profitability of Pharmaceutical Manufacturers, 1995–2009

Note: Percent is the median percent net profit after taxes as a percent of firm revenues for all firms in the industry. NA = no longer available.

Source: Kaiser Family Foundation and Sonderegger Research Center, Prescription Drug Trends: A Chartbook Update, November 2001, Exhibit 4.11, at http://www.kff.org/insurance/3161-index.cfm, updated with data from *Fortune*, Fortune 500 Industry Rankings: April 14, 2003, Vol.147, No.7, p. F-26; April 5, 2004, Vol. 149, No.7, p. F-26; April 18, 2005, Vol. 151, No.8, p. F-28; April 17, 2006, Vol.153, No.7, p. F-26; April 30, 2007, Vol.155, No.8, p. F-32; 2007 and 2008 numbers from Fortune 500 online at http://money.cnn.com/magazines/fortune/; 2009 numbers from personal communication with Fortune magazine.

Pharmaceutical Manufacturers

All Fortune 500 Firms

If the R&D costs are so high, and if, as the PhRMA site claims, five to ten thousand candidate drugs are investigated for every one that ultimately finds its way to the medicine cabinet, how can an industry burdened with such astronomical costs see any profit, to say nothing of having become the most profitable industry on the planet?

It's simple. Drug companies don't pay for most of their R&D—you do. University research is typically subsidized by your tax dollars. Whether the university researcher partners with the corporation, whether she starts a biotechnology company that the corporation buys, or whether the corporation enters into a contract directly with a department of the university, the result is the same. The corporations market, sell, and profit from a patent that is the product of largely taxpayer-funded university research.

Generic Strategies

Generics are often hailed as the key to taming high medication prices. After the patent expires for a medication's active ingredient, it can no longer sell licenses or extract royalties, and other companies are free to manufacture it without engaging in the extensive testing that the FDA requires for the approval of new drugs. The FDA instead requires only an Abbreviated New Drug Application, or ANDA, for generic versions that are simple, rapid, and far less expensive. A generics manufacturer can begin this truncated approval and testing process before the patent actually expires without legally infringing on the patent, so that it can begin selling the cheaper generic version the day after the brand-name patent expires.

This makes generic medications much cheaper to produce, and these savings are usually passed on to customers, especially in the United States. The availability of generic versions of branded drugs has sometimes eased patients' difficulty in paying for them.

Pharmaceutical makers have historically opposed generic medications because of the competition from these low-priced drugs. But more recently, they've pursued other strategies to reduce the competition from generic versions. The rivalry between generics and brand-name manufacturers has been marked by conspiracies that violate antitrust laws.

For example, the Drug Price Competition and Patent Term Restoration Act of 1984, popularly known as the Hatch-Waxman Act, grants 180 days of market monopoly to the generic manufacturer that is first to file an ANDA for a generic version of a brand-name drug.[51] However, in 2006 the Department of Justice charged Bristol-Myers Squibb and generics maker Apotex with conspiring to violate the Hatch-Waxman Act by agreeing that Apotex would delay bringing clopidogrel, the generic version of the blood thinner Plavix,[52] to market. This left the field free for BMS and its high prices, effectively extending BMS's monopoly on the drug beyond the legal limit.[53] In return, BMS agreed to share the resulting profits with Apotex. Both companies stood to increase their earnings, but Americans continued to pay inflated prices.

The Department of Justice filed criminal charges against BMS and one of its officers, Dr. Andrew G. Bodner. Both BMS and Bodner admitted lying and pled guilty, resulting in a $1 million fine for the firm and two years' probation for Bodner. There are many other similar cases where pharmaceutical companies have been accused of skirting the law to continue profiting from patents. These include the 2009 complaint that Solvay paid generic drug makers Watson and Par to delay generic competition to Solvay's best-selling branded testosterone-replacement drug, AndroGel, whose 2007 sales topped $400 million.[54] In 2004, Warner Chilcott agreed to pay Barr $20 million if Barr delayed entering its generic version of the very profitable Ovcon 35 oral contraceptive for five years, and a 2001 complaint alleged that Hoechst Marion Roussel Inc. paid generics maker Andrx millions of dollars to delay bringing to market a competitive generic alternative to the hypertension and angina drug Cardizem CD.[55] Such cases resulted in fines, probation, or consent agreements in which drug makers admitted to wrongdoing.

Moreover, a 2010 Federal Trade Commission report, "Overview of FTC Antitrust Actions in Pharmaceutical Services and Products," describes 104 such legal actions it has undertaken,[56] mostly between patent holders and generics companies that were trying to maintain monopolies on drugs whose patents had legally expired or that had otherwise conspired to evade or to delay lowered generic pricing.[57]

Are such "pay for delay" arrangements between pharmaceutical houses to delay generic manufacturing legal? As recently as 2010, one analysis stated that "The Circuit Courts are split. While the Sixth Circuit agrees with the FTC that reverse payment settlements are per se violations of the antitrust laws, . . . the more recent wave of decisions in the Second, Eleventh and Federal Circuit Courts of Appeals have held reverse payments to be acceptable restrictions within the exclusionary scope of patents."[58]

Life-Cycle Management

Drug makers often complain of a limited time to exploit their patents, but they do have remedies, because they use a variety of legal strategies to extend the period during which they can capitalize on their monopolies. Drug firms call these strategies for maximizing their monopolies "life-cycle management" or "evergreening," on which they expend a great deal of creativity and lobbying to stave off laws that might enforce or tighten patent expiration.

Patents usually grant twenty years of exclusivity but typical patent extensions of five to fourteen years are granted to cover the periods of FDA-mandated testing[59] and certain other conditions.[60]

Patent life management strategies include patenting polymorphs, which are simply new physical forms of the medication—in powders, pills, extended-release, capsule, gel, topical tablet, or liquid versions, or using different solvents. These may involve minor changes in dosage strength, but they needn't do so to buy the company varying amounts of extra time to exploit its monopoly.

Chemical tweaking of drug compounds pays off in new patentable drugs as well. For example, some active ingredients exist in "left-handed" and "right-handed" forms—chemically different structures that are mirror images of each other. These are called *enantiomers*, which the USPTO recognizes as separate inventions. Although enantiomers may have different biological effects, they can be similar enough for one to be patented for the same use after the patent on the other has run out.

Moreover, creative industry chemists are not limited to patenting the right- or left-handed versions of these drugs. An equal mixture of the two forms, called a *racemic* mixture, can be patented in addition to the right- and left-handed enantiomers.[61]

The antidepressant drugs Lexapro and Celexa, for example, are differently "handed" versions of the same molecule. Lexapro contains only the left-handed version (S-citalopram), and Celexa is a racemic mixture of equal parts of the left- and right-handed versions (S-citalopram and R-citalopram). Yet each was awarded its own patent. If only one version of the drug is active, then separating it into a drug with the racemic mixture and another drug consisting only of the active enantiomer, as the maker of Lexapro and Celexa did, imparts no clinical benefit to the patient and may dilute its action, but it benefits the company by providing it with another twenty-year patent for the same medication.[62]

In order to win a new patent, the drug company need only show the USPTO that its proposed "new" drug is marginally better than the old one. This is easier than it sounds, because scrutinizing the various components of a clinical trial will often reveal some subgroup or application where a medicine pulls slightly ahead of its very similar competitor.

Take the popular heartburn medication Prilosec, which is a racemic mixture of two enantiomers. This blockbuster drug earned AstraZeneca $26 billion and was cryptically popularized in early direct-to-consumer advertisements as the "purple pill." As Prilosec's 2001 patent expiration date loomed, AstraZeneca tested a single enantiomer of Prilosec, which it dubbed Nexium, and found that its activity was similar to Prilosec's. Testing Prilosec against its alter ego showed that for one uncommon condition, erosive esophagitis (a condition in which areas of the esophageal lining are inflamed and ulcerated, often by chronic acid reflux), Nexium worked slightly better. Nexium was awarded a patent to become the second-generation "purple pill," sold at a similarly high price to unwitting patients who did not realize that the nearly identical Prilosec was now off-patent and available as a cheap OTC pill at the same pharmacies where they filled their pricey Nexium prescriptions.

The only demonstrated differences between the two were a barely perceptible difference in effectiveness for an uncommon complication of gastric reflux—and an enforceable patent.[63] The *Wall Street Journal* observed: "The Prilosec pattern, repeated across the pharmaceutical industry, goes a long way to explain why the nation's prescription drug bill is rising an estimated 17 percent a year even as general inflation is quiescent."[64]

The Copycat Tradition

The selling of copycat or "me too" drugs did not begin with modern drug design. In *The $800 Million Pill*, Goozner writes of how they were already common in 1960 when Senator Estes Kefauver of Tennessee held hearings to probe the extent of copycat drugs.

Kefauver pressed the former head of research at E.J. Squibb to estimate how much corporate drug research was driven by the desire to come up with me-too drugs. The retired executive replied that "more than half is in that category. And I should point out that with many of these products it is clear while they are on the drawing board that they promise no utility. They promise sales."[65]

Today, these patented products of questionable utility—doppelgänger medicines in various physical forms and tweaked chemical structures—require very little in the way of development and minimal testing, yet they are not sold at low prices. Other me-toos include combining two medications into a dual pill such as Pfizer's Caduet, which is a patented combination of Norvasc (amlodipine besylate) and Lipitor (atorvastatin calcium), a "statin" drug used to protect the heart by reducing low-density lipoprotein or "bad" cholesterol while raising high-density lipoprotein or "good" cholesterol levels. Similarly, BiDil is a patented combination of isosorbide dinitrite and hydralazine, two generic medications for the treatment of congestive heart failure. "Repurposing" a drug for new uses is a practice so widespread that 84 percent of the fifty top-selling pharmaceuticals in 2004 were approved for additional indications after their first licensing.[66] And, under the pediatric exclusivity section of the Food and Drug Administration's Modernization Act of 1997, testing a medicine for use in children adds six months to its patent's life, allowing it to be sold to both children and adults under extended patent protection. Claritin's six-month extension in patent life meant an additional $1 billion in earnings for Schering-Plough. Both FDA medical evaluators and patent officers complain they are under pressure to approve such measures and patents based on them.[67]

The "patent cluster" is another useful patent-extension tactic. A company keen to hold on to a blockbuster drug's expiring patent may file dozens or even hundreds of closely related new patent applications, often of dubious merit, to confuse and intimidate potential generics firms and to maintain its monopoly. Drug firms have taken out as many as 1,300 patents across the European Union for a single drug.[68] Pharmaceutical companies have recently begun teaming up with generics manufacturers to make out-of-court settlements that delay the market entry of cheap generic versions of expensive branded drugs.

Pharmaceutical Pricing Strategies

So we return to the key question: If research and development costs are more often borne by the government than by large drug firms and if these companies deftly employ various stratagems to ward off patent expiration—and do all this so well that their profits consistently place them at the global corporate apex—why do medications cost so much?

The prices are high because the structure of the U.S. patent system leaves us no choice but to meet their demands.

It is no accident that the highest drug prices are for the most serious illnesses. The highest drug prices reflect not R&D costs, but rather what desperately sick patients are willing and able to pay to stay alive. Erbitux costs less in Canada than in the United States simply because Canadians struck a hard bargain when they contracted to pay less than the $208,000 U.S. price tag for John Colacci's treatment. Consider also the cost of treatment with the breast cancer drug Herceptin (trastuzumab), which is $35,000 a year. Herceptin was produced by twenty years of research at several universities and was largely financed, as is usual, by federal funds. When it was ready for market, Genentech obtained a patent *via* the Bayh-Dole Act. Yet Genentech justified its price by explaining that it had cost $150–200 million to develop the drug—costs that were, of course, largely borne by taxpayer-subsidized university research, not by Genentech. Roche, which acquired Genentech,[69] now generates $2 billion a year from Herceptin sales although it did not invest in its R&D costs: this $2 billion, then, reflects not Herceptin's R&D costs but what cancer patients are able to pay to stay alive.

The United States does not pressure drug companies to lower their prices, and individual patients like Heather and John Colacci lack the clout to negotiate them, but one private U.S. industry does wield enough power to force the negotiation of lower medication prices—pharmacy benefit managers, or PBMs.[70]

PBMs such as CVS Caremark and MedCo Health Solutions manage the medication-benefits portion of health insurance for 210 million Americans. They are hired by most health insurers for corporations and for the government, including large insurance plans such as Medicare. PBMs also procure drug prices for other organizations that provide health insurance to their members. The leverage provided by their vast base of insurees enables the PBMs to force drug makers to accept lower prices. Mark Merritt of the Pharmaceutical Care Management Association, the major PBM group, told the *Wall Street Journal* that "one of the great services PBMs provide is to play drug companies off one another and get big discounts on drugs."[71]

PBMs often are expected to retain part of the difference between the regular price and the negotiated price of the drugs as compensation, but because PBM–drug company negotiations are conducted in closed-door meetings, their clients cannot know the size of the difference between the price the PBM wrangles from the pharmaceutical firm and the price it extracts from the insured. Therefore, secrecy surrounds the savings the PBM retains and how much is passed on to employers and consumers. (See "Pharmacy Benefit Managers," below.)

Pharmacy Benefit Managers (PBMs) Control the U.S. Prescription Drug Market

Company	Number of Prescriptions Filled*	Share of Market
Medco Health Solutions	695 million	19.7%
Argus Health Solutions	578 million	16.3%
Express Scripts	425 million	12.0%
CVS/Caremark	384 million	10.9%
ACS	250 million	7.1%
Top 5 PBMs combined	2,331 million	66.1%
Next 5 PBMs	799 million	21.7%
Top 15 PBMS, inclusive	**3,397 million**	**96.3%**
Total	3,528 million	100%*

*The sums may differ due to rounding.
Source: *Drug Benefit News*.

Critics such as former New York congressman Anthony Weiner called for greater transparency. Weiner protested that the secrecy hides the fact that too little of the savings reaped by PBMs are passed on to the employers and the insured. But Merritt disagrees: "The thing that drives prices down is competition, not this kind of transparency which tends to help suppliers keep prices higher." Representative Weiner drafted provisions for an early version of the 2010 health-care reform bill that would require accounting to "cut down on inside deals that benefit only the PBMs and the drug companies,"[72] but the provision did not appear in the final bill.

Employers and insurers seem to be increasingly distancing themselves from PBMs. McDonald's and IBM are among the sixty major U.S. employers that spend more than $4.9 billion on medications annually, and they are calling on PBMs for greater transparency.

Old Drugs Don't Fill the Bill

Consider, too, the corporations' claims that they focus on producing the lifesaving medications that prolong our lives and promote our health. To bolster this claim, they point to such triumphs as the polio vaccine and new antibiotics and take credit for the U.S. life span's growing nearly thirty years within a century as well as for the control of many once-fatal diseases.

At PhRMA's 2009 annual meeting in San Antonio, its then-CEO Billy Tauzin (a former congressman who was key in getting the pharma-friendly Medicare Prescription Drug Bill passed), declared: "You have called for a war against cancer to find the cures that, in our lifetimes, will put an end to cancer, just as we once managed to put polio behind us." Without the industry's willingness to invest heavily and to take huge risks, drug makers claim, our children would still be crippled or dying en masse from diseases like polio.[73] However, the polio vaccine was never patented and was subsidized by the March of Dimes, not private industry, so it doesn't make the best argument for PhRMA's monopolistic drug-research framework.

More important, penicillin, which was found to tame syphilis, and antibiotics against tuberculosis were developed in the 1940s. Drug makers no longer focus primarily on medications that target current health crises; those days seem far behind us.

And although TB has enjoyed a disturbing renaissance due to burgeoning antibiotic resistance, drug makers have given us precious little to fight it. As the existing antibiotics lose their effectiveness because of disease resistance, nothing has emerged to take their place. Similarly, cures for childhood leukemia are important success stories, but they are old ones. When it comes to the contemporary mass killers and cripplers of Americans, the industry has offered us too little against AIDS, hepatitis C, and other contemporary scourges.

Do New Drugs Extend Life?

Are the newest drugs offered by the pharmaceutical industry primarily responsible for extending life, as the industry so often suggests? The question is complicated by the fact that the rate of increase in U.S. life expectancy has flagged, and life expectancy even fell briefly in 2009. However, in 2007, Columbia University economist Frank Lichtenberg wrote a Manhattan Institute paper titled "Why Has Longevity Increased More in Some States than in Others? The Role of Medical Innovation and Other Factors." The paper compared health status in states that rapidly adopted new drugs with that of states that did not, and it ascribed increased longevity to the rapid adoption of new medicines generated by the pharmaceutical industry, thereby finding, or at least strongly suggesting, that using new drugs increased life expectancy, increased productivity, and lowered health-care expenditures.[74]

According to an analysis by Dean Baker, PhD, and Adriane Fugh-Berman, MD, however, the paper used peculiar yardsticks to measure drugs' impact, and it was rife with flawed logic and glaring omissions.[75] Among its failings were:

- Lichtenberg's paper failed to take into account the overweening effect of reducing infant mortality, which is the single greatest factor in increasing life expectancy. States with lower infant mortality rates will have higher life expectancies independent of how rapidly they use the new drugs in question.
- The manner in which the paper characterized the age of a drug—its "vintage"—is not only unusual but profoundly flawed. The vintage is defined as the average year in which its active ingredients were first approved by the FDA, but two-thirds of what are deemed "new drugs" are actually different doses, formulations, or combinations of older drugs—not "new" at all.
- The paper determined health status by looking at AIDS, obesity, and smoking rates. But these are not appropriate measures for determining health status. For example, AIDS is an illogical measure because it is compartmentalized in

groups with a much higher risk for disease and early death, and AIDS is not a leading cause of death in any U.S. state.

- Finally, the paper doesn't sufficiently correct for "reverse causation." This is the situation when a paper's research findings can be explained not only by the explanation that the author adopts, but also by an opposite conclusion.

In the case of the Manhattan Institute paper, for example, Lichtenberg observed that in states where people were early adopters of new drugs, many people lived to older ages. He interpreted this correlation as a causation, concluding that taking newer drugs soon after they are released on the market helped people live longer. But, as Baker and Fugh-Berman point out, "Rather than new drugs extending lives, older people may use newer drugs."

Conversely, Lichtenberg's theory implies that using older drugs is tied to a shorter life span. But again, the causation can be just as easily reversed. Opiates, for example, are older drugs that are often used to treat cancer and chronic pain, and so they may simply be more commonly used by people with life-shortening illnesses instead of actually shortening lives.

This paper is important because it is one of many influential studies written by Lichtenberg that extol the health benefits of quickly adopting new drugs: in fact, observe Baker and Fugh-Berman, "Many citations for claims that improved health offsets the higher costs of new drugs can be traced back to studies by Frank Lichtenberg."[76] So, despite the wealth of references supporting the value of new pharmaceutical drugs to extending our health and lives, Lichtenberg's paper does not demonstrate that the pharmaceutical industry's newest offerings have a marked effect on life expectancy after all.

In many cases, older drugs have been proven equally effective or even superior to newer ones, which tend to be more expensive and unavailable in generic form. The federally funded Antihypertensive and Lipid-Lowering Treatment to Prevent Heart Attack Trial (ALLHAT)[77] determined that the inexpensive diuretic (water pill) chlorothiazide was superior to newer, more expensive hypertension drugs.[78] Another federally funded study, Clinically Antipsychotic Trials of Intervention Effectiveness (CATIE), found that older antipsychotics were as effective as newer ones against schizophrenia.[79]

Certainly, some new drugs have important positive effects on our health, but the *cumulative* positive effect of these drugs may have been dramatically exaggerated. In fact, writes University of Toronto professor Joel Lexchin, MD, "Assessments of the value of new drugs from Canada, France and the USA all show that at best one-third of new drugs offer some additional clinical benefit and perhaps as few as 3% are major therapeutic advances."[80]

Some carry deleterious effects as well, as the well-publicized injuries, death, and recalls from drugs such as Fen-Phen, Rezulin, and Avandia and COX-2 painkillers remind us.

What the Government Can (and Might) Do

What is the answer to medications that are priced beyond the ability of Americans—and others—to pay for them? One powerful, if neglected, solution lies in the U.S. government's power to overrule a patent, sweeping it aside in order to guarantee access to a needed drug if the patent holder refuses to sell the drug at an accessible price. These "march-in" powers allow the U.S. government to issue a compulsory license to another drug company that permits it to make and market the medicine. But such powers are rarely invoked, even in the face of pressing need. The government does not invoke them today to ensure that uninsured patients get expensive medications, and it did not use them in the 1980s and 1990s when the price of the antiretroviral medications drained the funds of the government ADAP (AIDS Drug Assistance Programs) plans that provided treatment to HIV-positive patients.

Yet the exercise of such powers seems appropriate because the federal government subsidizes so much of the research upon which the medication patents are based.

A great deal has been written on how patents have allowed companies to ignore health issues of the poor in countries such as Uganda, Nigeria, and Brazil or to charge prices that place life-sustaining medications beyond their reach. I examine these life-and-death issues in depth in chapters to follow. As noted earlier in this chapter, however, Western health-care corporations block vital health-care access at home, too, in the same manner: by pricing medications, devices, and other treatments far beyond the reach of those who need them, even with the help of insurance, Medicaid, and Medicare. Thus the United States and the

Third World share a problem with the same dynamics, but of course to dramatically different degrees.

Because the problem of overpriced medications presents a far more formidable barrier to health care in poor developing countries, their plight is detailed separately in Chapter 8, which discusses "biocolonialism." But we should note here that, because many pharmaceutical corporations are international companies whose products affect patients in many countries, and because they use the same legal devices in these nations to charge prices higher than patients can afford, these similar problems may have similar answers that can best be addressed by cooperation between nations. As we'll see, some poor developing nations, such as Brazil and Thailand, have been willing to wield the sort of "march-in" solutions that the United States eschews but should actually embrace.

Next Steps?

Health-care reform will be an ongoing process, and as the perennial debates continue, policy makers too often focus on the question "Who will pay the high drug prices?" This inevitably fuels rancorous discussions about the need to impose limits and rationing, which are not in the best interests of patients. Instead, we should ask, as I did with Erbitux earlier, "*Why* is the drug price so high?" We should be better prepared, like Canada, Brazil, and Nigeria, to pressure corporations for lower prices and more seemly profits, or, if necessary, to use the government's march-in powers to invalidate patents in order to ensure drug access.

Because lobbyists influence legislators to discount their constituents' widespread dissatisfaction with drug-pricing policies, lobbying by the pharmaceutical industry should be placed under stricter scrutiny and limited. Perhaps the revolving-door nature of the lobbyist-lawmaker dance (as seen notoriously in the case of former congressman Billy Tauzin, who, as noted earlier, helped ease the passage of the pharma-friendly Medicare Prescription Drug Bill) warrants ending pharmaceutical lobbying altogether. The unique importance and nature of health-care products justify such intensive government oversight.

We should, as I suggested earlier, adopt a more global perspective because we share a medication-affordability problem with the developing world, albeit on a much smaller scale. Drug-price regulation varies dramatically from country to country, as the Canada-U.S. disparities illustrate. I propose that we consider replacing this hodgepodge with better drug-marketing and payment models that provide uniform approval and pricing requirements. Consensus pricing could be enacted in a scheme that acknowledges the gradation of resources from the affluent West to the Third World, which should pay less.

Future health-care reform should be much less solicitous of the pharmaceutical industry's profits and far more mindful of the need of Americans to be able to meet drug makers' prices. With the current reform, this problem has not yet been solved, merely shifted from the consumer to the government and other insurers: consumers will ultimately pay these bills as well.

In evaluating these dramatic suggestions we must remember that the drug industry's pricing and marketing practices do more than price life-saving medications out of our general reach: they sometimes completely bar access to needed therapeutics, as the next chapter will illustrate.

CHAPTER 3

HITTING THE BRAKES

**How Monopolies Stymie the Production
of Needed Medicines**

*The progress of civilization is not wholly a uniform drift towards
better things.*

—ALFRED NORTH WHITEHEAD

On September 1, 2001, the excitement was palpable at the University of
Colorado Health Sciences Center as associate professor Dr. S. Gail Eckhardt strode to the lectern. Amid flashing lightbulbs, she gripped the
podium's sides, leaning slightly forward with excitement, and flashed
a megawatt smile. Her luxuriously tousled blond bob, the earrings that
dangled fashionably over her oversized pearl necklace, and her vis-
ible joy warred with the staid image of a pedant in white that the word
"researcher" can still conjure.

Eckhardt is every inch a scientist, a veteran of forty clinical trials
and a co-investigator in fifty more, and is widely recognized as a leading
oncologic researcher. She was there to announce the beginning of the
human clinical trials for a drug known cryptically as PI-88. "PI-88 is a
compound that is unique," she enthused. "We are looking forward to
investigating its potential in treating cancer patients."[1]

For Christopher Parish, PI-88's inventor, a dream hung on the trial
results—to say nothing of his life's work. Parish, an immunologist at
Australian National University, had spent innumerable hours at the lab
bench in his mission to develop the promising anticancer drug throughout the early 1990s. PI-88 is a double-action drug that slows both the
growth and the metastasis of tumors. It works by preventing angiogenesis, the development of new blood vessels that feed a tumor, and

by blocking the spread of cells from the tumor, all by tempering the influence of an enzyme called heparanase. Heparanase is normally produced within the body, and it promotes growth in many sites, spurring everything from wound healing to hair growth. Unfortunately, it also encourages the growth of cancerous tumors.

By inhibiting the production of heparanase, Parish believed that PI-88 could discourage the growth of tumors and the spread of cancer throughout the body.[2] And now it was about to prove itself, thanks to welcome support from an unexpected corner.

After years of toil, Parish had been "just delighted" when Progen Pharmaceuticals Ltd., a biotechnology company "committed to the discovery, development and commercialization of pharmaceuticals primarily for the treatment of cancer," offered to partner with him as he developed it for market.[3] We have already seen that in such university-corporation partnerships, drug companies require the university to sign the patent or other intellectual-property rights over to them in exchange for funding support. In this way, the university and researcher share funds, including support for the research, and the companies appropriate the rights to profits, licensing fees, and any new discoveries associated with the patent, which is now the company's to control. Assigning the intellectual-property rights to Progen was no problem for Parish, who just wanted to see his drug used to treat people with cancer. "My aim was to translate my research to the clinic."

As was the norm in 1993, Parish says, the university provided him not with the entire written agreement, but just the portions of it pertaining to his responsibilities. He was unconcerned with its details. "To be quite honest, I was just delighted to get a commercial partner." After all, did not he and Progen have the same goal—to develop an effective cancer drug that would save as many lives as possible?

The partnership thrived through the years of hard work it took before Eckhardt made the breathless announcement that placed Parish squarely on the threshold of his dream to vanquish cancer, specifically liver cancer, which the World Health Organization ranks as the third greatest cancer killer in the world.[4] Each year, at least 625,000 cases of liver cancer kill 396,000 people worldwide. (In the United States alone, an epidemic of hepatitis C is driving rates of liver cancer, which kills fifteen thousand Americans a year.) Liver cancer has few treatment options beyond surgery, and most sufferers do not survive beyond three years.

Seven years later, by late 2008, the Phase I and Phase II clinical trials of PI-88 had demonstrated that over twelve months, it reduced recurrence rates in liver cancer patients by 35 to 40 percent. PI-88 had been shown to work against cancer and now was ready for Phase III clinical trials, the last stage before approval and availability to the public.[5]

Then, abruptly, Progen shut down the trials, voicing concerns about factors "that impacted the commercial return" of PI-88, including the successful joint launch of Nexavar (sorafenib), a competing drug, by the Bayer and Onyx pharmaceutical companies.[6] (By 2007, Nexavar had been approved in seventy countries, including the United States, but it was refused approval in both the UK and Scotland on the grounds that its modest extension of survival—only three to six months—did not warrant its high price of $3,000 a month.)[7] Progen's new anticancer medication would likely face too much marketplace competition to become its next blockbuster. So the drug maker simply pulled the plug on PI-88, Parish's lifework, and on the hopes of imperiled liver-cancer patients. Because Progen holds the patent on PI-88, Parish cannot go elsewhere to conduct the Phase III trial and pursue its approval.[8]

Progen could have returned the rights to Parish, but it had no legal obligation to do so, and it certainly had no financial incentive. Quite the opposite, in fact: the company had paid Parish and the university for the PI-88 patent, and neither Progen's managers nor its shareholders were likely to approve giving away their considerable investment, especially since PI-88 worked well and would make whoever developed it a lot of money. In 2009, Progen struck an agreement to license the PI-88 patent to another firm, Global TransBiotech, but the agreed-upon additional clinical trials never materialized and their agreement fell apart.

In 2010 Progen agreed to grant drug maker Medigen, a Taiwan biotech and Progen stockholder, a license to test and finish developing PI-88, now dubbed Muparfostat. It has announced that it anticipates continuing Phase II trials and pursuing FDA approval. Perhaps this partnership will be more successful, but Parish is guaranteed no role in it.[9]

Australian National University professor Lawrence Cram blames such disappointing outcomes on the imbalance of power that characterizes universities' agreements with industry. "At the time that you're licensing something, the university's in a weak position," he told the *Canberra Times*.[10] When pharmaceutical firms complain that only one of every ten thousand candidate drugs on which they expend R&D resources ever graces pharmacy shelves to become a viable drug,[11] they cite external roadblocks such as drug flaws, safety issues, and FDA denials. They never mention cases such as Parish's, where the company's desire to maximize profits led Progen to abandon a badly needed drug and where the possession of a patent allowed it to do so over the objections of the drug's inventor.[12]

Moreover, the industry sets the bar high in these profit-driven decisions, and a "blockbuster drug" with $1 billion in sales is the goal. In choosing not to market less-profitable drugs, the industry denies us important medications.

And now? Parish says, "I think we need some other ways of translating research to the public good that doesn't necessarily require the commercialization."

Greed Proves Infectious

Unfortunately, PI-88 is no anomaly. In the summer of 2007, Bayer HealthCare slapped a patent-infringement lawsuit not against a competing researcher or corporation, but against an Ontario hospital. Thunder Bay Regional Health Sciences Centre is a four-hundred-bed hospital in a city of 120,000 people located very near the continent's geographic center and just above the Great Lakes. In 2007, Bayer sued Thunder Bay for using a generic antibiotic to treat patients who were suffering from stubborn urinary-tract and kidney infections. The hospital's health workers prepared the medication by diluting a concentrated, generic version of the drug ciprofloxacin, also known as Cipro.

Cipro is best known in the United States as the antibiotic given to victims of the 2001 and 2005 anthrax attacks. The pills went off-patent in 2004, but Bayer still sells pouches of an unconcentrated liquid form to hospitals for intravenous infusion into patients who cannot tolerate it by mouth, and this liquid was protected by patent until 2008.

The practice of diluting the concentrated generic solution is medically necessary to produce a safely therapeutic concentration of the antibiotic, and is exactly how the much-cheaper concentrated formulation was approved for use by Health Canada. Bayer claims that by diluting the generic antibiotic, its maker, Sandoz Canada, allowed hospitals to duplicate Bayer's patented form of the drug. However, Bayer had already tried and failed to use this argument to obtain an injunction against Sandoz Canada, and the courts had validated Sandoz's right to sell its version of the drug.

Nevertheless, Bayer now demanded that the hospital stop giving diluted ciprofloxacin concentrate to patients. When it did not, Bayer, an international corporate heavyweight, sued Thunder Bay, a modest-sized hospital.

Bayer called its actions necessary to protect its investment of hundreds of millions of dollars in research and development. "We have always vigorously defended our patent rights and will continue to do so," said Emily Hanst of Bayer HealthCare's Toronto office. "We do defend our patent rights to the end."[13] Hanst confirmed that on July 22 Bayer had also sued Calgary Health Region, part of the health-services network in Alberta, for patent infringement.[14]

Bayer sells $24 million worth of Cipro in Canada annually,[15] according to the research firm IMS Health Canada, and because relatively few patients were given the generic drug, Bayer's aggression puzzled many. Joel Lexchin, MD, an emergency-room physician and professor of health policy at York University, called Bayer's action "pretty petty" and worried that it would raise costs: such patent lawsuits tend to cost about C$1 million to defend.[16] The high price of the litigation prompted some to wonder whether the suits were attempts to intimidate the medical centers into abandoning legal cost-cutting measures in order to protect Bayer's monopoly, even in the absence of a Cipro patent. As of December 2010, more than three years later, lawyers for both sides were still filing motions and responses in Canada's Federal Court, with no resolution in sight.[17]

E. Richard Gold, director of McGill University's Centre for Intellectual Property Policy, characterized Bayer's as a desperate, and an ill-advised, move: "Pharmaceutical companies tend not to sue hospitals because, (a) they are their customers, and (b) it looks bad in the press. And," he mused, "it's not like the pharmaceutical industry is a well-loved industry."

Bayer's lawsuits against hospitals illustrate how pharmaceutical companies do not merely rely on patents as a shield to protect their intellectual property and profits.[18] These patents are also wielded as a sword not only against competing drug makers but also against health-care providers in order to maintain high prices and profits—even when doing so means withholding lifesaving drugs from patients. This harms not only potential future patients, as in the case of the aborted PI-88 trials, but also living, breathing patients who depend upon a medication to enable them to walk out of the hospital rather than be carried out.

Patenting the Pandemic

Hard-to-treat infections such as those treated at Thunder Bay are hardly our only looming health threat. After all, epidemiologists have made us all too aware that we are overdue for a major pandemic on the level of the 1918–1920 influenza that killed one hundred million people worldwide. H1N1 flu's 2009 advent was dramatic, killing more than sixteen thousand people in 213 countries, territories, and other communities,[19] and this has exacerbated the tension as we continue to look over our collective shoulder for the next viral threat.

Moreover, hyperbolic media accounts sometimes inflate our fears by failing to place such deaths in context. Much of the devastation we witness through televised accounts has struck nations without viable health infrastructures and reasonable access to medical professionals. Their death rates, inflated by this medical deficit, nevertheless feed widespread fear and churn a sense of urgency, even in Western nations where more people enjoy greater access to prompt medical care and correspondingly lower complications and death rates.

Severe acute respiratory syndrome, or SARS, is a spectrum of respiratory illnesses caused by a virus that was identified in 2003, after which a global outbreak spread to 8,098 people in more than two dozen countries throughout North America, South America, Europe, and Asia. Alarmingly, 774 people died before it was contained. Scientists have not yet found a specific treatment for the SARS virus, but a race is already on to patent the pathogen, symptomatic of the tendency to see genetic information as grist for the profit mill before envisioning it as a source of cures.

In the wake of the outbreak, a number of biotechnology and pharmaceutical companies as well as researchers in Canada and Hong Kong filed SARS-related patent applications, claiming exclusive rights to portions of the genome or to the virus itself. These groups realize that holding such a patent could ensure not only a monopoly on specific treatments but also exclusive profits from generating improved tests to identify SARS. As it is, many people with SARS are not diagnosed quickly, and some not until after supportive treatment has been completed. A company that holds the SARS patent could not only generate treatments and tests but could also prevent others from doing so.

For this reason, the federal government also entered the fray. The Centers for Disease Control and Prevention claims exclusive control of the virus and its entire genome via the "defensive patenting" it undertook not in order to reap profits but rather to place the information in the public domain and establish its status as prior art, which will prevent others from patenting the research, said CDC spokesman Llewelyn Grant. "The whole purpose of such a patent is to prevent folks from controlling the technology. This is being done to give the industry and other researchers reasonable access to the samples."[20] You might think that the development of remedies for high-profile emerging infectious diseases such as avian flu, swine flu, and SARS would be exempt from this sort of profit-driven therapeutic injunction. In view of all this global tension, with the world avidly watching, it would seem unlikely that anyone would tolerate placing profits above protecting the populace, and yet this is exactly what has happened, as a patent gold rush has taken the focus off treatment and cures for SARS.

A precedent for the CDC's maneuver had been set in 1990 when the Human Genome Project (HGP), a consortium of academic laboratories coordinated by the U.S. Department of Energy and the National Institutes of Health, began to identify all the approximately twenty-five thousand genes in humans.[21]

Progress was sluggish, hampered in part by simmering competition and jealousies among the various constituent laboratories, until 1998. That year, Celera Genomics, a private firm headed by Dr. Craig Venter, announced that it would sequence the human genome before the HGP, patent the genome, and charge fees to anyone who wanted access to significant amounts of the information. Most scientists and much of the public objected to this plan because they felt that the human genome should be available to any researchers and specifically that it should not become just another industrial commodity for sale.

Francis Collins, director of the National Human Genome Research Institute, spurred his often-fractious coalition members to efficiency by reminding them often of their responsibility to keep the "code of life" out of a private corporation's grasp.[22]

To prevent this, HGP researchers released the data they amassed into a public internet database every day. By publishing the gene sequences on the web, the government ensured that the information was no longer new and so failed the USPTO's novelty test: it became unpatentable.

However, another clear advantage emerged: when it removed the jealous contests for patents from the equation, the HGP became a model of efficiency and was completed two years ahead of schedule—unusual, to say the least, for a government program.[23] It's no wonder that when confronted with its own competing patent conflicts, the CDC did the same with SARS data.[24]

Although the HGP was marketed to the American people on the basis of disease cures it promised to enable, the connection between finding and mapping a gene and devising a disease cure can be long and tenuous. The data are still being analyzed, but that they are freely available to everyone means research is proceeding more quickly than if it was hampered by a thicket of patents and licenses.

However, during the widely publicized race to map the genome, many people wondered, "How can genes are patented?" After all, they are not created by man, but occur naturally in nature. The perennial "hand of man" conceit was argued, with patent seekers arguing that the act of purifying the gene and gene fragments removed them from the realm of the naturally occurring to become manufactured items that exist only when experts isolate and/or purify them. The argument was that isolated genes, divorced from their genomes, existed only because of the specialized work of researchers. Although it does not seem clear that the additional criterion—that the process behind such "purification" must not be obvious to a practitioner skilled in the art—is met in all such cases, the USPTO grants gene patents anyway.

However, patenting genes and gene fragments seems to fall short of another patent requirement as well: patent applications require that the inventor specify the function and potential uses for an invention, but scientists did not know what most HGP-identified genes did, and certainly had no idea what function was performed by the other fragments of DNA they were industriously patenting. In fact, the HGP illuminated the breadth of our ignorance about our genome. For one thing, scientists began the studies thinking that the human genome encompassed about one hundred thousand genes but ultimately discovered that we have fewer than thirty thousand, about the same as the lowly roundworm.

Money Never Sleeps: Patent Profits Trump a Trypanosomiasis Cure

In 1987, the news that Merrell Dow had developed a new medicine that quelled sleeping sickness threw other economic tensions into sharp relief. Even today, as doctors, politicians, and headlines decry AIDS, malaria, and starvation, African sleeping sickness, or trypanosomiasis, seems forgotten, shrouded by darkness and silence. Yet sixty million West and Central Africans are at risk of this parasitic disease caused mostly by protozoa of the species *Trypanosoma brucei gambiense*. Trypanosomiasis is transmitted by the tsetse fly, and the disease is endemic to regions of sub-Saharan Africa. It kills half those it infects in the Central African regions of Uganda, the Democratic Republic of Congo, Sudan, Ethiopia, Malawi, and Tanzania. According to the World Health Organization (WHO), "Sleeping sickness was the first or second greatest cause of mortality in those communities, ahead of even HIV/AIDS."[25]

Three regional outbreaks have ravaged the continent within the past decade. In 2005, between fifty thousand to seventy thousand people were infected—a very broad range, but in countries where the dearth of physicians and public-health infrastructures make accurate disease surveillance impossible, such epidemiological imprecision can occur.[26] Uganda endured an epidemic in 2008.

In some nations of sub-Saharan Africa,[27] death is often a silent denouement, because the dying slip away exactly as they have lived for the preceding year: silent, unmoving, and usually invisible. For months before their death, those stricken by African trypanosomiasis seemed neither living nor dead, their fate scaled by the bite of the tsetse fly. (A similar disease, American trypanosomiasis, or Chagas disease, threatens twenty-one South American countries but is caused by a different organism and requires different treatment.)[28]

The bite leaves a painful chancre, followed a few weeks afterward by the disease's first stage, also known as the hemolymphatic phase, wherein the parasites reproduce in the victim's tissues, blood, and lymph fluid. Its early symptoms—joint pains, bouts of fever, headache, and itching for a few days—seem disarmingly innocuous, especially because they resemble those of the malarial fevers that are common in affected areas. The parasite has to be detected in a blood sample, in lymph, or in cerebrospinal fluid to establish the diagnosis, but health-care workers are rare in the affected sub-Saharan areas, so accurately recording the number of cases can be a futile effort.

The body unsuccessfully tries to fight off the infection, and after several months the second stage ensues. It is also known as the neurological phase because the parasites, or trypanosomes, cross the blood–brain barrier and infect the central nervous system. The multiplying parasites cause the inflamed brain to swell, compressing blood vessels and evoking more dramatic signs and symptoms such as confusion, poor coordination, behavioral changes, and sensory disturbances. These include an irresistible daytime drowsiness that is followed by nighttime insomnia. The course of this phase varies from six months to several years.[29] Without treatment, a victim may die within six months from heart failure or from the infection itself.[30] The intensity and prevalence of infections vary from region to region and even from village to village, wreaking their worst damage on children. The parasite can also be transmitted to infants through breast milk.

The first stage can be treated with pentamidine, which is safe, and Suramin, which elicits side effects but is far less toxic than Melarsoprol, which is used to treat the second stage of disease when treatment becomes much more difficult. Until 1995, second-stage treatment was often futile because the only effective medication was injections of Melarsoprol, a compound of arsenic and of ethylene glycol, better known to us as antifreeze. Melarsoprol is as toxic as it sounds, killing one in five people who take it. And once the victim falls into a coma, Melarsoprol cannot cross the blood–brain barrier to cure him.

The lingering sufferers from sleeping sickness finally expire on mats in darkened rooms or in forgotten corners of their untended farms.

Although sleeping sickness is usually a rural disease, the least fortunate die unregarded in the streets and alleyways of thronged Third World cities.

The "Resurrection Drug"

At last, another drug was found to cure even late-stage sleeping sickness because it crosses the blood–brain barrier, and does so safely. Albert Sjoerdsmanot, former chief of Experimental Therapeutics at the National Heart Institute in Bethesda, Maryland, discovered eflornithine (also called DL-a-difluoromethylornithine, or DFMO) in the 1970s, and the drug was developed and tested in the 1980s.[31] Instead of simply relieving symptoms like most other sleeping sickness medications, eflornithine is a true cure, eliminating the parasite itself by targeting an enzyme within it, ornithine decarboxylase, that metabolizes eflornithine differently than does the human version of the enzyme. This allows the parasites to be selectively killed.

The FDA approved eflornithine tests for sleeping sickness in 1990, but the drug immediately hit a development roadblock: many pharmaceutical firms strictly enforced a stated or tacit prohibition against testing medications for use against tropical diseases. Why? Because these diseases struck people without the means to pay high prices for their drugs. There was no profit in it. As shocking as this sounds, it is consonant with recent Western pharmaceutical policies: of the 1,233 drugs licensed globally between 1975 and 1997, only thirteen targeted diseases that strike in the tropics.[32] (See "Diseases for Which 99 Percent or More of the Global Burden Fell on Low- and Middle-Income Countries," p. 105.)

Merrell Dow, however, hoped that eflornithine's selective enzyme-targeting would also prove efficacious against cancers that Western patients were willing to pay hefty sums to treat. So it began testing eflornithine in Europe as a cancer treatment.

At the Institute for Tropical Medicine in Antwerp, Simon Van Nieuwenhove, a doctor working for the Belgian-Sudanese Sleeping Sickness Control Project, had hungrily absorbed an article in *Science* that spoke of eflornithine as a possibly safe treatment for second-stage trypanosomiasis. On their frequent clinical visits to Sudan, Van Nieuwenhove and his colleagues were drowning in trypanosomiasis patients who did not

Diseases for Which 99 Percent or More of the Global Burden Fell on Low- and Middle-Income Countries in 1990

Disease	Disability Adjusted Life Years (Thousands, 2000)	Deaths per Year (2000)
Chagas disease	680	21,299
Dengue	433	12,037
Ancylostomiasis and necatoriasis (hookworm)	1,829	5,650
Japanese encephalitis	426	3,502
Lymphatic filariasis	5,549	404
Malaria	40,213	1,079,877
Onchocerciasis (river blindness)	951	___
Schistosomiasis	1,713	11,473
Tetanus	9,766	308,662
Trachoma	1,181	14
Trichuriasis	1,640	2,123
Trypanosomiasis	1,585	49,668
Leishmaniasis	1,810	40,913
Measles	27,549	776,626
Poliomyelitis	184	675
Syphilis	5,574	196,533
Diphtheria	114	3,394
Leprosy	141	2,268
Pertussis	12,768	296,099
Diarrheal diseases	62,227	2,124,032

Sources: Global Burden from WHO (1996), quoted in Lanjouw and Cockburn (2001, Table I). Figures updated from Lanjouw and Cockburn (2001), using WHO (2000).

respond to medicines for second-stage disease or who were killed by the medicines themselves. He also knew that the vast majority of patients did not even reach medical care (or did not reach it in time) despite the doctors' vigorous incursions into affected rural areas.

Van Nieuwenhove quickly discovered that pharmacologist Paul Schechter was managing the clinical cancer trials for Merrell Dow in Europe. He had to meet Schechter, so he set off for France.

Sitting across from Schechter at a table in a Strasbourg café, Van Nieuwenhove began earnestly to belabor the talking points behind his plea for a supply of eflornithine to test against sleeping sickness. No witnesses recorded this conversation, but Van Nieuwenhove knew that pharmaceutical companies took a dim view of testing their candidate drugs for tropical diseases, and he felt he had to make a powerful case. He armed himself with arguments that doubtless dwelt on the wholesale deaths of children, the clinic shelves that displayed drugs as dangerous as the disease they were meant to cure, the desperation and poverty of his patients, his helplessness once they had slipped over into coma, and the urgent need for something that could rescue still-living sufferers from that neurological void. But it is doubtful that Van Nieuwenhove got very far in his catalog of pleas.

"Of course I'll get you a supply of eflornithine," Schechter interrupted. "Right away."[33] Not only did he provide the eflornithine, but he did so without red tape, so that just a few days later, Van Nieuwenhove flew to Sudan with enough eflornithine in his carry-on bag to treat twenty patients.

Van Nieuwenhove gave the medicine by mouth to twenty of the fading patients in his Sudan clinic, eighteen of whom had second-stage disease. He was rewarded by prompt improvements and only one relapse—unparalleled in his, or anyone else's, clinical experience. Over the next months, just as Schechter was beginning to realize that the European cancer trials were failing to show effectiveness for eflornithine, Van Nieuwenhove oversaw trials in the Ivory Coast and Congo that not only confirmed eflornithine's dramatic ability to safely cure sleeping sickness, but also revived comatose late-stage patients who had never been helped by any medication and who had been given up for dead,[34] earning eflornithine the sobriquet "the resurrection drug."[35]

Finally, sleeping sickness could be eradicated, and eflornithine was rechristened Ornidyl for use against trypanosomiasis. But despite demonstrating that Ornidyl is a safe and uniquely effective replacement for the toxic Melarsoprol, very few sub-Saharan Africans with sleeping sickness could afford any modern treatments, to say nothing of expensive branded Western medications. Aventis halted production of Ornidyl in 1995,[36] citing its low earning potential, and it began seeking other, profitable, uses for its drug.

It soon found one: eflornithine effectively banishes facial hirsutism in women. Its direct-to-consumer ads admonish, "Although you tweeze, shave or wax your unwanted facial hair (UFH), when you're with people up close and face-to-face, you may still worry that others will notice, since unwanted facial hair is difficult to cover up." The scourge of African sleeping sickness would have to wait: unwelcome moustache and chin hairs, which Aventis (which now held the patent on eflornithine) medicalized as "UFH," took precedence, and eflornithine was reborn as Vaniqa.

In 2000–2001, Aventis Pharma (now Sanofi-Aventis) and Bayer HealthCare partnered with Doctors Without Borders (or Médecins Sans Frontières) and the World Health Organization to manufacture and donate $5 million worth of drugs, including two hundred thousand vials of eflornithine for sleeping sickness. Later, Bristol-Myers Squibb, Bayer, and the Bill and Melinda Gates Foundation contracted to provide eflornithine to Africa through 2006. According to MSF, this happened only after "years of pressure" and in the wake of Ornidyl's withdrawal and Vaniqa's subsequent debut, a source of embarrassment for the drug makers.[37]

Such mixed motivations aside, the drug makers' act was a highly ethical one with a laudable result: the number of trypanosomiasis cases fell to an estimated thirty thousand by 2009. If we want drug makers to place human lives above profits, it seems as important to praise and reward them for doing so as it is to castigate them for placing profits above patients. This is especially true when they act against their financial interests, as Aventis did.

Unfortunately, the pharmaceutical largesse was short-lived and provided only five years of free eflornithine. In 2008, when researchers tracked more than one thousand of the adults and children who were given eflornithine in Ibba, Southern Sudan, this study once again validated the drug as a safe, effective preferred treatment for sleeping sickness. But there are not nearly enough resurrections to go around: Although sixty million people remain at risk of sleeping sickness, today only 7 percent of these have access to adequate medical treatment.[38]

Aventis and Bayer's partnership with MSF and the WHO to provide eflornithine to desperately ill patients is an example of corporate altruism at its best—but it was cut off far too soon. It is completely understandable that Aventis would focus resources upon the profitable, if trivial, use of its medication as a depilatory, but it is disappointing that it does not also choose to make the drug more widely and cheaply available to poor Africans in order to vanquish sleeping sickness—perhaps dedicating a portion of its profits from its expensive cosmetic application to the cause of saving lives.

Ornidyl can no longer be had for love or money, but SkinMedica markets Vaniqa as a prescription-only depilatory cream because more U.S. women can part with $50 a tube to keep their faces hair-free than Africans can to save their lives. The human cost of pharmaceutical companies' misplaced values is starkly illustrated by this example of a lifesaving medication that has been pressed into service as a more lucrative lifestyle drug.[39]

Selective Cures

This is a domestic issue as well as a problem for the global South. In 2008, for example, Pfizer announced that it would spend up to $410 million to acquire the rights to the drug Xiaflex (clostridial collagenase) from Auxilium Pharmaceuticals so that it could develop and market it for use against Peyronie's disease. In this disorder, a collagen plaque builds up on the shaft of the penis, causing it to curve and reducing its flexibility. This condition affects 1 percent of U.S. men. In what reads as an afterthought, accounts of the acquisition noted that the drug might also be useful for adhesive capsulitis, or "frozen shoulder," and for Dupuyten's contracture, a similar collagen accumulation in the hand that affects the use of the fingers: the latter condition affects six times as many people as Peyronie's.[40]

Some may be tempted to excuse the preferential attention to Peyronie's on the grounds that choosing to address noncritical conditions that affect relatively few people is the company's prerogative. But as I've noted earlier, the case for that prerogative is weakened by taxpayers' substantial contribution to drug discovery. Others may argue that developing a drug for one condition such as Peyronie's does not rule out prescribing it for other, off-label uses, so that no one is actually harmed by this emphasis.

But some *are* harmed. Testing and seeking FDA approval of Xiaflex for Peyronie's does mean that a doctor can also prescribe it for off-label use for frozen shoulder or Dupuyten's. But without clinical testing for these uses, side effects or other problems may emerge only slowly and after harming many patients. Also, many insurers do not pay for such off-label uses, so the drug may be priced out of the reach of many.

Admittedly, opinions differ concerning which are the most important disorders and by what measures one should gauge that importance. But most reasonable people would agree that saving the lives of people who die of sleeping sickness trumps providing smooth, hairless chins; and that ensuring mobility by addressing frozen shoulders and painfully contracted hands trumps improving genital cosmetics. Similarly, huge differences in death rates, disability, and quality of life loom between the lifestyle issues that the drug industry clamors to address and the major killers that go unchallenged.

Malaria is one such killer. A child dies every forty-five seconds of malaria, which struck 247 million people worldwide in 2008 and killed at least one million of them, according to WHO figures that some call woefully underestimated. We have eight drugs to deploy against the four major strains of malaria, but some of them, like quinine, have been in use since the seventeenth century and are outdated.

Multi-drug-resistant tuberculosis (MDR-TB) is another deadly foe. It infects approximately nine million new individuals each year, and it is a key factor in many deaths from AIDS. On its own, MDR-TB causes 1.7 million deaths every year: its four-drug treatment regimen has been complemented by just a few others, and if none work, you die. Vaccines are still "in development."

By contrast, the diagnosis of erectile dysfunction (ED), a vague term[41] coined by drug makers to define a quasi-medical market for their amorous wares, kills no one, although more than 570 men have died, many of heart attacks, after using one of the more than fourteen medications developed since 1996 to treat it. Most of the dead were under sixty-five and had no preexisting heart problems.

The nebulous nature of ED's symptoms allows drug makers to make customers of fifteen to thirty million U.S. men. (Boehringer Ingelheim assures women that "pink Viagra" for orgasmic dysfunction is en route to them.)

The National Ambulatory Medical Care Survey (NAMCS) estimates that in 1985, 7.7 office visits were made for ED for every 1,000 American men. By 1999, the rate of ED office visits almost tripled, to 22.3, undoubtedly driven by a barrage of advertisements urging men to see their doctors for prescriptions. These ads have mutated from the gravitas of medicalized exhortations for couples to recapture their intimacy to today's frank invitations to sexual athleticism, e.g., "Gentlemen, start your engines!" and the Elvis-themed "Viva, Viagra!" Experts such as Dr. Jeffrey Klausner, director of STD prevention and control for the San Francisco Department of Public Health, think that recreational Viagra use is rising. His study found that 31 percent of his male clinic patients reported taking Viagra without medical supervision.

By the measure of drugs developed, erection on demand seems a higher priority than surviving malaria and tuberculosis. And waiting in the wings is Johnson & Johnson's drug Priligy (dapoxetine), for premature ejaculation (PE), which the company defines as taking place within one minute of the initiation of coitus. Johnson & Johnson's public-relations department assures us that one in three men suffer from PE, but at least one survey backing up the one-in-three claim is based on a disputed study that was never designed to quantify PE. Experts such as Dr. Wayne J. G. Hellstrom of Tulane also demur, estimating that from 20 percent to 30 percent of men experience premature ejaculation at some point.[42]

But doesn't Johnson & Johnson's estimate of one in three men equal 33 percent, very close to the 30 percent in Hellstrom's upper range? Don't the two statistics agree? Well, no, because Johnson & Johnson is speaking of PE as a *chronic* condition, while Hellstrom is referring to it as an *occasional* occurrence that bedevils as many men.

As an occasional annoyance, premature ejaculation is common. But as a chronic condition, it is not thought as common as Johnson & Johnson implies in its public relations (and may eventually imply in its direct-to-consumer ads). The distinction is key, but Johnson & Johnson largely ignores it. The FDA rejected Priligy in 2005 in the midst of a firestorm over suicides among people who take antidepressants, and Johnson & Johnson is pondering whether and when to resubmit a U.S. application. Meanwhile the drug company's Janssen Cilag unit sells it in Sweden and Finland for a distressing but relatively uncommon condition by urging it on many potential patients, convincing them that it is chronic, common, and treatable. The drug is recommended for men with symptoms so broad that its maker can hope it will be very widely prescribed, and Johnson & Johnson is eyeing Austria, Germany, Spain, and Italy next.[43]

The real issue, though, is not the rationales with which pharmaceutical companies sometimes mask minor conditions as prevalent "diseases": it is drug makers' insistence on expending resources on lifestyle diseases instead of killers, revealing a troubling tendency to choose the most profitable medications over the most desperately needed ones.

Because, as the case of Ornidyl/Vaniqa illustrates, poor people in the developing world cannot afford to pay high prices for lifesaving drugs, their governments sometimes decide not to honor Western drug makers' patents. Even the United States, that bastion of medical patent protection, has distributed lower-cost antiretroviral generics for the treatment of HIV disease to the developing world via the President's Emergency Plan for AIDS Relief (PEPFAR) program. The program is not perfect, but Stanford researchers credit it with reducing African deaths from AIDS by 10 percent—a glorious achievement.[44]

This drop—and the drugs—were a very long time coming. One reason is that PEPFAR set an unusually high bar for generics' acceptability that lowered the poor's access to the AIDS drugs. Normally, a routine certificate of pharmaceutical product would be sufficient to establish the safety of the generic drugs used to treat the HIV-infected. But the Bush administration delayed PEPFAR for years by expressing concerns about the "quality" of the generic antiretrovirals that were to be distributed to the HIV-infected poor in the Third World, who otherwise had no access whatever to very expensive medications. In vain did humanitarian groups such as Doctors Without Borders argue that these concerns were without merit because they had been using the medications in question for years with an excellent safety and efficacy record. In the end, PEPFAR insisted on using more expensive generics, which meant that fewer people could be treated. (See "U.S. GHI as a Share of the Federal Budget," p. 112.)

What's wrong with the blitz of medicines for minor conditions? Some think it acceptable for drug companies to maximize profits by any legal means, even if patients suffer. They essentially deny that pharmaceutical corporations are accountable to the public. This is untrue, first, because the government underwrites the research that leads to most patents and the brand-name medicines on which they depend. Since

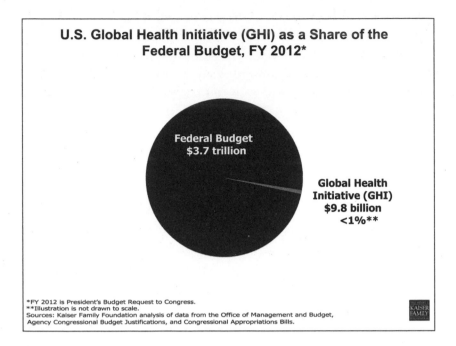

U.S. Global Health Initiative (GHI) as a Share of the Federal Budget, FY 2012*

Federal Budget
$3.7 trillion

Global Health
Initiative (GHI)
$9.8 billion
<1%**

*FY 2012 is President's Budget Request to Congress.
**Illustration is not drawn to scale.
Sources: Kaiser Family Foundation analysis of data from the Office of Management and Budget,
Agency Congressional Budget Justifications, and Congressional Appropriations Bills.

KAISER
FAMILY

American taxpayers have subsidized the research, they deserve to reap the benefits in the form of medicines that address important diseases and improve and extend life, just as pharmaceutical manufacturers promise in their advertisements.

There is also the moral dimension. Profiting from trivial and important drug applications is not mutually exclusive: drug makers can do both if they choose to. The firms could continue to earn handsome profits while making cheaper lifestyle medications *and* by making the more expensive novel drugs Westerners and the citizens of poor developing countries need against serious diseases. There is a market for both Vaniqa and Ornidyl, and laws against drug reimportation could protect companies against abuse if affluent Americans tried to import medications intended for poor Africans.

No Testing

Today, drug companies choose the path of maximal profit, which means, among other things, the path of least expenditure. There are many ways in which the pharmaceutical industry maximizes its profits from patents without the expensive R&D entailed by drug design.

Patent holders often opt to profit by licensing their patents to other companies and by litigation against others for infringement on their patents. A patent holder that is intent on positioning itself to collect licenses, royalties, and other financial awards through litigation, perhaps without any real intent to capitalize on the patent via development and innovation, is referred to slightingly as a "patent troll." These agents needn't be corporations: entrepreneurs and even universities have been characterized as patent trolls.

Developing tests for diseases caused by the pathogens or genes they have patented is another quicker, easier route to profit for drug makers than is onerous new drug design. The patent holder is paid whenever these tests are used by hospitals and doctors to diagnose patients. Many diagnostic tests are useful, and they are often necessary to identify illnesses, their nature and their severity; they can also be invaluable in treating disease. Tests determine how well a particular course of treatment is working, whether a cancer patient has entered or remains in remission, and whether an illness is progressing or a patient shows signs of cure. Having this information can be the difference between changing treatment tactics in time to save a life or pursuing a futile treatment for so long that the patient runs out of options.

The United States is the epicenter of tests based on the patented pathogens and genes because Europeans and other nations have been much slower and more conservative in permitting such "life patents." Europe has long shown a special aversion to gene patenting. European and developing nations tend to bar gene patents, or at least, with the exception of the UK, to approve far fewer than does the United States. Does this American proclivity for patenting genes and pathogens affect the ability of patients to get more accurate tests—and cheaper ones?

Yes, but as we shall see, not in a positive way.

Nations that don't permit gene patents or that sharply circumscribe them actually offer better genetic testing than we do. Those European nations that forbid gene patents, for example, offer better and cheaper tests than those that U.S. citizens can access, in part because the increased competition encourages both more accurate, sophisticated tests and lower prices.

But what happens when the patent-friendly United States and the more patent-wary Europe clash over testing?

In the late 1990s "David"[45] emailed me from Oxford, England, to complain that he was unable to persuade his doctors to give him a test for hepatitis C. This blood-borne liver infection causes a Pandora's box of signs and symptoms: profound fatigue, jaundice, hemorrhaging, abdominal swelling, and encephalopathy (organic mental confusion). It breeds many other dangerous complications, including cirrhosis and liver cancer. In fact, hepatitis C virus (HCV) infection is the leading cause of liver transplants in the United States and infects 4 million Americans and 170 million people worldwide. In the 1990s, only 15 percent of the infected were cured by interferon-b in its various formulations, such as pegylated interferon, sometimes boosted by ribavirin, which does not target HCV but which interferes with the virus's replication.[46] But escaping or surviving the worst consequences of HCV infection is linked to an early diagnosis, which allows early treatment and helps the HCV-positive avoid liver cancer and cirrhosis. "I know that an early diagnosis is key," wrote David, "but I could not convince my doctor to give me the test. He has this notion that only drugs users get hepatitis C."

David knew that although drug addicts are at significantly higher risk of contracting hepatitis C, so are many people who have never touched an illicit drug. Hepatitis C is a blood-borne illness, spread by pre-1989 blood transfusions, surgery abroad, tattooing, and even by shared razors.[47] Forty percent of people who acquire the virus have no idea how it happened, and most people are diagnosed by accident during blood tests for other reasons. David also knew that he had several risk factors and symptoms. But until I told him, David did not know that the real reason it had become more difficult to persuade a UK physician to test for HCV had less to do with drug-user mythology and more to do with a patent.

In 1994, the price of the test suddenly leaped sixfold, becoming too expensive for England's National Health Service, because the U.S. drug maker Chiron Corporation had stepped in to aggressively protect its patent—and its testing monopoly.

Chiron, of California, discovered and patented the hepatitis C virus in 1987, and it holds more than one hundred patents related to the HCV genome, some of which will be in effect until at least 2015.[48] The UK firm Murex had developed an inexpensive blood test for HCV that was in frequent use by the National Health Service. But in 1994, Chiron sued for and won an injunction from a London high court to prevent Murex from selling its cheaper tests: Chiron's patent on the virus meant that no researcher could use it, even to devise a needed test, without Chiron's license. As a result, Murex was banned from selling its test, and the price of a hepatitis C test in England[49] soared so steeply that the National Health Service had to ration the testing. What's more, Chiron's zealous patent-protection lawsuits frightened researchers away from investigating the virus, causing Professor Roger Williams, director of the Institute of Liver Studies at King's College School of Medicine and Dentistry, to warn London's *Independent* newspaper, "A situation where one company—Chiron—can limit the number of companies carrying out research into hepatitis C must inhibit our knowledge of the disease and our efforts to reduce its spread."[50]

Murex filed several appeals, finally challenging Chiron's "anti-competitive domination of the blood testing market" by seeking a European Commission review of Chiron's controlling role in the HCV market. However, Chiron's more than one hundred U.S. and EU patents and its right to prevent other companies from offering HCV tests were affirmed on appeal by both UK and European courts.

As this book went to press, the usual therapy consisted of a year of interferon-alpha with ribavirin, which cured only half of patients, often after they suffered life-changing side effects such as severe depression, fatigue, chronic flu-like symptoms, and anemia. But this frustration and pain seem to be at an end because we now stand on the brink of new and better cures. On April 27, 2011, the FDA's Antiviral Drugs Advisory met to evaluate Merck's boceprevir and telaprevir from Vertex Pharmaceuticals. Like many potent HIV medications, these drugs are protease inhibitors. They work by attacking NS3-4A protease, without which the hepatitis C virus cannot construct the proteins it needs to function.

Both show promising results in clinical trials. Each boasts a cure rate of 75 percent, a thrilling turnaround from the early days of the hepatitis C epidemic, when only 15 percent of the HCV-infected could hope for a cure from interferon. Sixty other anti-HCV compounds remain in development, so more and better cures are waiting in the wings.

In 2004, Chiron's tight grip on its one hundred–plus HCV patents was limiting research into hepatitis C cures and even driving other firms from the field. Not only was Murex forced to abandon its cheap effective HCV diagnostic test, but Gilead Sciences Inc. of Foster City, California, dropped work on a hepatitis C drug in 1999 after it was sued by Chiron, which was typically charging each company millions of dollars in licensing fees during research and development alone. How did today's burst of hepatitis C drug innovation come about?

It's simple: Chiron had a change of heart. On the heels of the scientific censure and negative publicity—resulting from its iron grip on the HCV patents and the chilling effect on research—Chiron decided to no longer demand that licensors pay up-front fees and make annual payments to obtain rights to the hepatitis C patents.[51] The firm is not suffering financially: it still earns millions more each year in royalties from HCV tests.

But by 2005, researchers from fifteen other companies flocked to HCV research, and today we see the initial fruits of this greater openness—the drugs we need.

Blood Rights

The United States has not been spared such tensions. One million Americans, including one in three hundred people of Northern European descent, suffer from hereditary hemochromatosis (HFE),[52] a genetic form of a disease[53] that compromises the body's ability to break down iron. As iron accumulates in the body, it imperils many organs, including the blood, liver, heart, pancreas, joints, and skin. Besides fatigue, abdominal discomfort, and joint pain, the high iron levels can lead to such serious conditions as arthritis, diabetes, cirrhosis of the liver, liver cancer, and heart failure. The discovery of the gene for HFE foreshadowed its troubles because, to discourage competing patent claims, the gene's finding was not announced in a scientific journal until a year after it was patented, even though this lag could have prevented or delayed the diagnosis of some affected people. This was not a rare occurrence, as a Harvard Institute of Health Policy study discovered: one of every five medical-science professors had held back reports of their research results for six months or more in order to further their monopolistic interests.[54]

Male sufferers of HFE are not usually diagnosed until they reach forty or older, and in a woman, the disease is usually detected only after menopause, when she is no longer protected by the monthly blood loss that can keep symptoms in check. An early diagnosis, however, can prevent complications by allowing the doctor to begin treatment to reduce iron levels, usually by phlebotomy—limited blood removal—and by treating organ damage.

Getting an early diagnosis can be tricky, though, because standard blood-iron tests do not reliably detect the disease—special diagnostic tests must be performed. Checking levels of ferritin, a protein that stores iron, is not an effective way to arrive at a diagnosis because so many conditions can result in aberrant ferritin levels, and hemochromatosis is one of the least common. Checking levels of both ferritin and transferrin, a blood protein that binds iron, makes sense for people with symptoms or with a family member who has the disorder: half the people with abnormal readings on both tests have HFE, and it is more logical to test based on symptoms and a suggestive medical history.

For people with HFE, the genetic test is doubly valuable, both in diagnosing them and in warning them that their children may be affected and should be tested.

Two mutations of the HFE gene,[55] C282Y and H63D, are associated with 85 percent of cases, and in 1998, the USPTO granted patents to Mercator Genetics on both mutations. These patents exclude others from testing for the HFE mutations. Progenitor bought the Mercator patents and licensed them to SmithKline Beecham Clinical Laboratories (SKB) for about $3 million. It then offered expensive sublicenses to several U.S. laboratories to test for the gene.

Other researchers, however, had already developed tests for hemochromatosis, and yet others were still planning to do so. They were intimidated by the prohibitive costs of the sublicenses, coupled with the specter of being sued for patent infringement. Cowed, fully 30 percent of 119 surveyed U.S. laboratories that offered diagnostic genetic testing for hemochromatosis stopped performing their tests because of the SKB patents.[56] The licenses' high costs and royalties are reflected in higher charges to patients for the HFE tests, which offer specific information about their disease that cannot be obtained elsewhere. In addition, fewer hospitals and clinics now use genetic HFE tests, which makes fewer data available to researchers who seek to better characterize the disease.

In Europe, other diagnostic tests have been designed to screen for hemochromatosis, but European companies have now followed the U.S. lead, and patent applications for the gene variants have been filed abroad as well. If a European patent is issued, tests on the continent may also become scarce.[57]

Similarly, tests for Dravet syndrome, a severe form of childhood epilepsy, have become devastatingly rare due to patent-protection issues. Dravet syndrome appears during a baby's first year and is characterized by repeated fever-associated epileptic seizures until the child reaches age five. Afterward, epileptic seizures can escalate to *status epilepticus*—continual, life-threatening seizures that require emergency care. The resulting neurological damage causes hyperactivity and impairs the child's development, including language acquisition, motor skills, and social interaction. If the disease is not diagnosed early and the seizures prevented before brain damage ensues, Dravet syndrome children often lose the ability to function independently by the time they are teenagers.

About 70 to 80 percent of children suffering from Dravet syndrome can be diagnosed early using a test for the SCN1A gene,[58] and a Melbourne, Australia, firm called Genetic Technologies (GT) holds the patent. Because no royalties for tests on the gene were paid to it, GT determined to stop laboratories and hospitals from impinging on its patent by testing babies for SCN1A. The firm has threatened to sue Australian public hospitals, as Bayer HealthCare did in Canada, to prevent them from screening newborns and young children.[59] In defending this stance, Genetic Technologies CEO Mervyn Jacobson demanded, "The question is, are public hospitals allowed to break the law and breach patents granted by the Australian Government?"

Although no lawsuit has yet materialized, the threat alone has made an early diagnosis impossible for some infants. According to John Christodoulou, director of the hospital's Western Sydney Genetics Program, his laboratory cannot risk performing another version of the SCN1A test because Genetic Technologies may bar him from testing or may impose a prohibitive royalty.

Among the more surreal consequences of GT's legal threat is that Australian hospitals have had to send infants' blood samples to Scotland for testing, and when the cost of this medical tourism quickly proved prohibitive, Australia stopped screening all but those children whose medical profiles were most dramatically suggestive of this dangerous condition.[60]

Deepak Gill, head of neurology at the Children's Hospital at Westmead, said that if they could conduct the test on-site, its clinic would test 50 percent more infants for the gene. What of the other children? Their diagnosis is often delayed until the child is twelve to eighteen months old, well beyond the best window of time to start treatment that prevents brain damage. Luigi Palombi, an Australian National University intellectual-property law expert, calls for reversals in the laws that permit the patenting of human genes. "Why should these people have a patent over DNA, and over treatment?"

Thus the issuance of expensive licenses and the suppression of cheaper tests mean that needed tests cost more, which in turn means that fewer people will have access to the tests that allow them to save their lives and health. As Dr. Gill summarized: "[Patenting the gene] may have helped initially to define and produce the test, but in 2008 it's not helping kids right now to access the test."

The Tragedy of the Anticommons

If patents are meant to increase medical innovation—in the form, say, of more, better, and cheaper tests for HFE, HCV, and Dravet's—why do they so often block it? Do patent rights stifle the innovation they are supposed to inspire? Some experts think that patents have an inherent paradoxical tendency to slow the development of new inventions and, by extension, to slow economic and medical progress.

In 1759, famed economist Adam Smith put forth the concept of a self-regulating "invisible hand" that he believed governed the market and would maintain economic justice, or at least prevent the financial oppression of the poor.

He was answered in 1833 by an amateur mathematician named William Forster Lloyd, who warned that this invisible hand of economic justice was a fantasy. Lloyd published *Two Lectures on the Checks to Population*, a small book on population control that introduced "the tragedy of the commons."[61] Lloyd was speaking of "the commons" as a medieval communal space in which every resident shared ownership and which everyone could use for his own ends, such as grazing sheep; and he was speaking of tragedy in that Greek dramatic sense described by Alfred North Whitehead—not mere unhappiness, but "residing in the solemnity of the remorseless working of things."[62]

According to Lloyd, the tragedy is this: Because the commons is shared and its costs are borne by all, each owner finds it in his best interests to increase the number of his sheep that graze there. The advantages of feeding additional sheep accrue wholly to the owner, while any costs are shared equally by the many owners, rendering the cost to the individual owner small or even negligible. But if every owner adds more sheep to his grazing flock, the advantages wane inexorably as the commons' resources gradually become depleted and there remains no grazing available for anyone.

More than 150 years later, Rebecca Eisenberg and Michael Heller raised questions about the patenting of biomedical science that turned Lloyd's warning on its head. They suggest that the patent system has created the same problem of lost opportunity through the *opposite* policy—rather than *no* monopolistic claims, that of *excessive* monopolistic claims via patent "ownership."

In this scenario, which their 1998 *Science* paper dubbed "the tragedy of the anticommons," the exclusive rights held by many parties in an area of innovation present many and often complex negotiations to navigate. As a result, promising roads to innovation are eventually cut off by a failure to agree upon licensing rights and fees, especially because these fees can quickly mount to exceed the value of the finished product.

In the case of drug development, licenses must be negotiated routinely for the use of many popular patented technologies. These include the key distinguishing portions of genetic material called single nucleotide polymorphisms (SNPs) and for certain gene mutations. Licenses also tend to be required for commonly used research technologies that expedite the discoveries of therapies, drugs, or diagnostic methods. These licenses cover such patented techniques as polymerase chain reaction (PCR), which expands small DNA samples to amounts large enough to test, and for "knockout" mice that are bred with hereditary deficiencies that mimic a disease under exploration. Licenses are also needed to negotiate the monopolies created by patented gene databases, enzymes, and many more biological tools. The frequent need to access several of these tools can easily create an impenetrable "patent thicket"[63] that requires many licenses and dollars to navigate. And of course, patent rights can enable the holder to block the claims of others altogether, as described above.

If the licensing is denied or the costs exceed the likely value of the potential treatment that is under investigation, innovation grinds to a halt.

Pharmaceutical firms often respond to complaints about high prices with evidence of their programs that provide free medications to the poor, and research into orphan diseases that affect so few people that there would seem to be no very lucrative market. But both of these can be exploited as well; such programs, unfortunately, do not necessarily offer evidence of pharmaceutical sensitivity.

As mentioned earlier, the FDA accepts funding from the pharmaceutical industry to evaluate their drugs, which not only poses a conflict of interest, but also prompts many to question whose interests the agency sees as paramount—those of American patients, or those of the drug industry. In early 2011, this question flared publicly amid widespread outrage over reports that the agency was acting as a pharmaceutical "enforcer," muscling mothers into paying prohibitive prices to save the lives of infants threatened by premature birth and miscarriage.

For years, pharmacies have compounded various formulations of a lifesaver cryptically named 17P. This medication is a synthetic progestin, or female hormone, named hydroxyprogesterone caproate, and when injected it protects high-risk pregnancies from ending in miscarriage or premature birth. The latter condition is tied not only to higher rates of perinatal death and infant mortality, but also to higher disease risks and lifelong disability for some children. The price of this protection? At $10 to $20 a dose, even the twenty-shot course of 17P therapy was $200 to $400, well within most U.S. women's reach.

But then the FDA approved KV Pharmaceutical's application to sell hydroxyprogesterone caproate, renamed Makena, under the terms of the Orphan Drug Act, which is intended to provide a fiscal incentive for drug makers to produce important medications for rare conditions that otherwise would have too few potential customers to attract attention. The FDA approval gave KV the exclusive right to sell Makena through its subsidiary Ther-Rx Corporation for seven years.

Armed with its FDA approval, KV Pharmaceutical set about recouping its investment by setting Makena's price at $1500 a shot, ten times the price of the costliest dose of 17P. This drove the price of a course of therapy to a whopping $30,000. The federal government—that is, you and I—funded the research upon which the approval was based, so KV cannot offer R&D costs as a rationale for the steep price hike. The drug maker followed its markup with muscle, sending letters to the pharmacies that once compounded 17P to warn them that the FDA would enforce KV's exclusive right to manufacture and distribute the medication. [64]

Widespread outrage followed as women, their physicians, and advocacy organizations decried the greed that threatened to doom unborn children whose mothers could not produce $30,000. When the protests showed no signs of abating after several weeks, both the FDA and KV distanced themselves from the prohibitive pricing. [65]

In April 2011, in belated response to letters from KV threatening aggressive FDA enforcement, the FDA issued a press announcement: "This is not correct. In order to support access to this important drug, at this time and under this unique situation, FDA does not intend to take enforcement action against pharmacies that compound hydroxyprogesterone caproate based on a valid prescription. . . ."

Note that the FDA did not rule out the possibility of taking enforcement action at a later date. Its statement went on to specify that enforcement action would not ensue "unless the compounded products are unsafe, of substandard quality, or are not being compounded in accordance with appropriate standards for compounding sterile products." This language echoes the concerns over the "quality" of cheap generics that were invoked by the U.S. government to delay the distribution of essential antiretroviral drugs to desperate HIV-infected people in developing nations via PEPFAR. Could FDA enforcement of KV's patent still ensue, cloaked in concerns about the quality of 17P?

For now, pharmacies can continue to sell cheap generic versions of Makena. For its part, on March 8, KV noisily rolled out its patient-assistance program, under which women with household incomes less than $60,000 may receive it for free, and those from households making between $60,000 and $100,000 pay only $20 a dose. But uninsured women with incomes between $60,000 and $100,000 are charged the average co-pay assigned by insurance companies: for such an expensive drug, the co-pay could be considerable.

Even more worrying than the attempted price gouging is the fast-track approval granted Makena. Typically, the FDA requires three extensive clinical trials; but since 1992, the agency approves badly needed drugs more quickly, with the condition that the company will conduct additional studies and monitor the drug's market use for issues.

Thus it was that Makena underwent only one trial—of 463 pregnant women who were followed for only 2.5 to 5 years to look for complications and stillbirths—in a study financed by the National Institutes of Health and published in 2003 by the *New England Journal of Medicine*.

Although the data showed Makena to be of no direct clinical benefit in preventing infant mortality and disease, the drug was approved despite the recommendation by its own Reproductive Health Drugs Advisory Committee, which voted 21 to 0 for additional study "to evaluate the potential association of (the drug) with increased risk of second trimester miscarriage and stillbirth."

Because the application fees paid by companies to the FDA are allocated for evaluating drugs, there is nothing left over for supervising the mandated post-approval studies—most of which are never performed, as drug makers flout the requirement with impunity.

Pharmaceutical Darwinism

Why did Genetic Technologies unleash a preventable tragedy by using lawsuit threats to withhold a test that stands between at-risk children and a lifetime of mental disability? Why did pharmaceutical behemoth Bayer flirt with public-relations suicide by suing a modest hospital for treating a handful of patients in strict adherence to the law? Why did Bristol-Myers Squibb, as recounted in Chapter 2, hold Erbitux for ransom after an unbroken tradition of cooperating with Canada's Patent Board?

Perhaps because the drug industry has lost its fiscal primacy, and despite its billions in annual profits, it is desperate. In 2006, the industry toppled from its customary number-one spot as the globe's most profitable industry and has not recovered, remaining in the number-three spot. Worse, the future looks bleak: one by one, the blockbuster medications that catapulted drug makers to the top have been going off-patent, a predicament that the industry has termed a "patent cliff." (See "Increased Spending, Declining Innovation," below.)

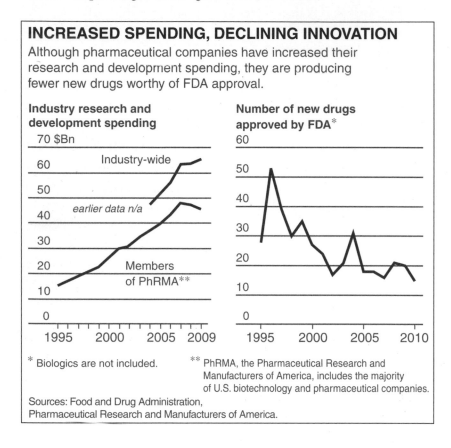

INCREASED SPENDING, DECLINING INNOVATION

Although pharmaceutical companies have increased their research and development spending, they are producing fewer new drugs worthy of FDA approval.

Industry research and development spending

Number of new drugs approved by FDA*

* Biologics are not included.

** PhRMA, the Pharmaceutical Research and Manufacturers of America, includes the majority of U.S. biotechnology and pharmaceutical companies.

Sources: Food and Drug Administration, Pharmaceutical Research and Manufacturers of America.

In 2008, Merck bid adieu to the Fosamax patent and its $3 billion in annual sales; the blockbusters Advair, Serevent, and Sonata also went off-patent that year, as drugs with annual profits totaling $20 billion lost patent protection.[66] Valtrex, Mepron, Prevacid, Topamax, Marginal, Matrix, and Lamictal went off-patent in 2009, and top earners Lipitor, Arimidex, Aricept, and Flomax are among those that expired in 2010.[67]

There is very little in the pipeline to replace the lost blockbusters. Although six hundred thousand scientists worldwide are working to develop novel drugs at a cost of billions of dollars, only twenty now emerge each year, according to Aled Edwards, a professor at the University of Toronto's Banting and Best Department of Medical Research.[68] Drug companies are still very profitable, but their considerable profits are in free fall, making tomorrow look uncertain—and tomorrow is all investors care about. With its moneymakers gone off-patent and to generics, and little in the pipeline to replace them, the pharmaceutical industry is fighting tooth and nail for survival.

The ability to bring new drugs to market is what carried pharmaceutical companies to the pinnacle of global dominance, and most experts agree with the 2007 Stanford Bernstein Report that the industry's future relies upon continued innovation. But where is that innovation? Until the late 1990s, each year ushered in about one hundred blockbuster drugs, but this fecundity has evaporated. The FDA approved twenty-four blockbusters in 1998 at a reported R&D cost of $27 billion, most of it borne by the government, but it approved only about half that many—thirteen drugs—in 2006. Moreover, the stated cost to do so more than doubled, to $64 billion, again largely provided by our taxes.

In short, drug makers still make very handsome profits, but they may not do so tomorrow: they are losing ground. Although the number of patent applications has more than doubled in the past thirteen years, there are far fewer new molecular entities, or NMEs, as opposed to copycat formulations.[69] Why are there fewer drugs, and where are the needed new drugs for diabetes, tuberculosis, AIDS, and SARS?

According to Stephen Schondelmeyer, PharmD, PhD,[70] professor of pharmaceutical economics at the University of Minnesota, one surprising reason for the loss of innovation is the longevity of the U.S. patent.[71] Twenty-year patent protection removes the incentives for innovation by allowing the patent holder to passively await the income from licenses, tests, and its monopolistic control over the market for its drug. "Patent exclusivity periods are too long and companies chase inexpensive modes of extending monopolies. The way to improve products and foster innovation is to shorten patent life, which will provide incentives to work faster, quicker and harder." In addition, the industry has outwitted itself with the many tactics by which its companies engage in life-cycle management, as was described in Chapter 2.

What's more, the innovation that fed pharmaceutical coffers was generated by university and biotechnology firms. At present, one-third of molecules in the R&D pipeline originated in biotech companies, so pharmaceutical firms have been buying up biotechnology firms in hopes that their innovation will save the industry. Between 2006 and 2009, $11 billion changed hands in fourteen sizeable pharmaceutical deals.

Large drug makers such as Pfizer and Merck made big acquisitions in 2009 after struggling to develop new hits of their own, and in the process they were able to cut billions of dollars by laying off workers and consolidating functions.[72]

Diving into Patent Pools

A thicket of patents on basic discoveries and necessary research tools has also created logjams that stifle innovation. At times, buying licenses and otherwise negotiating these constituent patents can drive the price of new-drug development above what the new drug would be worth. These patent thickets have also encouraged companies to forswear innovation in favor of wringing perennial exclusivity from their patents and other monopolies.

The most famous example is the 1917 patent thicket that encircled both Wilbur and Orville Wright's aeronautics firm, which they started in Dayton, Ohio, in 1909, and the rival Curtiss Company of Buffalo, New York. The Wrights were less interested in designing new aircraft or aircraft parts than in protecting their company's patents from interlopers, so they focused on earning royalties and heading off patent infringers.

Between them, the Wright brothers and Curtiss held most patents for airplanes; yet they had patented themselves into an impasse because neither could design new planes without infringing on patents held by the other, and the rivals refused to sell each other licenses. The industry was in danger of stagnating, but more important from the viewpoint of the U.S. government, America was about to enter World War I and the military refused to be thwarted in its need for warplanes.

Then–Assistant Secretary of the Navy Franklin D. Roosevelt strong-armed the reluctant companies into creating the nation's first patent pool, the Manufacturers Aircraft Association,[73] so that the patent thicket would no longer prevent the design of a suitable engine for warplanes. The patent pool proved so efficient and profitable that the companies merged in 1929, and by the end of World War II the resultant Curtiss-Wright Corporation became the largest airplane manufacturer in the United States.

A group of companies sometimes agrees to share intellectual property in patent pools. They do this by agreeing to cross-license patents covering a specific technology in which they share mutual interest. Patent pools can break up patent thickets, the intellectual-property logjams that can normally be so expensive to negotiate via licenses that innovation is utterly blocked. Although the competition law that regulates it is complex and some miscommunications and lawsuits are inevitable, such a pool may also be the only feasible method to bring a new discovery to the market.[74]

Some economists and life-sciences scholars express concern that the patent thickets resulting from the zeal for staking monopolistic claims on each discovery are hampering research and development within the pharmaceutical industry,[75] and disputes over these rights are burgeoning. Even in cases where one party agrees to pay for a license to use patented information, the costs may be passed on to consumers. But companies have increasingly resorted to litigation, especially in biotechnology. The number of such lawsuits exploded between 1978 and 1999, and they have become more expensive, according to the American Intellectual Property Law Association.[76]

More important, the tendency to pursue litigation varies widely across fields. Although the *average* rate of litigation for chemical patents is only 11.8 suits per 1,000, for example, it is more than double that for biotechnology patents and nondrug health patents; 25–35 lawsuits per 1,000 end up in court.[77] As companies await decisions over intellectual property, this litigation explosion means higher costs and greater delays—exactly what medical consumers do not need.

CHAPTER 4

POISON PILLS

How Patent Profits Spur the Proliferation of Questionable Drugs

Why is it we never get our bad medicine in small doses?

—EDMUND H. NORTH, 1960

On June 8, 2008, physicians, ethicists, and researchers of every hue from Seattle to Sri Lanka to Sudan filed into a cool subterranean auditorium of the Harvard School of Public Health. The purpose of the annual, weeklong Ethical Issues in Global Health Research Course was to help us mull, dissect, analyze, and perhaps even solve knotty questions about the conduct of medical research with the wretched of the earth. From the comfort of our seats in academe, we familiarized ourselves with and hotly debated nuanced theories for maintaining ethical research standards in poor developing nations, often under conditions of privation. Yet, despite the drama of these global challenges, we spent the first day distracted by an ethical crisis erupting much closer to home.

That very day, the *New York Times* had trumpeted the news that Harvard psychiatrists Joseph Biederman, Timothy E. Wilens, and others had violated federal and university rules that required them to report outside payments in excess of $10,000. These rules, designed to manage conflicts of interest, were invoked by Senator Charles Grassley, an Iowa Republican who was then the ranking member of the Finance Committee, as he confronted the doctors with what he and his staff had discovered.

Grassley found that the influential Biederman and his colleagues flouted regulations by failing to report many of their considerable payments from drug companies until Grassley's office detected them. For example, Biederman initially reported to Harvard that he had received no payments from Johnson & Johnson in 2001, but when confronted by Grassley, he admitted having received $3,500. Johnson & Johnson, however, says that it paid him $58,169 that year. Biederman earned at least $1.6 million in consulting fees from drug makers between 2000 and 2007, but reported only about $200,000 to the university. Wilens also earned $1.6 million, but admitted this only after being apprised of Grassley's accusations.[1]

Much more than money is at stake here. The mental health of the nation's children hangs in the balance, because Biederman is one of medicine's most influential proponents of administering powerful antipsychotic medications to young children like the thirteen-year-old son of Liza Ortiz.

Her son—let's call him Guillermo—began hearing voices when he was eleven. A year later he was diagnosed with schizophrenia and was prescribed an array of antipsychotic drugs, a "cocktail" that he took for a few years without serious incident. Then the drug Seroquel was added, and four days later Guillermo was dead. The use of these drugs in children remains hotly contested by experts, and none that Guillermo took had ever been tested in clinical trials with children.[2] On June 10, 2009, Liza Ortiz told an FDA advisory panel looking into the effects of prescribing powerful antipsychotic drugs to children that Seroquel had killed her son. "His hands twisted in ways I never thought possible in the I.C.U.," she recalled.[3]

This is a problem because many parents and physicians believe that medications like Seroquel and Risperdal, despite their steep price, are laden with side effects when given to children.

By the time her son, Kyle, was eighteen months old, twenty-two-year-old Brandy Warren of Opelousas, Louisiana, had grown unable to cope with his tendency to scream, throw objects, and hit his head against the wall when he grew angry or frustrated. Although these behaviors are frequently displayed by toddlers, Brandy, a poor single mother living with her parents, felt overwhelmed by her situation and was ill equipped to understand or to handle Kyle's emotions. She was afraid that Kyle's temper tantrums might be more than a premature case of the "terrible twos," and she turned to his pediatrician for help.

Instead of advising family counseling, a neurological assessment by a specialist, play therapy, or parent-skills training, Kyle's doctor told her that the boy was autistic, Brandy said, and that the best remedy for her infant's difficult behavior was antipsychotic medication.

As children in his waiting room played with Legos inscribed with the drug's name, he wrote a prescription for Risperdal, a powerful antipsychotic. But at that time, Risperdal was FDA-approved only for schizophrenia and acute manic episodes in adults. The next year it was approved only for very aggressive autistic children age five and older. It has never been approved for children younger than five, although doctors can legally use their clinical judgment to prescribe a medication for off-label use.

Over the next months, Kyle was diagnosed with an assortment of other disorders—hyperactivity, oppositional defiant disorder, bipolar disorder, and insomnia. For these he was given, every day, a cocktail of Risperdal, Prozac, several sleeping pills, and medication for attention-deficit disorder. He was two years old.

The barrage of drugs took its toll: if Kyle did not have serious medical problems before he was placed on the medications, he had them now. He was overweight, inactive, and drooled constantly, common side effects of the sedatives he was given. Some of these side effects, such as drooling and involuntary movements, can become permanent if the drugs are given for long enough. What constitutes "long enough" for two-year-olds? No one knows, because the drugs have not been evaluated in children Kyle's age. Diabetes is a common side effect as well.

Worse, Kyle's behaviors were indeed quieted: he no longer exhibited anger and frustration, but he was sluggish, glassy-eyed, and vacant, leading his mother to tell the New York Times, "I didn't have my son. It's like you'd look into his eyes and you would just see just blankness."[4]

Fortunately, Brandy made her way to Tulane University's Early Childhood Support and Services, where a special program is devoted to helping wean low-income children like Kyle from powerful antipsychotics that they should never have received. Why low-income children? Because, as a 2009 Rutgers University study revealed, poor children on government-sponsored programs such as Medicaid are four times more likely than privately insured children to be prescribed powerful antipsychotics, often without proper evaluation. Medications are far cheaper than family counseling. Texas alone spent $96 million on antipsychotic drugs for children, including some given to three infants less than one year old.

At Tulane, Kyle finally received a mental-health assessment that revealed his attention-deficit hyperactivity disorder, for which he now takes only a single drug, Vyvanse. At six, he is now an energetic, fit child who performs well in school, and his bouts of anger have been replaced by laughter, teasing, and other normal, childlike behaviors.

He never suffered from the dire diagnoses he was treated for with a cornucopia of pills, and his tantrums had sprung from the effects of family turmoil, due in part to the challenges Brandy was facing. This fact would have quickly emerged in family counseling had counseling been offered to them.

The antipsychotics that *were* offered to them constitute the nation's top-selling drugs by revenue, grossing $14.6 billion last year, with prominent promotions aimed at treating children. Given that the drugs present medical risks for children and they cannot ferret out or address the sort of family dynamics that caused Kyle's distress, why do so many doctors prescribe them? "This is a recent phenomenon, in large part driven by the misperception that these agents are safe and well tolerated," said Dr. Ben Vitiello, chief of child and adolescent treatment at the National Institute of Mental Health.

Joseph Biederman's assurances that these drugs are well tolerated did much to promulgate giving children antipsychotic drugs in general, and Risperdal in particular. Although he told the *New York Times* that his work and opinions on the administration of psychiatric drugs to children were "solely in the advancement of medical treatment through rigorous and objective study," his message to Johnson & Johnson was quite different.[5] According to court documents, Biederman's presentations promised the company that the studies he conducted of its medications in children would yield results benefiting Johnson & Johnson. And indeed, his studies of the firm's medicines, such as Concerta for attention-deficit hyperactivity disorder (ADHD), did yield favorable results.[6] They also assuaged physicians' fears by reassuring them that Concerta did not interfere with the growth of children. Because many neurologists now believe that human brain development continues into the twenties, some experts fear that the use of antidepressant drugs may affect the still-developing brains of children. Biederman's studies seemed to lay these fears to rest.

Biederman's relationship with Johnson & Johnson did not end there. He solicited financing from the pharmaceutical giant to fund a Massachusetts General Hospital research center of which he was director—the Johnson & Johnson Center for Pediatric Psychopathology Research. Johnson & Johnson gave $700,000 to this center in 2002 alone. "The rationale of this center," Johnson & Johnson internal documents explained, "is to generate and disseminate data supporting the use of risperidone [Risperdal]" in children and adolescents.[7]

Characterizing the rampant payments to "independent" medical experts as buying departments of the university or the hospital may seem without nuance or even unfair, but corporations sometimes also underwrite or even contract to patent all the research emanating from an academic department or center. This is exactly what Johnson & Johnson did when it funded the Johnson & Johnson Center for Pediatric Psychopathology Research.[8] And nearly ten years earlier, Japan's Shiseido contracted to fund all the research at Harvard's Division of Dermatology in exchange for patents on commercially significant findings, leading Marcia Angell, MD—professor of social medicine at the Harvard Medical School and former editor in chief of the *New England Journal of Medicine*—to muse whether cosmetic research might take precedence over research into life-threatening cancers and other serious disorders.

A Modest Proposal

The pediatric center delivered. Biederman's work did heavily support the use of Risperdal for ADHD children. From 1994 to 2003, it catalyzed a fortyfold increase in the diagnosis of pediatric bipolar disorder and a correspondingly impressive rise in the use of powerful and pricey antipsychotic medications in children.[9] The vast sums Biederman received have caused many to conclude that this premier proponent of antipsychotic drugs for children was paid by the pharmaceutical industry to influence the prescribing behavior of physicians and to promote the medication of children with powerful drugs that were designed for and tested in adults.

Thousands of parents have reported serious harm done to their children who were given the medications, and they have sued not only Johnson & Johnson but also AstraZeneca and Eli Lilly for hiding or downplaying the drugs' risks.

Their claims were validated in 2008, when a panel of federal experts concluded that Risperdal and similar powerful new psychiatric medications were being used too often and without appropriate safeguards in children. The panel urged that doctors must be better warned of their substantial risks.

There is more at stake for the companies here than the selling of antipsychotic pills for use in vulnerable children. Children are doubly valuable pharmaceutical consumers, because under the Best Pharmaceuticals for Children Act of 2002, if a company can extend its market to children, it will receive an additional six months of patent life for its medication, allowing it to profit by many more sales for both children and adults.[10]

In July 2011, Harvard punished Joseph Biederman, Thomas J. Spencer, and Timothy E. Wilens by banning them from any paid industry-sponsored activities for one year, followed by a two-year monitoring period during which they cannot engage in paid activities without obtaining approval from the Medical School and Massachusetts General Hospital. Harvard also warned the trio that they faced a "delay of consideration for promotion or advancement."[11] In a letter dated July 1, 2011, the researchers apologized for their actions but added, "We always believed that we were complying in good faith with the institutional policies and that our mistakes were honest ones."[12]

Biederman and his Harvard colleagues were hardly the only prominent psychiatrists who promoted the use of powerful but risky antipsychotic drugs for children while in the pay of drug firms.

From 1998 to 2004 and from 2006 to 2008, for example, psychiatrist Dr. Frederick K. Goodwin hosted an acclaimed radio program, *The Infinite Mind*, which was heard on National Public Radio and its affiliates. On his show, Goodwin relentlessly touted the use of potent antipsychotic drugs for children, frequently hosting guests who were as passionate as he in their advocacy for the medications. These guests had affiliations with the drug makers that Goodwin did not disclose to listeners or even to his producers at Lichtenstein Creative Media. Lichtenstein maintains that it was unaware of the $1.3 million Goodwin earned from delivering marketing lectures for drug makers. GlaxoSmithKline alone paid Goodwin in excess of $329,000 in one year for promoting its drug Lamictal. While in the pay of these firms, Goodwin even warned his listeners that bipolar children who were not given the "safe, effective" medications he espoused could suffer brain damage,[13] a distinctly minority view.

Goodwin's defense was startling. Instead of denying that he is bankrolled by pharmaceutical companies, he claimed that he was paid by so many different drug makers—a *New York Times* account lists nine, including Pfizer and Novartis[14]—that their competing interests canceled out any bias in his promotions. This logic is obviously faulty, especially because accepting funds from pharmaceutical companies incentivizes experts to discount nondrug therapies such as the talk therapy, family therapy, and behavior modification that helped Kyle Warren far better than the psychoactive pills he was prescribed. Accepting pharmaceutical-company funding also tempts doctors to favor newer drugs that are still profiting under patent protection over older medications that have gone generic and become inexpensive. This gives new drugs a marketplace monopoly based not upon clinical effectiveness and safety but upon their ability to maximize pharmaceutical profits. A paid clinical expert who fails to adopt such a pro-industry stance will not remain in its pay for long.

Moreover, NPR touts itself as the only major U.S. radio network that will not accept advertising—and by implication, as less vulnerable to industrial ties that promote conflicts of interest. To this end, public radio programs declare each source of funding to their audiences at the end of each program. For NPR to provide a home for the program of a psychiatrist who rakes in $1.3 million in undisclosed drug-industry payments is an especially egregious betrayal of trust.

While Biederman influenced prescribing behavior through his academic positions and affiliations at Harvard and Massachusetts General Hospital, as well as through his academic publications, Goodwin covered another front for the drug industry: popular medical journalism. For more than a decade, *The Infinite Mind* reached a million listeners in over three hundred markets, won sixty journalism awards, including the United Nations Media Award, six National Headliner Awards, four Gracie Awards, and honors from the National Institute of Mental Health, the National Mental Health Association, and the National Alliance for Research on Schizophrenia and Depression. The show billed itself as "public radio's most honored and listened-to health and science program."

But like Biederman, Goodwin enjoys multiple spheres of professional influence. He has written an influential textbook on bipolar disorder, and is the former director of the federal Alcohol, Drug Abuse, and Mental Health Administration. In the latter position, Goodwin was no stranger to controversy: he resigned under pressure when he outraged many Americans with his statements in support of a conference investigating the genetics of criminal behavior in children. Members of Congress, scientists, and laypersons alike expressed concern that the conduct and design of many of the studies featured disproportionate attention to blacks and could stigmatize African American children as "born criminals." As a result, the National Institutes of Health withdrew its $78,000 funding, but, partly in response to the complaints of an angry Goodwin, later restored it.[15]

Hardly mollified, Goodwin gave an address on February 11, 1992, that drew parallels between young inner-city (read "black") males and violent, oversexed primates.

> If you look, for example, at male monkeys, especially in the wild, roughly half of them survive to adulthood. The other half die by violence.
> . . . [M]aybe it isn't just the careless use of the word when people call certain areas of certain cities "jungles," that we may have gone back to what might be more natural without all of the social controls that we have imposed upon ourselves as a civilization over thousands of years in our own evolution.[16]

Widespread outrage greeted these statements, swiftly followed by calls for Goodwin's resignation. However, this brouhaha did nothing to retard Goodwin's political rise. Immediately after his resignation, he was appointed director of the National Institute of Mental Health, a move widely regarded as a promotion but curiously characterized as a demotion by then–HHS secretary Louis Sullivan.

Most experts agree that powerful antipsychotic medications have an important place in the management of adults' mental health issues and disorders. But their use in children, and their serious adverse events, including suicide, have always been questioned. Despite the paid opinions of Biederman, Goodwin, and their ilk, these drugs are dangerous for many and possibly for most children.

Funds such as those lavished upon Goodwin and Biederman are not drug makers' only investments in popularizing questionable or even frankly dangerous medications. Stark cash payments represent the tip of the iceberg. In this era of evidence-based medicine, pharmaceutical manufacturers not only pay experts for favorable opinions but have also adopted and sponsored strategies to appropriate or undermine the medical-reviewing and publishing process itself.

In some cases, corporations have controlled and distorted the conduct of clinical trials and of medical investigators to produce favorable results or to hide troubling or dangerous features of their patented medications.

Before discussing the details, it is helpful to know how clinical trials of medications and biologicals—blood, vaccines, and other biological treatments—are ideally conducted.

The Trials of Life

The FDA requires that clinical trials of medications and biologicals be conducted in humans before it will grant approval for marketing them. Usually these trials must be preceded by tests in animals. The process can take five to fourteen years, although the FDA also grants some approvals more quickly, after "fast track" testing for drugs that serve an urgent medical need. Fast-track trials are most prominent in the face of emergencies such as the development of AIDS medications and the H1N1 flu vaccine. Each clinical trial requires a protocol, which is a detailed blueprint of how the trial will be conducted. Before a clinical trial using human subjects—living individuals about whom an investigator obtains data or identifiable private information—can be conducted by a research institution, its Institutional Review Board, or IRB, must evaluate and approve it. IRBs seek to ensure that the study conforms to the law and to hospital regulations, and that it preserves the safety, privacy, and dignity of subjects. IRBs are also supposed to ensure that the trial meets prevailing ethical standards as well as the law, including informed consent for subjects.

After IRB approval and other requirements are met, the trial volunteers must verify their willingness to give informed consent after being thoroughly apprised of the study's intent, design, and known risks. (There are a few exceptions where informed consent is no longer offered.)[17]

Each clinical trial is conducted in several phases:

- Phase I: The candidate drug is tested in humans to determine its safety profile.
- Phase II: This study is done in persons who might benefit from the drug should it be approved, usually people with the disease or condition that is being treated. It seeks to determine whether the drug works as hoped and the optimal dosage.
- Phase III: This study is conducted in a large number of people to maximize the chance of discovering any side effects or problems and seeks to establish whether the drug works as hoped and is safe.
- Phase IV: After the drug is approved and is on the market, data collection continues to determine whether any safety or other issues emerge.

A great deal of care goes into a well-conducted clinical study to ensure that it is accurate and as free of bias as possible. The best clinical trial asks a clear, medically important question, is properly randomized (to avoid bias), and is conducted on a large scale (to avoid getting the wrong answer by chance). Most trials contain a control group of matched persons who are given the standard of care rather than the drug being studied, for the sake of comparison. In some cases, where ethical considerations permit it, the control or comparison group is given a placebo or "sham" remedy that has no active ingredients. Statistical experts are often involved in a trial's design.

These and other meticulous requirements were not always in place. IRBs were mandated after human medical-research scandals involving unwitting subjects in the 1970s. Other important requirements included the 1962 Kefauver Harris Amendment or "Drug Efficacy Amendment" to the Federal Food, Drug, and Cosmetic Act. This law introduced a requirement for drug manufacturers to provide proof of the effectiveness and safety of their drugs before approval and was enacted in the wake of a global tragedy based on poorly performed clinical trials.

Thalidomide and Friends

Amid all its considerable achievements—and failures—a momentous act of prudence stands out as the FDA's shining hour. In 1962, pharmacologist and physician Frances Oldham Kelsey refused to approve the German drug thalidomide for the prevention of insomnia and morning sickness in pregnant U.S. women, even though it had been distributed in Europe since 1957 by the German drug firm Grünenthal. In doing so, she—and a supportive FDA—defied Richardson-Merrell, the pharmaceutical company that sought to market the drug to the lucrative U.S. market. Dr. Kelsey, now ninety-six, gave thalidomide a thumbs-down because she determined that the safety tests had been performed incorrectly. The FDA refused its approval, even though Merrell threatened a lawsuit in response.

Dr. Kelsey was right, because thalidomide proved horribly unsafe. It is a teratogen, or medication that causes birth defects, and it crossed the placental barrier to cause profound prenatal injury to ten thousand children in forty-six countries. These children were born with gross deformities such as phocomelia, which is characterized by missing or dramatically shortened limbs and internal-organ malformations. But only sixteen American children, whose mothers were given the drug in a "marketing trial" meant to spur the drug's popularity among doctors,[18] suffered these profound birth defects, and the FDA takes justified pride in having saved Americans from sharing in this global tragedy.

Dr. Kelsey's achievement is a refreshing, even reassuring, reminder of the blessings that the U.S. medical-research system can impart at its best. The FDA's practices and culture have changed dramatically, however, since 1962, to say nothing of the legislative landscape. Today's largely overwhelmed FDA lacks the effectiveness and independence of the agency Dr. Kelsey knew, according to a 2006 report by the Institute of Medicine titled "The Future of Drug Safety: Promoting and Protecting the Health of the Public."[19]

The IOM report found major deficiencies in the FDA's system for ensuring that medications on the U.S. market are safe.[20] Today, FDA drug evaluations are largely funded by the pharmaceutical companies themselves—the agency is now deeply dependent upon the very drug makers whose products it evaluates for approximately 40 percent of testing costs. This causes a conflict of interest that seems to have upset the balance of power between the agency and the industry it is supposed to regulate.[21]

Many scientists now fear that a laissez-faire attitude prevails in which far too many medications become FDA-approved through questionable drug trials and less-than-meticulous evaluations. Even more ominous, some FDA insiders are among those who criticize the agency as loath to deny approval to even the most troubled drugs. In 2005, for example, Dr. David Graham, currently the associate director of the FDA's Office of Drug Safety, testified before the Senate Finance Committee that "finally, the scientific standards CDER [The FDA's Center for Drug Evaluation and Research] applies to drug safety guarantee that unsafe and deadly drugs will remain on the U.S. market."[22]

In stark contrast to the responsiveness with which it met Dr. Kelsey's thalidomide warnings, evidence is rife of a "Cassandra effect" as the United States has been bedeviled by a recent spate of FDA-approved bad drugs. Initially decried as dangerous by their FDA evaluators, medications such as the diabetes drugs Rezulin and Avandia as well as the COX-2 pain relievers Celebrex, Vioxx, and Bextra[23] were approved, marketed, profited handsomely from, and then ignominiously withdrawn from the market in the wake of injuries, deaths, and reports of unacceptable medical side effects and risks.

In fact, according to a 2010 analysis by Concept Capital, a division of Sanders Morris Harris, the FDA ignores one of every four recommendations by its advisory committees.[24] Although this selective dismissal ignores more calls for drug approval than rejection, the apparent diminution of overall standards makes one wonder how thalidomide might fare at the hands of today's corporate-friendly FDA.

Few of the internal FDA critics are willing to be publicly identified. And no wonder: as you will read below, physicians who question the safety and usefulness of potentially profitable drugs sometimes find themselves ignored, marginalized, or even targeted.

When Sidney Wolfe of the medical watchdog agency Public Citizen conducted an anonymous survey of physicians who evaluated medications for the FDA, more than a third expressed a belief that standards had dropped since 1995. Many thought that too many medications were being approved despite serious safety questions. Of the fifty-three medical officers who responded to Public Citizen's surveys, "Nineteen Medical Officers identified a total of 27 new drugs in the past three years that they reviewed that they thought should not have been approved but were approved. Asked how they would compare the current standards of FDA review for safety and efficacy to those in existence prior to 1995, seventeen medical officers described the current standards as 'lower' or 'much lower,' thirteen described them as 'about the same,' and six described them as 'higher.'"

One medical evaluator wrote, "My feeling after more than 20 years at FDA is that unless drugs can be shown to kill patients outright then they will be approved with revised labeling and box warning." Another wrote, "We are in the midst now to approve everything but to describe drug weaknesses in the label. As one high ranking official said, 'Everything is approvable. We can use the labeling creatively to lower the problems.'"

The complaint of yet another evaluator is especially chilling: "In the last two years, I recommended that two drugs not be approved. They were both approved without consulting me. This never happened before. In one case, the drug did not meet the standards set up by the division, so they nullified the standards."[25]

The Cassandra Effect

The fairly recent spate of bad drugs includes the diabetes drug Rezulin (troglitazone), which is used to lower blood sugar that is not controlled by insulin or other medications for blood-sugar control. It is used by Type 2 diabetics whose disease tends to arise after childhood and is frequently linked to being overweight. Rezulin was developed by the

Japanese biotech Daiichi Sankyo in 1982 and eventually patented and manufactured by Warner-Lambert. On a May 2000 visit to my elderly diabetic father, I was horrified to find a bottle of Rezulin nestled within the small pharmacy in his refrigerator. I called his doctor, who was equally disturbed. "I told your father to stop taking Rezulin a month ago. As you know, his memory isn't very good: he must have forgotten." I threw out the pills, and my father survived his brush with risk.

Ismael "Milo" Valenzuela was not so fortunate. "They killed my wife—that's the way I feel about it," he told the *Wall Street Journal*. Valenzuela was a Thoroughbred-horse-racing Hall of Fame jockey who won 2,545 races, including the Kentucky Derby—twice—before his retirement with his wife, Rosa, to California. Rosa, like my father, was taking Rezulin to help control her diabetes when she died suddenly of liver failure in December 1999. Three months later, the FDA persuaded its maker to withdraw Rezulin from the market.

Rezulin had been branded as a killer almost from the beginning, but most doctors would not learn of this for years. By 1996, before Rezulin even reached the market, FDA evaluating medical officer Dr. John Gueriguian discovered that it was associated with drug-induced heart and liver toxicity and with hepatitis. His report recommended that the FDA reject the drug.

Far from bestowing the same gratitude it had heaped on Dr. Kelsey, however, the FDA responded to pressure from Warner-Lambert by stripping Gueriguian of his evaluative role. In October 1996, Murray M. Lumpkin, MD, then director of the FDA's Center for Drug Evaluation and Research, reacted to complaints by executives of Warner-Lambert that "Gueriguian had used intemperate language in a meeting to discuss Rezulin," and set aside Gueriguian's report. A physician who spoke on condition of anonymity recalls, "He [Lumpkin] just said that the Gueriguian review doesn't exist because it was in draft form and hadn't been finalized. . . ."[26] In 1997 the FDA gave the drug not closer scrutiny, but fast-track approval within six months. According to a 2001 Pulitzer Prize–winning series in the *Los Angeles Times*, many of the FDA evaluators who advocated for Rezulin's approval were paid consultants for Warner-Lambert.

Almost immediately, Rezulin, which was promoted as devoid of significant side effects, was linked to high rates of liver failure. In 1997, the UK's Medicines Control Agency supervised Rezulin's withdrawal from their market, and in 1999 the agency refused to allow the drug to be sold again in the UK. In the United States, however, the FDA and Warner-Lambert were satisfied with revising the drug's warning label on four occasions and allowed it to stay on the market.

These events did not deter Warner-Lambert from deploying three hundred physicians to speak on Rezulin's behalf, for pay, to venues that included not only medical meetings but also the 1996 Olympic Games in Atlanta, where the company hosted doctors at the Château Élan Winery and Resort.[27]

The *Los Angeles Times* also recounts how Rezulin's maker focused its marketing on doctors with many Hispanic patients, who have a high incidence of diabetes. Spanish-speaking doctors in Miami, for example, were enlightened by drug reps' talking points that stressed "differences between Hispanic and American patients," such as:

"The Hispanic patient is less informed and educated about medicines," "The Hispanic patient is less disciplined," and "The Hispanic patient is easy to intimidate because they are afraid of having to go on insulin."[28] In addition to targeting Latinos, Warner-Lambert paid doctors up to $350 each to switch diabetic patients from safer drugs to Rezulin. In 1999, it even took the suspiciously prescient step of "offering to indemnify doctors nationwide if they were sued for prescribing Rezulin."

By the time Rezulin was pulled from the U.S. market in 2000, it had been implicated in ninety known liver failures and sixty-three deaths. It had also garnered U.S. sales totaling $1.8 billion. According to the *Wall Street Journal*, an FDA epidemiologist estimated that liver failure was afflicting twenty additional patients who took Rezulin every month.[29] By 2003, Pfizer (which acquired Warner-Lambert in June 2000) was facing thousands of lawsuits from Rezulin victims or their survivors.

The blockbuster diabetes medication Avandia (rosiglitazone), distributed by GlaxoSmithKline, is closely related to Rezulin and was widely touted as its replacement. Unfortunately, its users fared no better after it was approved by the FDA. In 2007, a *New England Journal of Medicine* article tied Avandia to increased risks of heart disease and found that its users were 43 percent more likely than others to suffer heart attacks.[30]

GlaxoSmithKline fought back, quickly publishing a clinical study of more than four thousand people that noted how, although twenty-nine Avandia users died from heart attacks or heart disease, more—thirty-five—died while taking other diabetic drugs, metformin and sulfonyl-urea.[31]

The study was conducted in a curiously sloppy manner, however. Atypically, the study was not blinded, meaning that the doctors and patients all knew who was taking which drug, a classic source of bias. Expectations color the results of trials that are not double-blinded so that neither the doctors nor the subjects know who is taking which drug. Moreover, one group took metformin and sulfonylurea, which carry risks of heart problems, while the other group took these *and* Avandia, which made teasing out the effects and comparing them quite difficult. Comparing a group on Avandia alone and another taking metformin or sulfonylurea would have yielded clearer data.

Moreover, many patients dropped out of the study, and their absence was not adequately explained. It was important to have more information about these defectors—for example, did they leave the trial because they developed side effects or serious illness? All these factors could have skewed the results, including the death rates.

Yet it is a mistake to assume that sheer carelessness underlay these errors: pharmaceutical companies have repeatedly demonstrated that they are masters of manipulating medical studies and scientific data to present their products in the most positive light or even, as happened in this case, to throw doubts on the seemingly clear hazards of taking their drugs.

COX-2 Medications: The Hard Sell

Thirty-two million Americans suffer some degree of daily pain from such common conditions as arthritis, back, and hip problems. In 1988, Dr. D. L. Simmons of Harvard University identified a cyclo-oxygenase-II, or COX-2, gene that causes pain and inflammation. Simmons moved to Brigham Young University the next year, where he contracted with Monsanto to develop painkillers based on the COX-2 enzyme. At BYU he fully sequenced and characterized the enzyme. Some might have gleefully announced their achievement to colleagues or broken out the champagne, but Simmons's savvy actions in the immediate aftermath of discovery showed that he was attuned to the importance of documenting his primacy as COX-2's discoverer. He had his laboratory notebook notarized that very day to legally validate his status, and in 1991 his findings were published in the *Proceedings of the National Academy of Sciences.*

If this act can also be read as Simmons's suspicion that Monsanto might balk at providing the royalties and profits to which Simmons believed himself entitled by their agreement, it was a prescient move on the researcher's part. Monsanto, which developed its COX-2 inhibitor drugs in partnership with Pfizer, patented the enzyme, refused to pay Simmons, and instead directed its in-house researchers to explore the development of COX-2 painkillers. Simmons promptly sued Pfizer with the backing of Brigham Young.[32]

While Simmons battled Pfizer for a share of the profits, pharmaceutical companies began racing to block the enzyme and create potent painkillers worth millions as replacements for cheap, over-the-counter (OTC) pain relievers.[33] For its part, Pfizer developed the blockbuster COX-2 painkiller Celebrex, cutting Simmons out of all patents and profits, claiming he "played no role in the development of Celebrex." The suit was amended in 2010 to reflect BYU's claim that Pfizer had concealed pertinent documents, but as this book went to press the suit remained unresolved.[34]

When it comes to cheap, effective, and safe pain relief, the older nonsteroidal anti-inflammatory drugs, or NSAIDs, such as ibuprofen (Advil), acetaminophen (Tylenol), and aspirin fit the bill for most people.[35] As a bonus, small daily doses of aspirin offer heart protection for many people. But no medication is perfect, and in the eyes of some drug makers, aspirin has two serious flaws: first, it can cause stomach upset and bleeding in some people; and second, it has long been off-patent, and therefore cheap.

By 1999, pharmaceutical firms sought to remedy both these failings by promulgating COX-2 inhibitors. Like aspirin, these are NSAIDs prescribed for relief of common pain including osteoarthritis, rheumatoid arthritis, painful menstruation, and menstrual symptoms. Pfizer's Celebrex (celecoxib), Merck's Vioxx (rofecoxib), and Bextra (valdecoxib) sold by G. D. Searle & Company, a Pfizer subsidiary, were COX-2 drugs. Because these were new patented medications, they were priced at hundreds of times the cost of aspirin, acetaminophen, ibuprofen, and other off-patent NSAIDs.[36]

The manufacturers did not claim that the COX-2 drugs relieved pain better than aspirin or other older, familiar medications. Instead, they sold these very expensive painkillers to the U.S. public on the basis that they did not cause the stomach upset and bleeding that aspirin can infrequently trigger, at least according to industry-financed studies.

Some questioned this claim, noting that the research backing it was largely funded by the drug makers themselves, so that a conflict of interest existed. Furthermore, a 2002 meta-analysis of serious injuries and deaths in COX-2 clinical trials revealed that serious adverse events, including admission to hospital, serious disability, and death, were significantly higher with COX-2 NSAIDs.[37] Today, the *Physicians' Desk Reference* entry for Celebrex warns of "serious gastrointestinal (GI) adverse events, which can be fatal. The risk is greater in patients with a prior history of ulcer disease or GI bleeding, and in patients at high risk for GI events, especially the elderly."[38]

Moreover, Stanford University researchers revealed that gastrointestinal-related serious illnesses and deaths related to over-the-counter ibuprofen and aspirin have dropped dramatically since peaking in 1992, well before Celebrex and Vioxx appeared on the market.[39] The current risk of gastrointestinal problems with other, cheaper NSAIDs is small: Only one user in two hundred develops bleeding ulcers from aspirin, and only one in five of those, or one user in a thousand, usually an elderly or frail person, dies from it.

Twenty million Americans suffer from osteoarthritis alone, and another four million take painkillers for rheumatoid arthritis, so there was a great deal of profit to be made in weaning them from cheap aspirin to expensive COX-2s. Thanks in part to the most expensive advertising campaigns in pharmaceutical history, the industry successfully sold COX-2 drugs to the public as safer replacements for the aspirin they had been taking to relieve menstrual cramps, back pain, and all manner of minor pain.

Drug firms also employed fleets of salespersons to cajole physicians into prescribing the drugs at high doses, in contravention of FDA recommendations. It is legal for physicians to use their clinical judgment to prescribe FDA-approved medications for unapproved or "off-label" uses, but it is illegal for drug makers to actively *promote* drugs for such unapproved uses. Unfortunately, some companies routinely do so.

"Duty, Honor, Country." Like the military elite it educates, West Point's motto is one that admits of no compromise. As a West Point graduate and Gulf War veteran, John Kopchinski took this motto to heart, and he carried it with him when he left the army in 1992 to work as a sales representative who promoted Pfizer medications to physicians in South Florida. But despite an impressive performance in the military academy and a decade at the front, working for Pfizer proved Kopchinski's rockiest challenge.

He did not endear himself to his superiors when he complained, for example, about the marketing of Bextra for uses that were not approved by the FDA. His complaints went ignored. In November 2001, the FDA had found that Bextra was unsafe at the high doses required for surgical procedures or for migraine headaches, and so it denied such uses and recommended doses no higher than 20 mg.[40] It approved Bextra only for lesser arthritis and menstrual pain and declared it unsafe for patients at high risk of heart attacks and strokes. Yet Pfizer continuously promoted and rewarded these uses, and its drug reps were trained to target anesthesiologists, foot surgeons, orthopedic surgeons, and oral surgeons—anyone who wielded a scalpel.

Pfizer not only routinely promoted risky high doses of this COX-2 medication for unapproved uses; it also paid reps a $50 bounty for each doctor they persuaded to prescribe high doses of Bextra to patients before and after surgery. Kopchinski, for example, was pressured to sell doctors on prescribing Bextra at eight times the approved dose for migraines.

Over six years of butting heads with company policy, Kopchinski felt that, as he told the Associated Press, "the ethical line kept moving in the wrong direction." Pfizer wielded a whip as well as carrot, he said, because "If you don't aggressively sell your products . . . you're labeled a non-team player." He could reach management's goals only by promoting and selling Bextra for unapproved uses.

In 2003, Kopchinski crossed his professional Rubicon by filing a *qui tam* lawsuit[41] against his employer. The individual complainant in a qui tam lawsuit will collect a portion of any penalty that is awarded. But his immediate reward was that Pfizer fired him. The timing was poor because the Kopchinskis had a baby boy, and his wife was pregnant with twins. His $125,000 salary plummeted to $40,000 when he was unable to get employment with another pharmaceutical company and he had to take a position with an insurance firm. This was an unsurprising development, says his lawyer, Erika Kelton. "In Pharma, it's no secret that it's an industry that can blackball former employees."[42] In short order, Kopchinski's 401(k) was depleted. He was forty-five years old.

But he was not defeated. For months before his dismissal from Pfizer, Kopchinski had been getting support from a different quarter—his lawyers. The qui tam suit sparked federal and state probes, which he had abetted by accruing invaluable evidence that Pfizer was illegally marketing its blockbuster Bextra.

In 2005, two years after Kopchinski's firing, Bextra was pulled from the market amid safety concerns that it raised the risks of heart attacks and stroke. The evidence that Kopchinski and five other whistleblowers had carefully collected over more than a decade with the pharmaceutical giant proved priceless to the Justice Department. It supported a federal case against Pfizer and its subsidiary Pharmacia & Upjohn that culminated in a $2.3 billion settlement, the largest health-fraud settlement ever won in the United States.[43] Pfizer's response read in part:

> We deny all of the civil allegations set forth in the *qui tam* complaints, including those in which DOJ intervened, with the exception that Pfizer acknowledges certain improper promotional conduct related to Zyvox and the Bextra conduct involved in the plea agreement.

Was it worth it? "In the Army I was expected to protect people at all costs," Kopchinski's response read. "At Pfizer I was expected to increase profits at all costs, even when sales meant endangering lives." But Kopchinski walks away with more than the satisfaction of having served "Duty, Honor, and Country." His share of the DOJ settlement is $51.3 million.

This conclusion may have a satisfying feel, but the apparent justice of the settlement is largely illusory. The government trumpeted the settlement as evidence of its take-no-prisoners reaction to pharmaceutical fraud, but is it really? Although the evidence that Pfizer perpetrated the greatest corporate health fraud in history—its fourth such fraud settlement within a decade[44]—would seem more than enough to indict the drug behemoth, it actually was let off lightly. True, the $2.3 billion settlement Pfizer paid is a fortune by any estimation. But that $2.3 billion is dwarfed by the $44.2 billion in pharmaceutical sales the world's largest drug maker rang up that year.[45] Some might suggest that it is just the cost of doing business, Pfizer's way.

Even more significant, a close reading of the settlement reveals that Pfizer paid the fine, but only its subsidiary Pharmacia & Upjohn pleaded guilty to one criminal count of violating the U.S. Food, Drug, and Cosmetic Act by its illegal promotion of Bextra.

Why does this matter? Because firms that are convicted of major health-care fraud are excluded from participating in the Medicare and Medicaid programs and cannot bill the government for products. The federal government pays for one-third of all medications, so such a ban could easily cripple even Pfizer. Lewis Morris, chief counsel of the U.S. Department of Health and Human Services, worried, "We have to ask whether by excluding the company [from Medicare and Medicaid], 'Are we harming our patients?'"

"We" would certainly be hurting Pfizer, because a fraud conviction for its illicit Bextra activities might lead to the collapse of the firm. The fallout, however, would also include the lost jobs of uninvolved Pfizer employees and of its numerous contractors, as well as massive losses to its shareholders. Medical education and research institutions as well as medical journals that depend upon Pfizer sponsorship could also be financially crippled or go under.

So instead of persisting with fraud charges against Pfizer, prosecutors ended by indicting and obtaining a guilty plea from Pharmacia & Upjohn Co., Inc., which is owned by Pharmacia & Upjohn, LLC, which is owned by Pharmacia Corp., which is owned by Pfizer Inc., which retains its ability to do business with Medicaid and Medicare and to bill the federal government.

Perhaps, like some huge banks and General Motors, Pfizer has been deemed too big to fail. Or perhaps it is just too big.

Pharmaceutical Omertà

Drug makers instructed their sales representatives to heavily promote COX-2 inhibitors both legally and illegally. But what ultimately closed the deal and led physicians to prescribe COX-2 drugs in huge numbers was the publication of two major clinical trials, the Celecoxib Long-term Arthritis Safety Study (CLASS) study in the *Journal of the American Medical Association* (*JAMA*) and the Vioxx Gastrointestinal Outcomes Research (VIGOR) study in the *New England Journal of Medicine*. Both journal articles reassured physicians that COX-2 NSAIDs triggered far fewer intestinal problems than did aspirin and the older, off-patent OTC painkillers.[46] Celebrex became a blockbuster drug: by 2000, 60 percent of Americans with arthritis were taking it. Celebrex and other COX-2 drugs were used for a wide range of pain, including osteoarthritis, rheumatoid arthritis, and menstrual pain, in doses from 200 to 600 mg daily. Fueled by a pervasive direct-to-consumer advertising campaign, COX-2 inhibitors became the most frequently prescribed drugs in the history of our nation.

What the advertisements did not mention and the journal articles tried at length to hide was that Celebrex, Vioxx, and perhaps other COX-2 drugs were triggering heart attacks and strokes. The FDA had data that revealed the increased risk of myocardial infarction, heart attack, and stroke, but these data were being withheld from the published studies.

To date, thirty-one thousand claims have been filed against the makers of Bextra, Celebrex, and Vioxx, and Merck has paid $2 billion to forty-four thousand Vioxx users without, however, acknowledging any responsibility for their injuries. Worldwide, Vioxx was prescribed to over eighty million people.[47]

As Vioxx was tied to heart attacks in users around the globe, English physician and journalist Ben Goldacre wrote that when the injured approached British health minister Ivan Lewis, he promised to help them. But, says Goldacre, within hours "Merck launched an expensive lobbying effort that convinced the minister to back off." In Australia, the *Guardian* newspaper unearthed email messages documenting Merck's efforts to silence, "neutralize," and "discredit" its "hit list" of various doctors who were critical of Vioxx and of Merck's efforts to shroud its dangers. "We may need to seek them out and destroy them where they live," read an email from a Merck employee.

The *Guardian* added that Merck staff were also accused of having "tried to interfere with academic appointments, and dropping hints about how funding to institutions might dry up."[48] This targeting of fractious doctors was not an isolated incident: as recently as 2008, Senator Grassley chastised Pfizer in print for having taken photographs of Harvard medical students who were protesting the pervasive influence of pharmaceutical companies in their classrooms and laboratories.[49]

An assailed Merck pulled Vioxx from the shelves in 2004, but the FDA allowed Celebrex to stay on the market. By letting the drug makers initiate voluntary recalls—or none at all—rather than pulling the drugs from the market itself, the FDA has given the companies deniability. The firms have thus avoided the permanence of a mandatory recall and often can control when and where the drugs will reappear. In June 2005, the FDA issued major new warnings for other COX-2 NSAIDs; in May 2006, Celebrex was found to cause twice as many heart attacks as older arthritis drugs; in December 2008, these NSAIDs were linked to high blood potassium; and in February 2009, they were demonstrated to dangerously raise blood pressure.

Merck replaced Vioxx with the COX-2 drug Arcoxia, which itself was linked to the risk of stroke and heart attack. Despite this, the path to FDA approval was eased when four prominent COX-2 critics[50] were excluded from the FDA panel convened to decide upon Arcoxia's approval. The FDA's own Dr. David Graham, like Frances Kelsey forty years earlier, protested that safety data on the drug could not support Arcoxia's approval. "What you're talking about is a potential public health disaster," Graham said. "We could have a replay of what we had with rofecoxib [Vioxx]."

Risk is inherent in research, and sometimes problems with medications do not emerge until they are marketed and large numbers of people take them, even in well-designed studies. This may not be avoidable and is not unethical.

The true significance of the flawed COX-2 medications, however, is that the deaths and injuries *were* avoidable, because they had been detected during FDA testing. But a pattern has been established by which flawed medications are loosed on the market, often over the objections of evaluators and abetted by flaccid scrutiny from the FDA—to say nothing of armies of paid physician boosters.

Consider that when Rezulin was finally found to be too dangerous for the American market, it became the eighth branded drug to be similarly withdrawn within thirty months. Besides the COX-2 painkillers and the other drugs described above, other dangerous but approved medications included the "Fen-Phen" weight-reduction duo of fenfluramine (Pondimin) or dexfenfluramine (Redux) and phentermine, which caused pulmonary hypertension and heart injury. A year before the Fen-Phen recall, FDA medical evaluator Leo Lutwak wrote a colleague to complain that the drug had few benefits and that American Home Products, its patent holder, "has gotten away with much manipulation these past three years, of the public, of the press, of the FDA."

Conflicts of Interest

Despite the omnipresent mantra of "evidence-based medicine" to which medical scientists pay homage, drug makers' payments have led some physicians, researchers, medical journals, and even the FDA to champion or shield medications that are unproven, dangerous, ineffective, or unnecessarily expensive. "Evidence-based medicine" refers to conclusions based upon scientific evidence applied to clinical decision-making. By implication, such conclusions avoid flawed logic and bias—cultural, social, historical, or financial.

Yet a curious lack of skepticism pervades journals about the propensity for bias in experts who accept money from the makers of the products they evaluate.

A medical reviewer is supposed to be an expert in a field of medicine who writes articles setting forth the best practices and evaluating the known tests, medications, techniques, and surgeries. The need for objectivity is clear, and so journals do not pay the authors of such articles. But the makers of the drugs and products in question often do.

To preserve objectivity, it is the usual policy of medical journals to set a ceiling on the funds that evaluating doctors are permitted to accept from drug makers, but these ceilings are usually high and vaulted, with the top-tier journals tending to publish reviewers who receive the fattest drug-industry paychecks. The *New England Journal of Medicine,* for example, has set a maximum of $10,000 a year from each drug company in speaking and consulting fees for doctors writing reviews. "So if a doctor is doing . . . business with four or five companies, he or she can get as much as $40,000 to $50,000 a year and not violate the *New England Journal* policy," summarized Dr. Sidney Wolfe of Public Citizen's Health Research Group.[51]

The practice of being a medical reviewer in the pay of drug makers has grown so widespread that it has become normal. By June 1992, conflicts of interest had grown so rife that the *NEJM* gave up its search for objective reviewers, announcing that it could find no reviewers who did not accept industry funds and so had abandoned its attempts to do so. It did so because, as medical journal editors estimate, *95 percent* of the academic researchers who assess which treatments work safely have financial relationships with pharmaceutical companies.

By 2000, drug makers were paying $6 billion a year in gifts to physicians, including $2 billion for 314,000 "educational" events like junkets to Caribbean islands. This does not include the speaking and consulting fees that the pharmaceutical industry pays friendly—that is, "high-prescribing"—researchers to discuss its products. Its long arm touches virtually all medical researchers.[52]

The industry also pays writers who are not experts in the field or who are not even doctors to "ghostwrite" review articles. In these cases any pretense of independence or objectivity is pretty much thrown to the wind. The writer is hired by the pharmaceutical company to write the article to the company's satisfaction, or in some cases company staff members write it, and the drug maker finds a doctor who is willing to append his name to the article for a few thousand dollars.

In September 2010, Adriane Fugh-Berman, MD, of Georgetown Medical Center, published a detailed case history of how ghostwriters from the publicity firm DesignWrite generated ghostwritten journal reviews that helped Wyeth Laboratories promulgate Premarin and Prempro, its brands of hormone replacement therapy (HRT), to prescribing physicians.[53]

Fugh-Berman's analysis, published in the journal *Public Library of Science* (*PLOS*), recounted how Wyeth paid DesignWrite to champion HRTs. These drugs were prescribed to women in order to address the escalating health risks they face beginning with the onset of menopause, when female hormonal levels shift and women lose the heart-protective effects of estrogen. Menopause-related hormonal changes trigger many signs and symptoms, from troubled skin, thinning hair, and brittle nails to fading libido and insomnia, but by shoring up hormone levels, HRT promised to safely preserve health and femininity indefinitely.

Some medical data, however, suggested links between HRT and cancer, so Wyeth chimed in to counteract these using ghostwriters who promulgated the company's sales messages in medical journal articles. Wyeth sponsored dozens of review articles and commentaries that denied the HRT-cancer link or downplayed these risks by, for example, falsely claiming that the cancers associated with HRT were less aggressive than other breast cancers. They implied that estrogen use was safe for breast cancer survivors, which is usually untrue. Other scientists denied HRT's cardiovascular risks, with claims that were not supported by the medical evidence, and promoted off-label uses of HRTs for everything from Parkinson's disease, dementia, eye problems, and even wrinkles. Some HRT research data were used, but in strict accordance with Wyeth's mandatory messages, scripts, and talking points.

We know this because lawsuits against pharmaceutical companies have resulted in rulings that forced the publication of the Drug Industry Document Archive, a searchable database of thousands of pages of industry documents on the internet, just as major tobacco companies were forced to do as a condition of successful lawsuits against them in the 1990s.[54] Fugh-Berman, who served as an expert witness, and the lawyers who represented people who were injured by HRT successfully fought to have the Wyeth documents available on the public database (http://dida.library.ucsf.edu).

The ghostwritten articles by DesignWrite scribes followed Wyeth's instructions to "Mitigate perceived risks of hormone-associated breast cancer," to "Promote unproven, off-label uses, including prevention of dementia, Parkinson's disease, and visual impairment," to "Raise questions about the safety and efficacy of competing therapies (competitive messaging)," to "Defend cardiovascular benefits, despite lack of benefit in RCTs," and to "Position low-dose hormone therapy."

When the clinical data conflicted with the marketing message, Fugh-Berman found, "the clinical trial reports were sometimes modified for marketing purposes." For example, in 2003 when Wyeth wanted the effects of a Premarin/trimegestone combination included in its report, DesignWrite emailed James H. Pickar, MD, of Wyeth, to explain its absence: ". . . it is highly desirable for them [the marketing team] to not have the metabolic data included in the lead paper, as this would cause labeling problems, *making the lead paper unusable for promotional purposes* [italics mine]."[55]

After papers were completed by DesignWrite, they were signed by a scientist, usually a physician, chosen by Wyeth. This violated the ethical guidelines of many medical journals, which specify the exact sort and extent of contribution required in order to qualify as a paper's author. Yet Fugh-Berman notes that the physician "authors" were considered interchangeable. One document states, "I moved Dr. Creasman as an author to the patented piece (with Blackwood, Weiss, & Speroff) and left Horwitz and Boman on the basic science manuscript."[56]

Fugh-Berman's article also revealed a permissive attitude toward recycling papers in a manner that would be described as plagiarism in most academic settings.

> In response to a question about whether previously commissioned papers could be reused, Gerald Burr of Wyeth wrote: "You can't just put another name on the article, but you can plagiarize the way we did when we wrote papers in college. What you need to do is give your potential authors Karen's version of the article before the author modified it. Then have your authors modify it for publication under their name. Wyeth owns Karen's draft, not the final publication."[57]

Such ghostwriting has been widely documented. In 2004, Forest Laboratories used ghostwriters to market Lexapro (escitalopram).[58] Drug makers also commissioned flack-written journal articles for many other drugs, including the antidepressant Paxil (paroxetine),[59] the recalled weight-loss drug Fen-Phen (fenfluramine and phentermine),[60] for the anti-epilepsy drug Neurontin (gabapentin),[61] the antidepressant Zoloft (sertraline),[62] as well as for the painkiller Vioxx (rofecoxib).[63]

But not every made-to-order research result was produced by a ghostwriter. Some came from credentialed researchers with a patent to profit from and a monopoly to protect.

Heart of Darkness

"Never bleed a negro," declared Thomas Jefferson, Revolutionary statesman, future U.S. president, and amateur physician. Bloodletting was once de rigueur treatment for illnesses, but his era's medical philosophy held that blacks suffered from different diseases and required different treatments than whites. Pellagra and cholera were racialized as black diseases. So were the imaginary "black diseases" drapetomania, hebetude, Struma Africana, and even the unique disorder "freedom," which doctors offered as the cause of mental illness in blacks. Physicians claimed to have found subtle physiological differences that imparted dramatically different reactions to treatment in blacks who were held to have uncomplicated nervous systems, to be relatively insensate to pain, and to be prone to diseases that struck only them.

And for "black diseases," physicians promulgated "black" remedies—to significant profits for those doctors who made a living ministering to the special diagnoses and treatments and certifying the fitness of enslaved black Americans to work the fields and farms of landowners. Such claims of medical difference have arisen often through American history, and they have rarely been interpreted in favor of black Americans: most often, they revealed or certified some manner of physical and mental inferiority. Rarely, too, have the scientific rationales stood up to disinterested scrutiny: Most medical beliefs about a "different" black physiology have been long on politically and economically convenient theories. Often quite outlandish, they tended to be short on demonstrated facts.

Today, however, scientists point to the evidence of humankind's genetic fraternity, one of the most ballyhooed products of the Human Genome Project. Now medical science's most consistent racial mantra is that race has no genetic basis. And yet these egalitarian utterances are belied by another burgeoning product of genetic technology: drugs tailored to racially distinct populations that are thought to share specific genetic profiles.

We may hope that at least some of these drugs will bear fruit by quelling disease. But already others have proven as unsubstantiated as the eighteenth-century nostrums that were put forth for the imaginary black diseases of the time.

The "black" heart drug BiDil became the first drug ever to be approved by the FDA on the basis of race when it was approved in 2005 for use in blacks only. BiDil, a patented combination of two generic medications, isosorbide dinitrate and hydralazine hydrochloride, supposedly was tailored to meet a special genetic profile shared by blacks in congestive heart failure.

Some tout BiDil as the future of genomic medicine. But will it actually return us to the era of race-based medicine, with its attendant social risks of reifying race and pathologizing difference? If the drug is truly a specialized boon for black hearts, such risks will have to be faced, because it would be folly to allow social concerns to threaten the lives of the seven hundred thousand black Americans who suffer from congestive heart failure.

But BiDil is not the savior it appears. In this era of evidence-based medicine, a disturbing degree of illogic and error infected the attempt to bolster faith in BiDil and to promulgate a fervent belief in the racialized medical difference that is its raison d'être. But unlike nineteenth-century "black" nostrums, BiDil was driven less by racial animus than by a company's hunger to exploit its monopoly on a patented medication.

In 2007, I sat on a Bayer-sponsored panel (I appeared without compensation) that discussed African American health issues. I was uncomfortably sandwiched between two black cardiologists who repeatedly pointed out to the audience that although medical research has long excluded blacks, "*This* drug has been tailored *for us.*" One of the doctors was affiliated with the Association of Black Cardiologists, or ABC, which was paid to conduct the clinical trials of BiDil; I was unable to determine the affiliation of the other.

In a preemptive strike, the ABC-affiliated cardiologist deftly framed any dissenting opinion of BiDil's approval in terms of blacks' emotional response to an abusive history of medical experimentation. "I know a lot of us have fears about medical research based upon things that have happened in the past. But this time we are included: This is *our* trial and this drug is for *us*. *We* tested BiDil." The other doctor echoed his statements, singing the praises of this new drug in their heart-disease armamentarium. "BiDil is the drug for us, tested *by* and *for us.*"

They were correct in that both the Association of Black Cardiologists and the International Society on Hypertension in Blacks (ISHIB) conducted the clinical trials that support BiDil, but I harbored doubts that the drug's selective efficacy has been proven, or that it is as demonstrably "black" as they claimed. My discomfort soared with their every word, because as a nonphysician, I usually lack the hubris to contradict physicians on points of their own specialty. BiDil's involvement with both of these excellent professional organizations of black cardiologists made it doubly difficult to ask the hard questions of the drug and its researchers.

But ask them I did, because the FDA's approval of BiDil raises concerns not only about race, but also about the cynical manipulation of science in the service of profit.

BiDil was not tailored for African Americans, as its proponents often claim. It began life as a general drug for congestive heart failure (CHF) developed by the Lexington, Massachusetts, biotech start-up NitroMed. In 1987 the FDA rejected NitroMed's application based upon the feeble results of its clinical trials. The company, which held patents only on BiDil, scrutinized the drug's data in search of another testing and marketing option that would allow it to approach the FDA again. It employed a frequently abused practice known as "data mining," wherein researchers, often aided by statisticians, examine an unpromising drug's test data in search of some group where it seems to have efficacy. In 2000, Dr. Peter Sleight, professor of cardiovascular medicine at Oxford University, mocked this practice when he published the results of stratifying some drugs' effectiveness by astrological sign, illustrating that disparate drug effects are easy to evoke whether they exist or not, and that nearly any medication can be made to seem worth developing if one scrutinizes enough subgroups closely enough.

Sleight and his team analyzed the data of the International Study of Infarct Survival (ISIS-2), a seventeen thousand-person clinical trial in the UK that asked whether aspirin helped people who had suffered a recent heart attack. It found that the beneficial effect of aspirin for patients having a heart attack was quite as powerful as that of streptokinase, a highly effective clot-dissolving medication. But when Sleight sorted the patients' responses by astrological subgroup, taking aspirin was associated with a good outcome for all birth signs, except for Libra and Gemini, for whom aspirin was harmful: they were more likely to die when given aspirin. Leos, on the other hand, would do well to consider taking the beta-blocker atenolol, in the wake of a heart attack, because another large study, ISIS-1, found a 71 percent reduction in the death rate of people born between July 24 and August 23 who took atenolol, as compared to all other birth signs, who enjoyed a mortality reduction of only 24 percent.[64]

Of course, birth signs have no effect whatsoever on your chances of benefiting from a remedy in the wake of a heart attack. Sleight and his colleagues concluded with this warning: "When in a trial with a clearly positive overall result, many subgroup analyses are considered, *false* negative results in some particular subgroups must be expected."[65]

Peering hopefully into BiDil's efficacy in women alone and in some other subgroups yielded no encouragement, but before NitroMed had to resort to astrology, the National Institutes of Health passed the FDA Modernization Act, an initiative for the inclusion of racial minorities in clinical trials. NitroMed said it found evidence in the rejected 1980s data that the drug might work better for blacks than it had for whites, and in 1997 BiDil was reborn as a "black" drug.[66]

NitroMed bolstered this claim of disparate racial efficacy with two biological statements. First, it claimed that physiology was key, declaring that "Death rates from heart failure are more than twice as high in black patients than in white patients." But this is untrue: whites and blacks die at almost exactly the same rate from CHF, in a ratio of 1.1:1.0.[67] The company also posited a biological difference—a racial "pathophysiology"—to explain the fictive doubled death rates. It was vaguely described as a genetic difference that "may involve nitric oxide insufficiency." Of course, the practically identical death rates negate any such claim. In a scientifically unwarranted leap of faith, subsequent discussions transformed this putative biological difference into a *genetic* difference, without evidence.

Among the BiDil proponents who published studies supporting this racial claim in medical journals was Jay Cohn, MD, who is one of its patent holders and thus had an important financial stake in promulgating this theory. Some black physicians who helped test BiDil also buttressed the arguments for a biological difference in the etiology of black heart failure, but they did so by giving short shrift to important environmental and behavioral differences between blacks and whites. For example, their papers discounted the contribution of stress to high blood pressure and ignored African Americans' different nutritional and exercise habits as well as their greater prevalence of smoking. Later, these physicians were paid by NitroMed to help conduct BiDil's clinical trials.

Once the theory of black genetic susceptibility to CHF was established in the medical literature, the NitroMed publicity machine went into full swing, and its marketing acumen proved far sounder than its

scientific logic. In order to cast BiDil as a "black" drug and win the new
FDA trial that would give it a new lease on life, NitroMed courted black
associations: not only ABC and ISHIB, as noted above, but also the
NAACP, which received $1.5 million from NitroMed in 2005 "to estab-
lish an organizational infrastructure to allow the NAACP to develop
health advocacy initiatives towards equal access to quality healthcare."
(Two years later the NAACP's loyalty to BiDil continued unabated. The
organization sent a "sharply worded" letter to the Centers for Medicare and Medicaid Services (CMS) castigating Medicare for "declining
to promote insurance coverage" for BiDil.[68] Many issuers did include
BiDil, but the NAACP, and presumably NitroMed, wished for the drug's
inclusion to be made mandatory, even though the two generic drugs
from which it is made have the same effect at a much lower cost.[69] Thus,
promoting NitroMed's monopoly trumped the NAACP's long-standing
interest in maintaining access to affordable medications.) Buoyed by
the influence of these prominent black organizations, NitroMed won
the FDA green light for a new round of testing to see whether BiDil
might work exclusively in blacks.

The new trial, dubbed A-HeFT, an acronym for the African American
Heart Failure Trials, was a Phase III study of 1,050 black subjects jointly
sponsored by NitroMed and the Association of Black Cardiologists. The
trial included only black subjects, no white ones. And despite the claim
that the BiDil mechanism is a genetic one, these were people who had
self-identified as black: no one knew or had quantified their genetic
complement. Furthermore, BiDil was not tested alone: it was given
only with congestive heart failure medications that are already known
to work, including diuretics (94 percent of patients), beta-blockers (87
percent), angiotensin-converting enzyme (ACE) inhibitors (93 percent),
angiotensin II blockers (62 percent), and digitalis (39 percent). This
prompts the question of how NitroMed planned to tease out the efficacy
of BiDil from the other drugs.

The published results of the trial were heralded as a success when
subjects taking the drug combination that included BiDil enjoyed 43
percent fewer heart-failure deaths and a 39 percent decrease in hospi-
talizations than subjects who did not take a medication regimen that
included BiDil.

At the subsequent FDA hearing on June 16, 2005, testimonials poured in from the Congressional Black Caucus Health Braintrust, the International Society on Hypertension in Blacks, and Dr. Lucille Norville-Perez, the national health director of the NAACP and former president of the National Medical Association. No one questioned the drug's efficacy. On June 23, the FDA approved BiDil as the first-ever drug for blacks only—a fateful step. Or perhaps a stagger, because this was a single clinical trial that admitted only black subjects and incorporated other troubling design choices.

I wished to ask NitroMed about these choices, but I could not, because their public-relations spokesperson insisted on scheduling an interview date after the FDA's final approval decision. On the day that my interview with chief medical officer Dr. Manuel Worcel was scheduled, NitroMed reneged, saying it would not speak with me "because the company has become a moving target" in the wake of the FDA approval.

If I had NitroMed's ear, I would ask, "Why was the drug tested only on African Americans?" The data that led the company to suspect (not know) that BiDil would work only in blacks are from a clinical trial that was designed more than twenty years ago and that was rejected by the FDA as unconvincing. That early trial involved a relatively small number of blacks, so that the drug's assumed greater efficacy could have been a random statistical artifact. When the black cardiologist declared before a largely African American audience that "usually we are excluded from clinical trials: this time we are included," he was wrong. Blacks were not included in the BiDil trials; they were segregated and targeted in a trial designed to reinforce a self-fulfilling prophecy: an ethical misstep married to a scientific one. A trial that included other ethnic groups is necessary for an accurate picture of BiDil's efficacy and whether that efficacy is actually greater in only one group.

I would also have asked NitroMed why BiDil was not tested for effectiveness on its own, but only in concert with other CHF drugs that are already known to work well. The positive results could signal synergistic effects, which would mean that BiDil may not work alone or may not work as well on its own.

Finally, I would also like to ask NitroMed whether it really considers BiDil's target group of black patients to be biologically distinct, sharing a discrete physiology. I ask because its clinical trials tested only people who "self-identified" as blacks. Thus the tests were not conducted on a genetically distinct group at all, but rather on a social cohort.

There may be one answer to all these questions: patent profits. Perhaps the testing did not include whites because it is possible that tests would show it worked in whites as well or even more efficiently, robbing NitroMed of its already thin rationale for calling BiDil a black drug. And BiDil could not be profitable unless it were labeled a black drug, because the patent covering its use in all ethnic groups expired in 2007, but the patent "for blacks only" allows NitroMed to profit until 2020.[70]

The decision to test BiDil only in concert with other effective heart drugs and not on its own also carries financial advantages for NitroMed: it means that BiDil will be FDA-approved only in concert with other drugs and so will not compete in the marketplace with these drugs. For this reason, other drug manufacturers will have no incentive to block its approval or promotion and may even profit by being partnered with BiDil. But blacks with heart failure will be prescribed two medications, not one, and thus will pay more for the privilege of taking "a black drug."

BiDil is not a black drug at all, however. Even the black cardiologist who praised it on the health panel admitted that "I fully expect to use BiDil in whites," and each physician with whom I have spoken agrees that this will be the case. Already, it has emerged that a BiDil component, hydralazine, raises the risk of lupus, a serious autoimmune disorder that strikes black women at three times the rate of whites. Such revelations may encourage physicians to consider it for whites, while withholding it from some blacks.

But because they were barred from the clinical trials, BiDil is not FDA-approved for whites, and if they benefit from it, some whites may have to pay more when insurers balk at paying for such an "off-label" use. Thus, BiDil may carry a high price for white patients with heart failure, who, in an unusual twist, may be barred by their race from access to a drug that could help save them.

The dearest costs of BiDil's triumph of racial labeling over scientific logic, though, are social, not financial. African Americans are about to pay the costs in a dangerous renaissance in stereotyped racial medicine. Stigmatized by an imaginary nitric-oxide pathophysiology, black sufferers may find that mainstream research efforts into congestive heart failure bypass them in the mistaken belief that their disease is too "different" for them to be included. Moreover, environmental, nutritional, and behavioral approaches to lowering CHF rates may be neglected in blacks because of a belief in their inherent genetic susceptibility. Finally, BiDil's approval on rather shaky evidence supports a dangerous return to separate-but-"equal" medicine.

In the case of BiDil, the expiring time limit on a patent, not a negative racial animus, encouraged shabbily conducted science that greased the slippery slope into neo-racial medicine. This cautionary tale should open our eyes to how the monopolistic biotechnology economy is perverting medical research and the quest for cures.

The extent to which the desire to maximize patent profits encouraged the production and adoption of BiDil is revealed when one learns that the glaring illogic of the way BiDil's clinical trials were conducted—unblinded, with no white controls, and in concert with drugs already known to work—is not as sloppy and nonsensical as it seems. It is consistent with strategies that often are employed to make medications look safe and effective even when they are not.

Blind Faith

How? The skepticism so treasured in scientific medicine often evaporates in the hot pursuit of pharmaceutical company funding, another symptom of the university researcher's loss of independence bemoaned by Sheldon Krimsky. In the case of BiDil, researchers too mindful of the bottom line used data mining of peculiar groups in order to ferret out supposed positive effects where there may actually be none. As in the cases of BiDil and Avandia, drug makers may structure the clinical trials so that the real cause of any therapeutic effects is unclear. NitroMed also loaded the statistical dice by claiming special efficacy in blacks, then testing the medication only in blacks.

But the most enduring type of clinical-trial manipulation is purchased bias. Although many assume that peer-reviewed studies, which are published only after they have been critiqued and evaluated by experts, are objective, several recent empirical studies suggest otherwise, at least when drug companies are involved. This extensive conflict of interest is important not only for medical publications but for vetting medications: groups such as the National Institutes of Health, the Institute of Medicine, and health-care insurers, including Medicaid and Medicare, examine the peer-reviewed medical literature to determine which drugs should be made available to patients and entered into formularies.

But clinical-trial results favor the products of those who fund them. We've suspected this since at least 1994, when Paula Rochon and her team analyzed all the trials bankrolled by the makers of nonsteroidal anti-inflammatory drugs (NSAIDs), painkillers for arthritis. Every one of the fifty-six trials found the funder's drug study superior to the medication to which it was compared. Not one study published results unfavorable to the drug maker.

Drs. Paul M. Ridker and Jose Torres at Harvard Medical School found that two-thirds of the results of industry-sponsored trials published between 2000 and 2005 in the three most influential medical publications—the *Journal of the American Medical Association*, the *New England Journal of Medicine*, and the UK's *Lancet*—favored experimental heart drugs or medical devices. Trials funded by nonprofits, however, were about as likely to support the drugs or devices as to oppose them: only 49 percent of these articles were positive. Studies that combined industry funding with nonprofit support fell between the two on the spectrum, with 57 percent offering favorable results.[71]

These findings, in a recent issue of the *Journal of the American Medical Association*,[72] indicate how large pharmaceutical and device makers pay for many of the major studies on new medical treatments, in hopes of replacing the current standard of care with their new therapy.

Similarly, Lisa Bero, professor of clinical pharmacy at the University of California, San Francisco, looked at two hundred trials comparing similar medications in 2007 in medical journals that were chosen because of their reputation for publishing high-quality, peer-reviewed studies.[73] She found that clinical trials that compare medications are twenty times more likely to favor the one made by the company that funds the research. Also, when papers discuss the implications of their findings, those with positive implications are thirty-five times more likely to have been paid for by the drug maker.[74]

A great deal of care goes into a well-conducted clinical study to ensure that it is accurate and as free of bias as possible. The best clinical trial asks a clear, medically important question, is properly randomized (to avoid bias), and is conducted on a large scale (to avoid getting the wrong answer by chance). Most contain a control group of matched persons who are given the standard of care rather than the drug being studied, for comparison.

However, there are many ways to debase the clinical-research process for marketing purposes. Some drug companies encourage or engineer sophisticated distortions in which the trials eschew evidence-based medicine in favor of large leaps of logic to unsubstantiated but profitable conclusions.

Medical journals are revered as bastions of scientific truth by everyone from journalists who educate the public about medications to the practicing physicians who must decide which treatments to adopt. But this once-rigorous system of medical publication can be defeated in many ways. This is such an open secret that in 2003 the esteemed *British Medical Journal* published a tongue-in-cheek article instructing researchers in the fine art of "HARLOT—How to Achieve Results without Lying to Overcome the Truth." The authors wittily summarized strategies by which drug makers can use clinical trials to tart up bad drugs. Their advice was to "test against placebo," "test against minimal dose," "test against maximal dose," and "test in very small groups."[75]

What does all this mean? It means that companies sometimes seek to make questionable drugs look good by:

- Comparing their drug to a competitor's medication, in the wrong strength. Too low a dose makes the rival drug look ineffective; too strong a dose tends to elicit worrisome side effects.
- Comparing their drug to a placebo. A placebo (the Latin word means "I will please"), such as a dummy or "sugar" pill, has no active ingredient, so it is much less likely to evoke a medically helpful response. Although placebos do convey poorly understood health benefits for some, they are weak, and nearly any medication will perform better than a placebo. Using a placebo typically introduces an ethical violation as well because it means that one group in the trial is given a "treatment" that has no adequate efficacy.
- Pairing their drug with one that is known to work well. This strategy, which was employed in the clinical trials for BiDil, can hide that a tested medication is weak or ineffective.

- Truncating a trial. Drug makers sometimes end a clinical trial when they have reason to believe that it is about to reveal that serious side effects are widespread, a lack of effectiveness, or that the trial is otherwise going south.
- Refusing to release or to publish data. If trial data look bad or troubling, companies sometimes refuse to release them, sometimes even to the researchers who collected them.[76]
- Publishing "ghostwritten" review articles. As we have seen, these externally produced reports selectively summarize the data with a spin that is approved of by the company.

Drug-funded researchers also conduct trials that are too small to show differences between competitor drugs. Or they use multiple endpoints, or therapeutic goals, in the study, then selectively publish only those that give favorable results. Furthermore, clinical trials sometimes consist of multicenter trials (conducted at several sites), and the investigators selectively publish results only from those centers that obtain favorable results.

There's more. Just as unscrupulous brokers will sometimes initiate frequent activity on their clients' accounts just to rake in fees, a practice called churning, researchers employ similar tactics by "seeding" and "switching" trials simply to get doctors to prescribe their drug. As we saw in Chapter 2, "seeding" trials are often scientifically meaningless, posing no clear question to answer and no logical control groups. But they tend to use large numbers of subjects, and the doctors who test the drugs are paid substantial sums for each subject they enroll into the trial. In a "switching" trial, the doctor changes the drug patients have been taking to the new drug. Any positive-sounding results are selectively publicized and influence physicians to adopt the medication.

HARLOT and other shady practices are less than amusing when you consider that all these techniques, and more, are deployed by companies seeking approval of drugs that sometimes wreak medical havoc once they go on the market. This happened with hormone replacement therapy, for example, and with Vioxx.[77] The esteemed *Annals of Internal Medicine* published what its editors regarded as a legitimate study of Vioxx in 2003. Only when a letter from lawyers, accompanied by an incriminating Merck intra-office memo providing "clear evidence that the intent of ADVANTAGE [Assessment of Differences between Vioxx and Naproxen To Ascertain Gastrointestinal Tolerability and Effectiveness] was to increase prescriptions of Vioxx," arrived at their offices did they realize that they had been duped into publicizing a seeding trial.[78] Thus the pharmaceutical industry manipulates even the most august medical media, which sometimes are duped into publishing incomplete, misleading, or false information.

Worse, publications are sometimes complicit. When Mark Abramson, MD, the author of *Overdosed America: The Broken Promise of American Medicine*, spoke at the 2008 Harvard global research-ethics conference mentioned at the beginning of this chapter, he dismissed much of the content of contemporary U.S. medical journals as "little better than infomercials." What provoked his harsh assessment?

Abramson was reacting to the fact that even in the most prestigious journals, medical assessments are bought and paid for as ethicists and journalists look the other way.

Caveat Lector

Beginning January 1, 2009, about forty members of the pharmaceutical industry agreed to a voluntary moratorium on branded goodies such as pens, mugs, soap dispensers, and other kitsch that it distributes to doctors at a cost of $1 billion a year. To many people, this widely publicized promise represents an important step away from pharmaceutical merchandising.

But while we debate whether physicians' loyalties can *really* be bought for a cheap pen or free lunch, the third-most-profitable industry in the nation is also buying and selling something far more influential: the contents of medical journals.

Flimsy plastic pens that scream the virtues of Vioxx and articles published in the pages of the *New England Journal of Medicine* and the *Lancet* would seem to mark the two poles of medical influence. Scarcely any doctor admits to being influenced by the former: everyone boasts of being guided by the latter and most regard medical journals as bastions of disinterested scientific evaluation and as the antidote to the fiscal influence of the pharmaceutical industry. And yet "All journals are bought—or at least cleverly used—by the pharmaceutical industry," claims Richard Smith, longtime editor of the *British Medical Journal*.[79]

The industry's editorial influence starts with advertisements, the lifeblood of every medical journal. Overworked physicians, pressed for time, will rarely admit to being swayed by advertising claims, but drug makers clearly don't agree and advertise copiously—and inaccurately—in journals.

In 1992, the editors of the esteemed *Annals of Internal Medicine* decided to gauge how well their own advertisements met the explicit 1981 FDA standards for accuracy and "fair balance" in medical-journal advertisements. They tested 109 advertisements along with the references cited by them, sending each ad to three expert reviewers who evaluated it in light of the FDA standards. Fifty-seven percent of the ads were judged to have no educational value, 40 percent failed the fair-balance test, and 44 percent, the reviewers believed, would result in improper prescribing. Overall, reviewers would have recommended against publication of 28 percent of the advertisements, as the *Annals* revealed in its published report.

Subsequently, from August 1997 to August 2002, the FDA issued eighty-eight letters accusing drug companies of advertising violations. But the *Annals* editors were in no position to bask in this validation: the journal was fighting for its life after large pharmaceutical companies withdrew $1.5 million in advertising. "Finally, the editors felt that to save the journal, they must resign," recalls Smith. A co-editor of *Annals*, Robert Fletcher, remarked as he departed, "The pharmaceutical industry showed us that the advertising dollar could be a two-edged sword, a carrot or a stick. If you ever wondered whether they play hardball, that was a pretty good demonstration that they do."

A decade later, with a different editor at the helm and a restored pharmaceutical advertising base, the *Annals* planned an editorial on high drug prices. But this time, it took care to first invite commentary from the premier drug makers' organization, the Pharmaceutical Research and Manufacturers Association (PhRMA).

Pharmaceutical advertising impinges heavily on the editorial sphere of medical journals, sometimes with surprising brazenness. The drug epoetin is widely accepted for its role in prolonging survival in people with end-stage renal disease: Medicare alone spent $7.5 billion on the drug in the decade preceding 2002. Dennis Cotter is president of a nonprofit institute that scrutinizes conventional medical wisdom, and his group's analysis suggested that epoetin's benefits for people with end-stage renal disease were largely chimerical, based on flawed logic. In 2003, Cotter submitted an editorial that detailed his questioning of epoetin's role to *Transplantation and Dialysis*, whose editor and peer reviewers agreed that it should be published. However, as the *British Medical Journal* reported in January 2004, Joseph Herman, *Transplantation and Dialysis*'s editor, rejected the piece because, "unfortunately, I have been overruled by our marketing department with regard to publishing your editorial. The publication of your editorial would, in fact, not be accepted in some quarters . . . and apparently went beyond what our marketing department was willing to accommodate."

After a hue and cry was raised in the medical press, the journal reversed itself and offered to publish Cotter's work, but he demurred, preferring to publish in a less commercial venue.

Medical journals are utterly dependent upon pharmaceutical advertising, which can provide between 97 and 99 percent of their advertising revenue. By 2005, some major journals, including *Consultant, Geriatrics*, and *American Family Physician*, carried more advertising than editorial pages and boasted glossy, full-color inserts that were longer than the journal's longest article. This explains why medical journals themselves advertise to drug makers, flooding the pages of pharmaceutical-industry publications such as *Medical Marketing and Media* to vie for the attentions of Big Pharma. The *Journal of the American Medical Association* bills itself in advertising as "a priceless audience at a price you can afford," while the *Annals* boasts: "With an audience of more than 90,000 internists (93 percent of whom are actively practicing physicians), *Annals* has always been a smart buy."[80]

Pharma's journal ads tout not only products, but also its hundreds of thousands of subsidized "educational opportunities." Drug and medical device makers spend $2 billion annually for more than 300,000 seminars and training opportunities, often held in the Bahamas or the Caribbean. The wolfed-on-the-run free pizza for harried medical residents that the industry has so sanctimoniously forsworn bears little resemblance to the sumptuous feasts, flowing wines, chartered flights, cruises, luxurious lodgings, golfing, snorkeling, and remarkably attractive sales reps that characterize these island educational junkets.

"There's a lot of bribery involved—the kids get pizza, the grown-ups get trips to Hawaii," observed Marcia Angell, MD, the author of

2004's *The Truth About the Drug Companies: How They Deceive Us and What to Do About It.* These pedagogic playdates familiarize doctors with pharmaceutical companies' patented products to the exclusion of cheaper—and sometimes safer and more effective—alternatives.

By 2000, drug makers were paying physicians a total of $6 billion a year for trinkets, island "educational opportunities," and financial grants for their pet projects, from golfing jaunts to clinics; this doesn't include the speaking and consulting fees that the pharmaceutical industry pays influential and "high-prescribing" clinicians to discuss its products. "Drug companies have moved their gift giving from drug reps to hiring 'thought leaders'—the best drug reps of all," says Angell. "They send experienced physicians out to give talks and ensconce them on well-paid speakers' bureaus. Then they claim that this is education, not marketing."

Moreover, those physicians who claim that they ignore the ads and are influenced only by the peer-reviewed articles cannot always tell the difference between the two. The lines are blurred because drug makers sometimes agree to buy journal advertising only if it is accompanied by favorable editorial mentions of their products. Or their in-house stables of writers or hired pens generate "advertorials," a Frankenstein mix of medical content and marketing messages that can be indistinguishable from editorial material. "Pharmaceutical firms also inform journals," Richard Smith, former editor of the *British Medical Journal* observes, "that they are receptive to buying huge volumes of reprints that favor their wares: The profits for the journal can easily reach $100,000."

Worse, journals allow their actual medical content to be subverted in many ways. The well-established "negative bias" of medical journals—their tendency *not* to publish studies with negative findings—is related to the drug industry's bottom line. "Any reputable journal is at the mercy of what is submitted to it," Angell says, "and must choose from whatever comes over the transom. Many studies never see the light of day because their findings are negative. There is a heavy bias toward positive studies, and this negative bias is a real problem. A company may conduct 100 trials; if two are positive, they get FDA approval and are published. The other 98 never see the light of day." In fact, half of all study data are never published.

One might think that physicians, with their scientific training and medical expertise, would be able to see through negative bias and data manipulation, but according to Eddie L. Hoover, MD, editor of the *Journal of the National Medical Association*, "A busy pediatrician who is seeing patients until eight at night doesn't have time to figure out whether an article has been vetted. He depends upon the journal editors to make sure he is not reading trash."

"When you are published in a medical journal, especially one of the top ones, this gives the article a certain imprimatur that makes people less critical," adds Joel Lexchin, MD, a bioethicist at York University in Toronto. "'If it's in the *New England Journal of Medicine*, it's got to be good': this mentality diminishes the critical reading of the study." Moreover, many inaccuracies cannot be detected because neither the journal nor the reader has access to all of the original trial data. In the end, explains Angell, "Journals get a heavily winnowed-out selection of trial findings, and so doctors come to believe that medications in trials are more effective than they are. Many psychiatric medications are little more than placebos, yet many clinicians have come to believe that SSRI [selective serotonin reuptake inhibitors, a newer class of antidepressants] drugs are magic, all through the suppression of negative studies."

We have already seen how widespread is the practice of hiring ghostwriters who typically are not physicians or even scientists to write review articles to the company's satisfaction, signed by a prominent physician. The nadir in medical publishing, however, was reached in 2003 when Elsevier, the august Dutch publisher of both the *Lancet* and *Gray's Anatomy*, sullied its previously impeccable reputation by publishing an entire sham medical journal solely to promote Merck products. Elsevier publishes two thousand scientific journals and twenty thousand book-length works, but its *Australasian Journal of Bone and Joint Medicine*, which looks just like a medical journal, and was described as such, was not a peer-reviewed medical journal but rather a collection of reprinted articles that Merck paid Elsevier to publish. At least some of the articles were ghostwritten, and all lavished unalloyed praise on Merck drugs, such as its troubled painkiller Vioxx. There was no disclosure of Merck's sponsorship. It was not peer reviewed or objectively vetted in any way. Instead of original articles based upon contemporary research, it contained nine articles praising Merck's Vioxx, and twelve on another Merck drug.

It was, in short, just as Mark Abramson described such publications: an infomercial. Unfortunately, Elsevier did not stop at the single sham journal.[81] It passed off five similar mock-journals, also paid for by Merck, as genuine. Medical librarian Jonathan Rochkind recently discovered not only that the ersatz journals are still being printed and circulated, but that fifty more Elsevier journals appeared to be pharmaceutical advertisements in medical-journal clothing. His forensic librarianship has exposed the once all-but-inaccessible queen of medical publishing as a high-priced call girl.

Elsevier first reacted by denying that the publications in question *were* medical journals, and insisted that they should not have been taken as anything but advertising. This prompted psychiatrist and journalist Ben Goldacre to wonder in print why the word "journal" appeared in the titles.[82] Later, according to the *Bibliographic Wilderness* blog, "Elsevier apologized for its publication of AJBJM, stating that in publishing the fake journal, it did not meet its own criteria for 'high standards for disclosure.' "[83]

The worst fallout is not the fatal blow to Elsevier's reputation, but that physicians rely upon such publications to give them the best possible assessments of new medications. Instead, they often are duped into prescribing dangerous or ineffectual drugs to their patients without adequate warning of their limitations or side effects.[84]

October to March

How do cozy relations between the FDA and the pharmaceutical firms whose products it regulates threaten the health of Americans? Earlier I explained how BioPort's troubled anthrax vaccine was championed by its only customer, the U.S. Department of Defense, and approved by the FDA. This book has also detailed how medications have been approved over the objections of, and even without the knowledge of, FDA drug evaluators, at least one of whom was stripped of his evaluative role after pharmaceutical firms complained about him. The fast-track approvals of medications such as Vioxx have been followed by thousands of deaths and eventual recalls. We have even seen that the FDA violates its own rules to further the interests of drug makers, as when the experimental anthrax vaccine was elevated to "approved" status in order to sidestep

federal judge Emmet G. Sullivan's ruling that the DOD could no longer force it on soldiers. I have also recounted how, under the rationale
of devising newer and better emergency treatments for trauma victims,
the FDA green-lighted at least fifteen drug-company studies that bypass
informed consent, resulting in the widespread conscription of tens of
thousands of U.S. citizens into medical research without their knowledge or consent. These have included testing of patented products such as
Northfield Laboratories' blood substitute PolyHeme and products tested
as part of the wide-ranging Resuscitation Outcomes consortium.

In an exhaustive investigation published by the *New York Review of
Books* in April 2011, Helen Epstein questions whether needless and even
frankly harmful medications are being pressed onto alarmed citizens
under the aegis of emergency preparedness.

Every year the vigilant state laboratories of the world face the same
deadline: to identify, analyze, and devise a vaccine against what will
become the primary strain of influenza virus, and to do so in time to
arm its populace immunologically before "flu season" is in full swing.
This process is a complex alchemy that combines immunological analysis, disease-pattern prediction, and the painstaking production of vaccine, on deadline. It requires not a little public-relations flair as well in
order to sell the public on taking the hard-won prophylactics.

For the influenza vaccine can be something of a hard sell in the
United States, where good nutrition, a rich public-health infrastructure, and abundant physicians and medications means that most of the
336,000 Americans who die of the flu each year[85] are especially vulnerable types. They tend to be those at the poles of life—95 percent of the
dead are elderly or children under five—or people with lung disease
and respiratory problems, including the obese. Or they are immunologically weakened people such as the HIV-infected and cancer or
organ-transplant patients who take immune suppressant drugs. Finally,
many people pass on flu vaccines because they consider themselves at
low risk for dying and do not know that death is not the only life-altering
legacy of influenza, which can also cause heart disease, loss of hearing or
the sense of smell, various brain injuries, or Reye's syndrome, an infection of the liver and brain that kills 40 percent of its victims.

However, those familiar annual bouts of influenza from which most
of us fully recover occasionally give way to killer pandemic strains that

decimate the globe. Most iconic was the 1918 flu pandemic, called the "Great Plague," which was a swine flu that had its origin in domesticated pigs and ended by killing 20 million people and leaving a terrible assortment of disabilities in its wake, such as encephalitis lethargica, a Parkinson's-like syndrome that left survivors in a permanently coma-like state. Such pandemics of influenza occur every eleven years on average,[86] but the most recent were the 1957–58 Asian pandemic and 1968–69 Hong Kong pandemics.[87] This means that as epidemiologists have been warning us, we are long overdue for such a pandemic. It may explain why an eighteen-person avian flu outbreak in Hong Kong in 1997 led governments to an excess of caution as they stockpiled a new class of influenza medications—neuraminidase inhibitors—even though these treatments were not yet FDA-approved. The most frequently used of these is Tamiflu, manufactured by Hoffmann–La Roche.

Despite the history of flu pandemics, some Americans are wary of the flu vaccine, largely because of the swine-flu fiasco of 1976. On February 5, 1976, Private David Lewis contracted the flu at the army's Fort Dix, New Jersey, boot camp, and within twenty-four hours he was dead. When government epidemiologists revealed that Lewis had died of a swine-flu strain and that five hundred other Fort Dix soldiers were infected, the Centers for Disease Control feared another worldwide scourge, so it advocated for mass immunizations across the nation and warned that all 220 million Americans must take the vaccine to avoid a possible pandemic, at a cost of at least $135 million.

"When lives are at stake, it is better to err on the side of overreaction than underreaction," wrote Dr. David J. Sencer, who was then CDC director, in 2006.[88] President Gerald Ford also wished to err on the side of caution, so he recruited Albert Sabin and Jonas Salk to lobby for rapid mass production of a treatment that the pharmaceutical manufacturers, who had an obvious financial interest in selling doses of their sera and vaccines, were happy to supply. Public-service announcements and unquestioning news stories urged all Americans to immunize themselves and their families against swine flu. Yet at the October deadline, drug makers proffered not the coveted vaccines, but an ultimatum: They would sell them to the federal government only if it first indemnified the companies against any legal claims arising from the vaccines' adverse effects. The suspicious nature of this requirement led some to wonder what might be wrong with the vaccines, but the government, its back against the wall, caved; on October 1, just eight months after Lewis's death, vaccines were urged on Americans at doctors' offices, places of employment, schools, firehouses, and medical centers.

But within two weeks, people began dying from heart attacks within mere hours of immunization. After inoculating 40 million people, so many had developed heart problems, Guillain-Barré syndrome, and other neurological problems that the government suspended the program. No swine-flu epidemic ever emerged, and, in fact, Lewis was the only casualty—unless you count the people who died after developing chronic illnesses from the vaccine. They or their survivors sued the government, and faith evaporated in the government's ability to predict pandemics and to provide a safe vaccine.

Thus, in 2009, when the H1N1 swine-flu strain emerged in Mexico, the CDC again decided to urge adoption of a vaccine, but it knew that it would have an uphill battle in gaining acceptance. This was not an American problem: the World Health Organization announced an H1N1 pandemic in June, warning that 2 billion across the globe would contract the virus and that a million could die. China slaughtered its pigs and closed its borders; Mexico closed government offices and canceled air flights; Egypt killed every pig in Cairo, ruining small farmers.

However, it's an ill wind that blows nobody good. Pharma reaped hundreds of millions in sales for vaccines and antiflu medications as part of the $10 billion governments spent on emergency preparedness, $4 billion of which was disbursed by the United States. Fully half the U.S. spending went to Hoffmann–La Roche for Tamiflu, reports Epstein. The United States and Europe bought $3 billion worth of Tamiflu and considered buying more for use in the developing world where few could afford it at $15 a dose.

Just as in 1976, the pandemic failed to materialize. Only eighteen thousand people died worldwide during the 2009–10 season from H1N1—fewer people than usual. Moreover, most of the dead had the sort of underlying chronic conditions that are always associated with higher mortality.

This was no surprise to some. The Council of Europe determined that WHO had known that H1N1 was a mild strain and it questioned whether pharmaceutical companies had influenced the agency's decision to generate the very expensive worldwide alarm.[89]

While the cost was being questioned, a 2003 report by Swiss physician Laurent Kaiser had already partially exonerated the use of Tamiflu by determining that people who took it were 55 percent less likely to develop pneumonia or other life-threatening complications. Tamiflu, he wrote, lessened the severity of flu symptoms, so it may have been worth the billions spent on it even in the absence of a pandemic.

But in Japan, Toshiharu Fujita studied 9,386 influenza patients under eighteen and found that loss of consciousness was 80 percent higher in those who had been given Tamiflu. In 2005, Osaka physician Dr. Rokuro Hama, who investigates the safety of pharmaceutical products through the Japan Institute of Pharmacovigilance, fielded dozens of reports of children dying from confused behaviors just after being given Tamiflu: one jumped from a ninth-floor balcony; another ran onto a freeway and was killed by a truck; still others died inexplicably in their sleep.[90] He cited a nationwide study that found no greater percentage of such neurological behaviors in children taking Tamiflu, but when Hama himself reviewed the data, he determined that the study's analysis was faulty and that children taking Tamiflu actually exhibited a fourfold greater incidence of hallucinations and other neuropsychiatric symptoms. Later he learned that the Japanese Roche subsidiary Chugai had funded the study. In fact, Keiji Hayaski, MD, found that *all* pertinent studies on Tamiflu had been funded by Roche, says Epstein.[91] Tom Jefferson, MD, of the Cochrane Collaboration, which independently reviews medical research, found the study's methodology was flawed: it was not properly randomized, and there was evidence of data mining, calling the touted benefits of Tamiflu into question.

Initially, the FDA had been similarly wary. In 2000, its panel of evaluators had rejected Tamiflu's active ingredient in its original powdered incarnation called Relenza. But the FDA approved it over their objections and subsequently fast-tracked Tamiflu based on Relenza's approval.[92]

Jefferson found conflicting journal articles: some reported serious side effects, and others reported few or none. This confusion was complicated by Roche's reluctance to release original data: in fact, in some cases, even the authors of articles about Tamiflu had never seen these original data, because these articles were ghostwritten, and neither the paid writers of Adis, a self-described "drug pipeline database," nor the putative "authors" who appended their signatures had been given the original clinical data for review. Instead, Roche had handed them tables of compiled figures and told them to emphasize the virulence of influenza and the merits of the Roche vaccine Tamiflu.

Epstein points out that the spending on emergency preparedness for the nonexistent H1N1 epidemic "exceeds the entire annual budget of the FDA." Thus, abetted by a compliant FDA, companies such as Tamiflu's maker reaped huge profits from the selling of "emergency preparedness," even as they escaped legal action arising from claims of injuries.

Thalidomide Redux

This chapter has explored how and why the pharmaceutical industry's monopolistic interests have come to trump safety to the extent that dangerous medications are protected and even promulgated. To establish a barometer of this tendency, I earlier posed the rhetorical question of how thalidomide might fare in today's pharmaceuticals-friendly climate at the hands of a weakened FDA.

We have our answer: thalidomide is back, with the FDA's blessing, but it is being tested almost exclusively in poor developing nations. Within the past decade, clinical trials of the infamously teratogenic drug—a drug that induces birth defects—have been conducted in Africa, Brazil, and India as a treatment for leprosy, HIV disease, and cancer.

In 1998, the FDA approved thalidomide for the lesions of Hansen's disease, or leprosy, and later approved its very close analog lenalidomide, derived from thalidomide and carrying its risks of phocomelia, for the fatal blood cancer multiple myeloma. Today the maligned drug graces pharmacists' shelves in Europe and the United States and occupies center stage in at least thirty-six ongoing research studies in the developing world—with the FDA's blessing.

How could this be? "We will never accept a world with thalidomide in it," declared Randolph Warren, head of the Thalidomide Victims Association of Canada, who was born with phocomelia.

But we have accepted it. One reason may be that our memory of the tragedy fades with each succeeding generation, especially in the United States, where so few were affected. And of course, people in Third World test sites have no experience with thalidomide. This collective amnesia shrouds thalidomide's renaissance in secrecy. The drug's identity is further blurred as it is marketed under unfamiliar names such as Synovir and lenalidomide.[93] Its FDA approval means that physicians can prescribe thalidomide for off-label uses, and it is currently being tested with research subjects in Brazil, Nigeria, and other areas of the developing world.[94]

Is thalidomide's renaissance warranted? That is, is it medically desirable, reasonably safe, and ethically acceptable? Despite the staggering emotional impact of its side effects, a logical evaluation of thalidomide suggests that its risks alone do not necessarily make it an undesirable drug, because these risks must be weighed against the drug's potential benefits. The risk of birth defects, for example, is clearly unacceptable in the context of its 1950s usage to stem vomiting and sleeplessness, especially because less harmful medications address these noncritical symptoms.

But today thalidomide is prescribed for leprosy and multiple myeloma, life-threatening conditions with few alternative treatments. The risk of birth defects may be worth these benefits because, unlike in the 1950s, this risk is now known and steps can be taken to minimize it. These include mandating the use of two contraceptive methods to all but banish the risk of imperiled pregnancy.

Unfortunately, thalidomide's side effects are not limited to missing limbs. Thalidomide is linked to the deaths of 2000 babies in the UK alone. Many of the UK's 466 thalidomide survivors suffer internal-organ damage, and the musculoskeletal strain of such damage has taken a toll on their fiftysomething bodies. Moreover, it is a mistake to assume we know everything about thalidomide's effects: some researchers fear that men who take thalidomide may transmit it in their semen, contributing to birth defects as well.[95]

In the industrialized West, where robust ethical protections, monitoring, and two forms of contraception are widely available, the risks seem manageable, although recent studies suggest that women who are advised to use contraceptives while taking teratogens often fail to do so. Even so, widely available medical care and contraceptives may make thalidomide an acceptable, even desirable, treatment for critical illnesses.

But the FDA and European drug-monitoring bodies have made a huge mistake in approving U.S. thalidomide studies in the developing world, where the risks are not manageable, and that error has been compounded with desultory monitoring. "WHO did not set up any advisory body to monitor the side-effects, or even to record how many patients were being treated," accuses Dr. Colin Crawford, a leprologist at London's Imperial College School of Medicine.[96] Women are not adequately warned of the need for such contraceptive precautions: warning labels are sometimes missing or in languages with which research subjects are unfamiliar, and subjects in the global South are more likely to be illiterate than are Europeans. Moreover, beleaguered women in developing nations lack the funds and the social power to negotiate the use of contraceptives, which are widely unavailable in such locales.

As a result, a 1994 Brazilian study found, sixty-one people were born after 1965 whose limb defects and exposure history were compatible with thalidomide embryopathy, and prescriptions for the drug were documented in about 64 percent of these cases.[97] It has not helped that until 1979, West African promotional materials still described thalidomide as "completely harmless."

So, forty years after it produced ten thousand horribly deformed babies around the world, evidence suggests that Third World subjects of thalidomide trials for leprosy and AIDS are not warned of the horrible birth defects the drug can cause, and photographs of black and brown babies who are missing limbs bear testament to the tenacity of pharmaceutical firms' greed.

Although some researchers cited Brazil's high rate of leprosy as a rationale for conducting trials there, the research is not meant to benefit Brazilians and Nigerians, who, as a rule, cannot afford expensive branded Western medications. As a November 2009 study in the *New England Journal of Medicine* revealed, one in three U.S. clinical-study sites is located abroad, mostly in developing countries.[98] Yet of the 1,233 drugs licensed globally between 1975 and 1997,[99] pharmaceutical companies developed only four new medications to treat human diseases in the developing world.[100]

Countries like Nigeria and Brazil bear the risks of thalidomide without reaping its benefits. This inequitable distribution of risks and benefits means that thalidomide trials should be suspended in poor developing nations. Such research should be confined to the United States, the United Kingdom, and Europe, and other nations whose citizens can benefit and where its hazards can be better controlled.

This would mean an ethical sea change in our habitual use of the Third World as the laboratory of the West. I don't pretend that this will be easy, but neither was Dr. Kelsey's decision to place American lives above medical "progress."

Dr. Kelsey cannot save us this time, however: she has run her race, and we must look to ourselves now. Can we, like her, be trusted to advance medicine, but not at the cost of innocent lives?

CHAPTER 5

GENE PATENTS

Buying the Disease

Genes are naturally occurring things, not inventions, and the heritage of humanity. Like a mountain or a river, the human genome is a natural phenomenon that existed, if not before us, then at least before we became aware of it.

—SIR JOHN SULSTON, 2002 NOBEL LAUREATE IN PHYSIOLOGY OR MEDICINE

"Pigs fly!" marveled the March 30, 2010, headline of the *Genomics Law Report*, which went on to clarify, "Federal Court Invalidates Myriad's Patent Claims."[1]

In a development the *GLR* described as "jaw-dropping," "radical," and "astonishing," Judge Robert W. Sweet of the Federal District Court in Manhattan ruled that seven of Myriad Genetics' twenty-three patents on the breast and ovarian cancer genes BRCA1 and BRCA2 are not made by man and that, for this and other reasons, they are invalid.

A few years earlier, Genae Girard of Austin had been astonished, too, when she learned that Myriad's patent meant that she and similarly stricken U.S. sufferers could obtain the genetic testing they needed to quantify their risks and to direct the best treatment for their breast cancers only by paying Myriad's $3,400 fee. Moreover, she learned that there were other tests that could help define her treatment by better characterizing her cancer, but these tests were unavailable to her, and to other breast cancer patients, because of Myriad's vigorous defense of its patent. It was Girard who brought the successful case against Myriad's patent because, as a health educator and advocate, she refused to accept the limitations on her care that the patent tests imposed.

Most, but not all, of Myriad's breast cancer gene patents were restored on appeal in July 2011; however, the matter will be taken to court again, very likely to the Supreme Court. Whatever the final result, it is clear that the federal ruling will resound far beyond the BRCA genes, for an astonishing one in every five human genes has been patented. Biogen Idec controls your kidney's essential KIM gene; the University of California holds patents on the TCP1, -2, and -3 genes that enable your tongue to sense taste; Trinity College of Dublin has filed for a patent on the human eye, and patents have been granted for genes that control the functions of human bones, heart, teeth, tongue, colon, skin, brain, ear, lung, liver, kidney, sperm, blood, and immune system. Disease genes and parts of genes have been patented, often even before their function was known. A specific isolated gene-sequence discovery, its biochemical composition, the processes by which these can be obtained and used, or a combination of such claims all can form the basis for a gene patent. Half a million gene patents have been granted in the United States alone.[2]

Redefining Nature

Patents are limited to entities that are novel, non-obvious, and manufactured, created by the hand of man. No one doubts the novelty of these genes, and the mode of their discovery was far from obvious, but are they "manufactured"? Since the 1980 *Chakrabarty v. Diamond* decision, which paved the way for patenting living things, the USPTO has sidestepped this stumbling block with the tenuous argument that the process of isolating and discovering a gene transforms it into a new, manufactured entity that is not found in nature but only exists *via* the "hand of man."

But "the essence of a gene is the information it provides—the sequence," demurs Sir John Sulston, Nobel laureate and chair of the Institute for Science, Ethics and Innovation at the University of Manchester. "Copying it into another format makes no difference. It is like taking a hardback book written by someone else, publishing it in paperback and then claiming authorship because the binding is different." Judge Sweet found the distinction between isolated and natural genes equally spurious and ruled the Myriad patents invalid.[3] Because the "hand of man" is the classic argument upon which gene and many other biological patents are granted, the implications for other gene patents is clear—if Sweet's ruling survives Myriad's appeal, many other gene patents also face invalidation.

BRCA1 is an enormous gene with a molecular mass of 220,000 amu, or atomic mass units, perched fatly on the long arm of the seventeenth of the twenty-three human chromosomes, chromosome 17; BRCA2 is nearly twice as big.[4] (By comparison, that of HBB, the gene for sickle-cell anemia, is only 15,000 amu, less than one-twentieth the size of BRCA2.) There is ample room for errors—mutations—on these big BRCA genes, and it is some of these mutations that are associated with breast and ovarian cancers. Cancer-causing mutations encode for the wrong proteins, which render affected family members susceptible to cancer. The prevalence of such BRCA1 mutations is also racially stratified, with the highest prevalence of BRCA1, 16.7 percent, found among young African American women,[5] and 8.3 percent of Ashkenazi Jewish women with breast cancer have a cancer-associated BRCA1 mutation.[6] However, the appearance of mutations does not mean that one will definitely develop cancer; instead, it increases one's *relative risk* of developing cancer compared to someone without a mutation. Calculating an individual's increase in risk can be complex because it is affected by other factors, including the exact nature of the mutation in question and other genetic anomalies.

The BRCA1 and BRCA2 tests are far from perfectly predictive. There are cancer-associated mutations on the genes that Myriad's test cannot detect. In fact, as many as 10 percent of all breast cancer cases may be hereditary, and although Myriad's patents are thought to cover just half of these, the patents have long given the company a lucrative monopoly.[7] Myriad cannot only devise diagnostic tests and treatments for familial breast cancer, but it can also license or exclude other researchers from working with the genes unless they secure Myriad's permission and pay its price.

Portions of the double helix of DNA that resides in our cells and tells them which proteins to make are constantly breaking under stress. Radiation, the act of cellular reproduction, and an assortment of other natural stresses constantly threaten the integrity of the code of life. The site of each break is a possible site of biological miscommunication that can result in disasters, from genetic illness to wide varieties of cancer. The helical molecule of life is in constant danger of unraveling, at least in part.

We all have BCRA genes, and we are fortunate that we do. Vigilant

BRCA genes are repair agents, called *tumor suppressors*, that constantly traverse our DNA, mending breaks in the genetic sequence. But what happens when BRCA itself is defective? A mutated BRCA1 gene can be bad news because it usually makes a protein that is abnormally short and does not function properly. Researchers believe that the defective BRCA1 protein is unable to help fix mutations that occur in other genes, and, as these defects accumulate, they may allow cells to grow and divide uncontrollably to form a tumor.

Women with certain BRCA mutations face a 60 percent higher risk than others of developing breast cancer by age ninety; the increased risk of developing ovarian cancer is about 55 percent for women with BRCA1 mutations and about 25 percent for women with BRCA2 mutations.[8] Men with the mutation also face higher risks of breast and prostate cancers. Researchers are not yet sure why the mutated genes specify for breast, ovarian, and prostate cancers.

Genae Girard is a multifaceted health advocate who makes her living by writing, advising, supporting, and freeing others from crippling anxiety, and she seems perfectly suited for the work. One-on-one, she's not only smart and knowledgeable about medicine, but warmly intense, affably pragmatic, and gifted with an irrepressible sense of humor. But when she learned that she had breast cancer, Genae took the offensive and gave the disease no quarter, deploying her sharp intellect and her ability to defuse anxiety. She energetically seized control of her treatment, voraciously educating herself and demanding that her doctors tell her exactly what she was up against.

"I'm passionate about education, especially when it comes to my health," Girard explained earnestly from her home in Austin, Texas. "My dad is a radiologist, and growing up in a medical setting, well, I'm a head-butter. It's in my constitution to question everything when it comes to my health."

But Genae had hit an immovable treatment roadblock—not the limit of her ability to absorb knowledge, nor her medication's efficacy, but Myriad's patents. The firm's near monopoly on abnormal breast cancer genes meant that Genae could find no "second opinion" test to better define her best treatment options for her cancer.

This is because, like most other American pharmaceutical and biotechnology companies, Myriad charges steep licensing fees to other researchers working with them. Patent holders defend their intellectual property with "cease-and-desist" letters, lawsuits, usurious fees, and financially painful settlements, and Myriad has fully exploited these, threatening legal action against other researchers who were working with the genes to effect a cure or treatment.[9] These researchers could not afford to defend themselves against a legal challenge and dropped their BRCA1 research, a development that has had a chilling effect on other American researchers.[10] And no wonder—according to a 1999 survey by the American Intellectual Property Law Association, bringing and defending the average patent lawsuit carries a $1.5 million price tag.[11]

A patent holder may also deny a license and so refuse access to its gene, molecule, or test at any price. Companies may exercise that right if they suspect that research would reveal flaws or inadequacies in their own patented treatments or tests, suggests Lori Andrews, a professor at Chicago-Kent College of Law.

This is not just a theoretical problem, as 2002 developments in Paris revealed. That year, the Parisian Institut Curie and Institut Gustave-Roussy joined to protest Myriad's European patents on BRCA genes. The European Patent Office had granted Myriad patents in 2001, but it provides a nine-month period to challenge patents, and scientists from laboratories and genetics societies in Belgium, the Netherlands, Germany, Denmark, and the United Kingdom swiftly joined the Parisian scientists' attempt to condemn Myriad's cancer patents.

This biotech cold war began when, after winning the European patent, Myriad demanded that European labs that had been performing their own tests for hereditary breast cancer send all their samples to Myriad's U.S. labs for testing and pay a $2,600 fee for each. Many European scientists and physicians responded by simply ignoring the patent.

But more than money and inconvenience were shown to be at stake when French scientists detected a deadly flaw in Myriad's tests. Dominique Stoppa-Lyonnet, MD, PhD, of the Institut Curie wrote a June 2002 report in the *Journal of Medical Genetics*, describing a new BRCA1 mutation her researchers found in a patient in Los Angeles's Cedars-Sinai Medical Center. The patient had been diagnosed with hereditary breast and ovarian cancers even after Myriad's test failed to find any BRCA mutations, and Stoppa-Lyonnet's team charged that Myriad's test cannot discern some large DNA aberrations such as large deletions or reshufflings of the code. Using a technique they call "DNA combing," she and her team found a sizable deletion of three coding regions that they think account for up to one in three BRCA1 mutations. In short, she claims that Myriad's test misses some 10 percent to 20 percent of BRCA1 mutations and insists that the combing technique, which was developed by Pasteur scientists, should be available as an alternative to Myriad's test.

As Stoppa-Lyonnet wrote in the *Journal of the National Cancer Institute*, "It's clear that the Myriad test is not the gold standard. It only detects small mutations and deletions, but not large rearrangements of the gene. There are many different techniques that can be used."

Håkan Olsson, MD, professor of oncology at the University Hospital in Lund, Sweden, went further: "In the long run, the patent is dangerous."[12]

In the end, the European Patent Office invalidated all but two of Myriad's patents and whittled their scope dramatically, to cover only part of the gene sequence. The EPO also narrowed Myriad's BRCA1 screening-test rights to a specific test for Ashkenazi Jewish women,[13] clearing the way for Europeans, unlike Americans, to avail themselves of the full scope of breast cancer tests.

David Bests Goliath

Back in the United States, Genae Girard was convinced that the restrictions imposed by Myriad's patent were hazardous to her health. She resorted to wide-angle legal buckshot, suing not only Myriad and the United States Patent and Trademark Office, but also other companies that hold patents on human genes. The American Civil Liberties Union rallied to her side, organizing a lawsuit joined by other civil libertarians, other cancer patients, medical activists, a body representing 100,000 pathologists, and a varied collection of genetic researchers. All call for an end to gene patents.

This extensive coalition of patients, their advocates, and scientists is a heartening rara avis that has already resulted in Judge Sweet's ruling against gene patents. The ruling could revolutionize U.S. medical care and research,[14] although it would likely apply only to gene patents, not cell lines tissues or medically important animals and devices.

Should any company be able to patent a gene? A key point in the federal ruling turns on the very nature of the gene. Judge Sweet ruled that, rather than genuine inventions manufactured by man, genes are products of nature, which cannot be patented. The laws governing the many types of patents are stultifyingly complex, but the basic requirements for patents remain those laid out earlier in this book: To be patentable, an entity must be novel, non-obvious, and manufactured. The patented item must also have *utility* or usefulness, and proving this tends to entail a description of how the entity will be used. The discovery of the genes was certainly novel, and the scientific work required to identify them was anything but obvious, at least to laypersons. Many scientists, however, have disparaged the discovery process as routine, easily mastered by the scientists whose skill the USPTO holds as a standard for determining whether the process is obvious, requiring little real imagination or skill.

But is a gene really manufactured? No, wrote Judge Sweet, this "hand of man" argument is, at best, a stretch. Judge Sweet wisely swept aside the distinction that patent holders make between the "isolated gene"—appropriated and "improved" after having been "discovered" in much the way that European explorers discovered continents that were filled with people—and the pristine genes that naturally populate our bodies. As Pasteur isolated and purified yeast and Takamine isolated adrenaline, the gene patents claim they have made of the genetic code a "a new thing" by manipulating them. From the gene in its natural state, Judge Sweet maintained that the only way to satisfy this "manufactured" requirement was through the "lawyer's trick" of positing that the gene gained its therapeutic value only through the technological manipulation involved in identifying—discovering—it, thus making the gene useful to research.

Shifting Sands

If the edifice of gene patenting is founded on such sandy soil, why did so many experts express shock to learn that in Judge Sweet's estimation, a legal sleight of hand rather than a legitimate act of creation enables profitable gene patents? Their consternation seems misplaced. *Newsweek* called it a "surprise ruling," one patent lawyer's blog likened the ruling to a *Twilight Zone* episode, and Duke University professor Robert Cook-Deegan called it a "bombshell." But the experts had been aware of the possibility that Myriad's BRCA genes could be invalidated in U.S. courts because they had already been questioned in Canada. And as we've seen, they were first invalidated, then subsequently narrowed to exclude genetic testing, by the European Patent Office in 2004.

In fact, just a month before Sweet's ruling, a U.S. appeals court revoked an even more pivotal patent on Ariad Pharmaceuticals' gene NF-κB, which dictates the method by which our bodies replicate DNA to make genes.[15] The broad scope of NF-κB's medical applications affects the production of many drugs. The patent was controversial because of its breadth: it controlled a ubiquitous biological pathway that governs many disease processes, such as cancers, inflammation, and osteoporosis.[16]

Gene-patent apologists' false sense of security may have been based not upon the logic of patentability claims, but rather on a nearly unbroken history of researcher victories and patient defeats in U.S. courts. As noted earlier, jurists in key patent disputes have tended to rule in favor of research scientists over patients, even when the claims to patented wonders were reaped from those patients' very bodies.

Such conflicts between research and patient interests were inevitable, and today they are legion, for the genes in question reside within our bodies, but their control increasingly rests with the biotech and pharmaceutical companies that dictate their uses through patents. These companies charge us for access, in effect becoming our biological landlords. Those who favor researchers' and corporations' rights habitually cast such conflicts as medical research *versus* aggrieved patients, but Girard's case undercut this view because geneticists, researchers, pathologists, and other scientists joined her in castigating gene patents.

Girard calls the U.S. patent invalidation a "turning point for all women in the country who may have breast cancer that runs in their family." But it is more. Judge Sweet's ruling resounds far beyond BRCA because, as we've seen, the USPTO has granted 40,000 to 50,000 gene patents[17] that cover only one-fifth of the human genome.[18] Some control the most basic processes of human life, while the functions of others are unknown: in fact, a single for-profit corporation, Genetic Technologies Limited, owns 95 percent of all noncoding DNA, or as it was once widely called, "junk DNA." This DNA is not known to code for proteins, and its function is still unknown, but despite its misnomer it *is* functional. Many patents are issued for genes whose functions are incompletely or murkily understood, even though the patent application requires an inventor to explain the likely uses of the patented entity. To demonstrate the patent's utility, applicants resort to broad aims and conjecture that, once patented, the DNA sequence will hasten the development of needed medications. Such widespread patenting of medically questionable entities nurtures a "patent thicket" that prevents others from investigating the nature and value of these genes, which in turn has exerted a chilling effect on health-care research.

Why, then, do we tolerate such profligate gene patenting? Gene-patent expansion has been sold to the American public just as other medically important patents have been—as a strategy to stimulate creativity, reward ingenuity, and spark the development of important new therapies, especially the tailoring of medications to genetic features or vulnerabilities. Actually, the expansion of gene patents has achieved the exact opposite: today, it stifles creativity by quelling competition and thus retarding the development of important new medicines. All too often the patent system fails dismally to reward creativity. Instead, it discourages cooperation and encourages a premature rush to patent, sacrificing the interests of many patients and researchers who worked to identify medically meaningful genes. Gene patents can also directly hinder access to necessary medical care and tests.

After Myriad was awarded a Canadian patent on the BRCA1 and BRCA2 genes in April 2001, the company deluged advocacy and public-health organizations that offered tests free to the public with cease-and-desist letters. Most of these groups operated on small budgets and paid practitioners little or sometimes nothing to conduct the examinations. When Myriad's lawyers warned that the company would now be protecting its patent and insisted on performing *all* BRCA screening, the advocacy groups could not pay Myriad's fee and so could no longer afford to offer the test cheaply or for free.

British Columbia's Health Professions Council (HPC), for example, was screening at a price of C$1,200 per patient, but Myriad immediately began charging C$3,850 for its gene-sequencing test, which it character-ized as the "gold standard." The costs now fell on the patients.

Two years later, the Canadians, like the Europeans before them, had had enough. In February 2003, British Columbia's Ministry of Health Services instructed its Cancer Agency and the HPC to sim-ply ignore Myriad's patents and resume the old screening procedures. Ontario swiftly followed suit when it resumed performing its own BRCA screenings at C$1,100 per test. The provinces told Myriad that the issue would be resolved in court. Translation: sue us. The U.S. ambassador to Canada, acting on Myriad's complaints, threatened trade sanctions if non-Myriad testing was not stopped, but Canada was not cowed.

Despite such pockets of defiance, Myriad now dominated breast cancer screening and research throughout the industrialized Western world through its patents in the United States, Canada, Europe, Aus-tralia, and New Zealand. Academic researchers who wanted to develop other breast cancer screening methods could not do so without pay-ing Myriad's licensing fees, although its patents on the genes had been obtained because of the generosity of collaborative researchers like geneticist Mary-Claire King who, while working at UC Berkeley, had first located the BRCA1 gene on chromosome 17 using tissue samples that were generously donated by people with breast cancer and their families. Myriad refused to grant others access to the samples, arguing that to do so imperiled its intellectual-property rights.[19]

Myriad compounded its aggression with unconscionable manipula-tion of direct-to-consumer (DTC) advertising for its gene tests. The ads exhorted women to take the test to see whether they suffered a genetic anomaly that could raise their breast cancer risk. It played on women's fears of breast cancer and failed to present the risk information, inac-curately leaving the impression that all women would benefit from the screening when actually the anomaly is rare, accounting for 5 percent of all breast cancer cases in the United States. This includes the approxi-mately 1 percent of Ashkenazi women who carry the BRCA1 anomaly; and, as mentioned above, it is found most often among young African American women (16.7 percent).[20]

Such advertising behavior offers a clear example of why every West-ern nation except for the United States and New Zealand bans pharma-ceutical companies from taking their sales pitches directly to consumers.

Without the intercession of independent physicians who advocate for the patients, not the patent holders, ethical lapses and frank deceptions abound.

Myriad's patent enforcement is so overbearing that even if a scientist uses a different detection technology from Myriad's direct sequencing method for BRCA1 and BRCA2 screening, Myriad claims that she is guilty of patent infringement. Myriad also compels laboratories as well as hospitals and clinics to send their DNA samples to its Salt Lake City laboratories for analysis.

By forcing samples to be sent to them and by jealously guarding its own samples and data from others, Myriad has positioned itself to become virtually the exclusive global custodian of breast and ovarian cancer samples, and it has compiled the largest breast cancer and ovarian cancer database in the world. Myriad's patent-suit threats have had a chilling effect on other researchers and thus have minimized their tissue collection. "This monopoly on patent exploitation will lead to a loss of expertise and information among physicians and research scientists in Europe, as they will no longer be allowed to improve diagnostic technologies and methods," summarized the Institut Curie in an official statement.[21]

The Tragic Gifts

Some reason that because genetic researchers and patients share the same goals—tests, treatments, and care—there is no basis for conflict, and nothing to be lost by patients who lend their support, tissues, and DNA to hospitals and corporations. Dan and Debbie Greenberg might disagree.

On June 12, 1981, their fourth wedding anniversary, the Greenbergs held their perfect newborn for the first time. Jonathan was everything you could wish for in a baby: beautiful, chubby, and alert, with shining brown eyes and a wealth of black hair. When they brought him home from Ingalls Hospital, Debbie, who worked with disabled children, was concerned because Jonathan wouldn't nurse. But the nurses she anxiously consulted chalked up his lassitude to fatigue after the exertion of birth.

Debbie knew too much to be reassured. She had also noticed that

Jonathan lacked a normal startle reflex: instead of simply jerking his head, he would cry incessantly in response to a sudden noise. In fact, Jonathan stopped crying only when she or Dan held him. Months after his birth, he still couldn't hold up his head. Although he smiled and giggled easily when tickled or hugged, the missed developmental milestones began piling up alarmingly. Half a year after his birth, Jonathan could not hold up his head, make eye contact, sit up, or grasp objects. He had never rolled over and did not crawl.

Debbie was reassured by the knowledge that long before Jonathan's birth, she had taken a test for Tay-Sachs disease, so she knew she did not carry the recessive gene for this genetic scourge of the Ashkenazi, who constitute 90 percent of U.S. Jewry. But Jonathan's head grew large in proportion to his body, and one day Debbie saw with horror that his hands had contracted into clawlike fists. She flew with him to the pediatrician, who dismissed her as a "neurotic first-time mother."

But she knew *something* was wrong, so she sought out another doctor, who took one alarmed look at Jonathan and sent them to Children's Memorial Hospital. There, pediatric neurologist Dr. Cynthia Stack performed the series of tests with practiced motions until, crestfallen, she paused a moment to whisper in his ear: "I think I know what's the matter with you. But I hope I'm wrong." The tests confirmed her worst fears. Gravely, she summoned the Greenbergs to hear the bad news: Jonathan had Canavan's disease.

Like Tay-Sachs, Canavan's is a mercifully rare genetic disorder that can strike anyone, but it has been studied most extensively in Ashkenazi Jews, one in forty of whom is an asymptomatic carrier. Shocked into silence, Dan and Debbie listened to Dr. Stack foretell their baby's fate, as Debbie realized for the first time that "I had been hoping that it was 'just' cerebral palsy."

Canavan's is much worse, a genetic killer that stalks children who seem happy and healthy at birth but quickly fall behind. These children never learn to crawl or sit and suffer racking seizures that can end in blindness and paralysis. The white matter of their brains begins to seep away and ossify like a drying sponge until the tissue becomes a matrix of spaces that fill with fluid. The resulting neurological devastation includes mental retardation and cerebral palsy. Although most affected children die before they are ten, some survive into early adulthood. And for their bereft parents, there was no warning, no test to alert them that their children would be at risk.

"Quick as thought" is more than a cliché: it is a biochemical reality. Our nervous system rests on an engineering marvel that allows the rapid conduction of electricity along our invisibly tiny nerve cells, up to 120 meters a second. Like insulation on an electrical cord, sturdy myelin sheaths—made of a specific type of fatty proteins—coat and protect each nerve fiber, but with strategic gaps at regular intervals that are called nodes of Ranvier. Instead of traversing the entire length of the nerve cell, electricity needs only to jump from node to node, which hastens the conduction of the electrical impulse and correspondingly speeds our physiological reactions, including the ones that govern thought. In general, the more extensive the myelin coat, the faster the nervous conduction. This accelerated conduct of electricity allows us to think on our feet, to respond wittily, to sprint, to jerk our heads in response to a loud noise, to immediately feel the prick of a needle on our fingertip. All these everyday wonders depend upon myelin, and Jonathan's myelin was already deteriorating, and eventually doomed to vanish.

Canavan's gene causes the wrong myelin protein to be produced, one that makes an aberrant, flimsy sheath. The resulting myelin is fragile and easily degraded. As it turns spongy, nervous-system signal transmission slows, becoming weakly intermittent and finally disappearing completely. This can destroy the nervous system and brain in a matter of three years, and it explains why Jonathan could not hold up his head, make eye contact, turn over, or sit up. He would never say "Mama" or take his first steps.

Like sickle-cell disease, Canavan's is an autosomal recessive disease, meaning that both parents must be carriers and that each of the Greenbergs' children faced a one-in-four statistical probability of developing it. But unlike sickle-cell and Tay-Sachs disease, no screening test or antenatal test existed for Canavan's. If the Greenbergs wanted a large family, they would be at the mercy of a cruel game of genetic roulette.

For his part, Dan intellectualized his grief, seeking out information about Canavan's and discovering the National Tay-Sachs and Allied Diseases Association. He found nothing good. As they gradually came to accept that there was no help for Jonathan, the Greenbergs focused on trying to save others from their heartbreak. They supported the Chicago chapter of Tay-Sachs, which offered well-publicized and inexpensive screenings within the Jewish community. These allowed carriers to know their status and manage their risks by avoiding marriage or childbearing with other carriers. Such screenings have reduced the national incidence of Tay-Sachs by 90 percent. A University of Illinois geneticist, Dr. Reuben Matalon, also helped by performing Tay-Sachs tests for $10 each instead of the usual $50.

Dan and Debbie still yearned for a large family, and they knew that the odds of having a healthy child were 75 percent in their favor, so they conceived again. But when Amy was born in 1982, she, too, had Canavan's.

After their years of struggle and fruitless searches for help, the couple's spiritual and physical energies were depleted by the crushing burden of caring full-time for two terminally ill children who now were immobile. They placed Jonathan and Amy in the Misericordia residential-care facility, where they visited them often, and they adopted two baby girls, Stephanie and Michelle.

It became clear to Dan and Debbie that the same tests that had helped tame the risk of Tay-Sachs were needed for Canavan's carriers, so in 1987 Dan urged Dr. Matalon to develop that genetic test, and he eagerly agreed. The first step was identifying the gene, for which Matalon would need tissues. So Dan allowed Matalon to take blood, skin, urine, and other tissue samples from Amy and Jonathan. He then brought Matalon together with other parents of Canavan's children who also allowed him to take samples. They set up an independent Canavan's foundation, which provided Matalon with blood, tissue, and other biological samples, as well as financial support. Parents of affected children spent time detailing their family's medical history. The Greenbergs knew this would not help their own ailing children who were imprisoned in their bodies, but helping others gave them a measure of relief.

Within two years, Matalon summoned the Canavan families to his lab to announce that the enzyme aspartocyclase was missing from the brains of Canavan's children, which allowed levels of N-acetylaspartic acid to mount, damaging the brain's white matter. Matalon then asked them for skin samples so he could design a carrier test. His N-acetylaspartic acid antenatal test already enabled him to determine whether a fetus in utero had Canavan's.

Armed with this knowledge, the Greenbergs conceived again, and the test confirmed that the fetus was unaffected. In 1989 Debbie gave birth to Joshua. She watched him keenly for signs of difficulty in feeding, unusual irritability, and weakness, but Joshua was a robust child who nursed vigorously, sat up, rolled over, and smiled easily—a happy, healthy baby, without Canavan's.

For a while the test freed the Canavan's carriers from anxiety, but then a child was born who, despite a negative antenatal test, suffered from Canavan's. Then another. The test was not accurate enough. Matalon determined to identify the gene that would enable an accurate predictive test.

Matalon's successes had eased his transition to director of research at Miami Children's Hospital, replete with gleaming new laboratories and financial support. He sped his quest to identify the Canavan's gene, and the Greenbergs were instrumental in this, connecting Matalon with even more families of Canavan's children and with the Canavan's Foundation, which secured nearly five thousand more samples for Matalon. They also introduced Matalon to Dor Yeshorim,[22] Hebrew for "the upright generation," which was devoted to the elimination of genetic diseases that affected Jews, and to the United Leukodystrophy Foundation. Dedicated parents such as Frieda Eisen journeyed from Brooklyn to Miami for annual MRIs and tests in support of Matalon's research, and one Melbourne, Australia, family, the Szwarcs, who had lost two sons to Canavan's, flew to the United States with preserved autopsy samples. When Jonathan died at eleven, Dan and Debbie made the wrenching decision to donate part of his brain and organs to Matalon. Amy died just short of her sixteenth birthday.

The families' generosity and altruism and Matalon's dedication were rewarded in 1993, when he identified the gene for Canavan's. Children's Hospital flew the families in to acknowledge their pivotal role and to praise their sacrifices.

Not wishing to impede research by imposing licensing fees, the Canavan's parents decided not to patent the genes, just as the March of Dimes and Jonas Salk before them had declined to patent the polio vaccine, ensuring that it would remain cheap and freely available to all and resulting in the eradication of polio from the United States and most other industrialized countries. The Canavan's Foundation offered free testing at New York's Mt. Sinai Hospital, and Dor Yeshorim tested more than thirteen thousand people a year. In 1998, the test's accuracy and usefulness were validated when the American College of Obstetricians and Gynecologists (ACOG) pronounced the test the "standard of care," which meant that doctors were obligated to recommend it for at-risk couples. Now the Greenbergs and other affected families could imagine a world in which, thanks to their sacrifices, Canavan's, like Tay-Sachs, could become largely a thing of the past. This was a boon for everyone: although Canavan's risks are highest and have been studied most often in Ashkenazi Jews, the disease strikes people of all ethnic groups.

But the families' satisfaction was short-lived. Lawyers contacted Dor Yeshorim with the abrupt announcement that Baylor University would no longer perform the tests, and they soon discovered why: without the knowledge of the Canavan's Foundation, Dor Yeshorim, or any of the families that had contributed tissues, time, and money, Miami Children's Hospital and Dr. Matalon had patented the gene—a full year earlier.

Moreover, Children's Hospital had withheld the announcement of the patent for a year and then had their lawyers enforce it at a strategic juncture, just after the ACOG announcement, which meant that legal liability could dog those who did not offer it to vulnerable couples. This announcement greatly increased the test's use and the potential profits from its patent.

The hospital began charging $25 for every prenatal or carrier test, without exception, and today Miami Children's Hospital continues to restrict and charge fees for the use of the Canavan's gene in medical research.

"We were shocked," recalls Dan. "This is a desecration of all the good that came out of Jonathan and Amy's lives. We gave our DNA and that of our children to help develop testing and prenatal diagnosis. We sent our blood and skin samples to a doctor at Miami Children's Hospital." Dr. Judith Tsipis, a Brandeis University biologist whose son Andreas died of Canavan's disease in 1998 at age twenty-two, told *Salon*: "Is it right that they use our genes—given to help others—in a way that restricts access and increases cost to testing?"[23]

The outraged Canavan's parents sued, protesting that the hospital's duplicity had denied them informed consent. They also claimed a property interest in the tissues and sought control of the gene whose discovery was predicated on their families' support and tissues.

Their lawyer, Lori Andrews of Chicago-Kent College of Law, also invoked the Moore case that had found Dr. Golde guilty of a breach of fiduciary duty when he failed to inform John Moore of the potential commercial value of his tissues. Under Florida law, DNA analysis results belong to the persons tested. Andrews charged that the parents gave permission for identification of the Canavan's gene, but they never agreed to gene patenting. Andrews alleged a breach of informed consent, unjust enrichment, conversion, misappropriation of trade secrets, and fraudulent concealment.

But in a drearily familiar scenario when patients confront corporations and medical institutions over patent rights and body-part ownership, the Florida court ruled against them and for the University of Miami and Dr. Matalon, citing the John Moore case and voicing fears that to award rights to the families would have a chilling effect on medical research.[24] Radhika Rao theorizes that "perhaps this is attributable to a labor theory of property that values the intellectual work that researchers perform more than the 'raw materials' patients provide,"[25] but she goes on to observe that it was the families and children who contributed the only uniquely valuable materials to the research.

Matalon denied that he desired patent rights to the Canavan's gene, telling the New York Times, "I am a research person. If they make money on me, I don't care. My understanding from the hospital was we needed to file the patent just so I could work with the gene myself. I had nothing to do with their licensing decision and I got no penny from any patent."[26] But a former colleague, Rajinder Kaul, says it was Matalon's idea to patent the gene.

In 1993, Matalon had recognized the Greenbergs and other Canavan's families when he wrote, "This is a disease where partnership between researchers and the families of affected children is critical for advancing knowledge." But by 2000, Matalon denied that the Greenbergs played a role in the gene's discovery.

Because access to the tests is most important to them, the families eventually made a settlement with Children's Hospital whose terms are confidential. Today Children's Hospital has licensed about fifteen labs in the United States and Israel to perform the Canavan's tests at $200 to

$400 each. The license is too costly and restrictive for most laboratories because it caps the number of tests that can be performed, charges a royalty in addition to the test fee, and does not allow other researchers to study the genes.[27] As a result, only a few laboratories continue to test parents and fetuses.[28] Dor Yeshorim has had to curtail most testing. And Canavan's sufferers are not alone: a 2000 survey revealed that nine of every ten U.S. clinical genetics laboratories have withheld some sort of testing because of oppressive patent terms.[29]

Test of Life

Genetic tests can liberate at-risk couples from fear by allowing them to avoid the birth of affected children. They can also alert people to their potential vulnerability, allowing them to change their lifestyles to minimize the chance that their tendency to diabetes or heart disease becomes a reality. Genetic tests offer these benefits to a person's children as well as to themselves. But tests have another advantage for companies, which can devise and market a test far more easily and cheaply than they can perfect a cure. Selling genetic tests has become a lucrative endeavor, but one that may also encourage the abandonment of needed medications predicated on lengthy and often costly R&D.

Tests for genetic conditions have become common. But as pharmaceutical firms seek to maximize profits by having such tests adopted as widely as possible, companies distort their messages to alarm consumers into embracing the tests whether they are truly at risk and likely to benefit or not. At least twenty human pathogens are patented by private corporations, including *Haemophilus influenzae* and the hepatitis C virus (HCV). Aside from the question of whether it is ethically and morally acceptable to patent body parts, animals, and genes, enforcement of the patents underlying the tests themselves has exerted a chilling effect on disease research because some tests simply do not work as advertised.[30] Others, such as those in the prevalent direct-to-consumer advertisements for BRCA gene mutations that are rare in the general public, have been oversold.

Chapter 3 related how Chiron Corporation's 1994 decision to enforce its patent on the HCV test drove the price of the test out of reach of England's National Health Service, imperiling the lives of the unwittingly infected. As we've also seen, in 1998 the USPTO granted patents on both forms of the hereditary hemochromatosis (HFE) gene, and Smith-Kline Beecham Clinical Laboratories obtained an exclusive license that forced other researchers to abandon work on HFE because of prohibitive costs and the specter of being sued for patent infringement. In 1999, Athena Diagnostics notified laboratories of its new patent on a genetic test for Alzheimer's disease and accompanied its notice with a demand for licensing fees that doubled the charges to laboratories, pricing the test out of reach of government researchers.[31] No magic bullets exist for hepatitis C, hemochromatosis, Alzheimer's, breast cancer, or prostate cancer, nor is there even effective treatment for or prevention of some of these disorders. The list of vigorously defended patents unaccompanied by cures continues ad nauseam.

Some such tests carry serious risks as well, however. Makers tout their accuracy as identical to those given in a physician's office. But even if this is true, the expert clinical judgment is absent. The test is less meaningful when conducted by a layperson, who may make errors in administering it, and worse, who may not be able to properly interpret its meaning. Moreover, tests for serious conditions such as HCV deliver shocking news over the telephone, which is not only a psychological blow but may also breed despair in someone who has no clinical expert available to explain what the results do and do not mean, including what treatments may be available.

Although genetic tests are frequently marketed as allowing customers to save money in lieu of an expensive, time-consuming visit to the doctor's office, many tests for serious ailments must be confirmed by a doctor, and so they end up costing the customer more rather than less. The profits from these patented tests encourage the development of easier, cheaper genetic tests that are used to justify treatments. This is not always a good thing. As we'll see, sickle-cell anemia and prostate cancer tests are sensitive but not specific, meaning that they give positive results for the disorder in many people who are not actually ill. At least some of these people subsequently undergo treatment that they do not need, and that treatment can be damaging or expose them to risks.

Other flawed or limited tests can do harm by a *lack* of sensitivity that allows them to miss the disease altogether, as in the case of Myriad's touted BRCA1 and BRCA2 gene tests.[32] There have even been occasions when genetic tests were widely misinterpreted, stigmatizing thousands of people needlessly. This is what precisely happened in the case of Sickledex.

The Blind Judge

In 1979, Stephen Pullens was forced to resign from the U.S. Air Force Academy when he reacted positively to the Sickledex test for sickle-cell disease, which had been made mandatory for all potential cadets. Although sickle-cell disease has long been mischaracterized as a "black disease," it actually affects people of most ethnic groups. Sickling of blood ensues when the S variant of hemoglobin causes the red blood cells, normally shaped like concave discs, to deform so that they become "sickle-shaped" and sticky. This typically happens under conditions of biological stress, such as the low-oxygen conditions at high altitudes. The sticky, deformed red blood cells clump together and block blood vessels, which causes very severe pain and a compromised blood flow that can lead to lesions, stroke, heart attack, limb paralysis, and other debilitating conditions.

Pullens's expulsion was rationalized on the basis that a positive Sickledex test meant he had sickle-cell disease, so that the requisite exposure to high altitudes could trigger a potentially fatal sickling crisis, making him hazardous and undependable in the air. Clearly, the air force argued, Pullens was incapable of surviving rigorous high-altitude training,[33] and this is why it barred anyone who tested positive from admission.

But this speculation warred with the facts. Pullens is a mountain climber and former state champion hurdler who particularly excelled at high-altitude races. As a four-sport athlete he had never experienced sickling crises, which was unsurprising because, despite the positive Sickledex test, he did not have sickle-cell disease. It is worth noting that by barring anyone with a positive Sickledex test, the air force had partially restored its onetime nakedly race-based bar to black Americans, which had been struck down by a lawsuit. The air force was unswayed by his arguments, so Pullens sued and won. The air force then announced that it would no longer predicate admission on the basis of the flawed Sickledex.

Genetic experts had known since the 1970s that Sickledex was so profoundly flawed that it could not discern who had sickle-cell disease.[34] But by the time of Pullens's challenge, half a million Americans had been tested for sickle-cell disease at about $40 each: the test was too profitable to put aside.

In the 1970s and '80s, Sickledex promoted confusion among scientists as well as laypersons. Well sickle-cell carriers, or heterozygotes, who had one normal and one variant copy of the gene, were confused with sick homozygotes, who had both variant genes for sickle-cell disease and therefore had the disease.

The National Institutes of Health, hospitals, and private organizations disseminated brochures and booklets equating carrier status with the disease, and millions of well people were informed that they were ill and genetically tainted. Some were told that they had a life expectancy of only forty years. In fact, the very first sentence of the preamble of the National Sickle Cell Anemia Control Act, enacted in 1972 to foster sickle-cell research, screening, counseling, and education, is untrue: "Two million Americans suffer from sickle-cell disease." Actually, 1.9 million people were healthy carriers,[35] and fewer than 100,000 suffered from the disease. The erroneous claim, coupled with the constantly reinforced misperception of sickle-cell disease as a "black" disorder, left Americans with the mistaken impression that a good portion—one in twelve—of African Americans suffered from sickle-cell disease. This reflects the number of African American sickle-cell *carriers*.[36]

This confusion was not accidental: it was promulgated by Ortho Pharmaceutical Company of McNeil Laboratories, the company that sold Sickledex, the sickle-cell screening test that was championed by health agencies and African American health activists alike. Seventeen states enacted laws mandating sickle-cell screening even though Sickledex could not differentiate between the sickle-cell carrier status and sickle-cell disease. It detected the presence of hemoglobin S, but at too low a threshold (10 percent) to discriminate between people with one or two genes for sickle-cell disease. By 1975, 500,000 blacks had been screened for sickle-cell anemia. In order to market the test, employers, military hospitals, and the government extended to well carriers[37] the same advice and restrictions that applied to people genuinely ill with sickle-cell anemia. Otherwise, these agencies would have had to admit that the test was of extremely limited therapeutic value because it could not tell a sick person from a well one, unlike screening tests for Tay-Sachs and Canavan's, which are accurately described with full disclosure and informed consent.[38]

The misrepresentation and flawed logic continues: as recently as 2007, the catalog for the Department of Defense of Aeromedical Evacuation Technician Schools of Aerospace Medicine indicated that a Sickle-dex test is mandatory for prospective students.[39]

Taking the Reins

Fortunately, genetic exploitation via patent is no longer the whole story, because prescient patients are now beginning to play the patent game—and play it well. "In 1994, we didn't know a gene from a hub-cap,"[40] recalls Sharon Terry, then a college chaplain, and her husband, Patrick, an engineer. But that year, their children, Elizabeth and Ian, were diagnosed with the rare genetic disease pseudoxanthoma elasti-cum (PXE), and the Terrys needed no other incentive to learn. Learn they did, in a painful but ultimately transformative process that left them two of the few people to traverse the boundary from patient to researcher—and beyond.

It was a brutal education. The Terrys spent their evenings studying PXE in medical textbooks and poring over (and sometimes crying over) the latest revelations in medical journals as they immersed themselves in the genetics and the mechanism of the disease that threatened to kill their children before age thirty.

PXE, also known as Grönblad-Strandberg syndrome, is thought to affect one in every 100,000 children, dooming them to vision problems, premature sagging and wrinkling of the skin, heart disease, and gastro-intestinal disorders. The Terrys learned that research into this orphan disease was uncoordinated and sporadic. They also learned that when a researcher asked them for blood or tissue samples, they couldn't simply refer him or her to a doctor who'd already taken them: such samples were guarded jealously, and competing researchers refused to share. They learned that this lack of coordination and cooperation meant that it was up to them and people like them to save their children.

The Terrys courted, cajoled, and pushed researchers, suggesting new approaches even as they organized a large group of PXE parents to produce the necessary blood and tissue samples. But the researcher with whom they worked most closely refused to share "his" information with other parties.

"The researcher in whose lab we banked our samples actively tried to thwart access to the bank by other researchers," recalled Sharon. "We were appalled, maybe naïvely so, that researchers would put their needs for publications, funding, promotions, and tenure ahead of the needs of people living with disease."[41]

The Terrys knew that their best chance for success was to work with many researchers, so they set up the PXE International foundation to link not only parents of PXE children but also researchers dedicated to PXE. The Terrys pooled the contributions of PXE members and created their own centralized tissue bank to which they gave a number of researchers access—for a steep price.

The Terrys had learned enough to grasp the value of these tissues as a commodity with unique leverage for researchers, and they recognized patent rights as a rich source of income and power in making medical-research decisions. Knowing that the licensing terms for the PXE gene patent could make or break medication development and the generation of tests, "we saw early on," Sharon said, "that we needed to keep control."[42]

They did retain control in a unique fashion, by changing the nature of payment for access to the coveted tissue banks. Any researchers who wanted access to PXE tissues had to agree to name the Terrys or the patient group as a coapplicant on any patents they filed. When a Hawaiian researcher discovered the mutated gene that causes PXE, he and Sharon Terry were named as coinventors of the PXE gene. The patent was awarded, a biotechnological landmark as the first time a layperson had secured a gene patent. To get justice, the Terrys had bypassed the courts. "We consider ourselves stewards of the gene," Sharon explained in 2003, "and know that the real issues will be played out in its licensing."

The income from the patented gene now funds PXE International, a thirty-three-laboratory research consortium with fifty-two offices worldwide, which investigate new therapies and diagnostic tests. But this medical-research empire is no faceless corporation: the nonprofit also solicits funds while providing information and support for affected children and their families.

The Terrys had perceived how affected people suffered when others patented their genes, commandeered tissue data banks, and placed profit ahead of patient welfare and cures, so they determined to turn this model on its head, taking control of and reversing the monopolistic agenda. They hope for a cure but are secure in the knowledge that the affected maintain some control over whether and how this happens.

It is worth noting, however, that in order to do so, they had to buy into the "hand of man argument," and to treat the gene like property. Sharon Terry, for example, refers to herself as the inventor of the PXE gene, as do other gene patent holders. But she dramatically breaks with convention where it counts, by enshrining a patient-centered agenda of support as well as research. "My work with PXE International has taught me that consumers can be central to the research endeavor," she summarized. "We can be a catalyzing force for translating research into the services we desperately need."

A Reversal of Genetic Fortunes

Not only the ill remain at the mercy of life-related patents. We are all vulnerable to patent monopolies that can place caring for our health out of our reach.

Researchers benefit from increasing genetic knowledge, and so, in large part, does public health. But for individuals, the benefits are sometimes unclear because the price of genetic knowledge can be intolerably high. This is especially true when one is diagnosed with a genetic risk but can take no positive steps to protect one's health with the knowledge. In such cases, the diagnosis causes anxiety and stigmatization and can directly impede health, as in the past when insurers have used it to deny coverage. Today, genetic tests can screen for four hundred conditions, from cystic fibrosis to Down's syndrome to sickle-cell disease and Huntington's chorea. But there are no effective treatments or cures for some conditions, calling the usefulness and advisability of testing for them into question.

Some common misconceptions lead people to believe that gene patents are the concern only of the sick or of those who are vulnerable to genetic disease. We hear and read most about those people who suffer by dint of possessing the genes for Tay-Sachs, breast cancer, sickle-cell disease, or Canavan's. These are diseases linked to a single gene, the presence or absence of which dictates the medical fate of the sufferer. But these diseases are the exception. Most genetic disease is far more subtle, depending upon several genes or upon the interaction of a gene and environment, or upon imperfectly understood interactions between genes, environments, and behavior.

Such issues affect more than the small populations of people at risk for exotic genetic disorders: as early as 1997, then–HHS Secretary Donna Shalala reported that more than 20 percent of Americans reported testing positive for a genetic disorder for which they or their family member had been refused health insurance.

Fortunately, the May 2008 federal Genetic Information Nondiscrimination Act (GINA) bars employers and health insurers from penalizing those with flaws, anomalies, or atypical disease risks when they are revealed by genetic testing. This is a very positive advance, yet its health protections are not universal because GINA does not prohibit life insurance and disability insurance companies from considering genetic data in making coverage decisions. These facts lead some ethicists to worry that genetic testing may yet create an uninsurable biological underclass.

We all have genes, however, and the patents on genes that control processes in the human heart, teeth, tongue, colon, skin, brain, bone, ear, lung, liver, kidney, sperm, blood, and immune system affect us all. So it is unsurprising that the resentment felt by the sick has been joined by trepidation among the well. In 2007, California Democrat Xavier Becerra and Florida Republican Dave Weldon crossed party lines in the House of Representatives to seek the end of genetic patents when they introduced the Genomic Research and Accessibility Act.

Some argue that gene patents are necessary to generate the profits essential to funding the medical cures. But as the cases of breast cancer, hepatitis C, and hemochromatosis illustrate, genes are more commonly used for faster, easier routes to profit, such as marketing tests, selling licenses, and suing those patent infringers who step on the corporation. In countries where genes are not patented, patients get better tests for genetic diseases than in the United States.

Although gene-patent apologists tend to characterize the mounting resistance as "anti-science," the Becerra-Weldon bill was supported by the College of American Pathologists, the American College of Medical Genetics, the American Society of Human Genetics, the Association for

Molecular Pathology, the Academy of Clinical Laboratory Physicians, and other scientists, just as Genae Girard was joined in her suit against Myriad by the College of American Pathologists, the Association for Molecular Pathology, the American College of Medical Genetics, the American Society for Clinical Pathology, and the College of American Pathologists.

The legislative movement of the 1980s that married the university to Big Pharma created a medical-industrial complex that eventually robbed universities of their independence and seized control of medication design, costs, and even the evaluation of medication in medical journals. This complex has exhibited a zeal for patenting an expanding swath of life and its components. But this achievement has not produced the important new cures we were promised but rather these patents have stymied them. The facile generation of patent profits, not the difficult production of cures, has become the new medico-industrial focus. Becerra and Weldon think that the marriage made in the courts is now best dissolved in the very courts that once defended it without exception. Whether or not it is upheld in the appeals process, the federal ruling against Myriad may be just the first blow against profligate gene patenting.

Silicon Valley venture capitalist Bryan Roberts has predicted that the revocation of gene patents, which will dramatically lower their profit potential, could cause universities to reclaim their independence and primacy in discovering genes and diagnostic tests, saying, "The government is going to become the funder for content discovery because it's going to be very hard to justify it outside of academia." Should this happen, the betterment of human health, not profit, may again dictate the use of genes, and we may see the welcome "turning point" that Girard has begun to celebrate.

CHAPTER 6

LIQUID ASSETS, LETHAL RISKS
Patents, Research, and Blood Rights

Make thick my blood,
Stop up th'access and passage to remorse,
That no compunctious visitings of nature
Shake my fell purpose

—MACBETH, V.V.43–46

With near-parodic gothicism, Friday the thirteenth was plagued by gray clouds, frigid rain, sleet and snow in succession—a foul day, even by the low standards of January in Detroit. As night fell, Martha Milete finished dinner and padded into her bedroom.

After a moment, she remembers, "I heard a thump."

It was probably nothing, Milete thought, maybe a dog outside, but she sighed softly, rose to open the bedroom door, and found herself staring at two men brandishing large handguns. Wordlessly, one masked intruder held a gun against her temple as the duo shoved her into her dining room and thrust her onto her knees, snarling at her to keep her hands behind their head. As one thug batted drawers open and pawed through sideboards and chests, the other barked, "Give me all the money, all you've got."

"But I had no money, and I told them so. 'I have no money. There's nothing in the house.'"

"Yes, you do," the first invader said slowly and distinctly, his gun steadily trained on her.

"I looked in his eyes: they were dead, and I knew. I knew. I begged him, 'Don't! Please don't! Don't shoot me.' I was still begging him when I was blown backward by the force of the gun's blast. I couldn't breathe and felt a searing pain in my eye. They ran though the front door, and I was alone. I couldn't see much, but I was able to call my son and say, 'I've been shot' before everything went black."

Milete had just become a victim of urban violence, one of 100,000 Americans shot in 2006: a statistic.

"My son called 911: he saved my life," she recalls. The ambulance screamed to her home and picked her up, and while she was en route to the hospital in the hurtling vehicle, she woke up. "I was conscious while an EMT gave me blood,[1] but then I passed out, and I don't remember anything after that until I was in the hospital." Minutes after her son's frantic 911 calls, Milete lay in Detroit's Sinai-Grace Hospital, where she underwent six hours of surgery for the gunshot wound to her chest, the force of which had also injured her retina, requiring specialized ocular surgery. For days, she hovered between a vestigial consciousness and oblivion. "I would come to in the hospital and hear a little conversation, and then I'd black out again. For days, two people—a guy and a girl—kept drawing blood from me: at first I thought it was part of the hospital routine. When I became a little more alert I realized that the people who were drawing blood from me several times a day were not part of the team caring for me. They wore insignia that read 'Wayne State University,' and all they wanted was my blood, which they took twice a day. I remember getting real upset one day. I shouted, 'You're not taking one more ounce of blood from me. Stop and leave me alone.'

"Then my daughter Cathy told me why, that it was part of the medical experiment that I was in. She explained that when I was bleeding heavily, lying between life and death, they had given me an experimental liquid instead of blood, the artificial blood. It was called PolyHeme."

Did no one from the hospital or research team tell her that she had been enrolled in the PolyHeme study? "No, my daughter told me," insists Milete. "The medical staff never told me. They never asked me anything. They were still studying me as part of an experiment. There was a coordinator at the hospital, she didn't say much. She kept telling nurses to 'take more blood, take more blood': she was in cahoots with the research people.

"I could not believe it! I told them that I wanted no part of it. It was wrong. Although I survived, it was wrong. How can they make you a guinea pig without asking your permission?"

Between 2003 and 2006, 720 trauma victims at thirty-two U.S. medical centers were "enrolled" in a research study to determine the efficacy of PolyHeme, a patented blood substitute manufactured by Northfield Laboratories. Its maker claimed that PolyHeme could safely and efficiently replace the standard saline solution and blood that keeps heart-attack, car-crash, gunshot, and other accident victims alive. None of these victims was asked for his or her consent, yet this PolyHeme study broke no law. This is because since 1996, federal regulation 21 CFR 50.24 has allowed research with uninformed and unwitting trauma victims to be conducted in emergency settings such as aboard ambulances and medical-evacuation helicopters.

I wished to discuss the case of Milete, Northfield's use of the 50.24 exception, and other events concerning the testing of PolyHeme with the company. Spokesperson Sophie Twaddell promised to call me back, then failed to do so over eight weeks of unreturned phone calls. She finally responded to an email with a refusal to allow me to speak with any Northfield representative or even to respond to emailed questions.

This media silence in response to probing questions was not unusual for Northfield, and its omertà even extended to medical communication around clinical questions. Instead of releasing data in peer-reviewed medical journals, researchers communicated study data through press releases and apparently issued gag orders to researchers. Of the ten Poly-Heme researchers I asked for interviews, only one, Dr. Andrew Bernard of the University of Kentucky at Lexington, agreed to speak with me, which he did openly and frankly. The other medical investigators cited the Health Insurance Portability and Accountability Act of 1996, or HIPAA, regulations that govern disclosures that might violate patient privacy. Or they claimed that releasing requested information would threaten Northfield's proprietary information. Or they simply refused to speak to the inquisitive.

How did our nation come to determine that informed consent, and even consent of any kind, is disposable? Unsatisfied with the occasional waivers of informed consent that were issued on a case-by-case basis, in May 1994 a congressional subcommittee charged the FDA and the Department of Health and Human Services with developing consistent guidelines that would allow institutional review boards, or IRBs, to green-light such research. Two years later, FDA Regulation 21 CFR 50.24, which detailed the procedure for exempting research from informed consent, became law.

Today many researchers defend this ethical sea change by invoking the need to provide quicker, better, evidence-based responses to traumas.

Blurring the Line

But laws on the books already enabled health-care providers to treat trauma victims who were unable to give consent, and some states' Good Samaritan laws go so far as to protect bystanders who treat seriously ill people, even should the injured worsen or die afterward. So let's be clear: The exception is not necessary to *treat* people who are too sick to give consent. It is necessary only to *study* them. The trauma victim requires intervention, but the "50.24" exception law allows *experimental* treatments that, unlike the federally approved treatments that constitute the standard of care, are not known to be safe.

"Research is not treatment," the late Jay Katz, MD, reminded us in 1997, in the wake of the 50.24 approval. Katz, who was Elizabeth K. Dollard professor emeritus of law, medicine, and psychiatry at Yale University, added: "And whenever clear distinctions are not made between the two, the waiver of informed consent becomes problematic because some human subjects are being recruited to serve the ends of others."

Daniel Nelson, PhD, director of the Office of Human Research Ethics at the University of North Carolina at Chapel Hill, offers reassurance on the basis of the presumed rarity of such exceptions. "You know in 1996, when the rules changed, we discussed the exception proposal at length, we agonized over it, over the language and protections. When we finalized the legislation, we braced ourselves for an onslaught of proposals to use the exception, but they never came. It's very rarely used."

However, from the beginning other experts reacted with deep misgivings regarding research with the 50.24 statute. "It's a fateful step," proclaimed Katz, who, just a few months after the statute was adopted, wrote in the *Hastings Center Report* of his "many problems with the way the legislation was drafted."[2] Chief among these were "the vast and vaguely defined discretion granted to IRBs in administering these fateful regulations" and his fear that the affected communities would be duped regarding the true nature of the research into which they were conscripted. "The informed-consent dialogue in research with competent patient-subjects," he wrote, "must be stripped of the 'therapeutic illusion,' which misleads patient-subjects into believing that they are receiving the most advanced and beneficial treatments available, when instead they are being asked to serve the interests of science."

That same year Adil Shamoo, PhD, a University of Maryland professor and the editor of *Accountability in Research*, wrote that there may be a limited role for nonconsensual research but warned, "In ten years we'll have some abuses and people will start rethinking the rules."[3]

Commerce versus Consent

In this chapter I focus on the PolyHeme study as an example of the pitfalls and ethical failings of 50.24 research, but it is far from the only recent episode of investigative servitude for patients unwittingly conscripted into the studies that are often conducted in order to make or to save money for corporations.

Wartime military expediency has often escalated the erosion of human rights in research, and recent events have proved no exception. The military fired the first modern legal salvo against informed consent in the shadow of the impending Gulf War and subsequent Middle Eastern hostilities—and besides the military, at least one private drug maker, then called BioPort, stood to profit.

The Department of Defense (DOD) sought and secured the FDA's permission to dispense with informed consent as it forced 2.4 million soldiers to accept injection with an experimental anthrax vaccine, a patented product of BioPort Laboratories, via its 2000–2005 Anthrax Vaccination Immunization Program (AVIP). So, just four decades after the army had overseen the Nuremberg trials of twenty Nazi physicians on charges of conducting experiments upon the powerless without their consent, the DOD opted to experiment on its own soldiers without their consent.[4]

This odyssey into research without consent proved a medical and legal disaster that eroded many soldiers' trust in medical research. Soldiers suffered miscarriages and were maimed, blinded, and killed, all of which they blame on experimental anthrax vaccines. The *Washington Post* raised questions about the safety and quality of the vaccine and alerted the public that the factory in which it was manufactured had been the subject of repeated FDA evaluations, which found substandard hygienic and production conditions.[5]

By a conservative estimate, 2,500 soldiers refused the experimental vaccines, and as a result many were court-martialed, jailed, or forced to leave the service with less-than-honorable discharges. They literally had no recourse, because the Feres Doctrine stipulates that soldiers on active duty cannot sue the U.S. government for personal injuries experienced in the performance of their duties, and their families cannot sue for wrongful death.[6]

One of these soldiers was Jamekia Barber, a private first class in the Seventh Infantry Division stationed at Fort Carson, Colorado. She and her husband were alarmed by reports of devastating side effects, including miscarriages in soldiers who had taken "the shot."

"We did research and found other people who were disabled because of the shot. Another man, an African American, had 20/20 vision before he took the shots: he lost 80 percent of the vision in one eye and 40 percent in the other eye. After the third shot he feared he would die, but the army says it was a reaction to Tylenol." A lawsuit was not an option for this soldier, because of the Feres Doctrine.[7]

"We were taken to a hospital on post and given printouts saying that there were no adverse reactions and that the various drugs had been approved by the FDA in 1999 or January 2000. But a pregnant girl in my command had taken two anthrax shots, and when she went to the doctor one day he said, 'The baby is gone.' I didn't want to take the shot. I could not agree to that, because having children was important to us." Barber's concerns about the vaccine and pregnancy are supported by the admonitions in the vaccine's product insert, including, "Studies have not been performed to ascertain whether Anthrax Vaccine absorbed has carcinogenic action, or any effect on fertility."

But the army did not need Barber's permission. Barber tried to resolve the issue through legal means and requested a transfer to a unit where she would not need to submit to the injections, but she says her commanding officer blocked it, intending to "make an example" of her, and that he encouraged others to harangue her into compliance.

"I was bothered by the blatant disrespect of the men around me, who were pushing me as they shouted at me to take the shot." She relates being physically assaulted, followed by confinement to a barracks until the day she jumped out of the second-story window because "I learned that I was being detained in a building where a gang rape had taken place on the same floor just two weeks earlier."

In the end, demoralized and suffering from PTSD, Jamekia accepted the proffered "Chapter 10" resignation from the army in lieu of a court-martial because, she says, she was assured that she would not receive anything less than an honorable discharge. But on May 11, 2000, a less-than-honorable "administrative discharge" was exactly what she received. She unsuccessfully appealed the decision in 2003, by which time her husband had also been released with an administrative discharge.

Later that year, Judge Emmet G. Sullivan of the United States District Court in Washington, D.C., ruled to end the forced experimentation. The FDA responded by rapidly elevating the anthrax vaccine from a questionable investigational drug to an approved therapeutic, which allowed the DOD to sidestep the intent of the law and force the medications on soldiers as part of fitness-for-battle measures.[8]

This move returned U.S. soldiers to a state of investigative servitude—"investigative" because the data collection and evaluation of the anthrax vaccine risks, including death, continued. In rapidly approving the vaccine, the FDA had violated not only the intent of Sullivan's ruling but also its own regulations by failing to hold the required public hearings.

In 2004, half a dozen unnamed soldiers filed a class-action suit protesting the vaccinations.[9] Judge Sullivan, again presiding, finally drove a stake through the heart of this *pro bellum* experimentation with a decision that read in part, "The women and men of our armed forces put their lives on the line every day to preserve and safeguard the freedoms that all Americans cherish and enjoy. Absent an informed consent or presidential waiver, the United States cannot demand that members of the armed forces also serve as guinea pigs for experimental drugs."[10]

Between 2004 and 2011, more legal cases were brought by soldiers who had been forced into the vaccination program while the DOD attempted, on several occasions and with limited success, to restore mandatory vaccinations. The FDA issued a string of actions against the vaccine manufacturer, which were triggered by quality issues such as failed potency tests and unapproved changes in manufacturing as well as the soldiers' injury lawsuits.[11] The vaccinations are currently voluntary, but will they remain so? Currently, Emergent BioSolutions, now the parent company of Bioport, has committed to preparing 1.45 million doses of anthrax vaccine by 2011.[12]

After Sullivan's decisions ended forced research on soldiers, Barber renewed her appeal and won an honorable discharge. But the price of her vindication was high: she and her husband divorced. Although she has remarried and she and her ex-husband remain friends, Barber attributes the breakdown of their marriage to the strain of fighting the DOD. "Sometimes I wonder what our lives would have been like without 'the shot.' But I don't allow myself to dwell on it."

There have been many more recent instances of U.S. citizens conscripted into medical research without their knowledge or consent. In a 2001 Maryland appeals court decision, Judge Cathell condemned a Kennedy Krieger Institute study of lead levels in children whose parents were urged by its staff to rent homes that the institute, which serves children with pediatric developmental disabilities, knew to be tainted with lead. The study had been approved by the IRB of Johns Hopkins University, with which the KKI is associated, but its design was unethical because the KKI researchers told families with young children that they would help them find lead-free housing, then referred these families to housing that they knew to be imbued with lead. The motivation was financial: the KKI was trying to determine the cheapest way to reduce the homes' lead, and the bodies of the children were used to titrate the resultant lead exposure. Predictably, some children's lead levels rose, and they were visited by a Pandora's box of ills, including mental retardation. The court found the KKI guilty of using black Baltimore children like "canaries in a coal mine" in a veiled experiment to test lead levels.

In 1995, black and Hispanic children in Los Angeles were given experimental measles vaccines without their parents' knowledge, and that year the Medical University of South Carolina was accused of illegal human experimentation when it enrolled pregnant women in North Carolina, most of them black, in a drug-treatment research study without their knowledge, and then reported them to police as drug abusers. A year later, three New York City research institutions gave six- to eleven-year-old black boys the cardiotoxic drug fenfluramine as part of research into genetically mediated violence.

As early as 1996, a report by the *Cleveland Plain-Dealer* determined that 4,154 FDA inspections of new drugs that have been conducted since 1977 uncovered a dramatically broad abandonment of informed consent. The article noted, "More than half the researchers were cited by FDA inspectors for failing to clearly disclose the experimental nature of their work."[13]

Many of these nonconsensual studies, whether permitted by an FDA waiver as the anthrax vaccine was, licensed by the 50.24 statute as with the PolyHeme trauma trial, or pursued in violation of the law, like the South Carolina study, were conducted for financial gain. Bio-Port, which manufactured the patented anthrax vaccine that the DOD was testing on soldiers against their will, hoped to sell it widely—but could not do so without FDA approval via the heavily populated clinical trials that the waiver of informed consent guaranteed. As we've seen, the KKI's agenda was also financial, as it sought to determine the cheapest effective route to lead abatement. Money changed hands in the form of generous funding for the ethically indefensible South Carolina drug-treatment and New York City fenfluramine studies. And the very first trial approved under the 50.24 exception was that of HemAssist, a blood substitute that was a patented product of Baxter International of Deerfield, Illinois.[14] One hundred uninformed subjects were enrolled in the study, but it was halted when reviewers realized that the mortality rates were unacceptably high.

Given this blighted history, why was PolyHeme research thought urgent enough to merit this draconian testing scheme? One reason is that Northfield laboratories had only PolyHeme, its sole patented product, to sell. Time was running out on its window to complete clinical trials, and dispensing with informed consent was the fastest way to recruit the hundreds of subjects needed to complete them.

Such scenarios raise the question of how extensive a role such corporate financial goals play in promulgating research without consent.

True medical urgency exists with trauma victims because their lives depend upon hemoglobin, the scarlet protein that enables red blood cells to ferry oxygen throughout the body. Whether rent by steering wheels, blown aneurysms, or gunshots, the torn bodies of trauma victims crave blood. When an ambulance arrives at a trauma scene, whether it be a car crash or Martha Milete's gunshot assault, replacing the blood ebbing from the victim's body becomes a priority. Too much lost blood, unreplaced for too long, will starve tissues and organs, including the brain, of oxygen, and culminate in unconsciousness, organ damage, and finally death.

A blood transfusion is impractical within an ambulance, however; because blood can take up to an hour to type and match, it must be refrigerated, and storing the necessary types requires too much space. Fortunately, a cheap, plentiful, and portable blood substitute has been proven effective and safe: salt water. Salt water in a 0.9 percentage solution (called "normal" because it mimics the saline concentration in our bodies) can be quickly and easily infused into trauma victims. Saline expands the volume of blood, staving off shock in plenty of time to get urban victims to the hospital, where replacement blood is available. On city streets, saline is the safe, proven, pre-hospital standard of care.

But not outside cities. Saline has a critical limitation for rural residents and for battlefield casualties who may be hours from blood and hospital care: saline has no hemoglobin, leaving the tissues and brains of battlefield victims oxygen-starved and at risk for a cascade of vascular disasters leading to stroke, heart attack, and death.

Acutely aware of the danger to injured soldiers, the Department of Defense has been experimenting for decades with myriad blood substitutes, auditioning everything from the oxygen-saturated perfluorocarbons that inspired the divers' breathable liquid in the film *The Abyss* to freeze-dried "blood" powder: just add water. This obsession of military physicians continues a long medical crusade: In the seventeenth century, Christopher Wren infused wine into a dog's bloodstream, and a century later, American gynecologist Gaillard Thomas flushed milk into the veins of pallid, blood-starved postsurgical patients. Substitutes derived from human blood were first tested in 1933, when William Ruthrauff Amberson of the University of Tennessee boldly infused hemolyzed red blood, only to be rewarded with a stemmed flow of urine, bradycardia (a dangerously slowed heartbeat), and skyrocketing blood pressure, followed by ugly deaths from kidney failure. A host of other contemporary blood substitutes have proved equally disappointing.

By the 1990s, as wars and rumors of wars fed fears that U.S. battlefield traumas would escalate, the DOD and trauma surgeons elsewhere turned their attention to a species of blood substitutes called hemoglobin-based oxygen carriers (HBOCs). PolyHeme was one. Milk and wine may seem arcane blood-substitute candidates, but PolyHeme is made from no less gothic a substance—expired human blood, donated for transfusion but long past its shelf life.

PolyHeme contains hemoglobin. But it shares a devastating medical limitation with other HBOCs: Once sprung from the prison of its blood-cell membrane, an unrestrained hemoglobin molecule becomes a rogue agent tiny enough to indiscriminately penetrate the walls of veins and arteries. There, free hemoglobin molecules trigger inflammation, causing the muscular cell membranes to seize and contract, which can block a blood vessel to the heart, triggering a heart attack. Studies of the HBOC HemAssist, for example, had to be shut down in 1998 when nearly half of the fifty-two trauma patients infused with it died, [15] compared to only 17 percent who received standard therapy.

Each HBOC manufacturer in succession has claimed to have generated its own unique, patented process to transform free hemoglobin into a safe bearer of oxygen. So far, none has been shown to work to the FDA's satisfaction, and the biotech boneyard is littered with "definitively" modified HBOCs.

In PolyHeme, Northfield Laboratories claims to have found the holy grail of hemoglobin safe conduct: polymerization. Northfield's answer is to harness quadrupled arrays of hemoglobin, called *tetramers*, to one another in chains called polymers. This rearrangement, Northfield claims, will neutralize free hemoglobin's errant ways—and eliminate the risk of heart attacks and deaths.

If this worked, PolyHeme would allow medical institutions to do without much of the real blood they must buy, test, type, refrigerate, and store for the 3.5 million Americans who undergo blood transfusions every year. FDA approval would also allow Northfield to capitalize on PolyHeme's patent to corner the roughly $3 billion blood-substitute market.[16]

To this end, Northfield's CEO, Stephen Gould, MD, armed with an initial $1 million from investors, ultimately raised $194 million after taking Northfield public in 1994. He then turned his attention to winning FDA approval.

It is easy to understand that for-profit companies such as Northfield could be willing, even eager, to give personal autonomy and informed consent short shrift if they stand between them and the FDA approval they need. However, it is harder for the public to accept that money can compromise the independence of medical researchers and academics as well.

Northfield has thrown a lot of money around, beginning with the approximately $10,000 per patient it paid hospital research programs. The University of California at San Diego was paid $10,840 for each patient who completed the study, discounted steeply for an early withdrawal: the university was guaranteed approximately $73,000. Some researchers gleaned additional bonuses, such as the $556 per capita handling fee received by Scripps Mercy Hospitals. According to a *New York Times* account, Northfield paid the University of Texas Health Science Center at Houston $336,000 to test PolyHeme, and the University of Kentucky Medical Center garnered $132,468, funds the hospitals say merely covered operating costs. When pressed about this, University of Kentucky surgeon Andrew C. Bernard responded, "This is not a profit-making endeavor—it is a scientific one."

Actually it is both. This model has become the norm within the last quarter century, as pharmaceutical corporations and biotechnology firms in partnership with universities have muscled the government aside to become the chief patrons of research.

PolyHeme on Trial

After conducting several small "test-run" clinical trials, Northfield commissioned a larger 1998 multicenter hospital trial, the Acute Normovolemic Hemodilution investigation, nicknamed the ANH study. Northfield convinced the hospitals and the FDA to allow it to investigate whether infusions of PolyHeme would safely allow the use of less donated blood during surgery. In this experiment, PolyHeme was infused into subjects awaiting surgery at institutions such as the University of Kentucky to repair an abdominal aortic aneurysm, a ballooned, weakened area in the artery wall that could burst at any time, causing massive, frequently fatal, hemorrhaging.

Two measures would have signaled success in the ANH study: the ability to use less, or no, donated blood during surgery, and more important, no higher a rate of adverse events, complications, or deaths when using PolyHeme than with blood. However, its Data Safety Monitoring Committee, an independent panel of experts that scrutinizes the safety and efficacy of an ongoing clinical trial, detected differences in the health status of the PolyHeme and control groups and asked for an in-depth analysis. This revealed that 54 percent of the patients who received PolyHeme suffered serious adverse events, ranging from heart-rhythm disturbances to pneumonia to heart attacks, but only 28 percent of patients who received blood suffered such problems. The results generated serious concerns about PolyHeme's safety, concerns that were realized when ten of the eighty-one PolyHeme subjects died, in contrast to only four of those who had received blood. The difference was statistically significant, meaning that it was unlikely that it could have arisen by chance.

Northfield responded to these safety alarms by quietly closing the trial in early 2001. Its CEO, Stephen Gould, duly reported the excess morbidity and mortality to the FDA as was legally required, but he attributed it to putative disparities in the physical condition of the subjects. He also claimed that the doctors had bungled the study by infusing subjects who received PolyHeme with excess fluids.

In the wake of the ANH study, time was running out for PolyHeme. Its patent window was good for only about twenty years, and the longer it took Northfield to procure FDA approval, the greater the chance a competitor might emerge and the less time the company might have to enjoy any exclusive profits from its sale. A successful clinical trial was necessary for FDA approval, but the informed-consent process required that Northfield disclose to potential subjects the elevated rates of heart attack and death that dogged recipients of PolyHeme in the ANH trial. The revelation of these adverse effects would have made recruiting the necessary hundreds of subjects extremely difficult.

But Dr. Gould was an invitee to FDA meetings on the subject of HBOCs, where he presented the virtues of PolyHeme, including detailed technical arguments that fluid mismanagement and the profoundly ill condition of some subjects were to blame for the ANH medical disasters, not PolyHeme. These presentations apparently bolstered his arguments on behalf of PolyHeme enough for Northfield to convince the FDA to allow it to exploit the 50.24 exception and begin enrolling unwitting trauma patients in PolyHeme studies.

Flouting the Law?

Although the CFR 50.24 law builds in special requirements and protections in an attempt to compensate for the loss of informed consent, the PolyHeme trial violated many of these and was mishandled so dramatically that the targeted communities and eventual subjects were left vulnerable.

These rules stipulate that the medical condition and time constraints must preclude eliciting informed consent from the subjects or their legally authorized representatives; that the subjects must require treatment for a life-threatening condition; and that known treatments must be "unproven or unsatisfactory." In addition, the substance being tested must have prior study data suggesting that it provides "a direct benefit" to the subject. The regulations also mandate "community consultations" to inform people living in the targeted research areas—"communities" in CFR parlance—about the nature of the study that provides an opportunity for feedback from the affected residents.

But each rule was followed either in a desultory manner or not at all. The federal requirement that subjects' medical condition must preclude the ability to give informed consent is usually taken to mean that the patient is unconscious or not lucid. Because trauma victims spiraling down into hemorrhagic shock tend to fall unconscious before help arrives, those who defend these studies claim there is no way to secure their consent. But investigators present no empirical evidence for this, and they provided no means for securing consent from those patients who retain or regain consciousness. "Has anyone actually done the research to establish that this is infeasible?" asked Peter Lurie, MD, of the watchdog group Public Citizen. "The company will complain that it is too difficult; this doesn't make it impossible. Most reasonable people would want to be informed." Martha Milete, for example, was conscious and remembers receiving PolyHeme in the ambulance, yet no researcher ever asked her permission or even notified her that she was a subject.

Despite the requirement that an experimental product such as PolyHeme can be administered under the 50.24 exception only if other approved treatments are unavailable, unproven, or unsatisfactory, researchers continued to administer PolyHeme for up to twelve hours after patients arrived in the hospital, where blood, the approved standard of care, was available. During this period subjects were unnecessarily, and according to 50.24 regulations, illegally, exposed to the risks of the experimental substitute because the desire to prove the product's efficacy trumped the patients' best medical interests. Nancy King, a lawyer and professor of social medicine of the University of North Carolina, pointed out that "the waiver of consent is permitted only when available treatments are unproven or unsatisfactory, and in a hospital, blood is neither." Glenn McGee, PhD, director of the Bioethics Education Network (BENE), agreed and was largely responsible for Albany Medical School withdrawing from the PolyHeme study, as did other sites, including Boston University.

King had a personal as well as a professional interest, because "I live in the area from which the study drew subjects and could have become a subject." She also discovered that the Duke University study in Durham, North Carolina, violated her state's Patients' Bill of Rights, which guarantees informed consent to medical-research subjects. She and her colleagues publicized these and other concerns in the *American Journal of Bioethics*, and the North Carolina study was suspended. Unfortunately the state medical board chose to waive the bill's guarantee of informed consent in March 2005, and the study at the Duke site resumed.

Despite a legal requirement that the experimental treatment must offer a direct benefit to the unwitting subjects if approved, urban trauma patients could expect no such benefit even if PolyHeme were to work. Urban trauma victims typically reach emergency rooms within twelve to twenty minutes, so they can expect no benefit from the purported ability of PolyHeme to keep them from oxygen deprivation for hours. Moreover, the earlier studies, such as the ANH study, suggested that PolyHeme produced not a direct benefit but a direct *hazard* to patients.

The deaths and adverse events characterizing prior HBOC studies over more than a decade were equally alarming, according to an April 28, 2008, study titled "Cell-Free Hemoglobin-Based Blood Substitutes and the Risk of Myocardial Infarction and Death," which was published in the *Journal of the American Medical Association (JAMA)*.[17] This meticulous meta-analysis observed sixteen blood-substitute studies that evaluated five different HBOCs with 3,700 subjects. Charles Natanson, MD, and his coauthors found that people who received HBOC transfusions suffered a 30 percent higher risk of death and fifty-nine heart attacks, as opposed to only sixteen of those who received no blood substitute. In short, all these blood substitutes caused higher rates of death and disability than did blood. All the paper's data prior to the Poly-Heme trauma study were available to both the FDA and to Northfield and should have given them pause.

Equally questionable was the notion of "community consultation," in which the affected community was to be informed of the study's details and to offer feedback whose purpose was nebulous. This "consultation" was supposed to compensate for informed consent and was originally called, in an example of semantic duplicity, "community consent." The usually precise regulatory language of the Code of Federal Regulations suddenly gave way to vaguely defined goals when discussing the nature of this community notification. For example, the purpose of the meetings is ostensibly to solicit the will of the affected community group, but the protocol language left it unclear whether attendees' feedback could result in any change in the conduct of the trial or could result in its closure. In any event, most investigators did not seem open to such possibilities, because they presented the study to meeting attendees as a fait accompli, and researchers' scribbled marginalia characterized attendees who asked hard questions as "hostile."

In practice, community consultation was bowdlerized cheerleading for the study, carefully scripted and tightly directed, featuring hagiographic profiles of PolyHeme's principal investigators. Presenters deployed uncritical PowerPoint presentations using a template that did not vary from site to site. Q & A PowerPoint slides offered rosy therapeutic promises and unsubstantiated safety reassurances, such as:

Q: Is PolyHeme safe?
A: In clinical trials to date, PolyHeme® has demonstrated
    no "clinically relevant" adverse effects. That is, they didn't
    impact the patient's safety or recovery.[18]

Proponents employed artful semantic twists to make forcing subjects into research seem ethically palatable. Research subjects were called "patients," suggesting a nonexistent doctor-patient relationship, and PolyHeme was relentlessly referred to as a "treatment" and often as "safe." In perhaps the most dazzling deployment of jargon, some PolyHeme researchers invoked the ethical term "equipoise," which refers to the fact that in order for comparative research to be ethical, the investigator is supposed to inhabit a state of uncertainty regarding the relative merits of the substances being compared in the study. (If he knew one treatment to be superior, he would be obligated to offer only that treatment to the subject.) But the higher heart-attack and death risks for PolyHeme recipients of the ANH study, and similar injuries that plagued subjects in several earlier HBOC studies—all of which investigators were aware—called into serious question the vaunted "uncertainty" as to whether PolyHeme or blood was the safest treatment.

Worst of all, the few, sparsely attended community consultations failed dismally to notify affected communities of the study's existence and their own vulnerability. Ross McKinney Jr., vice dean for research at Duke University School of Medicine, estimates that its community consultations "reached about 450 people," which he acknowledged was only a "tiny fraction" of Durham County's 267,000 residents. News reports in cities such as San Antonio and Denver[19] televised what happened when a reporter posted at a busy downtown intersection at lunchtime asked every passerby, "Have you heard of the PolyHeme study?" Not one person had. While on the faculty of Albany Medical School, McGee conducted a telephone survey of ten thousand city dwellers and found that "essentially no one knew anything about the trial. Those who were presented with the possibility that they might get the substance were quite adamant that they would not want to be involuntarily enrolled—if at all." (The CFR requirements do not quantify how many community members must be notified.)

When directed by some IRBs and regulators to provide a way for people to opt out of the study, Northfield settled upon a bright blue plastic bracelet inscribed with "I decline the Northfield PolyHeme study" in black block letters to alert emergency personnel. The catch, of course, is that no one could request a bracelet unless she had heard of the study.

The PolyHeme study proceeded, and in May 2006, undeterred by the excess heart attacks and deaths in the ANH study, Northfield began building a larger facility for spinning the dross of expired human blood into PolyHeme gold.

Meanwhile, most accounts note that only twenty-three test sites in twenty cities remained enrolled by the end of the trial. The centers that withdrew include those in Albany, Boston, Cleveland, and Johnson City Medical Center in Tennessee. At least six of the defectors, including those in Albany, Boston, and Durham (which later resumed the study), cited ethical discomfort with the study's conduct and protocols.

But no center asked the important ethical question of whether minority-group members were more likely than others to be enrolled.

Reverend Charles Williams, president of the National Council for Community Empowerment of Detroit, thinks this was the case. "We African Americans have been treated like guinea pigs," he declared. "We have suffered a history of research abuse and this is yet another instance." The council's website[20] criticized the PolyHeme study as exploitative, and Williams held protests in early 2008 to air these concerns.

A few investigative journalists, notably Matt Potter of the *San Diego Reader*, also alleged that biomedical redlining directed the testing of Poly-Heme to disproportionately black and Hispanic neighborhoods. Potter forced the release of original memos and research proposals through the California Public Records Act that revealed how only the San Diego ambulances that consistently troll three of the city's black and Hispanic neighborhoods were selected to distribute PolyHeme. "The experiment is targeted at several neighborhoods south of I-8, where many poor and minority residents are unlikely to have heard of the study,"[21] he wrote. Detailed demographic data of each site may not exist. "Federal law normally requires that hospitals and researchers collect racial data on their subjects, but the law for private companies is unclear," points out Heather Butts, JD, of Columbia University's institutional review board. Columbia did not participate in the study.

Yet U.S. Census data buttress a damning racial-bias case against the PolyHeme trial. Only 10 percent of the 3,141 counties in the United States have "majority-minority" populations where minority-group members make up more than 50 percent of the populace. But according to U.S. Census data, 34 percent of the municipalities where ambulances carried PolyHeme[22] were majority-minority. Richmond, Virginia, for example, is 57 percent black; Memphis is 61 percent black; Macon, Georgia, is 62 percent black; and Detroit is 84 percent black. Racial disparities also characterize some of the few rural PolyHeme sites, such as the village of Maywood, Illinois, which is 83 percent black. Of the twenty cities that ultimately completed the trial, thirteen—65 percent—had black populations considerably higher than the national average of 12.9 percent, and some had disproportionately high Hispanic populations as well.

In 2007, the *Detroit Free Press* reported that blacks and Hispanics constituted fifteen of the city's sixteen PolyHeme subjects who were brought by ambulance to Detroit Receiving and Sinai-Grace hospitals.[23] Both of the Detroit PolyHeme subjects who died were black.

In Indianapolis, which is only 25 percent black, Wishard Health Services scientists report that 59 percent of those who received Poly-Heme and 71 percent of the study control group were black, suggesting that even cities that are not majority-minority employed recruitment schemes that targeted people of color.

Another racial filter feeds the disparity. Although the scenarios in media discussions and on the Northfield website focused on trauma victims who had suffered motor-vehicle accidents or heart attacks, the trauma caused by urban gun violence contributed heavily to the pool of research subjects of color like Martha Milete. "The silence in regard to this," observes Karla Holloway, PhD, a professor of English and law at Duke University who criticized the PolyHeme trial's subject recruitment in *The American Journal of Bioethics*, "suggests a failure to acknowledge the statistical evidence that undoubtedly pointed them [researchers] to these population centers."

National trauma-study data disseminated by staff at Wishard Hospital in Indianapolis validate this racial overrepresentation by revealing that 35 percent of the U.S. subjects who received PolyHeme were black and that 33 percent of study controls were black.[24] This is 2.76 times the national percentage of African Americans.

Blood Simple

In May 2009 the FDA denied PolyHeme approval, finding it not only devoid of clinical benefit but also unsafe. The April 2009 letter in which the FDA rejected PolyHeme's Biologic License application concluded, "The safety data of all controlled studies reveal that the administration of PolyHeme places the patients at a higher risk of significant adverse events. . . . Based on the totality of the data in the application, FDA has determined that the data submitted do not support the proposed indication."[25] The subjects who received PolyHeme suffered three times the rate of heart attacks of those who received saline.

After the FDA denied Northfield's ambitions for PolyHeme, stock share plummeted 51 percent, and it ceased construction of the new complex it had begun building in May 2006 to manufacture the blood substitute. On June 1, 2009, the firm filed for bankruptcy, and by July, Northfield's stock was valued at only five cents a share and the company had lost its stock-exchange seat. By then, many of Northfield's stockholders, convinced that the firm had lied to them about the deaths and heart attacks in the earlier ANH trial, had mounted a class-action suit against the company. But should they win, there may be little in the way of assets to disburse.

PolyHeme subjects may find justice equally elusive. "I was angry about being used without my permission," Martha Milete says, "but I didn't know that PolyHeme was harming people until I read it in the newspaper. I called a lawyer right away, but he wouldn't help me. He said, 'You didn't die, so you have no case.'"

The death knell to Northfield's hopes seemed almost anticlimactic, for by this time its failures were legion: the headlong rush to strip urbanites of their right to say "no" to medical research; the failure effectively to poll the public, to notify communities, or to adhere to even the diluted standards of the informed-consent exception; the withholding of information from stockholders, from the more exacting members of the press, and even from the very researchers who conducted the trials; and the credible accusations of racial targeting—all these must give us pause.

But we must add to these the shrouding of the excess deaths and heart attacks in the ANH hospital trial—and *JAMA*'s April 2008 excavation of the long, consistent history of HBOC deaths and deficiencies, which belatedly revealed that PolyHeme had promised nothing better from the start.

Is Informed Consent a Fading Concept?

On the heels of Northfield's demise, I learned that although PolyHeme may be history, our future includes a far more extensive assault on informed consent. A roll call of new medical innovations is even now being tested through the 21 CFR 50.24 exception. This is the $50 million Resuscitation Outcomes Consortium (ROC), a broader, more ambitious, and potentially more profitable network of eleven regional sites that are conducting nonconsensual studies, again in emergency scenarios. The University of Washington Clinical Trial Center coordinates the network, and the study chair, responsible for the overall scientific leadership of the research, is Myron L. Weisfeldt, MD, chair of medicine at Johns Hopkins University. Each research site is fed by at least one medical center, and some of these centers conduct several investigations.

Reading ROC's brochures and research proposals evokes déjà vu. As in the PolyHeme study, victims of trauma—people injured in car accidents, shootings, and cardiac arrest—will be "enrolled," and the studies will be conducted by paramedics and EMTs in ambulances and other emergency settings. As in the PolyHeme study, the likely unconsciousness of victims is invoked, without empirical evidence, to demonstrate the futility of obtaining consent from victims or their families.

The ongoing ROC plans to investigate approaches to neurological damage in six thousand trauma victims and to evaluate resuscitation methods on fifteen thousand people who have suffered sudden cardiac arrest. At least eleven Level I (top-tier) trauma centers in the United States and Canada host these studies, including hospital emergency departments in Seattle, Portland, San Diego, Dallas, Birmingham, Iowa, Milwaukee, Pittsburgh, Ottawa, Toronto, and Vancouver. Each Level I trauma center tests at least one arm, and in many cases several arms, of the trial. Thus a specific site may conduct arms of several individual studies, such as tests of saline solutions and tests of CPR assistive devices.

As in the PolyHeme study, the ROC is testing ways to reverse or to prevent shock that is triggered by traumatic injuries. And, as in the PolyHeme study, the profitability of corporate monopolies is at stake. Among its research protocols, for example, is a study to test a patented valve device made to assist in cardiopulmonary resuscitation, or CPR.

Unlike the PolyHeme study, the ROC studies enroll adolescents as young as fifteen, whose medical fates can now be determined by a computerized coin toss rather than by their parents.

Daniel Nelson, PhD, had reassured me in 2008 that 50.24 research was "very rarely used," but North Carolina lawyer Nancy King mused,

"The emergency-consent exception is supposed to carve out a very narrow window, but that narrow window seems to be expanding." In mid-2009, ROC study chair Weisfeldt of Johns Hopkins told me, "The ROC has already enrolled seven thousand subjects," eclipsing the 720 subjects in the PolyHeme study. The ROC study's published goal is the enrollment of twenty-one thousand people by 2012.[26]

No One Can Now Call Research without Informed Consent "Rare"

Like the PolyHeme trials, the ongoing ROC studies have lost both scientific and ethical footing at times, but, like Northfield's Dr. Gould, ROC investigators seek to cast these in the most positive light possible. One ROC experiment, for example, injected highly concentrated salt water into trauma victims' blood vessels. Brain injuries are usually treated by giving normal saline solution, but this multicenter ROC study tests concentrations of salt that are dramatically higher than the saline concentration in our bodies. Some arms of the study also randomly add dextran 26, which consists of daisy-chained sugar molecules that are intended to reduce blood clotting. The dangers of such a highly concentrated saltwater solution, including high blood pressure and seizures, have long been known, and dextran creates further risks with its potential to trigger allergic reactions. These concerns were validated on August 25, 2008, when the study's Data and Safety Monitoring Board (DSMB) suspended research because of concerns about patient safety.

During our discussion, however, Weisfeldt portrayed this suspension not as a safety issue but as a decision made because of "futility. There was so little difference between the study's two arms that there was no reasonable prospect that it would show a benefit." Only when pressed did he admit that the DSMB had suspended the study.

Weisfeldt insisted, "Seventy percent of people approve of the [ROC] study, according to a telephone survey." But once news coverage of the ROC familiarized some area residents with the study's intentions, the researchers, despite their claim of a mandate, were besieged by nervous potential subjects who wanted no part of it. In Portland, Oregon, seven hundred residents demanded and received opt-out bracelets. Researchers in the Seattle arm of the study were "overwhelmed" by the demands for bracelets: by June 2007, the high demand had rendered them unavailable for more than a year.[27]

But perhaps the wary needn't have bothered: ROC publications warn, "Even if you opt out, there is no guarantee. . . . You might still be enrolled in the study." When asked to clarify, Weisfeldt stopped short of an assurance: "In most cities, if someone objects, they are given a bracelet. Every effort is made to recognize the bracelet if he or she is a candidate. We do our best to honor that."

Why, I asked Weisfeldt, is it ethical to conduct research on people who have not given their consent? "It is the only way scientifically to learn what the best treatment is, by doing clinical trials. The [ROC] study is completely legal and is approved by IRBs." But does that make it right? "We live in a society that goes by the law." I explained that I was not questioning the legality of the study, but its ethics: Is it right to conduct research with no provision for consent? Weisfeldt paused, then said, "I'd better not answer that question."[28]

Ethics for Sale?

Withholding the right to consent, whether via 50.24 research, presumed consent, or frank deception, speeds research studies that would be difficult or perhaps impossible to recruit if potential subjects were actually informed of the risks they faced. This can be convenient and profitable for the pharmaceutical and biotechnology companies that embrace it. But why do academic researchers who conduct the studies for pharmaceutical companies put aside their sacred ethical obligation to inform patient-subjects? There is probably more than one answer to this question, but when a researcher or medical institution is dependent upon the largesse of a corporation, they risk behaving as if they were obedient employees rather than independent investigators.

An exchange of press releases by Northfield Laboratories[29] and Johns Hopkins University, whose researchers were being paid—well—to test PolyHeme, illustrates this tension by revealing the company's attempt to control a Johns Hopkins researcher's statements and behavior.

In early 2006, when Northfield was confronted about its failure to disclose the excess heart attacks and deaths among PolyHeme recipients in its ANH study, the company responded with a press release announcing that principal investigator Dr. Edward Norris of Johns Hopkins University would hold a press conference at a major medical meeting, during which he would explain that no deception existed because he had indeed been informed of the deaths by Northfield. The release assured readers that Norris would also deliver Northfield's party line on the subject—that researcher error, not PolyHeme itself, had caused the heart attacks and deaths.

However, Dr. Norris was apparently less tractable than Northfield thought, because on March 23, 2006, Johns Hopkins countered with a press release of its own:

> Contrary to a statement made as part of a press release by Northfield Laboratories of Evanston, Ill., on Feb. 22, 2006, a Johns Hopkins Medicine faculty member, Edward Norris, M.D., is not presenting information about a clinical trial of the company's blood substitute PolyHeme at the annual meeting of the Network for the Advancement of Transfusion Alternatives (NATA) in April 2006; was not given access to full study results from Northfield; and does not and cannot substantiate Northfield's claim that PolyHeme was unlikely to have been the cause of 10 heart attacks and 2 deaths in patients receiving the blood substitute as part of a clinical trial that ended in 2000.
>
> Johns Hopkins Medicine has asked Northfield to retract its February 22 release and to reissue a corrected version.[30]

Unfortunately, not all clinical researchers display such independence: They have motives to comply with a corporation's directives. Researchers want to recruit subjects and complete their research in the timely manner required by federal regulations. They also presumably want to validate effective treatments and preserve lives and often promulgate consequentialist arguments for cutting ethical corners—that the laudable ends justify the dubious means. For example, no one questions that a blood substitute would be a stellar advance if it worked safely, or that research to definitively establish the superiority of one resuscitation technique over another would be a good thing. So researchers often focus on these speculative benefits, not the certain abuse of impressing subjects into research.

Moreover, once they have carried out the research study, academic researchers have sometimes found themselves cut out of the process of data evaluation and publication, with no power to influence the interpretation of the study results. Northfield's policy of withholding information from the more critical members of the press and ethics community even extended to some of the doctors who conducted its research for them.

For example, despite repeated pleas from PolyHeme researchers Drs. Ronald M. Fairman and Albert Cheung at the University of Pennsylvania and from T. J. Gan, MD, of Duke University, Northfield did not provide data about the entire study to participating researchers and failed to publish the data, leaving investigators with only the limited information they could glean from their own subjects. Dr. Cheung told the *Wall Street Journal* that Northfield's Gould agreed to meet with doctors of the twenty-one hospitals that had conducted the ANH study in Philadelphia, then canceled the meeting at the last minute.[31]

And as we have seen, the hefty payments to medical institutions by pharmaceutical and biotechnology companies that are eager to fund promising research provide a financial incentive as well.

But the nonconsensual subject recruitment that has undergirded PolyHeme, the ROC, and many other recent investigations is an appalling ethical reversal. Worse, this forced participation in medical research has been adopted with an utter lack of transparency, so it is even harder to understand the tolerance of many medical ethicists for this broadening abandonment of informed consent.

Some undoubtedly share the consequentialist focus of researchers who fixate on the prospective benefits of a successful blood substitute or other desirable innovation. But naiveté or baser motives may drive some ethicists to defend research without consent.

Others have mulled the question before I: Are some corporations buying the ethics they need? Does pharmaceutical and medical-company funding influence the views of some ethicists, as it does some of the medical professionals and institutions discussed in Chapter 4? It is heresy to suggest that some ethicists are influenced by drug and device makers' money, even though they may not be conscious of their seduction. However, Carl Elliott, an ethicist at the University of Minnesota, suggests that we ask

... why bioethicists at the University of Toronto take funding from GlaxoSmithKline, Pfizer, and Merck to write editorials on bringing biotechnology to the developing world. Or why
the University of Chicago's MacLean Center for Clinical Medical Ethics cosponsored a recent conference with Pfizer, Merck,
and PhRMA, the pharmaceutical industry trade organization,
on inequities in American health care. Or why bioethicists
at the University of Pennsylvania take money from Pfizer to
write an article explaining why physicians should not accept
gifts from companies like Pfizer. We may take industry money,
bioethicists argue, but we're not industry stooges. We're doing
God's work.[32]

Elliott's insight is critically important: pharmaceutical companies
sometimes give ethicists money not because they expect unalloyed support, but as a component of their "third-party strategy." Independent
bioethicists are not expected to sell the companies' products—which in
this case are an ethical defense of its drug, manufacturing, or marketing
actions—directly. This is because the ethicist's independence is what
makes her opinion valuable, lending it power and making her an opinion leader. Instead she indirectly rationalizes, supports, or defends the
company's actions in grand rounds, radio programs, scientific presentations, journal articles, or even in discussions with colleagues. Perhaps
she merely raises questions about the condemnation of actions such as
Northfield's no-consent studies or the ROC's testing of a proprietary
device on unwitting subjects: this subtle support is valuable to the corporation, too.

Even if the ethicist devotes much of her writing to assailing a company's practices, any isolated statement of support or approval can be
taken out of context and publicized by a company that may also publicize its financial support of the ethicist. Some of these handpicked
ethical "opinion leaders" are undoubtedly convinced of their own
impartiality despite the drug makers' checks in their back pockets, and
that is all to the good as far as the industry is concerned.

Even revered bioethicists' groups such as the American Society for
Bioethics and Humanities and the American Society of Law, Medicine
and Ethics endorse Pharma's payments to ethicists, displaying the same

naiveté shown by publishers and readers who accept medical-journal review articles written by "objective" scientists in the pay of Pharma. In Chapter 4, we read how Frederick K. Goodwin, MD, defended himself against accusations of purchased bias by arguing that he took money from so many pharmaceutical companies that his opinions favored no one firm. Similarly, ethicists are sometimes encouraged to take money from several pharmaceutical companies to deflect accusations of bias.

The financial benefits that some ethicists enjoy have seduced them into defending, or at least failing to criticize, the erosion of informed consent and other coercive policies that benefit drug makers' bottom line. I hasten to add that I do not impute an impure motive to *all* ethicists who defend dispensing with informed consent: fair and reasonable scholars can disagree. I do suggest that some may find their ethical vision clouded by pharmaceutical-firm money.

Ethicists are only one of the many groups vulnerable to seduction by Pharma's money. We have seen how physicians are particularly vulnerable because drug and device makers pay fully half of the $1.4 billion spent annually on continuing medical education for U.S. physicians. So, increasingly, are medical-advocacy organizations as drug makers fund patient support and advocacy groups—as well as some prominent bio-ethics centers.

And what of Martha Milete, the story of whose assault opened this chapter? How has she fared, and what does she think of the increasing tendency to bypass the consent of research subjects in emergencies?

"I had suffered so much trauma," she recalls with a trembling voice. "My whole body was open from my breast all the way down my torso and they couldn't close me up for a long time. I returned to the hospital for several major surgeries, and the impact of the gunshot tore my retina, so I had to go in for eye surgery. My vision is pretty good now, I can see, but little waves make it seem as if something is always going across my field of vision.

"My body is disfigured now, I have incisions that cross my whole torso, but I am grateful to be alive and my clothing can cover my scars—imagine if I had been shot in the face! I'm disabled: there are a myriad of things wrong with me, and I can't do half the things I used to do; I just have to accept that."

Perhaps the psychological scars are the worst. Milete still cannot sleep well, haunted by nightmares and fear despite the dog she bought for protection. Her assailants were never apprehended.

"But I'm walking. I'm able to live in my own home. I'm just glad to be alive and independent. But when I think of the research they did on me, I lose my peace of mind: How can they do that? How can they use you in an experiment without telling you what they want to do?"

CHAPTER 7

A TRAFFIC IN TISSUES

If anything is sacred, the human body is sacred.

—WALT WHITMAN

In Chapter 1 we saw how, in 1950, wondrously long-lived cells taken from the body of Henrietta Lacks catalyzed the science of cell-line culture—and a persistent tug-of-war among corporations, researchers, and patients for ownership and control of "donors'" bodies. Thirty years later, Dr. Heideaki Hagiwara retreated to his native Japan from a University of California at San Diego laboratory with a specialized hybridoma and was promptly sued by UCSD for patent infringement. For more than a decade, John Moore fought, and ultimately lost, the battle for ownership of his uniquely productive and invaluable cells.

But today advances in biotechnology, such as the completion of the Human Genome Project and nascent pharmacogenomics (the study of how genetic variation affects the body's response to drugs), have changed the way tissues can generate medical and fiscal wealth. Today's techniques mine the medical value of our bodies by collecting large amounts of normal tissues, cells, and genes from many people, not just unique or unusually valuable ones from a few. One factor remains constant: the courts continue to rule that everyday individuals have no rights to their "discarded" body parts, leaving us at the mercy of the university-industrial complex, which does enjoy those rights.

Today "access to quality human disease tissue is becoming increasingly important to the drug discovery process," declared AstraZeneca vice president Jeff Hanke, PhD. The resulting medication patents rest on the fruits of our own bodies.[1] Amid calls to "share the gift of life," pharmaceutical companies, blood and tissue banks, tissue brokers, and other companies that profit from research and biotechnology that uses human tissue would have us believe that such amassing and patenting of human tissue allow us to pursue an altruistic agenda.[2]

But the only "altruism" is practiced by faceless patients and the dead, who are the uncompensated and often uncomprehending donors of tissue. While they are spoken of as altruists amid invocations of humanity and the noble "gift of life," everyone else in the tissue food chain are knee-deep in the stream of human-tissue commerce and act as hard-nosed capitalists who demand their share of the profits.

And this is the best-case scenario, because in many cases the "donated" tissue is appropriated, not given.

Sometimes it is stolen, as in the case of oral surgeon Dr. Michael Mastromarino and his for-profit human-tissue recovery firm Biomedical Tissue Services (BTS) of Fort Lee, New Jersey. After acquiring a tissue-harvesting license from the New York State Department of Health in 2002, Mastromarino hit upon a crude scheme to sell body parts without the knowledge of the dead or their families and without regard for the law, to say nothing of the health of recipients. The FDA shut down BTS[3] on October 8, 2005,[4] after Mastromarino and two employees were convicted of illegally removing human bones, organs, and tissue from cadavers awaiting cremation, of forging consent forms, and of selling the purloined body parts from hundreds of people to medical companies without the consent of their families.[5] The company's underground dissections netted Mastromarino $12 million over three years. Among BTS's victims was Alistair Cooke, a British-American broadcaster who from 1971 until 1992 was best known to millions of U.S. viewers as the lovably supercilious host of PBS's *Masterpiece Theater*.

BTS acquired tissue from at least 1,076 people whose tissues were not rare or unusually valuable. To the contrary, their tissues were often substandard, ravaged by disease and infection, dramatically illustrating how tissue volume has come to trump biomedical excellence or rarity.

This desire for large volumes of tissue is why, beginning in 2000, patients facing surgery at the Harvard-affiliated Beth Israel Deaconess Medical Center in Boston were given one more consent form to sign. This form gave permission for the hospital to send excised tissues from their surgeries to Ardais, a private for-profit genomics company.[6]

Tissues slated for *transplantation* are used to treat burns and traumatic injuries and for plastic surgery, cancer, and other therapies, and their collection and use are regulated by the American Association of Tissue Banks. But *research* tissue banks, such as those fed by Ardais, are not overseen by any formal regulatory body and need not meet the standards for human transplantation. Nearly any tissue type—skin, bone, cornea, fetal tissue, blood vessel—is a candidate for research and inclusion in various tissue banks.

Ardais wished to identify disease-causing genes and then create drugs to target and nullify their effects. To do this, the firm began to gather and bank large quantities of anonymized tissue (tissue that had been separated from its identifying information) and to collate data from it, especially genetic data, which it sold to other biomedical concerns. Ardais is freed by the signed patient-consent form to sell or to utilize the patient's tissue in its profitable research and medication development.[7]

For one arm of a study that sought to refine treatment for prostate cancer, the firm collected approximately fifty thousand samples every year. The consent forms given to hospitalized patients may not have been legally necessary, because collecting tissues for databases is largely uncharted territory in a field characterized by a decidedly laissez-faire atmosphere.

Margery Moogk, MS, who directs Seattle's nonprofit Northwest Tissue Bank, has observed that it may not be legally necessary to obtain patients' consent for using tissues that were removed during surgery. "If an organization is investing a lot of money in research or new product development, and they don't have a particular target in mind, they're using the tissue without any real knowledge of or guarantee that it will make a contribution, then it's not so clear that they have any kind of obligation to go back to an individual and say, 'We extracted DNA from your cells that we used to make the target RNA that is now an important component of our product'—because it's not really theirs [the patient's] anymore."

"We do have a general consent form with a sort of nebulous provision for materials to be used for research," says Alan D. Proia, MD, PhD, vice chairman of pathology at Duke University. "That's where a lot of institutions get into conflict, because the government says that for federally funded research you need fully informed consent, but others say the consent form for surgery allows them to use tissue."

Ardais and the hospital were being prudent because the signed consent form could conveniently deter any future John Moore, who might otherwise mount a lawsuit.

One might be tempted to think that if a patient decides to sign the form, the ethical duties of the physician and hospital have been fulfilled and no wrongdoing or exploitation can have occurred. But this is untrue. A signed consent form is *not* informed consent, nor is it proof of informed consent. It is merely a single piece of evidence offered to support a researcher's or provider's claim that she has provided informed consent to the patient. True informed consent must fully inform the patient of the nature and known implications of what he may be surrendering, including the patient's option to refuse the "donation," and it must advise the subject of the tissues' likely commercial value. This information should be delivered by the researcher—who is prepared to expand on the nature of the donation and to answer questions—not simply written on a form. Even the most conservative rulings, such as those of the California and Supreme courts that denied John Moore the rights to his appropriated tissues, have held that these fiduciary duties of physicians and researchers to their patient-subjects are sacred.

Far from fulfilling the criteria for informed consent, there is also a deceptive element in this transaction because surgical inpatients identify with their role of "patient" and with their doctor's role of "surgeon": they do not see her as a researcher and certainly do not see her or the hospital as an agent for a for-profit firm that traffics in human tissue. They are expecting to sign forms that permit procedures that are necessary for their health and may not recognize that the tissue-consent forms are for the benefit of a for-profit company.

Also, although treatment cannot legally be denied for a refusal to participate in research, a whiff of coercion also lingers, because despite a stated policy of "no interference with necessary medical procedures," one wonders how completely patients can uncouple the consent form from the surgery—and whether they are ever encouraged to do so. The ability to do so certainly varies from patient to patient, but 85 to 90 percent of patients sign the form, says University of North Carolina associate director for policy and ethics Lynn Dressler, PhD, adding that few realize the true nature and import of "donating" their tissues in this way or that they may opt out and still have the surgery.

At nearby Duke University, more than 99 percent of the subjects consent, says Alan D. Proia, "because medical research has everything to gain and they have nothing to lose." In 2001, approximately nine hundred patients gave consent for their tissue to be collected by Duke, which banked approximately half of it. By 2002, the number of consenting patients numbered more than 1,400: Duke banked about 800 of them.

Despite the signed piece of paper, however, true informed consent may not exist. Some patients are intimidated into acquiescence, and all are given too little information on the form to make a good decision, so that only that small percentage of patients who are especially savvy and are comfortable questioning their surgeons may obtain the information they need to make an informed decision. Furthermore, Dressler points out, "Some people agree and sign the form, then change their minds later."

In her position as a guardian of UNC's tissue-procurement policy and ethics, it is Dressler's responsibility to ensure that patients have given their consent to having their tissues used for research. On several occasions, Dressler recalls contacting surgeons to tell them that no informed consent form had been submitted, only to have the surgeons airily wave aside her concerns, saying of the anesthetized patient, "Oh, don't worry, she'll sign." In response, Dressler twice directed the surgical technicians she supervises not to accept the samples, and her institution's surgeons now comply with the requirement to obtain consent before banking removed tissue.

Faced with the troika of a powerful medical center, an ambitious physician-researcher, and a results-hungry biotech or pharmaceutical company, how much autonomy can a lone sick patient, who presumably needs the surgery he is about to undergo, wield? Might a medically naïve patient be cowed into signing the form, or will he fear that refusing to sign can affect his relationship with the care team or his ability to have the surgery he needs? There is a deliberately nebulous nature to this transaction that encourages ignorance and discourages questioning or refusal: both war with the attainment of informed consent.

The Code of Federal Regulations governing this area of human medical research (45 CFR 46) also stipulates that if the tissue is without identifiers—that is, if there is no clinical information that allows one to identify the subject who is the origin of a tissue sample—consent can be waived if the hospital's institutional review board (IRB) agrees. Furthermore, as we've seen in *Moore v. Regents of the University of California,*[8] the California Supreme Court ruled in 1990 that John Moore had no ownership interest in his excised tissues that were used for research, and the U.S. Supreme Court upheld this ruling. But the Moore decision did find that physicians are bound by a fiduciary duty to inform patients of any economic or personal interests that accrue in using or studying the tissues. Companies such as Ardais hope that the patient's consent will allay accusations that the physician has neglected this fiduciary duty.

Will the presentation of an informed-consent document in this context generate more questions than it answers? To what exactly has the patient given consent? To basic research with the tissues? To the patenting of any discovery whatever gleaned from or facilitated by the tissues? To the commercialization of the patent that results from the research? Should the form be required to state what specific research goals the researcher has in taking the tissue, and if these goals change or are supplanted by others, will the researcher be in violation of his fiduciary duty if he does not update the patient?

It's easy to envision situations where it will be impossible to update the patients on all the tissue's uses because there is no identifier on the tissue or because the tissue has been used for upstream research that results in the development of many other patented entities. Should specific prior information be dispensed as to the researcher's possible future inventions? And who exactly should be able to give—or withhold—consent? This question becomes even more complex when the same genetic resources (for example, a particular gene mutation) are shared among members of a family community, or even neighboring countries. Then we must worry about the possible effects not only on the subject but also on her family and community.

Harvard's Deaconess was merely the first academic medical center to partner with Ardais. After Duke University Medical Center followed,[9] eventually others, including Maine Medical Center in Portland and the University of Chicago, entered into similar agreements. Medical centers found this relationship attractive because Ardais paid them for access to the tissues. The agreement also allowed hospitals to minimize the sort of legal and financial risks posed by the Lacks and Moore cases.

This stratagem is profitable for the institutions but not for patients, because the medical center and the company each profit from the products of this research, but the patient, who is the source of the tissue, does not.

The College of American Pathologists agreed that "the rapid evolution of clinical genomics has transformed tissue banking from a relatively informal resource for academic researchers to a commercial linchpin of the drug and diagnostics industries,"[10] and in 2003 it predicted that the market for human tissues was on the brink of reaching $1.6 billion. Today, according to Proia, "everybody and his brother wants human tissue for genomic and proteomic research." Thousands of high-volume tissue banks now exist.

Research-tissue collecting did not burgeon before 2000 because surgically acquired tissue was very expensive and time-consuming to bank in a meaningful manner. Large amounts of clinical data about the donor had to be collected in order to make each sample useful. "To really create a lot of value for it, you need to provide a rich clinical annotation, with a lot of information about the patient, the disease, the organ site the tissue is taken from, and so on," explained Michael J. Becich, MD, PhD, chairman of pathology at the University of Pittsburgh Medical Center. By 2002, the money to fund the collection of that data was provided by the escalating demand from biotechnology and pharmaceutical companies for frozen tissue on which to perform genomic profiling for diagnostic biomarkers provided, and by 2003 tissue-collection firms were thriving. Ardais boasted 140,000 samples and similar companies such as TissueInformatics and Detroit's Asterand produced 22,000 samples. Both provided tissue to large pharmaceutical and biotechnology firms such as Lilly, Abbott, and Pfizer. In February 2003, Ardais announced that AstraZeneca had licensed access to Ardais's library of tissue samples and related information for its drug-discovery program. In 2006, Ardais was acquired by GulfStream Bioinformatics. Today Ardais has commercial agreements with twenty-five other pharmaceutical corporations and biotech firms, including Bristol-Myers Squibb, Aventis, and CuraGen.

There exist noncommercial tissue sources as well, notably the Cooperative Human Tissue Network funded by the National Cancer Institute, which distributes about eighty thousand specimens per year for research in North America through six participating institutions. But medical centers often cannot compete with profit-making companies: "A single tissue sample might reach four figures—out of range for many academic researchers," warned *CAP Today*, the house organ of the College of American Pathologists.[11]

Presumed Consent

In 1987, Thomas Seaborn lost control of his motorcycle on a Philadelphia street and was killed. The death of a child is every parent's most profound horror, but her son's passing propelled Doris Jackson into a labyrinth of grief whose bizarre twists she could never have imagined. As she told CBS's *America Tonight*, when she set out for the medical examiner's office, crushed by despair and nearly mute with grief, she needed desperately to see her son and had one thought: to hold him again. But when she reached the medical examiner's office, the staff refused to let her see his body for hours, as she doggedly repeated her demand to see him. When Jackson finally was ushered into a room where she was permitted to view his body, she was staggered by what she beheld. His skull had been opened, and his brain and eyes had been removed. No one had asked her consent for this, and her son had not opted to donate his organs.[12]

Jackson was one of several Philadelphians who complained that the eyes and brains of family members had been removed without their knowledge or permission, and, like the others, she was astonished to learn that she had no recourse. The desecration of her son's body was perfectly legal, for he, like the others, had fallen victim to Pennsylvania's doctrine of "presumed consent." Under this regulation (also called a "medical examiner's law"), coroners can take tissues from the dead without their prior consent and without the knowledge of their families.

In order to increase the availability of tissues and organs for transplantation and research, every state has passed laws that enable pathologists to remove certain tissues from deceased individuals. Permutations of the Uniform Anatomical Gift Act vary from state to state, and while some make provisions for obtaining the consent of the deceased person or his family, most do not.

The rationale for this tissue appropriation is that even with vigorous recruiting, the demand for tissues far exceeds the supply. In addition, policy usually dictates that the family must ratify an organ donor's wishes to give his body parts after death, and families sometimes refuse to honor the donor's wishes. Campaigns to encourage people to sign their driver's licenses have raised visibility and increased the availability of organs for transplantation, but the demand for tissue (and organs) still far outstrips their availability. Ostensibly to meet this shortfall, cities and counties within at least twenty-eight states, including California, Ohio, Florida, Michigan, and Texas, have adopted presumed consent as an aggressive strategy for procuring tissues.

But another motive drives the hunger for tissues. The burgeoning of biotechnology has created medical applications that increase the demand for corneas and brain tissue at the same time that far fewer routine autopsies are being performed than in previous decades, limiting coroners' access to tissues.

(Enabling the harvesting of solid organs such as kidneys would probably be worthless because preservative techniques must be employed and a family history and other screens are necessary, all of which would require the family's being informed of the harvesting, and one point of presumed consent would seem to be excluding the family from the process.)

Unlike shocked family members before her, Jackson contacted CBS News because she wanted to alert her fellow Philadelphians to the danger. When her story ran, *America Tonight* viewers learned for the first time that theirs was one of the localities with designs on the bodies of its citizens, and that this widespread appropriation is sanctioned by law.[13]

"Presumed consent" is an oxymoronic phrase that describes laws allowing the state to conscript tissues or organs from the bodies of the unwitting by assuming that the patient or subject *would* have given his or her permission to have tissues removed, unless there are signed documents to the contrary. The catch is, of course, that because the city or county makes no attempt to publicize the law or to explain how to opt out of such "donation," very few affected people know about the danger, and so few can register their dissent.

Cyril H. Wecht, MD, JD, medical president of the St. Francis General Hospital in Pittsburgh, is past president of the American College of Legal Medicine, the American Academy of Forensic Sciences, and the American Board of Legal Medicine. He agrees that the Philadelphia medical examiner's office does not tell families of its intention to take the organs, effectively denying them an opportunity to object. "If you get a call saying your husband's been killed at work, will you say, 'First thing, I better get in touch with the medical examiner, then I'll call my family, my minister or rabbi'? Who the hell is going to think of anything like that?"

So almost no one opts out (or is opted out after death), and the coroner takes the organs of many people who would have vehemently objected. But very few residents of Philadelphia know of the risk. Coroners are loath to discuss these laws because many people, even those who support organ and tissue transplantation, dislike such ghoulish opt-out schemes, which rob the public of autonomy in order to obtain large volumes of tissues not only for transplantation, but also for research. Presumed consent expanded the market from six thousand tissue "donations" in 1994 to twenty thousand in 1999, garnering millions in fees.[14] These sub rosa laws also helped reinforce the legal penchant for assigning body and tissue property rights to research institutions and corporations rather than family members, as we have seen.

Although the public is not warned about presumed consent, tissue firms advertise extensively to potential stockholders and to those in the market for hips, skin, knees, cardiac tissues, arteries, femoral veins, bones, tendons, ligaments, fetuses, cord blood: in short, for nearly any body part that can be transplanted or used in research. Corporations such as CryoLife, Regeneration Technologies, Hybrid Organ, Islet Technology, Ixion Inc., and VitaGen charge fees that are paid by the transplant surgeon's hospital. By appropriating the tissues of the unwitting, the medical-tissue industry's worth swelled to $20 million in 1996, and by 2003 it had become a $1 billion industry.

Why strong-arm the dead into surrendering their tissues? One reason is that the number of autopsies has been falling since the 1960s: by 1985, the national rate had dropped to only 10 percent of deaths.[15] This decline limits coroners' access to tissues and results from the failure of patients' families to request routine autopsies. Even should they wish to, many are prevented by the fact that insurance companies don't cover them. One indication that the routine autopsy has fallen out of medical favor is that the Joint Commission on Accreditation of Health Care Organizations has ceased requiring hospitals to maintain a minimum autopsy rate. Some observers also think that doctors and hospitals avoid autopsies for fear that the conclusions could heighten their vulnerability to malpractice suits.

George Lundberg, MD, editor of *Medscape* and the former editor of the *Journal of the American Medical Association*, decries this trend, calling the autopsy an important diagnostic tool. "[It] was just as important in 1996 as it was in 1956," he said, explaining that autopsies allow doctors to check the accuracy of their diagnoses and the effectiveness of their treatment plans, as well as to learn more about the patterns of disease progression. It is true that historically autopsies have provided key information about diseases and their treatments: for example, it was through autopsies conducted in the 1940s that Stafford Warren learned that most Hodgkin's disease patients at his institution were dying not of their cancer, but of the radiation used to treat it. This inspired doctors to seek and find better treatments for Hodgkin's, ultimately transforming it into a survivable illness.

In contrast to routine autopsies, forensic autopsies are mandated by law and performed by coroners or medical examiners whenever someone has died by violence, accident, or questionable circumstances: these are on the rise, according to 2006 statistics from the Centers for Disease Control and Prevention.

Ignoring the Law

Tissues can be legally taken only if the coroner knows of no objection by the deceased or the next of kin. Even this thinnest of protections, however, is routinely flouted in some jurisdictions, as the body parts of people who have managed to register their opposition to tissue harvesting are sometimes taken with impunity anyway.

Deborah Brotherton discovered this in 1988 when she explicitly refused, in writing, to donate her husband Steven's corneas after his death, explaining that he had always been vehemently opposed to the idea. Brotherton's case was unusual in that all parties agree that her refusal was well documented.

However, the Cincinnati coroner, Frank P. Cleveland, MD, like many other U.S. coroners, had been contacted by the Eye Bank Association of America (EBAA), a corporation that encompasses eighty-seven eye banks in forty states. The EBAA urged Cleveland to steer as many corneas as possible to its local member, the Cincinnati Eye Bank.

Cleveland ordered his staff to "cooperate with the Cincinnati Eye Bank to obtain as many corneas as possible," and he did his part by countermanding Brotherton's refusal. Her husband's corneas were harvested over her objections, as "an anatomical gift" slated for release to the Cincinnati Eye Bank and for subsequent sale. A total of 59,784 corneal grafts were supplied by U.S. banks in 2009, and 14,547 were used for research.[16] Although no good data stipulate how many were acquired through presumed consent, major counties in more than half of U.S. states use the doctrine, so half, or 37,166 corneal grafts, would be a conservative estimate.

Brotherton sued the United States District Court for the Southern District of Ohio, challenging the constitutionality of the cornea-removal statute, but the district court dismissed the case, finding that she held no property interest in her husband's body, as apparently, the coroner's office did.

Fortunately, Brotherton persevered. She added to her suit another plaintiff whose loved one's corneas also had been taken against her express wishes through presumed consent, then she filed an appeal with the Sixth Circuit court. That court affirmed that she did indeed have a property interest in her husband's corneas and further found that the coroner's office had failed to provide the necessary warnings before the tissue harvesting. What's more, by failing to heed her objections, the court found that "the coroner had violated due process protection afforded by the United States Constitution."[17] This decision was followed by a string of reversals and affirmative findings. In the end, the courts released Cleveland from the suits by barring Brotherton from taking action against him, but it did allow her to sue the eye banks, and she finally prevailed.[18]

Many families formally have complained that their refusals were ignored by coroners' offices that took tissues from their loved ones. In one dismaying Florida case, a family was sequestered in a nearby room while a deceased relative's corneas were being removed without their consent.[19]

Copious payments for tissues are received even by nonprofits, creating a powerful financial motive. This is typical, says Joye Carter, MD, a Houston forensic consultant who has served as the chief medical examiner of several major cities, including Washington, D.C., and Houston.[20] "There is an acquisition fee, money that is passed to insurance companies, for organs. The Los Angeles coroner's office, for example, takes corneas and makes a lot of money from it. This is unfair because no one is going to take organs from the rich and famous." She also observed, "The law that permitted harvesting of heart valves was passed in D.C. by a city council. This helped the hospital and the transplant center financially, but the law says the citizens who were affected don't have the ability to sue." While chief medical examiner there, she says, "I refused to adhere to that law."[21]

The dramatic size of the tissue markups from the coroner's office to market is suggested by a precursor to the Mastromarino case, the L.A. coroner's office scandal triggered by its financial relationships with the Doheny Eye Bank.[22] In 1997, the L.A. coroner's office sold five hundred pairs of corneas within a year to the Doheny Eye and Tissue Transplant Bank. The coroner received $335 for each pair of corneas, and Doheny sold them at $3,400 a pair. Fully 80 percent of these corneas came from Hispanic and African American bodies via presumed consent.

The fact that the traded tissue comes from people who never had a chance to say yes or no and whose families are unaware of the transaction carries a powerful financial consequence as well as an ethical one: everyday people, the source of these tissues and organs, are cut out of the transaction completely, unable to demand their share of this billion-dollar market based upon the unconscious "gift" of body parts. They cannot even decide whether they want their tissues to be auctioned off to the highest bidder. This is unjust.

Also unjust is the way this hidden economy robs the public of a voice in the tissue market, unable to express our opinion as to whether hospitalized burn victims should be deprived of the cadaver skin they need to recover so that tissue brokers can inflate the lips and smooth the cheeks of the well-to-do while profits from the tissue sales line the pockets of tissue-banking corporations.

Also, consider the small but fervent groups that militate against infant male circumcision. They would surely be interested in knowing that foreskins have become a popular ingredient in facial-cosmetics recipes. This would allow them to question whether such trivia influence the continuation of a practice they consider harmful. The foreskins are a lucrative source of fibroblasts, bits of human skin that are used as a basis of a culture to grow other skin cells. One foreskin processed in this manner can be amplified to produce $100,000 worth of human skin for grafts that can cover the wounds of burn victims and diabetics whose ulcers require external skin to heal.

But foreskins fetch a much higher price when they are used as a source of collagen that creates pouty lips to order and that smoothes wrinkles through a $150-an-ounce skin cream called SkinMedica. Adult foreskins will not do: only fibroblasts from infant foreskins possess the youth and vigor that permit the needed endless duplication. Because U.S. circumcision rates are dropping, we needn't worry that cosmetics sales may be inducing more widespread male circumcision. However, these falling circumcision rates worry the purveyors of foreskins because although the cosmetics can be manufactured using other sources of human tissue, doing so will make the products far more expensive.[23]

When pressed, researchers who favor presumed-consent statutes explain that the tissues and organs thus commandeered further medical knowledge. This is true, but they do so as part of an industry that generates $1 billion in profits from which the donors are excluded. And sometimes, bodies and body parts further research in a manner to which neither the deceased nor the family would have agreed, because some research initiatives are undignified or disturbingly exploitative.

In the research laboratories of automobile manufacturers, for example, the bodies of infants have been secured in cars and used to test the physical consequences of simulated car crashes.

Because of their small size and differing body proportions, child car-crash victims are prone to different injuries than are adults, notably more neck and brain injuries. The 1993 revelation that researchers in Germany, Scotland, France, and Great Britain were using the dead bodies of children in safety tests sparked outrage over similar research in the United States. Here, the National Highway Traffic Safety Administration (NHTSA) funds $2.5 million in cadaver-collision research each year, which is supplemented by funding from the Centers for Disease Control and Prevention and by the nation's private automobile companies. Although U.S. crash-test centers do not use children's bodies, they do use the bodies of adults who had donated their remains for scientific research. And NHTSA funds some of the research abroad in countries such as Germany, which does use the bodies of children.[24]

But unlike adults, children cannot legally give their consent to have their bodies used for research after death. Usually their parents have given consent when medical staff ask them (as they are required to do by law) to donate their children's bodies shortly after death. But parents are not warned that such lifesaving "research" can include grotesque scenarios such as auto-crash studies. And parental consent is not always sought. Dr. Claude Tarrière, former head of safety research for the French automaker Renault, explained that a child in his laboratory's tests was an orphaned murder victim. "A single mother had killed her child and then committed suicide. There was no family, so the medical faculty offered us the child's body."[25] This child's unspeakable final indignity may help Renault to create a safer car, and to compete in the market with that safer car, but I can't help thinking that the callousness of this act diminishes each of us.

When tissues are secretly appropriated, the act cannot accurately be characterized as a "donation": neither is the insensate victim a "donor"—one who has made a gift of his tissues. To "donate" entails the conscious act of bestowing, which is not the case here. Characterizing purloined tissues as "donated" maintains the illusion of a gift relationship; altruism is a necessary conceit if one is to pay the source of the tissues nothing and hide the coercive nature of the transaction. "Donation" also carries a connotation of permanence that is unwarranted in research scenarios where informed consent generally entails the right to change one's mind. To avoid these flaws, "I prefer the term 'contribution,'" suggests University of North Carolina ethics director Lynn Dressler.

Presumed consent is just one of several faux-consent paradigms that legally free up organs and tissues whether the source of the tissues is willing or not. (See "Bestiary of Consent," p. 249.) From "community consent," in which mass education substitutes for eliciting individuals' permission, to "deferred consent," in which consent for research or a medical procedure is requested only *after* the research in question has already been carried out, these schemes are united by their lack of actual consent. They are also united by their convenience for researchers and tissue harvesters, allowing them to proceed without clearing the hurdle of informed consent.

Such no-consent schemes are invaluable for corporations with patented products and devices to sell, allowing them to leapfrog over the

Bestiary of Consent

Bestiary of Consent	Definition	Informed? (Are you told the details of alternatives, risks, benefits, and unfolding information?)	Must family or a legal representative be notified?	Is subject's consent required before, after, or never?	Can subject choose to give or to withhold his consent?	Other
Informed consent	Consent elicited only after a detailed description of benefits, risks, and options; continues throughout study	Yes	No	Before	Yes	Mandated by first tenet of Nuremberg Code
Presumed consent	A presumption that every subject would consent if asked	No	No	Never	No	Practiced within most U.S. states
Community consent	An area's population is enrolled in a study without procuring individual consent	No	No	Never	No	Expedient, but is not consent; now often called "community notification"
Consent by proxy	A surrogate is asked for consent	Yes, but only after you are enrolled	Yes	No	No	Necessary with some incapacitated subjects
Deferred subject consent	Consent from subject after the procedure has already taken place	Yes, but only after you are enrolled	No	After	No	————
Deferred proxy consent	From next of kin after already taken place	No	Yes	After	No	————
Implied consent	A general assent is taken for consent to specific individual acts	No	No	Never	No	————
Blanket consent (waiver of consent)	Permission to use for any purpose	No	No	Before	Varies	Generally considered unacceptable by IRBs
Broad consent	Permission to use info for a variety of purposes	No	No	Before	Varies	Applies to some tissue contributions

hurdle of eliciting subjects' consent and proceed directly to amassing the necessary hundreds of research subjects who will permit rapid completion of the studies needed for FDA approval. For instance, as we've seen, despite repeated quality-control issues and FDA reprimands that might have scared off voluntary subjects, BioPort's patented anthrax vaccine underwent large-scale testing by forcing military ground troops to undergo immunization without their consent. Chapter 6 explained how for-profit companies such as Northfield Laboratories and Baxter Healthcare Corporation were able to test their patented artificial-blood products, PolyHeme and Hemassist respectively, by legally bypassing subject consent. Today such no-consent research schemes continue, as patented CPR valves, for example, are currently being tested without subject consent as part of the eleven-site, twenty-thousand-subject Research Outcomes Consortium.[26]

Proponents of presumed consent justify it by claiming that most Americans support organ and tissue donation. But even if this were true, a simple majority is not a sufficient empirical basis for presuming that people wish to consent. Ethicist Robert Veatch has pointed out that one would need a 95 percent approval rate before one could speak of a mandate for such involuntary actions. No surveys demonstrate this level of support. As mentioned above, many Americans do not even realize that a lucrative commercial traffic governs the distribution of donated tissues and organs, or that the tissues in question are used for research as well as transplantation.

Moreover, there is no implication that the potential donors or their families would have offered their consent had they been asked. Those who cite the generosity of donors and the prevalent atmosphere that supports tissue and organ donation forget that this support does not necessarily extend to research uses. They also neglect to consider that there are two components of this support. You must ask whether a person supports donation, and you must also ask whether a person supports *being compelled* to donate. A significant portion of people who support tissue and organ donation do not support being compelled to donate.

Then, too, some groups are adamantly opposed to presumed consent in principle. This includes religious groups such as some Orthodox Jews, and others who share a belief in the primacy of bodily integrity. Jehovah's Witnesses object to tissue harvesting and to transplantation

that entails blood exchange or transfusion. Presumed-consent proponents also ignore other large pockets of very specific opposition, such as
African Americans.

"African Americans presume *not* to consent," observes Clive O.
Callender, MD, chief of transplant surgery at Howard University. As
founder of the Minority Organ and Tissue Transplantation and Education Program (MOTTEP), Callender is the highest-profile proponent
of African American organ and tissue donation in the nation. African
Americans have responded generously to pleas for organ donation: the
success of programs such as MOTTEP gives testimony to that. So does
the enthusiastic nationwide response to calls for donations for individuals in medical crises such as that of then-seventeen-year-old Michelle
Carew, whose 1996 national call for bone-marrow donors sparked the
creation of numerous African American blood and tissue banks.

No one has done more than Callender to transform the acceptability and marketing of organ and tissue transplantation in the African
American community. Attitudes around organ donation for transplantation have warmed dramatically among African Americans as detailed
in Callender's 2010 *Journal of the American College of Surgeons* paper
titled "Minority Organ Donation: The Power of an Educated Community."[27] But presumed consent is anathema to this group. "There are
specific reasons why we are often suspicious of attempts to part us from
our organs," muses Callender. "You have only to think of Tuskegee to
understand our reluctance, but there's also the fact that more blacks
than whites have more hysterectomies and amputations."

African American attitudes are also important to take into account
because blacks are a major source of presumed-consent tissues. A much
higher percentage of African Americans and Hispanics die of accidents
and homicides than do whites. Eighty percent of African Americans live
in urban areas, and, proportionally, five African Americans die in accidents for every four whites. Autopsies are mandated for the bodies of
actual and possible crime victims, so theirs is the only group for which
the U.S. autopsy rate is rising instead of falling.[28] Because the homicide
rate is eight to ten times higher among blacks, black bodies are more
likely than others to end up where they fall prey to presumed consent.[29]

The 1980s escalation in the African American homicide rate coincided with the rise of a market for human tissue and organs. African

Americans always have been at higher risk for the involuntary use of their bodies after death, but twenty-first-century medical technologies have put an Orwellian twist on this exploitation.[30] I am not suggesting that the connection was deliberately engineered. But I am observing that organs harvested from the bodies of brain-dead African Americans in hospital emergency rooms and tissues spirited from their bodies on coroners' tables have fed both profitable organ and tissue banks and African American fears that they were being exploited and their lives truncated for profit.

Callender is not the only scholar who has quantified African American opposition to presumed consent. A survey conducted by Michele Bratcher Goodwin, the Everett Fraser Professor in Law at the University of Minnesota and the author of *Black Markets: The Supply and Demand of Human Body Parts*, revealed that 80 percent of African Americans surveyed reject presumed consent as an unacceptable method for procuring tissues.

Prostate Profits

Prominent cancer surgeon Dr. William Catalona, of St. Louis, Missouri, has earned his patients' gratitude, both inside and outside the operating room. In 1986, he devised an elegantly simple test for prostate cancer, using the prostate-specific antigen (PSA). Despite dissent over PSA's use in mass screenings (see Chapter 5), the test has been widely embraced: three of every four U.S. men over fifty have used it.[31] Catalona, like George Washington Carver and Jonas Salk before him, refused to patent his invention. He then went on to refine a type of nerve-sparing prostate surgery that saves men from such life-altering surgical side effects as incontinence and impotence, making him the favored surgeon of such high-profile patients as Joe Torre. Not one to rest on his laurels, Catalona determined to advance cancer detection and treatment even further by refining the detection of genetic markers of prostate cancer.

In the early 1980s, he began asking patients he treated at Washington University (WU) of St. Louis whether he could retain their blood, DNA, and prostate tissue samples for use in this research. He also solicited samples via advertisements and word of mouth as well as referrals from his medical colleagues. He acquired about 255,000 blood and tissue samples from more than 30,000 men who said yes, but not before asking each patient to sign an informed-consent form that seemed a model of transparency. Because the samples were paired with identifiers and contained genetic data, they could impart sensitive health and heredity information about individual men and their families, so Catalona scrupulously adhered to both the NIH laws governing such samples and to ethical considerations. The consent form laid out the conditions under which the tissue would be used, stored, and maintained, and the form's language specified a guarantee: "Your participation is voluntary and you may choose not to participate in this research study or withdraw your consent at any time." The consent form also included WU's boilerplate language indicating that each sample was "a free and generous gift of your [blood, tissue and/or DNA] to research that may benefit others." Catalona helped establish the Genito-Urinary (GU) Repository at WU, and he stored the samples there for use in his prostate cancer research, just as he had explained to his patients.

But the university had other plans for the samples, which it saw as human capital because biotechnology and pharmaceutical companies pay handsomely for such tissues as raw materials for research. To WU, these could be a lucrative source of industry income.

As Catalona and his university debated the proper use of the samples, he decided to present a comparison of all predictive prostate cancer tests at the American Urological Association's annual meeting. To help compile this information, he decided to send some samples to Hybritech, a San Diego diagnostic company that had created a new test.

An email from WU's office of technology management registered its dismay: "Bill Catalona wants to send nearly 2,000 documented samples to Hybertech [sic] for free. Just from a cost-recovery scenario, this should be worth nearly $100,000 to the university. The only consideration Hybertech [sic] is offering is the potential for Catalona to get a publication. It is my opinion this is an unacceptable proposal."

The nonfiscal collaboration that Dr. Catalona proposed with Hybritech was the model under which medical scientists once routinely worked, but it has been supplanted by the newer paradigm of maximizing profits by establishing a monopoly on research materials and findings, then selling them to the highest bidder, which is what WU espoused.

In 2001, Catalona decided to leave Washington University and the tissue conflict behind. Although six thousand patients indicated, in writing, that they wanted their samples to travel with him, WU sued him, claiming ownership of the tissues. Patients joined the defense, and the case was heard by the U.S. District Court for the Eastern District of Missouri.

In court, the university claimed that nothing in the signed consent forms compromised its exclusive rights to the tissues. One patient, Richard N. Ward, said, "Frankly, I was offended by that. I entered into this research project; I consented to it with Doctor Catalona; and no time did I transfer ownership to Washington University or to anyone else . . . and when I found out that they took the position that they owned my body parts, my tissue, I wanted to get involved." Of the six thousand patients who were party to the suit, only eight were permitted to testify against the university's claim that it owned their tissue. The others' statements were consistent with Ward's, as each affirmed his right, guaranteed in writing, to his tissue and to withdraw from the research at will.

During the trial, however, the university lawyer had each respondent read the portion of the consent form stating that the patients were making a "gift" of their biological materials for research. This is an exculpatory clause that appeared in WU's informed-consent forms even though the NIH policy explicitly bans any consent-form language that makes a subject "waive, or appear to waive" his or her legal rights.[32]

The university interpreted this exculpatory "gift" clause broadly, as granting the university unconditional ownership of the patient's blood, DNA, and tissue samples, and despite the NIH policy, the district court agreed.

As in the John Moore case, a number of organizations weighed in to support WU with amicus curiae ("friend of the court") briefs that urged the denial of tissue property rights to the patients. These friends included powerful research universities such as Cornell, Duke, Emory, George Washington, Johns Hopkins, and Stanford as well as the Universities of Michigan, Minnesota, Pittsburgh, and Rochester. The Mayo Clinic, the Association of American Universities, the American Council on Education, the Association of American Medical Colleges, and the American Cancer Society also filed briefs supporting the university, warning that "creating ownership rights in research samples would have unwanted negative effects on important specimen research."

However, the university was itself claiming ownership rights, and none of these friends expressed concern about the chilling effect that WU's financial agenda threatened to exert on Catalona's prostate cancer research. Moreover, in court records, the university's vice chancellor for research admitted having "stalled" the approval of Dr. Catalona's research in the past,[33] providing yet another example of how needed medical research is sometimes stymied when it conflicts with a corporation's or a university's desire to make a profit.

Why did so many illustrious medical-research and advocacy institutions support the university's claims to the tissue samples? "All of these institutions, including the American Cancer Society, have a financial stake in large research sample repositories, or represent institutions that have them," explains Dr. Catalona. "Therefore, they all have a conflict of interest. It doesn't surprise me that they would all want to be declared 'owner' of the samples." Catalona had hoped that the NIH would criticize the exculpatory clauses in the informed-consent statements, but the NIH did not weigh in.

And what of the men's right to withdraw from the study at will? Any reasonable interpretation of "withdrawing from the study" would seem to entail destroying or returning the samples. This is because Catalona's prostate research was the raison d'être for the samples for which they had given consent, yet samples could not be used for this purpose should he lose access to them—and because each man's identity was linked to his sample's genetic information, which could expose him and his family to many sensitive genetic revelations. It's hard to see how a patient could remove himself from the research study, as the form promised, while the sample remained in the hands of others.

The court took the narrowest possible view, however, finding that the right to withdraw meant only a man's right to refuse further active participation. As for the guarantees in the informed-consent forms themselves, the court responded with shocking indifference, as Judge Stephen Limbaugh Jr. waved aside the informed-consent documents as "inconsequential."

Based on the university's own broad claims to ownership that were supported by the exculpatory clause, the court ruled in favor of the university in March 2006, finding that WU "owns the biological materials and neither Dr. Catalona nor any contributing individual has any ownership or proprietary right in the disputed biological materials."

Only after the decision did the Office for Human Research Protection (OHRP), which oversees the regulation of research through the NIH, write WU to demand that it remove all the exculpatory language from its consent forms: *"OHRP recognizes the possibility that individuals may have certain legal rights in their excised tissue or other human biological materials, even the absence of a specific recognition or an affirmative establishment of any such legal rights in these materials by the relevant legal body of a particular jurisdiction"* (italics mine). In other words, the OHRP admitted—albeit in language that was as opaque as possible—that the consent-form wording that WU made its researchers use violated federal research guidelines. It illegally forced the subjects to give up some of their rights by stipulating that the patients were making a "gift" of their biological materials. The OHRP ordered the university to remove this language from its forms.

But WU's court victory had been largely based on this very clause, and if the OHRP had weighed in on this before the trial, the outcome might have been different. Accordingly, Catalona turned to the Eighth Circuit Court of Appeals, which upheld the decision but did note that the men had the right to order WU to stop using their tissue. The university could not simply delete their identifiers from the samples and continue to use it.[34] This ruling left the U.S. Supreme Court as the only recourse, so on October 18, 2007, Catalona and his patients filed separate writs to the Supreme Court. A month later Us Too International, the world's largest prostate cancer support group, filed a supporting amicus brief. But on November 29, 2008, the Supreme Court declined to take the case, prompting Catalona to ask, "If the research participants cannot rely on OHRP, IRBs, or the courts for protection, where can they turn?"

Today, Washington University retains outright ownership of the samples that carry intimate genetic information about each donor. It is now free to sell or license the samples, or it could choose to use them for research to which the donors would object. Despite the 2008 passage of the Genetic Information Nondiscrimination Act (GINA), which offers some protection from genetic discrimination in the medical sphere, there is also the danger that genetic information about the men and their families could open them to discrimination or stigmatization in employment, insurance, or society.

This case serves as yet another object lesson in how patenting human tissues or otherwise establishing legal monopolies on them hinders the sharing of data among scientists that is critical to medical innovation. Perhaps the greatest tragedy of the legal tug-of-war between Catalona and Washington University is how it deprives patients of the innovative prostate cancer treatment Catalona hoped to perfect.[35] Today, he is rebuilding the tissue collection in hopes that he can realize his goal to offer men the best possible diagnosis and treatment of prostate cancer.

Tissue of Lies

Susan Molchan, MD, program director for the Alzheimer's Disease Neuroimaging Initiative (ADNI) project at the National Institute on Aging, is passionate about ending the scourge of Alzheimer's disease. She is also resourceful. When she needed a way to publicize and recruit eight hundred people for research on early identification of the disease's memory decline—a rather complex and dry-sounding quest on the surface—she raised the profile of her study by recruiting famed poet Maya Angelou, who has lost friends to the disease, to appear in gripping media narratives and public-service announcements.

But in 2006 Molchan was frustrated, confused, and frankly at her wit's end. Over the years she had amassed 3,200 spinal-fluid samples, collected in a painful process from Alzheimer's patients and invaluable for research that she hoped would allow earlier and better treatments for this dreaded thief of the mind. Molchan had used only about 5 percent of the samples before moving on to other projects, leaving the rest safely stored in NIH freezers. The samples in the freezer had been gleaned over a fifteen-year period from 538 research subjects, and collecting them had cost the government $6.4 million.

Now Molchan and her colleagues needed some of the samples for the new Alzheimer's study, but when she asked her former boss, Dr. Pearson "Trey" Sunderland III, for them, he told her that 95 percent of the samples had been destroyed when storage freezers malfunctioned. Sunderland, chief of the National Institutes of Mental Health (NIMH) Geriatric Psychiatry Branch, could produce no proof of this, however, and he had made contradictory statements to other researchers requesting access, claiming that the donated tissues had been "lost," not thawed.

Where were these samples? It was not an exaggeration to say that the person who controlled them could control the future of Alzheimer's research. As the University of Pennsylvania's Arthur Caplan has summed it up: "The more tissue samples you can collect these days and extract genetic information about risk and benefit, that's the future of drug development around the world."

Molchan's repeated requests for clarification came to naught, and Sunderland's equally confused colleagues couldn't discover the fate of the samples, either, so she turned to the NIH administration.[36] But it, too, could discover nothing.

With millions in taxpayers' dollars at stake, the House Energy and Commerce Committee determined to trace the fate of this fortune in tissues. But at the ensuing two-day congressional hearing to which he was summoned, Sunderland became the first NIH official ever to "take the Fifth." After Sunderland invoked his right not to testify, the startled committee asked twenty-one drug manufacturers to supply information about their transactions with NIH researchers. In this way the committee learned of pharmaceutical-company payments to scores of NIH researchers who had not reported them as required by law.

One of these was Sunderland. An NIH ethics officer had earlier asked him whether he had outside consulting arrangements, and he had replied, "No."[37] Now the NIH was shocked to discover that Sunderland was actually under contract to Pfizer, which had paid him a total of $596,000 in fees, lectures, and travel expenses over the years.

Sunderland gave Pfizer something in return: nearly all the missing tissue samples, accompanied by their clinical data.

Perhaps "gave" is not the right verb. After he bestowed the samples on Pfizer, Sunderland is said to have received $285,000 and definitely was named coinventor of a patent titled "Nucleic Acid Molecules, Polypeptides and Uses Therefor, Including Diagnosis and Treatment of Alzheimer's Disease." He assigned the patent rights to Pfizer, as his contract with them required.

Sunderland was charged with federal conflict-of-interest violations, felonies that carried a five-year prison sentence for willful violations, but he and his lawyers downplayed the accusations, characterizing the conflict as a case of nonreporting of income—simply "paperwork violations." Unimpressed, the House committee called for Sunderland's dismissal. "Will a criminal conviction for conflict of interest be enough to get someone fired from NIH?" asked Representative John Dingell (D-MI).

Apparently not. In the end, Sunderland was allowed to plead guilty to a misdemeanor for which he received two years of probation and four hundred hours of community service at a geriatric psychology service. He also agreed to pay the government $300,000, about half his compensation from Pfizer.

Thus it was that Pfizer, which denies any ethical breaches, acquired samples that cost the government $6.4 million and fifteen years to collect for the bargain-basement price of Sunderland's approximately $600,000 in fees. The samples enabled the refinement of Pfizer's patented Alzheimer's drug Aricept, which is now the top-selling Alzheimer's drug in the world, with $2 billion in sales during 2011 alone.

In the end, the government received nothing for its investment in the embezzled samples. And worst of all, Molchan's quest to characterize and treat Alzheimer's disease at an earlier stage, before irreversible loss set in, has been derailed after taking a backseat to greed.

In 2005 the NIH had adopted ethics regulations that barred all its employees from consulting for outside entities and prohibited their owning stock worth more than $15,000.[38] Many NIH scientists took exception to the new rules, and influential scholar Richard A. Epstein, professor of law at the University of Chicago, wrote, "If the protests sound to you like the howls of a greedy biomedical elite, consider that the NIH's policy is likely to drive qualified physicians and scientists out of the national labs where they're most needed—and slow the pace at which treatments and cures come to market." But his consequentialist argument ignores the chilling effect of greed such as Sunderland's, which is what really threatens the pace of medical innovation. The case of the missing Alzheimer's samples offers the most powerful evidence that the policy is sorely needed and, if anything, overdue. We should never forget this.

Redefining Ownership

Writer James Kunen, himself a lawyer, once observed, "There is no greater example of the power of an adjective to modify a noun than the use of the word 'legal' before the word 'ethics.'" The legal decisions that have defined the ownership of American bodies and body parts amply illustrate Kunen's quip.

A proliferation of biotechnology arrangements between universities, researchers, and private industry has created powerful corporate entities focused upon generating profitable products of research and development. Is there any financial or moral obligation to compensate the tissue donors for contributing the material? And who safeguards the patient's safety, his medical interests, and his financial stake in the biological bounty emanating from his body?

In at least one case, it was the patient himself.

A vigorous debate rages about whether donors should be paid for their tissues, with many insisting that in the service of lofty ideals such as altruism and community, tissues should remain "gifts" from patients. But before his death in 1984, Ted Slavin, a hemophiliac, perceived the value of his own body's products, and, most important, he found a way to exercise utter control over them.

Slavin had been treated in the 1970s with clotting infusions derived from large numbers of human donors, and this imparted a very high concentration of valuable antibodies against hepatitis B to his blood. He knew this because his doctor told him so.

By so alerting Slavin, the doctor fulfilled the fiduciary responsibility that the courts had established in the case of John Moore but that so often remains ignored in such scenarios. Unlike Henrietta Lacks, John Moore, and the presumed-consent donors, the trustworthiness of his doctor allowed Slavin to bypass the courts by negotiating the rights to his valuable blood while he remained in possession of it and therefore in a position of negotiating strength.

Slavin's blood was so valuable because researchers needed a constant supply of B antibodies to develop a diagnostic test for hepatitis B (HBV).

Slavin, a savvy businessman, reacted with alacrity to the news, selling his blood to interested researchers and companies for $6,000 a pint. The blood that had so often triggered health crises that prevented him from working steadily now made him a wealthy man, and Slavin formed a corporation, Essential Biologicals, to market his blood. He went further, recruiting other similarly endowed hemophilia patients with unusual blood profiles to sell their blood as well. In doing so, he triggered a quiet revolution: today nearly two million people sell their blood that harbors unusual properties, although on a smaller scale than Slavin's.

Slavin understood that donating and selling tissues are not mutually exclusive, and he rewrote the rules. While he sold his blood to for-profit corporations, he also gave it away to noncommercial researchers and to fund charities. Slavin worked with research teams, including that of Baruch Blumberg, MD, who perfected the hepatitis B vaccine and tests for liver cancer as well. Blumberg, who won the Nobel Prize for Medicine in 1976 for his work with hepatitis B, recalled, "He very generously donated to us large quantities of his plasma, which we used extensively in our research over the course of many years and have preserved as a form of memorial to this remarkable man."[39]

After the HBV test was perfected, Slavin's blood remained in high demand from reagent manufacturers that produced the tests.

Some argue that patients should not be allowed to sell their blood and other tissues because this would dampen altruism. However, this book has repeatedly questioned the nature of the "altruism" these people seek to protect. I argue that our present system is not based upon altruism at all, but rather upon the exploitation of patients and subjects, including the dead and their loved ones.

Our tissue-market system is based in large part upon deception, as body parts are seized in secret through presumed consent and bodies are impressed into service as research subjects without consent, informed or otherwise—as the PolyHeme trauma study, the ROC studies, and other nonconsensual research demonstrates.

Slavin's actions contradict the binary assumption that tissues must be either sold or given, because markets can coexist with altruism. In fact the two do coexist, but our present system is unethical, abusive, and ridden with medical collateral damage.

Some policymakers share a long-standing concern[40] that allowing erstwhile donors to sell their tissues, including blood, will threaten the public's health by encouraging unsuitable donors to introduce infected blood and tissues to the donor pool. Less than fifty years ago, however, an alternative economy allowed the donor to sell his own blood, and many poor people, college students, and others strapped for cash availed themselves of this income source.

But selling blood was widely discouraged by sociologists and medical experts, and especially by Richard Titmuss's influential 1970 book *The Gift Relationship: From Human Blood to Social Policy.*[41] He theorized that paying blood donors imperiled public health by encouraging the wrong sort of people to donate. The poor, transients, and "Negroes" were those most likely to donate blood for pay, he argued, and they were precisely the persons who were likely to donate unacceptable blood that harbored disease. Titmuss insinuated that these persons were also less likely than well-to-do whites to be truthful about the infectious diseases they might be carrying. Their inferior sense of responsibility and low empathy for the larger community meant that they would donate even knowing that they were transmitting disease risks. These were important concerns in Titmuss's era, which predated the efficient screening of the blood supply for infectious diseases.

Mindful of the dangers Titmuss revealed, the government mandated the labeling of blood as either "volunteer" or "paid," and hospitals and companies predictably shunned the sales of "paid" blood, the demand for which then fell so low that paying people for their blood was discontinued. Today, FDA regulations prohibit paying people to give blood.

Of course, despite the ubiquity of volunteer blood, we have faced blood-safety issues in our own time. A plethora of emerging pathogens such as HIV and HCV as well as the prions that cause Creutzfeldt-Jakob disease (CJD) and other infectious diseases have imperiled the blood supply. Ironically, it was not the thoughtless greed of the lower classes but rather the unbridled altruism of HIV-infected people, many of them gay men, and of the HCV-infected from every walk of life, that introduced viruses into the blood supply. Refined tests for hepatitis, HIV, and many other feared pathogens have reduced the U.S. infection rates from blood dramatically, although the need to protect the blood supply, including the weeding out of unsuitable donors, continues to loom large.

Incidentally, today's continued exclusion of gay men from blood donation seems to have no scientific basis in a society where high concentrations of HIV also exist in other groups. Barring people from donation on the basis of actual risk factors, such as certain diseases, infections, certain forms of drug abuse, and unprotected sex with multiple partners, is more logical than discrimination based on social and sexual bias.

In addition to bans on donations from infected donors, there are still challenges such as the need to devise tests for disease-causing prions held responsible for Creutzfeldt-Jakob disease, the human equivalent of mad-cow disease. The risk of infection now stands at just one in a million transfusions.

Titmuss saw an interesting combination of moral and medical failings in paid, lower-class, and African American donors that made them unworthy to shore up the nation's blood supply. But he never thought to ask whether the financial ambitions of companies that buy and sell the donated blood might encourage these firms to cut safety corners and endanger the public's health.

One can still sell plasma, the clear, palest-yellow, fluid component of blood. To collect it, the donor's blood flows into a machine that separates the plasma from the red blood cells and then pumps the cells back into the bloodstream, in a process called plasmapheresis. Because the plasma expands blood volume and funnels needed water, sodium, and nutrients to all the body's cells, it can save the lives of trauma victims who have suffered shock, burns, or injury. Plasma also contains proteins such as gamma globulin, which are useful for a number of medical conditions. For example, gamma globulin typically contains enough antibodies against diseases such as measles and hepatitis to be effective against them when it is injected into an exposed person. Plasma donors are paid $35–$60 per donation at more than four hundred for-profit plasma collection centers in the United States.

It was improved blood screening, not the paid-donor ban, that kept the blood supply safe. Now the blood-transfusion risk of HIV or HCV infection hovers around one infection in a million. Sadly, though, the remarkable successes in blood screening came too late for some, including an entire generation of hemophiliacs who were infected with HCV and often also acquired HIV.

Moreover, as we have seen, the current corporation-mediated system of tissue harvesting and transplantation, with its unbridled financial rewards and lax oversight, has produced dramatic abuses, as illustrated by Mastromarino's nationwide distribution of cancerous and infected bone and tissues.

By contrast, the patient-enabling models of PXE's Sharon and Patrick Terry and of Ted Slavin are superior both scientifically and ethically. The Terrys' substitution of tissue access for financial payment encourages cooperation that speeds research and has been largely lost with the commercialization of medical research. Furthermore, their model, in which researchers and affected patients share the patent, can temper the drive for profit with the prominent interests of patients whose sacrifice made the gene discovery possible. This introduces a missing element of social justice by rewarding people's sacrifices and correcting the imbalance of power. Such balanced partnerships will also encourage research that will have maximal medical benefits, not just higher sales.

By establishing PXE International and Essential Biologicals, laypersons have introduced the sort of flexibility we will need as we decide how we want to adapt the market for the distribution of blood tissues and organs to become more fair—because make no mistake, a market already exists. The question is, how fair can we make it?

CHAPTER 8

BIOCOLONIALISM

"Discovering" Biological Treasures

License my roving hands, and let them go,
Behind, before, above, between, below.
O my America! my new-found-land,
My kingdom, safeliest when with one man man'd,
My mine of precious stones: my emperie,
How blest am I in this discovering thee!
To enter in these bonds, is to be free;
Then where my hand is set, my seal shall be.

—JOHN DONNE, "ELEGY XIX: TO HIS MISTRESS GOING TO BED"

John Donne's metaphysical paean to discovery, conquest, and exclusive appropriation, excerpted above, was not, of course, written to celebrate patents. Yet his verse does aptly invoke the lust for "discovery," license, appropriation, and, finally, exclusive ownership that excited seventeenth-century explorers, naturalists, and colonial entrepreneurs as well as lovers.

Centuries ago, colonial aggression was fueled by a desire for inanimate resources such as jewels, fuel, and minerals, but it now turns on biological riches, that is, on plants, animals, medicines, and even human capital in the form of genes, tissues, and cell lines. As in Donne's poem, the conquest of another's body serves as a proxy for the conquest of another's land and its riches.

A hunger for these riches, abetted by faith in a type of scientific manifest destiny, is still invoked in the medical arena to justify the literal appropriation of the bodies and tissues of the poor, the marginal, the weak, the subjugated, and the genetically distinct for the Western medical marketplace—and for the plants and animals under their dominion as well. This appropriation and commodification diminish the affected individuals, their communities, and human life itself.

Researchers travel to parts of the world rich in biodiversity to acquire and patent plants with medicinal value. They learn of these plants from native healers and guides who tell them where to gather them and how to use them as medicines.[1] When they return home, these scientists determine the plants' chemical structures, extract their active ingredients, and obtain patents. They do not offer to share credit or profits with the natives who determined the medicinal uses of the plants, and the new patents actually block the organism's use by natives and require the country of origin to pay for access to its own plant medicines.[2]

Environmental activists such as India's Vandana Shiva, PhD, of the International Forum on Globalization, as well as many indigenous advocacy groups, call these exploitative policies "biopiracy" or "biocolonialism" in a parallel of the economic policies that deplete the resources and reinforce the poverty of Third World denizens while enriching their Western guests.

Plant Medicinals

Researchers and pharmaceutical companies have designs on the diverse biological riches of poor countries because much of the biodiversity of the West has vanished, having fallen victim to the shortsighted agricultural behavior of industrialized nations. The United States and Europe have bred crops by selecting for traits that will maximize market performance such as hardiness, disease resistance, long shelf life, and even for shapes that ease stacking and storage, such as square tomatoes and watermelons. As huge farms crowd small ones out of business and giant supermarket firms dominate the market, botanical conformity sells, leaving little room for more exotic varieties of fruits and vegetables that are harder to stock and store. Reliance upon relatively few strains of each agricultural product has sapped Western genetic diversity. Ninety percent of all the vegetable varieties ever distributed by U.S. seed houses during the twentieth century are now extinct, and fully half of Europe's domestic animal species have become extinct over the past century as well.[3] For diversity, scientists must look to the developing world.

They have not been disappointed. Ethiopia alone is home to a rich diversity of more than 6,500 plant species, more than 800 of which are used as medicinals. Four of every five Ethiopians rely on traditional medicines from plants that are harvested from the wild.[4] Brazil is the world's most biodiverse country, home to one of every five animals, plants, and microorganisms on earth and to one of the highest densities of indigenous human communities as well.

Many familiar medications are derived from plants that were first studied or cultivated by people in the developing world or in marginalized, genetically distinct enclaves of Western nations. Aspirin was distilled from willow bark and meadowsweet, and it was used widely for pain relief by ancient peoples including those in Egypt, Rome, Southeast Asia, and Sumer, where a four-thousand-year-old stone tablet mentions it as a remedy. It was equally popular among Native Americans and Bronze Age Scots.[5] In 1853, chemist Charles Gerhardt distilled acetyl-salicylic acid from it, which the German drug firm Bayer tested and marketed as a less-irritating replacement for standard common painkillers in 1897.

The rosy periwinkle (*Catharanthus roseus*) originated in Madagascar and has long been used in Togo, Botswana, Uganda, and other parts of Africa as a diabetic medication that lowers blood sugar and that also treats malaria, dengue fever, dysentery, diarrhea, and cancer. Today, the medicinal alkaloids vincristine and vinblastine have been extracted from it and are in wide use as a cancer therapy as well as in a myriad of Western prescription medicines for neurological disorders.[6]

According to legend, the antimalarial drug quinine was derived from *Cinchona pubescens* when Ecuadorean physician Juan de Vega used the native Quichua remedy "quina bark" on the Countess of Chinchón, who had contracted malaria. English pharmacy worker Robert Talbor popularized the treatment in the late 1660s, and by the nineteenth century the Dutch had set up cinchona plantations in Java from which they cornered the market in quinine as a treatment against malaria. Pseudoephedrine is derived from the *ephedra* species, and digitalis from the purple foxglove, *Digitalis purpurea*.

Senna alexandrina, a shrub native to Arabia, yields senna, a commonly used laxative, and *Rauwolfia serpentina*, named after the famous sixteenth-century German physician-explorer Leonhart Rauwolf, yields reserpine, which is used both for hypertension and as an antipsychotic. The opium poppy (*Papaver somniferum*) is the source of the potent pain-killer morphine, whose popularity spread throughout Europe in 1546 when a French naturalist named Pierre Belon drew European attention to the widespread opium use among Turks. Today, the UN estimates that such drugs derived from plants are worth $16 billion.

The intellectual property of the Third World included medical techniques as well, as when Cotton Mather's slave Onesimus instructed him in the method of smallpox prevention through the African practice of inserting a bit of matter from an infected person into an incision. This procedure induced mild illness, fever, and permanent immunity. Mather in turn told Dr. Zabdiel Boylston, who proved that the technique worked during the Boston smallpox epidemic of 1721, and who was praised at home and abroad as the originator of smallpox variolation. Onesimus's name, and the role of the African healers, was forgotten.

Through the 1950s, major pharmaceutical companies still sold many plant-based medicines in tablet, liquid, and ointment form, and plants continue to provide the basis for 40 percent of the U.S. medicines in use today.

For all its storied biological diversity, Brazil, like most developing nations, has never patented a new drug. Its cultural heritage does not include monopolistic claims on living things for profit,[7] and it lacks the technological basis for turning its biological diversity into pharmaceuticals.

But the West has mastered that technology. According to the World Intellectual Property Organization (WIPO), the growth of patents worldwide increased by 5 percent a year between 1990 and 2000. Biotechnology patents rose even more quickly, at triple this rate within the United States and by 10 percent in Europe during the same period. But the growth of these biotech patents is "highly concentrated," because 74 percent are granted to the United States, Europe, Japan, South Korea, and China.[8] In response to the 1980 Chakrabarty decision, nations such as Brazil had passed laws to protect their traditional knowledge and natural resources by limiting access to their flora,[9] but researchers often flout such laws.

A concentration of biotechnology expertise and a lust for biotech patents drive industrialized nations, while a proliferation of biological resources and a technology vacuum characterize most developing countries. This variance has set these nations on a collision course that is typified by a hallucinogenic plant that has been coveted by everyone from scientists to Sting.

Ayahuasca

That plant is ayahuasca, also called yagé by the indigenous people of the Amazon who revere it and by William S. Burroughs and Allen Ginsberg, who immortalized it in *The Yage Letters*.[10] Celebrities from Paul Simon to Tori Amos to Sting have embraced ayahuasca publicly, describing their experiences with the hallucinogenic medicinal potion in countries such as Brazil, where its possession and use are perfectly legal. For indigenous peoples, it is more than a plant: one of its names, "Quechua," means "vine of the soul," or "vine of the dead,"[11] and they believe yagé possesses a living spirit.

But Ginsberg and Sting were only some of the more recent Westerners to marvel at ayahuasca. For centuries, journals and travelogues have documented a Western fascination with the drug that promises health and heaven, usually preceded by a sojourn in the depths of a psychological hell.[12]

Naturalists and anthropologists detailed the hallucinations or "visions" and cures that indigenous people ascribe to the ayahuasca plant, which scientists call *Banisteriopsis caapi*.[13] Ayahuasca is prepared by indigenous herbalists in a variety of complex recipes incorporating other psychoactive plants that enhance the plant's powerful hallucinogen, the alkaloid N,N-dimethyltrypamine (DMT). It is drunk under the direction of shamans who guide the user's experience.

Although ayahuasca has spawned a cottage industry in psychedelic tourism, most seekers are not chasing a high. Pilgrims from North America and Europe have claimed cures for everything from depression to colon cancer to cocaine addiction, and besides the treatment of physical and mental illness, the potion is key to shamanic rites of self-discovery. Chilean novelist Isabel Allende, for example, credited it with shattering her writer's block.

Nearly all the contemporary medical pilgrims claim to have found relief, just like the Westerners who documented the healing power of ayahuasca throughout the ages. On what basis, then, did American scientist Loren Miller claim to have discovered ayahuasca, and patent it as a "new" plant?

When Miller visited Brazil in 1974, an Ecuadorean tribal leader gave him a sample of an ayahuasca plant.[14] Miller hoped that a patent on the plant would enable his company, International Plant Medicine Corporation, to strike a deal with a pharmaceutical firm for the production of medicines. In 1981, he duly applied for a patent on the plant, renaming it Da Vine. Miller argued that his sample was a novel variety and thus patent-eligible because its flower color and markings differed from other known ayahuasca plants.

The USPTO granted Miller a patent that gave him the exclusive rights to breed and distribute ayahuasca. Miller had not shared these intentions with the healer who gave him the plant, and it was ten years before the Amazonians learned that their sacred plant was now under the exclusive control of a Westerner whose rights to it were protected by U.S. patent law.

For years, representatives from various indigenous groups asked Miller to surrender the patent, but he simply ignored them, and after the WTO's Trade-Related Aspects of Intellectual Property Rights (TRIPS) agreement became effective in 1995,[15] Miller did not need to answer to Amazonians.

TRIPS is an agreement among WTO nations that protects many aspects of intellectual property, from patents on computer software to pharmaceutical patents, and even trade names. TRIPS binds developing nations, even those without laws governing patents, as well as industrialized ones. It also validates and enforces patent monopolies by setting up the WTO as the arbitrator of disputes and by providing legal and financial penalties for breaches of intellectual property.

TRIPS standardized the patent's period of unfettered profitability at twenty years, the same period granted by the United States. These patents give their holders the right to prevent third parties from selling, distributing, importing, or using patented property or production techniques without the express permission of the patent holder.

Vandana Shiva of the International Forum on Globalization writes that U.S., Japanese, and European corporations joined to design

TRIPS,[16] which validates the rights of outsiders such as Miller who seize and patent the plants, animals, and processes of the developing world. It does not provide benefits to developing nations, because patenting is not part of the culture and practices of such technologically limited countries. Poor countries face immediate challenges to survival that tend to make blocking questionable patent claims a low priority. In short, the developing world is ill-equipped to defend its intellectual property and resources and is now bound to respect Western monopolies on that very property.

TRIPS also makes it harder for developing countries to surmount the hurdle of the patents on expensive Western pharmaceuticals that they need. Before 1996, developing countries such as Brazil and Ecuador had the option of legally opposing patents by exercising various march-in powers. This usually meant that they could acquire needed medications by means of compulsory licenses that give the right to produce a patented drug more cheaply to others. Usually the patent holder receives some compensation, but the country still realizes enormous savings. Or poor countries could rely upon cheaper generic versions. Or, as India did, a nation could simply ignore the patent and allow its own firms to reverse-engineer the needed drugs and then produce them at attainable prices. But TRIPS forced developing countries to honor foreign patents even if doing so mandates prohibitive prices for desperately needed medications. (See "Earlier Adoption," p. 272.)

In response to complaints from the developing world, the WTO agreed to extend its deadline for their TRIPS compliance until 2016. In November 2001, the WTO mounted a conference in Doha, Qatar, to allow poorer countries' input. The Doha Declaration on the TRIPS Agreement and Public Health (Doha) reaffirms each nation's right to evade patents during a public-health emergency by issuing compulsory licenses. But the conference's findings and requests have proved unpopular with more-affluent nations, and by December 2009, the deadline for acceptance, less than a third of member nations had signed it: the United States was not among them, and negotiations continue.[17]

The United States does, however, support the TRIPS obligation to permit the patenting of biological "inventions." These inventions are not limited to microbiological products of technology, and they also

Earlier Adoption
Under TRIPS, developing countries are being asked to adopt strong patent protection at much lower income levels than developed countries do.

	Year of Adoption	GDP per Capita (1995 U.S. dollars)
OECD Adopters		
Japan	1976	24,043
Switzerland	1977	36,965
Italy	1978	13,465
Netherlands	1978	20,881
Sweden	1978	21,896
Canada	1983	16,296
Denmark	1983	28,010
Austria	1987	25,099
Spain	1992	14,430
Greece	1992	10,897
Norway	1992	30,389
Recent Adopters		
China	1992–93	424
Brazil	1996	4,482
Argentina	2000	8,100
Uruguay	2001	6,208
Guatemala	Future	1,545
Egypt	Future	1,191
Pakistan	Future	508
India	Future	450
Malawi	Future	156

Source: Ianjouw, Jean, 2002, Intellectual Property and the Availability of Pharmaceuticals in Poor Countries, CGD Working Paper No. 5 (Washington: Center for Global Development).
Note: China GOP is for 1992. For countries adopting after 1999, the GOP per capita figure is for 1999.

include natural plants that have been used, cultivated, and revered by native peoples for millennia.[18]

Dr. Bernard Pécoul of Doctors Without Borders criticized Doha's restriction of compulsory licensing to national emergencies or other urgent situations, asking, "In Africa, pneumonia is the second biggest killer after HIV/AIDS. Will countries declare pneumonia a national emergency? It is hard to imagine. If they do, will they also declare emergencies for diarrheal diseases?"[19]

In 1999, the Center for International Environmental Law (CIEL) challenged Miller's Da Vine patent on behalf of four hundred groups of indigenous Amazonians.[20] CIEL asked the USPTO to revoke Miller's application because of the impropriety of ownership by U.S. citizens of a plant that has long been sacred to Amazonians. CIEL also argued that the plant's long use by Amazonians exempted it from patent eligibility under the provisions of TRIPS, especially in view of the power imbalance. CIEL's Rodolfo Asar declared, "Our goal is to have the ayahuasca patent annulled, and to teach all international biopirates a lesson."

The USPTO did reverse approval of Miller's patent, but not because of concern over the Amazonians' rights. Instead, the patent was revoked on the grounds that it was not novel.

Of course, Da Vine was not new: centuries of Western lore and shamans in eight countries had all paid testament to the long history of ayahuasca's medical and cultural use. The USPTO ignored this history, however, and instead based its reversal on the fact that a single specimen like Miller's had been on display at Chicago's Field Museum the year before he applied for a patent. The decision referenced only the narrow context of U.S. experience, giving centuries of Third World experience short shrift.

But if a single display could invalidate the patent, how did Miller obtain it in the first place? Because in determining whether an invention is new, Section 102(a) of the Patent Act looks for references to "prior inventions, patents, patent applications, and publications discussing prior inventions."[21] These include prior knowledge of the invention by others in the United States; prior use of the invention in the United States; prior patent of the invention in any country; and the printed publication of the invention in any country.[22]

Within U.S. borders, simply using an invention is enough to render it ineligible for a patent, which is why displaying the plant in a Chicago museum rang the patent's death knell. But using the invention abroad doesn't preclude the USPTO from issuing a patent unless the foreign use is published and available for anyone to find.[23] This means that the USPTO will grant a patent for an "invention" such as ayahuasca that is already known and in wide use in its own country, such as in Peru, Brazil, or India.

This law was defensible a century ago because it reflected a time when a U.S. citizen would not necessarily know that something he wished to patent was already in common use abroad. One might question whether this was the case with a naturalist who ventured abroad specifically in search of medically useful plants, but ignorance of foreign use was at least theoretically possible.

Today's digitized global telecommunications, air travel, pervasive education, and widespread knowledge of other cultures, however, rob this rationale of any credibility, especially for bioprospectors who travel abroad specifically in order to find patentable plants. Today, prior use of foreign inventions is easily discovered and widely examined by U.S. researchers, leaving little reason to excuse such appropriations.

CIEL complained that after the repeal, the indigenous groups it represents were specifically barred from participating in further discussions of the patent, but that the USPTO repeatedly allowed Miller to engage the patent office in appeals. Miller renewed the application with improvements and further arguments, and in 2001 the USPTO reversed its decision, confirming his patent on ayahuasca/Da Vine and allowing it to stand for another two years.

For his part, Miller argues that he never sold or profited from ayahuasca or from its patent: "This patent has been sitting harmlessly in a drawer gathering dust, and it does not affect the natives' use of their plants in any way, shape or form."[24]

But the patent didn't lie fallow because of any belated sensitivity on Miller's part. The argument he made to the USPTO precluded him from exploiting the patent, because Miller's appeal narrowly covered only the particular plant he owned and its cuttings, not the wider varieties of ayahuasca. His patent expired on June 17, 2003.

"The Ayahuasca case shows the total disrespect of the whites' world towards our beliefs and culture," responded Chief Darcy Marubo, of the Coordination of Indigenous Organizations in the Brazilian Amazon (COAIB).

The ayahuasca experience has been repeated over and over in different countries but with similar results. For example, neem, a semitropical tree native to the East Indian region, has been known throughout much of Asia and Africa for thousands of years as a living pharmacy. This is why at least twenty languages have names for it, including Urdu, Sanskrit, Vietnamese, Tamil, Marathi, and English. Perhaps most fitting is its Swahili name, "mwarubaini," or "the tree of forty," in reference to the forty diseases it is known to treat.

Although neem has long been inseparable from Indian healing traditions and culture, the European Patent Office (ERO) granted the U.S. firm W. R. Grace a patent on neem in 1994, for an antifungal derived from the plant—over the objections of the Indian government, which appealed, citing more than twenty centuries of domestic use for that and other purposes. India prevailed and the ERO ruled against W. R. Grace, but the company appealed this decision on the basis that no "prior art" had ever been published in a scientific journal. The ERO was unimpressed and revoked the neem patent on March 5, 2005.[25] Westerners have also obtained patents on medicinal plant extracts that others, such as Pacific Islanders, had discovered, processed, and used for millennia: these include kava, taro root, and the canarium nut.

This bioprospecting shows disregard for the cultural significance of living things in marginalized countries. "In South Pacific cultures a plant is a living ancestor—and even a drop of human blood retains its life spirit after it has been collected for medical research or synthesized and specific DNA qualities isolated," explains A. H. Zakri, director of the United Nations University's Institute of Advanced Studies. "Plants and animals are not seen as mere physical or biological entities but also as embodiments of ancestral spirits," adds Steven Ratuva of Fiji, a senior fellow at the University of the South Pacific.

"Researchers are harvesting and patenting the Pacific region's genetic resources by simply gathering and taking ownership over almost everything in their path," protests Aroha Mead, senior lecturer at Victoria University in Wellington, New Zealand, whose book *Pacific Genes and Life Patents* decries the inequity of intellectual-property protections supported by the WTO. To do so, these researchers routinely dismiss spiritual and cultural concerns of South Pacific Islanders, for whom the appropriation and patenting of plants violate values of "pono" and "tika," meaning to act virtuously or appropriately, because in their philosophy everyone is meant to share benefits from the use of plants.

Some countries, such as Tanzania, have sought to protect their resources, and its national institutions are involved in carefully monitored research management with other countries. Tanzania's ten thousand plant species, for example, are protected by a facility that "can collaborate with a technologically developed institution or country through mutual research agreement in short- and long-term programs." Tanzanian scientists collect and export the materials for testing by the Western collaborator, but only after a research agreement spells out the terms under which any discovery's benefits are to be shared by Tanzania and its guests.[26]

For example, one such 2006 cooperative research agreement from Muhimbili University of Health and Allied Sciences in Dar es Salaam requires that the university researchers share in any intellectual property such as copyrights and patents emanating from a partnership with an external company or university. It specifies the sharing of costs, the distribution of income, and the ability of each party to license and assign rights. The agreement even dictates how disputes will be settled should they arise, noting that the laws of Tanzania will govern the validity and enforcement of the agreement and that any changes must be agreed upon by both parties.[27]

Seeds of Change

A quarter million homes collapsed in the wake of the hurricane that hit Haiti in January 2010, leaving a million people homeless. The lives of three million Haitians would never be the same. Already the poorest country in the Western Hemisphere, Haiti endured the closing of its ports and airport, the collapse of communication, education, banking, and, worst of all, its already-enfeebled medical and agricultural systems. Even the morgues filled quickly as thousands of bodies were piled in the streets and inadequate medical supplies and food rations left the starving survivors with unbound wounds.

Sadly, hunger is no new development in Haiti. Even before the hurricanes had devastated fields and destroyed the roads to markets, and even before local farms had succumbed to competition from cheap foreign food and free food aid, 2.4 million Haitians, a quarter of the country, did not have enough to eat.

Understanding that two of every three Haitians depend upon farming,[28] the Monsanto Company of Creve Coeur, Missouri, announced in April that it was donating 475 tons of vegetable seeds—$4 million worth—to earthquake-devastated Haitian farmers.[29] This fit the mission stated on Monsanto's website: "We help farmers grow yield sustainably so they can be successful, produce healthier foods while also reducing agriculture's impact on our environment."[30]

The gift required some negotiating. The Haitian minister of agriculture rejected Monsanto's original offer of Roundup Ready genetically modified organism (GMO) seeds, explaining that Haiti has no law to regulate GMOs.

The Haitian government gratefully accepted hybrid seed instead, and among Haitian farmers, the announcement was met with a pledge. Chavannes Jean-Baptiste, a farmer and the founder of the Peasant Movement of Papay (MPP), vowed to burn the Monsanto seed as "a very strong attack on small agriculture, on farmers, on biodiversity, on Creole seeds."[31] On June 4, 2010, World Environment Day, ten thousand Haitian peasant farmers marched to protest Monsanto's seed donation and symbolically burned a mound of the seed, exhorting their countrymen to do the same.

These Haitian farmers fear that a gift of Monsanto hybrid seeds is a Trojan horse fated to undermine the development of local seed stocks and to create dependence on imported seeds. As this chapter will explain, this is a valid concern, but the seed is dangerous in other, more direct, ways. They are infused with extremely toxic pesticides such as Maxim XO and Thiram,[32] a class of toxin so hazardous that the EPA requires a prominent warning label and special protective clothing. These chemicals are banned from U.S. home sales for fear that noncommercial users will not have this gear,[33] yet Monsanto offered no warnings or protective clothing in its emails describing the seeds to Haiti's Ministry of Agriculture staff.[34]

Neither is "gift" the operative noun, since as Monsanto admits, although the company is donating the seed free to the Haitian government, the farmers are required to pay for the seed, albeit at reduced prices, "to avoid flooding the local economy with free goods."[35] Thus, despite the fact that the seeds are described by the company, the Haitian government, and the news media as "donated" and as a "gift," neither the Haitian government nor Monsanto is the benefactor it seems.

In brief, the seed is regarded as a poisoned kiss by advocacy organizations that have chronicled the relationship between Monsanto and farmers in the developing world.

From Colombia to India to South Africa, Monsanto has adopted a scorched-earth policy toward weed killing. It engineered its Roundup Ready seeds to be resistant to its ultrapowerful patented herbicide and pesticide Roundup (glyphosate). The company sells both the seed and the pesticide to farmers, who are instructed to douse literally everything in their fields with Roundup: only the treated seed will survive. Farmers are told that the yield will be much greater with less effort because Roundup seeds allow them to dispense with tilling the soil and applying pesticide strategically.

Farmers are not initially warned that second-generation seeds are rendered sterile through the use of patented terminator-seed technology, so that farmers must buy seed anew at the start of every season instead of saving portions of the harvest to seed the next year's crop. This leaves them with extra expenses for vast quantities of pesticide and perennial purchases of seed. Nor are agricultural workers warned that the seed thrives only in well-irrigated areas, although water is scarce and expensive in many of the regions where farmers eke out a hardscrabble existence from the exhausted land.

Hybrid seeds such as those distributed to Haiti are not sterile, but they yield such scanty, inferior, unpredictable growth that Monsanto allows, "When farmers choose to start planting hybrids, they usually also make the decision to begin purchasing new seeds each year because they want the quality hybrid."

Monsanto characterizes its biotechnological mission as feeding the planet by maximizing yield. But each seed feature, such as the utter dependence on the profligate use of a patented pesticide and the terminator-seed technology that requires new seed purchases every season, is carefully engineered to maximize Monsanto's profit and to encourage a dependency upon its products. So is Monsanto's especially broad patent, which allows it to sue farmers who "use" its seed without paying for it.

The latter group consists not of sticky-fingered seed-store customers but rather of hapless farmers who have been sued by Monsanto for patent infringement when the wind blew its patented seeds onto their fields. The company investigates about five hundred farmers a year, and by 2007 it had filed 112 lawsuits in the United States alone for alleged contract violations on its GMO patents.[36] These involved 372 farmers in twenty-seven different states from whom the company won at least $21.5 million in judgments.[37]

In November 2009, Monsanto also sued four Ontario farmers for saving and replanting its Roundup Ready soybean seed. The courts ruled that farmers must pay Monsanto their profits and court costs of $9,000 to $63,000 per person. The farmers were placed on Monsanto's Orwellian "Unauthorized Grower List" and denied all access to the company's current and future technologies—forever.[38] This is no small penalty, considering that Monsanto is the largest seed purveyor in the world[39] and is constantly acquiring smaller companies. Syngenta, DuPont, Bayer, and Monsanto together control more than half of the world's seeds.[40]

Vandana Shiva declares, "Every seed that is in the market in cotton [for example] is tied to one company or another licensed and controlled by Monsanto." This is handwriting on the wall for the United States, where 90 percent of soybean seed is now genetically modified and patented Roundup Ready. On the other hand, the European Patent Office has proved far more cautious, invalidating Monsanto's EP0301749 patent that covered all genetically modified soybeans in 2007.

There are health costs as well. In Colombia, farmers and human rights organizations charged that the highly toxic Roundup has destroyed food crops, fouled water sources, and promoted birth defects and cancers. It requires a more intensive, more expensive farming effort using large amounts of hard-to-procure water and leading to higher food prices, lower crop yields, rising farms costs, and more pollution of the land and water.

David Ehrenfeld, professor of biology at Rutgers University, observes that "genetic engineering is often justified as a human technology, one that feeds more people with better food. Nothing could be further from the truth. With very few exceptions, the whole point of genetic engineering is to increase sales of chemicals and bio-engineered products to dependent farmers."[41]

The costs do not stop there. Predictably, pesticide-resistant super weeds have arisen as a result of the overuse of Monsanto's glyphosate, a parallel to the antibiotic resistance that has been fed by indiscriminate antibiotic use.[42] In his *New York Times* blog, Michael Pollan points out that the rise of Roundup-resistant weeds was predicted by the Union of Concerned Scientists and by Marion Nestle in her 2003 book *Safe*

Food: The Politics of Food Safety, but Monsanto dismissed the predictions as "hypothetical."[43] Today, resistant weed species are quite real and can be found in at least twenty-two states, infesting millions of acres of soybeans, cotton, and corn. Resistance forces farmers to add other highly toxic pesticides into the Roundup regimen, creating a witches' brew of toxic substances and herbicides. Some allege that these exposures heighten the risk of non-Hodgkin's lymphoma and other serious health problems for consumers as well as for farm workers.

Monsanto denies the Hodgkin's link, but it is worth noting that Biotest Laboratories and Craven Labs, the laboratories it used for glyphosate testing, were charged with fraud by the EPA. Three Craven employees were indicted on twenty felony counts, and its owner was sentenced to five years in prison and a $50,000 fine. Craven Labs itself was fined $15.5 million, while Japanese researchers who examined its data on Monsanto products "found clearly intentional misinterpretation" of data.[44]

In June 2011, a report by the international nonprofit scientists' group Earth Open Source charged that glyphosate, the active ingredient in Monsanto's Roundup, causes birth defects in the embryos of laboratory animals, suggesting the possibility that it does so in humans as well. The report, which analyzed a large body of existing data, further suggests that regulators with the European Commission have known since 2002 that glyphosate causes these developmental malformations; but the European Commission disagrees, and has approved the pesticide's use through the next decade.[45]

These health concerns seem not to have stemmed glyphosate use. In 2011, the EPA released its Pesticide Industry Sales and Usage Report for 2006–7, which estimates that 180 million pounds of glyphosate were used by the domestic agricultural market alone.

Farmers in Haiti and in much of the developing world share a concern that Monsanto is exploiting a natural crisis to create a manufactured one. To fully understand why, we must consider the deadly experience of India with Monsanto's patent-heavy agriculture.

Rivulets slowly trace through the dust powdering Krisnabhai Tekham's cinnamon face as she quietly recounts the last hours of her husband, Dalit Tekham. "He came home from the fields, and he collapsed. His mouth was smelling of pesticides, so we put him on a cart and took him to the hospital in town. But he died on the way." Today, Dalit lies two miles from their home beneath a lonely clearing, his grave marked only by heaps of black stones. He leaves behind Krisna-bhai, his thirty-eight-year-old widow; their small daughter; and his aged father-in-law, as well as a farm whose deed has been signed over to moneylenders. Krisnabhai says not a word about herself, but saddled with debts she cannot pay, she soon will have to leave her home and farm and make her way in the world without any means of support.

In the Vidarbha region of central India, located within Maharash-tra, India's second-most-populous state, Dalit was one of 1,300 Vidarbha cotton farmers who committed suicide in 2006 alone, and one of 32,000 farmers who committed suicide in Maharashtra. In the decade between 1993 and 2003, 1,000,248 Indians have committed suicide. Dalit's trag-edy is typical, because the suicides are overwhelmingly triggered by debt, sometimes less than $214, and the means is often pesticide inges-tion. Some districts saw a suicide every eight hours, half of whom were between twenty and forty-five years old.[46]

Initially, the Indian government denied the high numbers of farmer suicides, but gradually the numerous reports convinced the government that farmers in India were imperiled and succumbing to anxiety and despair in staggeringly high numbers.[47] Government statistics now doc-ument that between 2002 and 2006, at least 17,500 farmers killed them-selves every year.[48]

For example, according to the National Crime Records Bureau (NCRB), the state of Maharashtra's 4,453 farmer suicides accounted for over a quarter of the 17,060 Indian suicides in 2006. NCRB documented the total since 1997 as 199,132. Another NCRB study found that farm suicides increased since 2001, but the number of farmers has fallen as thousands flee their ancestral lands and agrarian traditions.[49] At least 17,368 Indian farmers killed themselves in 2009, an increase of 1,172 over the 2008 count of 16,196.[50]

Between 1997 and 2003, the first seven years during which the increase in Indian farmers' suicides was documented, there were 113,872 farm suicides, an average of 16,267 a year. Over the next six years, 102,628 farmers took their lives—an average of 17,105 a year. Therefore an aver-age of forty-seven farmers killed themselves each day between 2004 and 2009: about one farmer every thirty minutes.[51]

Economist K. Nagaraj, who has written the most extensively detailed analysis of Indian farm suicides, told *The Hindu* newspaper, "That these numbers are rising even as the farmer population shrinks, confirms the agrarian crisis is still burning."

Many blame Monsanto.

The land planted by Vidarbha's cotton farmers is dry, exhausted, and haunted by pests and disease such as the Lal Rog fungus that spreads the color of blood over affected cotton fields. On occasion, the parched earth gives way to unpredictable floods that destroy crops and lives. Even worse, the price of cotton is falling, so after their endless days in the fields combating pests and drought, Vidarbha farmers earn little even in good years.[52] The government provides little in the way of technical support, and farmers see their yields and income plummeting as their debts to the bank balloon. "Almost half of all Agriculture Research Officer positions are vacant," observes Vandana Shiva. "Even those who are employed are virtually invisible: staff have neither the funds nor the willingness to travel to the fields[,] leaving farmers to the mercy of aggressive marketing by seed companies, moneylenders and with zero advice on pests, disease or new farm techniques."[53]

Many can no longer obtain bank loans and must turn to moneylenders, who may give them cash for the seed pesticide they need but only in return for their farm deeds.

Into this natural disaster stepped Monsanto. In a 1970 partnership with the Indian government and international aid organizations, the company first encouraged farmers to use its patented hybrid seed technologies that promise larger yields. But most of the farmers are illiterate and could not read the warning that the new seeds require special chemical fertilizers, large volumes of pesticides, and irrigated lands. Without these, the yield is less than before. Farmers were also not warned that the hybrids yield poor-quality seed.

More recently, Monsanto introduced genetically modified cotton seeds, such as Roundup Ready cotton. Flashy advertisements using movie stars and even Hindu gods promise immense yields, immunity to disease and pests, and great wealth. Monsanto websites and television advertisements feature testimonials from farmers who tell how profits enabled them to build homes, buy trucks, and generally prosper. The seeds are sold not under the name Monsanto but the names of well-known Indian seed companies, and they use the patented terminator-seed technology, so farmers must buy them anew each year.

Vandana Shiva explains: "That innocent farmer is grabbed by the agent who says, 'Here is a miracle seed that is going to double your money. Put your thumbprint here.'" The miracle seed is Monsanto's pest-resistant BT cotton, which was planted in a mere 0.4 percent of Vidarbha farms in 2002–3 but rose to make up 15 percent in 2005–6.[54] "Soon the farmer will have to take out loans for fertilizer pesticides and for water because less than 3 percent of cotton fields are irrigated." They must now buy seed every season, because, Shiva adds, "Saving the seed is now an intellectual-property crime and seed exchange is treated as theft." (See "Monsanto's Rapid Growth," p. 284.)

Despite a huge investment in Monsanto fertilizer pesticides and water, farmers tend to end up with lower yields and greater expenses and will end up defaulting on their debts to the bank. Then, when banks will no longer lend to them, they will go into debt to the village money-lenders. Of 3.2 million Indian cotton farmers, 2.8 million have already defaulted on their loans, which typically means losing the deeds to their farms. Blacklisted by the banks and moneylenders, penniless, and without land or any means to feed their families, many farmers resort to suicide by pesticide.

Monsanto has replied to these accusations with a statement that reads in part: "While some may suggest that BT cotton is to blame, the fact is that there are multiple social, economic and environmental factors that make agriculture challenging in India."[55]

Despite the outrage by numerous groups such as the International Forum on Globalization, Monsanto has persisted by eliminating market competition and farmer choice. Monsanto also controls the scientific image of its GMO seeds by ensuring that only data from studies it approves are published. In order to buy its seed, every end-user must sign the same type of take-it-or-leave-it agreement that is required to use computer software. This applies not only to customers who are scientists but also to small farmers who want to compare, for example, the output from two types of seeds or who want to see how well the seed fares in a low-water environment such as Vidarbha's.

Although companies have the right to impose end-user agreements that prevent customers from reverse-engineering or taking other steps

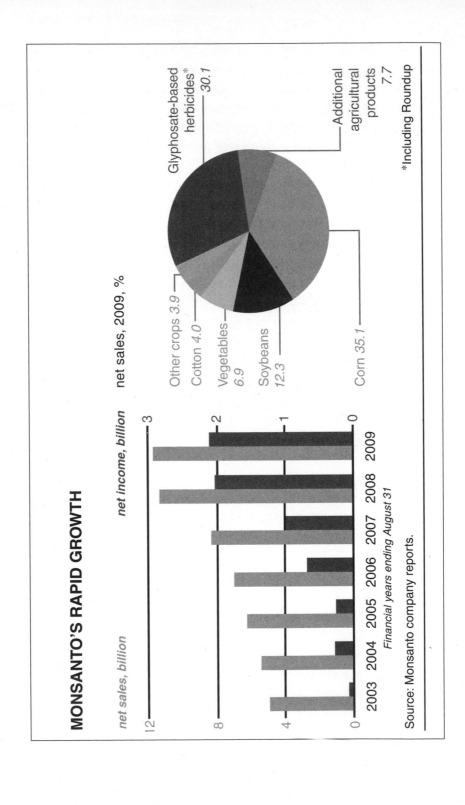

MONSANTO'S RAPID GROWTH

net sales, billion   *net income, billion*

net sales, 2009, %

Glyphosate-based
herbicides*
30.1

Additional
agricultural
products
7.7

Other crops *3.9*

Cotton *4.0*

Vegetables
6.9

Soybeans
12.3

Corn *35.1*

*Including Roundup

12

8

4

0

3

2

1

0

2003 2004 2005 2006 2007 2008 2009

Financial years ending August 31

Source: Monsanto company reports.

that violate intellectual property, Pioneer, Syngenta, and Monsanto include clauses that preclude such "research" to see whether seeds intended for use with highly toxic pesticides lead to unintended environmental side effects. If customers do so, they can be sued.

Amazingly, this means that if you want to study and publish independent research on Monsanto's seed, you must apply to the company first. Nelson J. Shields, an entomologist at Cornell University, complained to the EPA that "selective denials and permissions [are] based on industry perceptions of how 'friendly' or 'hostile' a particular scientist may be toward [the company's] technology."[56]

As with the pharmaceutical industry's intensive lobbying, described in Chapter 2, Monsanto has adopted the revolving-door model of lobbying, wherein officers of the company alternate roles as lobbyists with government regulatory positions. Some continuously rotate through these roles, ensuring that the government takes Monsanto's interests to heart. For example, before being named deputy administrator of the EPA in 2001, Linda Fisher spent a decade as a vice president for governmental affairs at Monsanto.[57] Today she is the vice president of safety, health, and environment and chief sustainability officer of DuPont.[58]

Animal Issues

Plants are not the only target of this Third World patent gold rush. Medically important animals have also been acquired and patented by Westerners with little regard for the animals' significance to the people who have long studied, cultivated, and used them.

New Zealand's AgResearch agency experimental facility was the setting in 2000 for genetic-engineering research with Maori cattle and human cells after obtaining approval from New Zealand's Environmental Risk Management Authority.[59] In a five-year trial, the team of Phil L'Huillier sought to produce therapeutic proteins from cows and introduced human cells into bovine embryos in hopes of producing human-cow chimeras. They hoped that the resulting organisms' milk would express the protein myelin, which is key to nervous-system transmission. Multiple sclerosis, a nervous-system disease, results from the destruction of myelin, and Canavan's disease, discussed in

Chapter 5, also results in demyelinizaton. L'Huillier theorized that drinking milk from the myelin-generating cows might provide a harmless alternative target for the myelin-destroying factors of the affected patients.[60]

This overture was followed by others, including the creation of bovine animal–human hybrids by British scientists at Newcastle upon Tyne who sought a source of plentiful stem cells for the possible treatment of Parkinson's and motor neuron disease. With the permission of Britain's Human Fertilisation and Embryology Authority and over the objection of Catholic bishops, Lyle Armstrong and his team inserted human DNA into cow's eggs whose contents had been evacuated. Then each egg was given a Frankensteinian electric shock, which induced it to develop into an embryo that was more than 99 percent human. The scientists claim that they used cow's eggs because of a scarcity of human eggs.[61]

Back in New Zealand, L'Huillier's project horrified the local Maori, who consider themselves caretakers of the land and animals at the AgResearch site. In their philosophy, each living thing is characterized by its own "whakapapa"—a direct genealogical line from the gods to its current incarnation. Blending human and animal cells disrupts that heritage and the natural order. "Is it animan or manimal?" one Maori wondered. Yet the Maoris' protests that such research creates a spiritual imbalance in the community of men and animals were ignored by researchers.

Brazilian diplomat Henrique Moraes also described the case of a poisonous Amazonian giant leaf frog, *Phyllomedusa bicolour*,[62] that was used by more than ten indigenous communities in the state of Acre, within one of the remotest corners of the rain forest. Anthropologists and writers who visited the rain forest described how the Matses and Mayoruna tribes used the frog's poison to burn their skins and explained that they did so in order to dull pain and protect against disease when they went hunting. Scientists in Europe and in the United States who read these accounts have collected the frogs, procured its toxins, and filed more than twenty patents on its components. They isolated dermorphin and deltorphin, anesthetics that are 33 percent stronger than morphine. They also patented an antibacterial substance that promises effectiveness against malaria and HIV.

A 1992 *Journal of Medicinal Chemistry* article praises "the recently discovered deltorphines, heptapeptides of frog-skin origin [which] are also highly selective and potent."[63] *Recently* discovered? By whom?

There isn't any record of the patent being enforced against the Matses and Mayoruna, although this remains a possibility whenever the patent holders and licensees choose to enforce it. The tribes do not have the funds to pay for access to the medications emanating from their birthright, so it seems unlikely that they will face such demands. But neither will they share in the profits from the development of deltorphines and heptapeptides, and "their" cultural biotreasures are now owned by others.

Identity Theft

In today's world of legal ownership of "discovered" tissues, bodies, and genomes, a similar sentiment of colonial entitlement carries the day, as the economic dynamic follows a gradient of wealth, power, technological advancement, and sheer numbers. When everyday citizens of the developing world resist Western researchers seeking to patent their body parts or intellectual property, they have tended to lose in the international medical sphere and in the courts.

In the name of science, frauds are being perpetrated on entire populations of mostly poor, marginalized people. Researchers and corporations who profit hugely from gene patents overwhelmingly hail from affluent nations: the United States, Western Europe, and Japan. Genset of France, for example, has applied for patents covering 36,083 human gene sequences.

Rapacious Western researchers and corporations are using patents as a tool to perpetrate colonial exploitation by "discovering" cultural treasures, patenting them, then using their newfound monopolies to force the people who have utilized the newly patented entity for centuries to approach patent holders as supplicants and pay to use their own discoveries and technologies.

The burgeoning commodification of our bodies is another dimension of this abuse. The tendency to determine a person's worth according to his body's fiscal value has had the effect of devaluing human life. The dream of American innovation catalyzed by patents has become a nightmare for many.

This book has described how individuals have been surreptitiously relieved of invaluable cells and tissues that made fortunes and reputations for physician-entrepreneurs. This practice has not been consigned to the past, nor only to individuals. What happened to Henrietta Lacks and John Moore is being practiced on entire populations from Brazil to Iceland, abetted by U.S. patenting practices.

Patents at the World's End

Consider the experience of those living at the end of the world.

Tristan da Cunha sits squarely in the middle of nowhere. This archipelago of volcanic islands lying 1,750 miles from South Africa and 2,090 miles from South America is the most remote inhabited location on earth. The sea all but envelops its main island, also named Tristan da Cunha, and whips so roughly that its remote rocky coast remains inaccessible to ships that often find that they cannot land there. Even Tristão da Cunha, the Portuguese explorer credited with discovering the islands in 1506, was unable to land due to the rough seas. He was, however, able to name the island after himself. Centuries later, Jonathan Lambert, of Salem, Massachusetts, settled there in December 1810, claiming the islands as his property, and six years later they were annexed to the United Kingdom.

So many have died trying to reach the islands that over the past three centuries the island has been populated chiefly by shipwreck survivors and their descendants, mostly English, who numbered 275 in 2010. So, in the middle of nowhere, the natives speak English, albeit flavored with Dutch accents and idioms from a handful of twentieth-century settlers from Holland.

Every native of Tristan is a farmer or fisherman, but its subsistence economy has fallen drastically due to a collapse in the crayfish market. This in turn augurs ill for Tristan's plans to improve its rudimentary educational opportunities, which top out at its sparsely attended grade schools.

Besides poverty, islanders are beset by a medical isolation. Only one doctor from South Africa lives on the island, running a bare-bones clinic equipped to deal with minor ailments. In medical emergencies islanders must signal passing fishing boats to transport the seriously injured to Cape Town.

In 2007, the Tristan government convinced IBM and Beacon Equity to partner with the University of Pittsburgh Medical Center on "Project Tristan," which provides the island's doctor access to long-distance telemetry help. This enables him to send EKGs and X-rays to doctors in other countries for immediate consultation.[64]

Although the male population was erratically augmented by shipwrecks and women immigrated sporadically, a few at a time, the isolation and small population have led to inbreeding: today the island's residents share only eight surnames.

They also share something else. Centuries of inbreeding and isolation among these descendants of errant sailors have yielded a genetically distinct population with medical peculiarities. In our age of ubiquitous air travel, transcontinental commerce, and transethnic marriage, such strict genetic segregation is no longer easy to find.

Isolated communities are more likely to contain the rare "disease genes" that the pharmaceutical companies seek. They hope to capitalize on them by taking out patents and then devising profitable diagnostic tests and therapies based upon them. The game plan is to interest corporations with deep pockets to fund the research, development, and marketing that will transform its samples into the next blockbuster genetic product.

In 1993, researchers from Axys Pharmaceuticals of California descended upon the poverty-stricken island and took extensive blood samples. Half of the island's residents suffer from asthma,[65] a propensity that was bequeathed by three of the earliest founders who suffered from the disease. Axys scientists did not introduce themselves to the Tristans as biologic entrepreneurs with a grand fiscal plan. Instead, they presented their plan for addressing the island's health challenges, then left a small cache of outdated asthma medical supplies and equipment in their wake as they carried off genetic gold.[66]

By partnering with Toronto's Samuel Lunenfeld Research Institute, Axys boasted that, in only two and a half years, they used DNA-analysis tools to isolate an asthma gene that proved to be the most common disease-susceptibility gene on the planet.[67] The journal *Science* speculates that the Axys-Lunenfeld partnership plans to collect many more samples from other remote, disease-prone communities.

Axys patented the samples and genes, and today it holds patent rights to the entire genome of Tristan da Cunha's residents.[68] Axys contracted to receive $70 million from Boehringer Ingelheim, which believes it will derive medically profitable asthma therapies with the cell lines from this asthma-ridden population.

Duke University professor Robert Cook-Deegan observed, "The main policy rationale for genome research was the pursuit of gene maps as scientific tools to conquer disease, but economic development was an explicit, if subsidiary, goal."[69]

The countries where Axys hunted for genes for asthma, diabetes, obesity, osteoporosis, schizophrenia, and manic depression are not affluent Western industrialized nations. Instead, Axys and its partners prospect for genes in developing nations, whose poor inhabitants lack adequate access to health care and often the education that would allow them to understand what they are surrendering when researchers depart with blood and tissue samples.

Axys has also contracted with a long list of international pharmaceutical companies to jointly exploit DNA largely from isolated communities in the developing world. Its partners include Bayer, GlaxoWellcome, and Boehringer Ingelheim of Germany, U.S. firms Amgen, Merck, Abbott, SmithKline Beecham, and Warner-Lambert, Switzerland's Novartis and Hoffmann-La Roche, and Sweden's Pharmacia & Upjohn.[70] Since its triumph in Tristan, Axys has announced that it is collecting and patenting the genome of "a small traditional Jewish community that settled in southern India more than 2000 years ago" and the one thousand Polynesian residents of Easter Island, which, like Tristan, is about two thousand miles away from the nearest population center, Chile (which annexed the island in 1888). Axys has also patented the genomes of "a family of 170 in the Brazilian highlands outside Rio de Janeiro," and a family of 120 living in a small Chinese village.

Axys is prolific, but it is by no means the only corporate genetic prospector. In fact, many companies follow the same business model. Millennium has entered into similar contracts with Johnson & Johnson and Eli Lilly, and it collaborates with Sweden's Astra. In 1996, Genset of France was also partnered with Johnson & Johnson and France's Synthélabo, which was then France's third-largest pharmaceutical company in seeking a prostate cancer gene. One agreement gave Synthélabo "exclusive worldwide rights to develop and commercialize small molecular weight drugs, therapeutic proteins and therapeutic antibodies to treat prostate cancer and other prostatic diseases derived from genes discovered as a result of this collaborative research programme."[71] Genset also works with the Technion Ruth and Bruce Rappaport Faculty of Medicine in Haifa to commercially exploit banked Israeli DNA and research in conjunction with the Chinese Academy of Sciences.[72] Genset has filed patent applications covering at least 36,083 human gene sequences.

Through these partnerships, the collectors of genomes can bypass federal funding for the deep pockets of Big Pharma. This means that some federal restrictions on their research do not apply, because the only penalties for breaching certain human-subjects research strictures is the loss of federal funding. Though this sounds unsettling, the U.S. government itself has practiced the same appropriation of bodies of aboriginals.

For example, in 1990, the U.S. government sought to patent a virus from the cells of a twenty-six-year-old Guaymí Indian mother of two from Panama. Her body harbored a unique virus whose antibodies made her tissues useful in AIDS and leukemia research. Like most people whose bodies produce valuable substances, she never knew of the uses to which her cells would be put nor of the patent application.[73] Her name does not appear on the patent records, which are labeled simply "Guaymi Indians from Panama." The Guaymí petitioned for the return of the samples and the withdrawal of the patent application, but the U.S. government initially balked at this, so the Guaymí took their protests to the United Nations. They were joined by groups such as the Rural Advancement Foundation International (RAFI), now known as the ETC Group, and the World Council of Indigenous Peoples. Under the scrutiny of a world that is far less accepting than we of owning the genes of others, the United States withdrew its patent application in November 2006.

However, our nation refuses to cede ownership of the cell line and has not returned it to Panama. Indeed, the Guaymí samples are still for sale at the American Type Culture Collection (ATCC), for $127.

On March 14, 1995, the U.S. National Institutes of Health (NIH) succeeded in patenting the T-cell line of a man from Papua New Guinea's Hagahai tribe and from others in the Solomon Islands as well. The

Hagahai were infected with a virus that researchers hoped would prove efficacious against a form of leukemia. Today Hagahai T cells, like the cells of Henrietta Lacks and the Guaymí, can also be purchased from ATCC. The late U.S. secretary of commerce Ron Brown defended our nation's right to patent these cells, declaring, "Under our laws, as well as those of many other countries, subject matter relating to human cells is patentable and there is no provision for considerations relating to the sources of the cells that may be the subject of a patent application." After the patent was awarded, however, the research yielded little of value, so rights to the patent were abandoned.

Aside from the financial exploitation, researchers and Western governments have shown too little understanding and respect for the divergent cultural stance that makes bodily appropriation, even in the name of science, an anathema to many distinctive peoples. Darcy Marubo, a leader of the Coordination of Indigenous Organizations in the Brazilian Amazon, said, "The whites created all these names like patent, intellectual property and biodiversity. It is very hard for us to understand them all, but we had to get used to them even though they have never brought any concrete benefit to us."

There has also been too little consideration of the element of coercion, or at least of undue inducement. Inhabitants of small, poor, or weak countries or of marginalized enclaves of larger countries enjoy few opportunities for medical care, except for submitting to tissue harvesting and to medical research.

Genetic Reservations

The Grand Canyon, a majestic chasm 277 miles long and 18 miles wide, is also the residence of the Havasupai nation, 650 strong. In their way, the Havasupai are as isolated as the Tristan islanders. Their ancestral home lies deep within the Supai region of the Grand Canyon in an area so rife with natural stone barriers that it can be reached only by horseback and helicopter. But its people would not dream of leaving, because their cosmogony teaches them that their land deep within the canyon is a Shangri-la, the birthplace of man. As original men, their home is not only sacred but an inseparable part of their identity. Even their name, Havasu 'Baaja, translated "people of the blue-green waters," refers to the arresting turquoise waterfalls within the canyon.

Their village boasts a small café, lodge, post office, school, church, clinic, police station, and a general store. Visitors can sleep in the camping grounds, and mail arrives on the nation's last pack train mail. There is one doctor, from the Indian Health Service.

Tourism is the chief source of income as the tribe shares its gorgeous flowers, hiking, and horseback trails and the canyon's Havasu and Mooney waterfalls. But the Havasupai expect their visitors to care for the earth as they do, leaving no trash behind, and they ask that visitors respect their cultural integrity, including the bans on alcohol, drugs, firearms, and even machetes, which are all illegal and forbidden anywhere on the reservation.[74]

In 1989, the Havasupai's invited guests included Arizona State University diabetes researchers whom the tribe had asked to devise some way to remedy high rates of diabetes disease among them. The researchers presented a protocol to the Tribal Council in 1989–90 that included diabetes education, collecting blood samples, and genetic testing to identify which genes, if any, were the disease culprits.

But in 2004, the Havasupai learned that 400 blood samples from 180 donors had been used to look at the incidence of schizophrenia within the group, and that researchers had studied the interbreeding within the tribe. The nation sued the university and the state Board of Regents, alleging that the research stigmatized the Havasupai nation as mentally ill and sought to establish migration patterns, all without the knowledge or consent of tribal members. Furthermore, the nation was outraged that researchers improperly obtained the medical charts of members. They further alleged that the university's Institutional Review Board (IRB), which is responsible for protecting human subjects and for ensuring that its research conforms to ethical and legal standards, had done nothing to prevent the research without informed consent or the misappropriation of the medical records.

Finally, the Havasupai sued for intangible harms resulting from the conduct of research that threatened to undermine their ancestral heritage. Research proposing that their origin was outside the Grand Canyon threw into question their belief in their origins. Verifying higher-than-normal rates of interbreeding could question one's identity as a member of the nation. Someone whose genetic complement failed to match others in the tribe could have his identity as Havasupai questioned, an important matter for peoples whose membership criteria are not limited to genetic ties but encompass adoption and other means of amalgamation.

It is indeed the responsibility of an IRB to ensure that "named populations" such as the Tristan islanders and the Havasupai are not stigmatized or negatively labeled by research when there is a question of increased disease incidence. Even if the disease rate is not actually higher than normal, the perception is enough to qualify them for special protections in a research setting.[75] The researchers had a responsibility to thoroughly educate the Havasupai about this risk and to elicit their permission before proceeding.

IRBs also must consider the consequentialist implications of research—that is, what foreseeable effects the research might have on the population being studied, or even, by extension, on others who are a part of the larger group from whom research subjects are culled. In this case, for example, it was clearly foreseeable that research that sought to quantify the risks for a stigmatizing disease such as schizophrenia could result in a perception of the Havasupai as prone to mental illness. There are more immediate risks of such a diagnosis as well. Psychoses such as schizophrenia often result in a loss of civil rights and even a loss of freedom if the person is deemed a danger to himself or others.

For these reasons, consent to research concerning diabetes prevalence is not equivalent to consent for research concerning schizophrenia prevalence, and the subjects should have been offered informed consent specifically for the schizophrenia studies.

Some may argue that informed consent may retard research because many subjects will not agree to the research in the wake of such informed consent. This is possible, and in this case the research should not be conducted. Although the idea is anathema to many researchers, the fact is that some research simply cannot be ethically performed, no matter what the putative benefits.

Corporations have also proposed to patent the genome of the Kanaka Maoli, native Hawaiians. The worth of this genome was calculated in the hundreds of millions of dollars, but the Hawaiian people, wary of surrendering their genome to companies, rejected the proposal.

Why is the Hawaiian genome so valuable? Differences in the genetic sequences of a population can cause disease outright or greater vulnerability to sickness. Testing for a disorder caused by a single mutation such as cystic fibrosis or sickle-cell disease is fairly easy. But testing for diseases caused by multiple genetic variations and by environmental factors is much more complex. If the genetic diversity in a given population is reduced, it is easier to test, track, and study genetic disease.

Before Western colonists interacted with the Hawaiian population in 1778,[76] 800,000 people lived on the islands. By the mid-1800s only 40,000 remained, a 95 percent reduction in population. A dramatic reduction in native Hawaiian genetic diversity made them more susceptible to multigene disorders such as hypertension, diabetes, and renal disease, and easier to test and study.[77]

Honolulu lawyer Le'a Malia Kanehe, analyst for the Indigenous Peoples Council on Biocolonialism, explains that the Kanaka Maoli consider their genome "sacred and inalienable," but this hasn't deterred subsequent attempts by patent prospectors, many of whom arrogantly dismiss the ethical and cultural beliefs and objections of native peoples.

The interests of corporations are protected by laws that reinforce these biological inequities, such as the World Trade Organization's Trade-Related Aspects of Intellectual Property Rights (TRIPS). The ethical implications are wide and deeply troubling. And these abuses may harm not only the distant poor but also affluent Westerners.

Icelandic Saga

Even the gene pool of a Western nation, Iceland, has been patented for profit under questionable models of consent.

In 1999, the people of Iceland surrendered their genetic complement and medical profiles to deCODE Genetics, a private biotech founded by neuroscientist Karí Stefánsson, MD, PhD, to collect, patent, analyze, and market Icelanders' private medical information. DeCODE explained that it was searching for genes associated with over thirty diseases such as heart attack, emphysema, and Alzheimer's. Hoffmann-La Roche Pharmaceuticals had contracted to fund research into a dozen of these disorders and had paid deCODE Genetics $200 million for the rights to the Icelandic genome.

Stefánsson's biotech was a visionary foray into population-based molecular genomics, which means that it planned to collate the genome of Iceland with its medical history to identify and patent genes associated with disease, then market them in concert with pharmaceutical companies to devise tests and treatments for those diseases.

Although Iceland is a small country of only 275,000 people, collecting any nation's genome and its medical histories would normally be a Sisyphean task. This is to say nothing of trying to mesh them to associate genes with the diseases and conditions they can trigger. Stefánsson sought to accomplish this, however, by exploiting some unusual features of Icelandic culture. Although Iceland's genome is not as homogenous as myth would have us believe,[78] it is uncomplicated by extensive immigration. Moreover, genealogy has long been a national obsession of Icelanders, 80 percent of whom take pride in being able to trace their ancestry far back, sometimes to a single Viking. In addition, the nation is blessed with a superbly efficient Health Sector Database, a system that maintains extensive personal medical data on each citizen going back many generations. This relative homogeny and uniquely comprehensive data keeping mean that it would be far easier to link the health of Iceland to its genome than it would be for most other nations.

In order to maximize participation in the database, deCODE expanded the use of presumed consent, under which the government assumes that everyone would consent to having his medical and genetic information acquired. As Chapter 7 noted, presumed consent is used in the United States to surreptitiously harvest cadaver tissues without the consent of the dead. Iceland's government agreed to acquire the medical records and genetic profiles of living Icelanders in mammoth databases[79] and to use presumed consent to compel citizens to share their genomes and medical histories with the commercial national database—unless he or she took the steps required to opt out. In the end, more than 140,000 Icelanders, or about 65 percent of the population, were included in the database.

Presumed consent gave rise to some ethical issues. Because of the way the opt-out period was structured, some children who gained their majority during the data collection were unable to opt out. The mentally challenged and elderly and some others may not have been able to express their desire to opt out.

More generally, the medical privacy and sensitive genetic information of individual Icelanders were now in the hands of a for-profit corporation, a concern that Stefánsson dismissed in the pages of *The New Yorker* as a "crock of shit."[80]

Ostensibly, a subject can opt out of the database at any time, but as with Dr. William Catalona's prostate cancer subjects in Chapter 7, "leaving the study" is defined extremely narrowly. No data already entered about a subject will be removed, making him a nonconsensual research subject. Nothing in the deCODE study's protocol promised that people would be informed of the type of research done with their personal data.

As Arizona State University did with the Havasupai research, Hoffmann-La Roche has funded schizophrenia research with the Icelandic data, opening the door to negative medical stereotyping. This is an economic threat as well as a social one. If a schizophrenia association is found, will insurers presume that an Icelandic heritage means a propensity to insanity?

Also, the monopolistic arrangements hopelessly obscure the line between deCODE as a private concern and the Icelandic government. Although the database belongs to Iceland's national health system that the government mandated and manages, deCODE's monopoly allowed it to market the data for profit for twelve years, during which time it sold the data to health-insurance firms and pharmaceutical companies and made arrangements with Hoffmann-La Roche to investigate twelve diseases that effectively block anyone else from studying these diseases in Iceland. What's more, Iceland's regulations guarantee deCODE that no one will have access to the data if this would harm deCODE's financial interests.

Thus deCODE's financial interests in what was essentially government property have been well protected and were bolstered by the fiscal security of Pharma's deep pockets.

But in exchange for donating their intimate medical data and privacy, Icelanders were given only financial promises backed by no guarantees.

The promises were substantial. Icelanders were promised health benefits: as Stefánsson explained, he made some free medications for Icelanders part of his deal with Roche. He proudly announced that "I thought it would be interesting to force Big Pharma to recognize the contribution of the population."[81] However, these were to be medications developed with the database, not at all a certain bounty.

DeCODE also promised that Icelanders would share in the profits from the medical tools forged from their genetic data because the biotech would bring an influx of biotechnology jobs to the economy.

But armed with a laptop, biotech scientists can perform and collaborate from anywhere in the world, so no phalanx of new scientists was hired in Iceland, and no pharmaceutical facilities were built there. This means that although the government had enthused about the financial gains from hosting deCODE, Iceland never received a sizeable tax influx, nor were fees paid to the government for the firm's vast and valuable monopoly or the staggeringly expensive database, because deCODE covered only the database's modest administrative costs.

The people of Iceland were also promised less-tangible treasures, such as national pride and greater prestige for the Icelandic nation as deCODE (run by Stefánsson, a famous neuroscientist born in Reykjavík) revealed nature's medical secrets and spun from them cures and novel therapies—to say nothing of the dollars.

DeCODE was successful in identifying many important disease genes. By 2007, the company had identified fifteen gene variants associated with an increased risk of disorders, from asthma, stroke, and diabetes to prostate cancer. These were by no means confined to Icelanders. DeCODE found, for instance, a variant gene associated with heart disease that substantially increases the risk of a heart attack in African Americans. In fact, by 2009, deCODE had discovered more genes than any other company on earth.

But like many other biotech companies, it never discovered a viable business model and never turned a profit. DeCODE was unable to transform its talent for gene identification into marketable products or generate a steady income stream. Instead it burned through its $676 million stake, and the situation was not helped when the firm entrusted its operating funds to Lehman Brothers, which shunted the money into speculative bonds that vanished by November 2008.

After its stock spent a year in free fall, deCODE declared bankruptcy in November 2009, never having delivered on its promises to Iceland, where public-health costs continue to soar, personal bankruptcies are fueled by disastrous investments in deCODE, and two hundred deCODE employees have been laid off.

The story hasn't ended yet, because the biotech rose from the ashes in January 2010[82] as "the New deCODE." Instead of searching for cures, it now sells a spectrum of genetic diagnostic tests, including deCODEme, a personal genome analysis service. Stefánsson now has partners with their own plans and vision, and this means that Iceland also has partners who will determine the future direction of the research with the nation's no-longer-private medical data. This raises privacy concerns because the security of the personal genomes is as uncertain as deCODE's fate.

Icelanders were persuaded or coerced into sharing their private medical profiles and genetic information. Now the promised medical benefits have proved illusory and the promised wealth has yet to appear—except for some shareholders who bailed before stock losses, including some of the scientists who promulgated the research. The citizenry of Iceland has lost its privacy for elusive benefits and broken pledges.

But the case of Iceland also reveals that Western populations are by no means immune to the penchant for biocolonialism. Although the nation's deception has been subtle rather than blatant, the ethical and medical and financial harms are no less profound as the Icelanders, like the denizens of the developing world, surrendered their medical identities for empty promises.

CHAPTER 9

THE LABORATORY OF THE WEST

**Pharmaceutical Corporations, Human-Subjects
Research, and the Developing World**

*No one should approach the temple of science with the soul of a money
changer.*

—THOMAS BROWNE, *RELIGIO MEDICI*

(THE RELIGION OF A PHYSICIAN)

The swath of Africa's "meningitis belt" stretches from Ethiopia to Senegal, within which the periodic pandemics have been arriving at shorter and shorter intervals.

During the height of a 1996 pandemic, the low-pitched drone of a DC-9 announced the arrival of a new group of doctors into Kano, Nigeria, seemingly just in time. They quickly set up a clinic right next to the teeming makeshift tents of the Infectious Diseases Hospital, a treatment center staffed by overwhelmed, sleep-deprived physicians from Doctors Without Borders (MSF) who, alongside a handful of local physicians, were treating ceaseless waves of desperately sick children and their worried families. All had good cause for concern: meningococcal meningitis strikes young children most frequently, but during epidemics older children and young adults also fall victim to its ravages. Without treatment, half may die.

The newcomers infused their expertise, energy, and even a new medicine, Pfizer's Trovan (floxacin), into the situation, and terrified parents, desperate for medical attention, lined up to grasp at Trovan's straw.

Among them were the parents of patient 6587-0069. She was ten years old, and because shortly after the time of her treatment many research records were lost, accounts of her story use her number.[1] A number is what she was to Pfizer because she, like the other children whose parents sought help for them in the new clinic, was an experimental subject. Trovan was an experimental drug that had not been FDA-approved, and although Pfizer hoped it would become the firm's next $1 billion blockbuster, its approval depended on the results the new doctors would have with the medication. So patient 6587-0069 was given 56 mg of Trovan.

But 6587-0069 was not getting the results she needed. As her fever soared and she slipped deeper into unconsciousness, her strength dissipated and an eye froze in place. In response to this, the staff noted that "the dose was continued unchanged." If she had been in an ethically conducted U.S. trial, she would have been switched from the experimental drug to one that is known to work, such as the chloramphenicol that was given to the control group. But she was not in Connecticut; she was in Kano, and because testing Trovan was the priority, she was given no other drug throughout her steady decline, and she later died.

It is impossible to know whether she would have lived had she been given another safe, effective drug because as many as one in twenty patients dies even when treated. But we do know that safe, effective drugs were available both from Pfizer and from the nearby MSF treatment center. We also know that Trovan is a drug so dangerous that it left deafness, paralysis, and death in its wake. At the trial's conclusion, the FDA refused to approve it.

By the time the experiment ended, two hundred children were left deaf, lame, blind, seizure-ridden, disoriented, and with other severe disabilities. Eleven were dead. Although the epidemic continued, the Pfizer doctors were gone, having flown out after they doled out their doses and collected their data, which took just three weeks.

In 2001, at least 211 Nigerian parents sued New York–based Pfizer, alleging that non-FDA-approved experiments had killed their children; that Pfizer failed to obtain the requisite prior approval from local leaders; and that the pharmaceutical giant failed to administer standard therapies with proven efficacy, such as Pfizer's own ceftriaxone, to those children who, like 6587-0069, continued to deteriorate after being given Trovan.

It did not help matters that, during the course of the epidemic, Nigeria's military government had amassed an execrable human-rights and corruption record, which guaranteed the silence of some local physicians who were disturbed by the Pfizer study. "I could not protest," Dr. Amir Imam Yola recalled for the *Washington Post*. "The system you have in America and the system we have here, there is a wide gap. Freedom of speech is still not here." He went on to call the study "a bad thing."[2]

Dr. Sadiq Wali, chief medical director of the Aminu Kano Teaching Hospital, insists that his hospital's medical-ethics committee never gave Pfizer the required approval to use the drug at the infectious disease hospital in Kano. "Pfizer did not do that. I am not sure if they had the consent of the people used as guinea pigs, because that means *informed* consent in medical parlance. Such consent has to do with the patients being told the good as well as the side effects of the drugs to be administered."

In the same vein, Peter Ebigbo of Child Rights Information Network told Inter Press Service, "Our leaders must not allow Nigerians to be used as guinea pigs by any company to make money."

Pfizer counters that it treated ninety children with Trovan and ninety-seven with the FDA-approved ceftriaxone, and that it obtained all the necessary approvals.

When the FDA audited the experiment, Pfizer claimed that Nigeria's Infectious Disease Hospital Ethics Committee division had approved the study as required by law; Pfizer produced a March 1996 letter to this effect. However, the committee was not even constituted until October of that year, and a Nigerian doctor in the case later turned whistleblower and admitted that his office created the backdated letter of approval in 1997, well after the research had been completed.

Pfizer also claimed to have consent forms, but they would have meant nothing because most of the villagers treated by Pfizer were illiterate. A local staffer elaborated: "You explain to them, 'It's a new medicine and you have a right to say no.'" "The patients did not know if it was research or not," affirmed a Nigerian laboratory technician. "They just knew they were sick."

But documenting what patients had been told of the drug's experimental status and determining Trovan's effects on these patients for the lawsuit would prove difficult: the medical records of 350 meningitis patients treated between April and June 1996 have disappeared from the hospital, as the records of research studies that are accused of cutting legal and ethical corners so often seem to do.[3]

"It could be considered murder," said Dr. Evariste Lodi, the supervising physician for the Doctors Without Borders treatment clinic in Kano, adding, "If I had the power I would take away their medical licenses."[4] The victims' $6 billion suit against Pfizer was bounced from continent to continent, having been conducted at various times in both Kano and Manhattan, and Pfizer was accused of unsavory political machinations in an attempt to dissuade Nigerian officials from pursuing the case of the Kano children.

A secret State Department cable, discovered and released by WikiLeaks, alleges that Pfizer levied corruption accusations against the Nigerian attorney general, Michael Aondokaa, in an attempt to get him to drop the case. The cable describes an April 9 meeting in Lagos with Pfizer's Nigerian manager, Enrico Liggeri, in which Liggeri indicated that Pfizer investigators had found evidence of corruption they were threatening to release to the news media, and the company wanted Aondokaa to drop the suit. Aondokaa denied any knowledge that he had been investigated by Pfizer, and Pfizer denied having done so. However, the same 2006 State Department cable also correctly describes the terms of a settlement for $75 million that Pfizer reached with the Kano families. Pfizer also paid an undisclosed sum to Nigeria in 2009.[5] But some of the Nigerian parents insisted that justice had not been served, and sought to invalidate the settlement and reopen a criminal case against Pfizer.

In addition, some victims have been frightened into dropping their compensation claims after Pfizer introduced DNA testing in May 2010 as a requirement for qualifying for payment. The tests entail the insertion of a sizable instrument that takes buccal samples, scraping the inside of the cheek to collect DNA-laden cells. Many parents say that they have already provided documents proving children were part of the trial, and they think the DNA test is designed to deny them compensation. But Pfizer says the test is designed to guard against fraudulent claims. Health Care/Meningitis Trust Fund spokesperson David Odiwo claims, "We have collected samples from 547 people and only 200 people participated in the study, so what do we do?"[6] If Pfizer has accurate numbers of study participants, and reference DNA samples from the study that allow meaningful comparisons, it is interesting that these survived the research chaos when so many other key study documents and data, some of which might incriminate the firm, were lost.

A lawsuit filed by the Trovan Victims Forum led the Nigerian Abuja

High Court to issue an injunction halting the screening process. But the Emir of Kano persuaded the victims to drop their suit, thus paving the way for DNA testing, which resumed in April 2011.[7]

Yvonne Ndege of Al Jazeera points out that "the subjects are poor and illiterate. They don't understand what DNA testing is and fear it is another attempt by Pfizer to make them guinea pigs in a new drug trial." Accordingly, some victims abandoned their claim when DNA testing was introduced as a condition of receiving payment.[8]

Pharmaceutical Tunnel Vision

The abuses of the Trovan trial are inexcusable. Africa most certainly does need new and better medications, however, and some Westerners have tried to provide them. It is laudable and heartening that Western medical systems and news media have given so much attention to the critical dearth of expensive, hard-to-administer HIV drugs that can save lives in those developing nations that have been devastated by AIDS. Government support, notably the PEPFAR (President's Emergency Plan for AIDS Relief),[9] has helped reduce the rate of infections and has kept many people in African and other developing nations alive. It has also provided some funds for programs to address tuberculosis and other endemic diseases. According to U.S. government budgetary figures, the 2012 budget requests $7.2 billion for PEPFAR, including more than $5.6 billion for bilateral HIV/AIDS programs, $1.3 billion for the Global Fund, and $254 million for bilateral TB programs.[10]

However, people in the developing world are also dying from a lack of medicines that are cheap and easy to administer. The 25 percent of sub-Saharan children who do not receive vaccines are deprived of drugs that cost a few cents a dose and are easy to deliver because they require no tests or diagnoses. In fact, "Seven million children under the age of five die every year as the result of infectious diseases. Ninety-nine percent of those children live in developing countries," according to Pari Shah and Ann Juergens-Behr of Brown University.[11]

People throughout the developing world die when they are deprived of hepatitis B and haemophilus influenzae b (Hib) vaccines, which cost just a few dollars each. One of every four people on the planet[12] suffers from worm infestations that can be disfiguring, debilitating, blinding, and fatal, yet each could be saved with medications that need be taken only once a year and cost less than a dollar. Chapter 3 documented the drug industry's lack of attention to crippling killers such as malaria and tuberculosis in favor of medicating the minor but lucrative gastroenterological and sexual-performance obsessions of the West. All of Asia (except Japan) and all of Africa make up only 5.1 percent of the global pharmaceutical market, according to Information Management Group.[13] This medical neglect costs millions of lives each year.

Michael Kremer, PhD, the Gates Professor of Developing Societies at Harvard University, brought this inattention into sharp focus when he noted that of the 1,233 drugs licensed globally between 1975 and 1997, only thirteen targeted diseases that strike in the tropics. You may recall from Chapter 3 that some drug companies have had a long-standing, albeit tacit, policy against testing medications that might demonstrate efficacy against diseases of the developing world, an animus that surely contributes to this studied neglect. What's more, five of these thirteen medications were developed for animals, two were "me too" replicates of existing medications, and two were developed by the military, not private concerns.[14] This means that within twenty-two years, the drug industry developed only four new medications for human diseases of the developing world. More recently, as we saw in Chapter 3, innovative partnerships of pharmaceutical firms with nongovernmental organizations such as the Gates Foundation have begun to supply some needed vaccines and other medications. (See chart below.)

Percentage of Disease Burden

Cause	World	Low-Income Countries	Middle-Income Countries	High-Income Countries
Infectious and parasitic diseases	23.1%	33.3%	13.9%	3.0%
Tuberculosis	2.4%	2.9%	2.2%	0.3%
HIV/AIDS	6.1%	9.7%	2.6%	0.7%
Malaria	2.7%	4.5%	1.0%	0.0%
Noncommunicable conditions	46.1%	33.2%	55.5%	82.7%
Malignant neoplasms (cancers)	5.3%	2.9%	6.7%	14.4%
Cardiovascular diseases	10.3%	7.7%	12.3%	16.4%

Sources: World Health Report (2001), World Bank (2001).

Even some of the medications developed by for-profit drug firms against diseases rife in developing nations, however, may not end up helping those in the Third World. Take malaria, which infects 500 million people a year and "kills one child in Africa every 30 seconds," as the GlaxoSmithKline (GSK) website notes.[15] In 2000, GSK launched Malarone, the industry's first new antimalarial in forty years. However, it is intended for prevention, not treatment, and it was marketed to the estimated seven million visitors to malarial regions, not to the people living there. Other research that investigates drugs for ailments that target the poor take inappropriate approaches, such as focusing on sophisticated AIDS drugs that are useful in developed countries, but are too expensive and difficult to use in developing countries, where obtaining refrigeration and administering injections can be a challenge.

Yet today pharmaceutical companies invoke the poverty of developing nations, not biased pharmaceutical-research agendas, as the reason for the widespread sickness and early deaths. The companies and their advocates are not referring merely to the industry's failure to develop and market needed medications and treatments priced within the reach of poor African and other developing nations. Instead they place the onus on the deficiencies of the societies themselves.

Perhaps the most influential exoneration of patents as the principal barrier to medicines for the poor was a November 2001 *Journal of the American Medical Association (JAMA)*[16] article coauthored by Amir Attaran, of Harvard University's Center for International Development, and Lee Gillespie-White, the director of the International Intellectual Property Institute. The 2001 study asked a simple question: How many of the fifteen recognized antiretroviral drugs against AIDS have been patented by their manufacturers, and in how many African countries were they issued?

Attaran found that only 22 percent of the 795 patents that could have been issued in Africa had been awarded, usually because the potential pharmaceutical patent holders did not trouble to apply for the patents.

And yet, antiretroviral drugs were then far too expensive for wide use in Africa. Attaran—and the drug makers—conclude that the antiretroviral patents are too few to be held responsible for high prices. And if patents are not responsible for the lack of access, poverty must be.

The study has a number of serious flaws, some of which are acknowledged within the report.

First, the study ignores that the average price of African antiretroviral therapy fell from $10,000 annually in 1998 to $350 annually in 2001 as a result of an energetic campaign by a coalition of African and Western health advocates and nongovernmental organizations.

This illustrates, among other things, that many factors that are independent of poverty *and* pharmaceutical patents affect pricing; and that Attaran's analysis is so narrowly focused that it misses many pertinent factors.

Attaran also downplayed other factors that lower drug prices. India was at that time supplying the developing world with generic antiretroviral cocktails that it patented very aggressively and sold very cheaply: in fact, most patented drugs were those produced by India. This is an atypical situation very different from the antiretroviral cocktails sold very dearly by Western manufacturers. Additionally, most of these patents are taken out in wealthier African countries where many of the Indian companies have offices and where many can pay for the drugs.[17]

Also, the analysis chose to focus on South Africa, but that nation is not at all representative of Africa's approximately fifty-four countries. It had the highest HIV-infection rate and was one of the wealthiest nations with an intact health-care infrastructure and thus was most able to supply and produce medicine. So it is unsurprising that thirteen of the fifteen drugs discussed the most were patented in South Africa.

The paper claimed that if patents were the culprit, the more patents that abounded, the less access there would be to antiretroviral medicine. It did not find this inverse relationship between patents and medication access, so it concluded that patents are not a factor in lack of access to medicine. But this is far from the only or even the most reasonable conclusion: where people have more wealth and poverty is less extreme, patents become more lucrative, which is a better explanation of why there was no negative correlation between patents and access to antiretroviral drugs.

Finally, the Attaran study does not exculpate Western patents on the matter of expensive medications in poor Third World countries, because it discusses the much narrower case of Indian patents on atypically inexpensive antiretrovirals in some wealthier African countries. It seems far more likely that a broader study would show that both patents *and* poverty bar Third World access to lifesaving medications.

The authors admit some serious limitations of their study, and the paper is couched in such qualified language that it does not claim to have proved that patents fail to make medicines unaffordable. The paper admits that patents can in some cases bar access to medication in Africa and also admitted that after 2006, patents, reinforced by new World Trade Organization treaties, would likely block access to new medications.

Despite these limitations and numerous qualifications, the weakness of this exoneration of Third World patents was underacknowledged. But beginning in 2001, this exculpatory theme became a mantra. Attaran has often reiterated his exoneration of patents, including in his 2002 letter to *JAMA* that asked, "Do Patents Prevent Access to Drugs for HIV in Developing Countries?"[18] And he followed up with such offerings as a 2004 *Health Affairs* study that concludes poverty, not patents, is the main barrier to access to essential medicines in the developing world.[19]

Other articles that sought to cast doubt on the exclusionary role of patents proliferated in academia and the news media and were echoed endlessly on public-relations news wires, all often couched in very similar language.

"Poverty, a market failure not curable by technology fixes," averred Chakravarthi Raghavan in July 2001; "Fight Poverty, Not Patents," urged Carl Bildt in a January 2003 *Wall Street Journal* op-ed; "Poverty, Not Patents, Is to Blame," declared James Shikwati in a June 2004 article on the website allafrica.com;[20] "Poverty, Not Pharmaceutical Patents, Leading Factor in Lack of Access to Medicine in Developing Countries," the press-release site PRWeb claimed in February 2009; "Poverty, not patents, imposes the greater limitation on access," summarizes a 2009 article in *Health Affairs* titled "Poverty, Not Pharmaceutical Patents, Leading Factor in Lack of Access to Medicine in Developing Countries."[21] "Poverty and sickness won't be cured by fighting patents," opined Franklin Cudjoe in a widely reproduced January 2011 opinion piece,[22] and in January 2011 Keith Martin, MD, MP, published an equally ubiquitous *Edmonton Sun* opinion piece, titled "Poverty, Not Patent Law, Blocks Poorest from Getting Medications."

Unfortunately, the subtleties of Attaran's *JAMA* paper were lost in the headlines, blogs, and pharmaceutical-friendly press releases. The politicized take-home message was a broad claim that patents have nothing to do with the developing world's ability (or lack thereof) to obtain lifesaving medications: instead, their poverty dooms them. As the *New York Times* noted, "The study is being used by pharmaceutical companies to support the view that it is not their fault that millions of Africans are dying of AIDS."[23]

But the pharmaceutical companies' PR offensive in defense of Western intellectual-property rights was actually triggered by a crisis that is even broader than that of AIDS in Africa.

These articles burgeoned after 2001, when embattled developing nations pushed back against the World Trade Organization's Trade-Related Aspects of Intellectual Property Rights legislation. As we've seen, TRIPS made patent enforcement against poor nations easier for pharmaceutical firms to enforce. The developing world did, however, win a concession: the Doha Declaration on the TRIPS Agreement and Public Health, which reaffirms each nation's right to dispense with patents in times of public-health emergency by issuing compulsory licenses. The ability to override patented medicines through these "march-in" rights did not sit well with drug makers and others whose livelihoods depend upon the ability to exploit Western intellectual-property rights.[24]

Such maneuvers alarm pharmaceutical companies and have already cost them a great deal—for example, when Brazil issued compulsory licenses for expensive medications such as the antiretroviral drug efavirenz for HIV infection. The forceful complaints from developing nations and their dismissal of several patents in order to provide low-cost drugs to their citizens triggered this media blitz in defense of patents.

But while some analysts and virtually all pharmaceutical companies blame poverty, not their patents and the resulting high drug prices, for the preventable deaths and plummeting life expectancies of poor foreign nations, the data tell a different tale.

Medications, not developing nations' wealth or per capita income, are critical to extending life in the Third World. To be sure, health improved and life expectancy first extended in *developed* countries as a result of the better nutrition and sanitation, such as cleaner water supplies, that resulted from higher incomes. As a result, death rates in the United States fell most precipitously between 1700 and 1910, at an adjusted rate of 70 percent, *before* the advent of important medications. But poor countries today are governed by a different dynamic, where life expectancy has increased dramatically when access to medications and medical technology has improved, even while poverty has remained static.

For example, the per capita gross domestic product (GDP) in low-income sub-Saharan African nations actually decreased 13 percent between 1972 and 1992, but life expectancy increased by 10 percent within this period, in concert with increased vaccinations and medications for important killers. (Seventy-five percent of the world's children receive patented vaccines through the WHO and, specifically, UNICEF, which are chiefly underwritten by governmental and nongovernmental organizations, not pharmaceutical companies. This saves at least three million lives a year.) Life expectancy then plummeted again, depressed by skyrocketing HIV-infection rates when the expensive antiretrovirals for HIV disease were withheld from poor sub-Saharan Africans.

Michael Kremer notes that by 2002, Vietnam enjoyed a life expectancy of sixty-nine years despite a per capita income that was less than one-tenth that of the United States in 1900, when life expectancy was only forty-seven years.[25]

Kremer adds: "An analysis of worldwide health trends in the twentieth century has found that most improvements resulted from technological advances rather than from income growth. . . . Income growth accounted for only 10 to 25 percent of the growth in world life expectancy between the 1930s and 1960s and suggested that the diffusion of technological advances was a major factor for the increase in life expectancy at any given income level." Improved medical therapies and access to them, not poverty, are the major determinants of health status.

According to WHO estimates, infectious and parasitic diseases make up one-third of the disease burden in all poor countries and nearly half in Africa, but only 3 percent of the burden of more affluent countries.[26] PhRMA estimates that Africa represents only 1 percent of its market. In 1998, U.S. health spending totaled $4,000 per person, while sub-Saharan African nations spent only $18 per person,[27] so little that drug makers often have not bothered to take out patents in small, poor countries.[28] (See "World Pharmaceutical Market by Region in 2005," p. 311.)

World Pharmaceutical Market by Region in 2005
(Ex-manufacturer prices)

Region	Sales ($bn)	Global Share of Sales (%)	Global Share of Population (%)
North America	268.8	44	5
Europe	180.4	30	8
Japan	69.3	11	2
Oceania	7.7	1	1
Commonwealth of Independent States	5.0	1	4
East Asia	28.8	5	30
Latin America	26.6	4	9
Indian subcontinent	7.2	1	23
Africa	6.7	1	14
Middle East	4.9	1	4
World	605.5	100	100

Source: Sales data: CIPIH 2006, p. 15. Population data extracted from Population Division of the Department of Economic and Social Affairs of the United Nations Secretariat, World Population Prospects: The 2006 Revision, http://esa.ul1.orglunpp, last accessed July 25, 2008. (There may be imperfect matching of regions between sales and population, as the sales data do not disclose region boundaries.)

Yet pharmaceutical firms doggedly attack attempts to make medications available to the poor, insisting upon full enforcement of their patent rights. The TRIPS treaty has made patent enforcement easier for pharmaceutical firms in developing countries. This treaty is disastrous for the economies of countries that are unable to defend their biological resources against predatory Western entrepreneurs. But TRIPS is also deadly for the people in poor countries, because drug firms price their medications in line with the resources of the rich and have no fiscal incentive to provide for the poor, who die of preventable, curable diseases such as malaria, tuberculosis, worms, and respiratory infections because treating them doesn't pay.

The Developing World's Health-Care Vacuum

The dearth of health care in much of the developing world leaves its people vulnerable to experimental exploitation and abuse. One cannot generalize about a continent as large and diverse as Africa, for example, because there are wealthy countries and people as well as poor ones, and a few health-savvy nations, such as Cameroon, can teach us a thing or two about providing health care to all our citizens.

But much of sub-Saharan Africa has been devastated by colonial rape and depletion that has left poor health, tattered remnants of health-care infrastructure, and few physicians in its wake. A mere 750,000 health workers care for its 682 million people. The Organisation for Economic Co-operation and Development (OECD) estimates that this represents a health-care force that is as much as fifteen times lower than in OECD countries. According to WHO, only 1.3 percent of the world's health workers practice in sub-Saharan Africa, but the region harbors fully 25 percent of the world's disease.[29] A bare minimum of 2.5 health workers is generally needed for every one thousand people, but only six African countries meet this standard. Instead, the average in sub-Saharan Africa is 0.8 health worker per one thousand people—less than one-third the minimal standard.

To achieve the minimum health-care staffing level would require an infusion of one million health workers into the continent, but health-care workers are actually fleeing in the other direction—to Western countries where they can earn more money and work under conditions that do not imperil their patients' health.

To a greater or lesser extent, this medical drought similarly applies to the less-affluent people of the Middle East, South Asia, Latin America, Africa, and Oceania as well. Enclaves of other nations suffer such medical deprivation, too, such as Eastern bloc countries and the Romani people, and so do some distinct populations of Native Americans, African Americans, and others within the United States and Canada.

Africa is far from alone in suffering medical neglect. India has one doctor for every 1,800 people, but the distribution is very uneven. The ratio of doctors to rural residents (who constitute 70 percent of the populace) is nearly six times lower than that in the urban population. The ratio of hospital beds to the rural populace is fifteen times lower than in the cities.[30] Moreover, the Indian public-health system remains grossly inadequate and underfunded. Only 17 percent of all health expenditures in India are borne by the state, and 82 percent come from out-of-pocket payments by individuals. Only five nations—Burundi, Myanmar, Pakistan, Sudan, and Cambodia—offer worse health-care access than

India.[31] This means that few of India's poor have needed access to care, including hospitalization.

Within poor developing countries in Africa and elsewhere, safe medical devices can be as scarce as doctors. Reused single-use devices (SUDs) and unsterilized needles help to spread AIDS and other infectious illnesses. The medically damaging injection practices and the practice of ethically suspect research have fomented a loss of trust in needed vaccines in countries like Nigeria.[32]

Much of the news coverage focuses upon the contentions by suspicious Africans that the administration of Western vaccines spreads HIV and causes sterility.[33] But whether these fears are accurate or imaginary, the practical result is unambiguous: suspicious patients avoid care, and this iatrophobia means that "conquered" diseases such as polio have seen a resurgence on the continent.[34]

The focus on the poverty and debt of former Western colonies is myopic in that it ignores the causes of such privation, which is very pertinent to ethical discussions. African nations were wealthy before encounters with European colonists. Their gold, diamonds, minerals, oil, exotic livestock, and medically important flora have been stolen by European countries as they divided the continent's spoils, including its people, many of whom were kidnapped en masse. National boundaries were redrawn for the convenience of colonists without regard for existing ties of kinship, amity, or enmity, abetting deeply entrenched conflict and warfare. African poverty is not a natural state; it was precipitated by Western greed and colonial policies. The exonerating argument that poverty and a health-care vacuum separate the poor of the developing world from the medicines that can keep them alive is factually unsubstantiated and morally feeble, and it violates the principle of legal equity, which does not permit a party to profit from its own wrongs.

Round Up the Usual Subjects

In the midst of this therapeutic vacuum and public-health black hole, a lucrative research culture paradoxically burgeons. While the developing world's wounds go unbound, research is big business in Africa, India, Latin America, and the poorer enclaves of Eastern Europe.

"To get around consent forms and a skeptical public, many researchers are turning their attention to African and other developing countries," Robert F. Murray Jr., MD, chair of the Division of Medical Genetics at Howard University, observed more than a decade ago. "I would say the greatest chance for injury is in the Third World, where people don't even know research is going on and don't have a clue."

His concern was prescient because a November 2009 study in the *New England Journal of Medicine* found that U.S. research has become globalized. Fully one-third of the Phase III trials from the twenty largest pharmaceutical companies are conducted outside the United States, and most study sites—13,521 of 24,206—are located in developing countries.[35] This number has more than doubled since Murray's observation, as clinical trials conducted in the United States and the rest of the West decreased.[36] Impoverished Eastern European nations contribute subjects as well. The number of FDA-regulated investigators who are based outside the United States has grown by 15 percent a year since 2002, while the number of domestic U.S. investigators has declined by 5.5 percent.[37]

Seventy billion dollars is spent each year on medical research, but not on malaria, tuberculosis, sleeping sickness, or other scourges of the poor: only 10 percent of this sum is dedicated to the diseases that cause 90 percent of the world's health burden.

This discrepancy provides an incubator for research abuses. Surrounded by pain, death, and infection, medically ignored peoples are confronted with a Hobson's choice: experimental medicine or no medicine at all.[38] U.S. researchers are supposed to adhere to our own ethical and protection standards when conducting studies abroad, and their protocols must be approved by their home institutions. But at every level, these protections have been weakening, and some studies flout them outright.

"Research in the Third World looks relatively attractive as it becomes better funded and regulations at home become more restrictive," agreed Marcia Angell, professor of social medicine at Harvard Medical School and former editor of the *New England Journal of Medicine*, in a 1998 essay.

Why conduct trials abroad? Clinical trials in the developing world are completed more cheaply and more quickly than those conducted in the United States and Europe. A top-tier academic medical center in India charges approximately $1,500 to $2,000 per subject, compared to the $20,000 charged by second-rate research centers in the United States.[39] Much of the savings are due to the cheaper labor of medical professionals in the Third World.[40] Pharmaceutical companies have therefore found it in their financial interests to move their trials to Africa, India, and Southeast Asia.

Western researchers also find Third World testing sites convenient because they conform to fewer and looser regulatory requirements. The language of the World Medical Association's Declaration of Helsinki, which dictates the ethical conduct of research abroad by Western physicians, is often ambiguous, as when it states that U.S. institutional review boards "should" (not "must") evaluate and green-light their organizations' research at home and abroad: there is no external penalty for failing to do so, although many medical centers and universities require such oversight. Even when consulted, these U.S. IRBs often have little information and experience of the conditions in foreign research sites and often rely upon the assurances of the very researchers who are eager to perform the studies.[41]

For example, most university policies align with FDA regulations that require treatments given to the control-group members to be the "standard of care" for the treatment of the illness. Thus, if one wanted to test the broad-spectrum antibiotic trovafloxacin, or Trovan, in Connecticut, the protocol or research plan would stipulate that researchers must give the control group the best drugs known to treat meningitis, such as the drug ceftriaxone. However, the FDA monitors less than 1 percent of clinical trials conducted outside our country.[42]

When no effective treatment for a condition exists, control-group members may receive a placebo, an inert substance, or a sham technique without intrinsic disease-fighting activity—a sugar pill that allows scientists to compare the results of a treated and an untreated group.

But placebo studies, which are falling out of favor in the West, are completely inappropriate for serious diseases when effective treatment exists. You cannot ethically justify withholding, for example, an efficacious drug such as AZT from HIV-positive people or people at high risk of contracting HIV just to determine whether protease inhibitors work better than nothing. You must give the tested group protease inhibitors and the control group the best-known standard therapy.

Giving HIV-positive people in the control group placebos, vitamins, or antibiotics would doom them and so would be an unacceptable ethical breach—at least in the West. However, U.S. IRBs treat Third World populations as second-class subjects and employ different standards for evaluating study designs in Africa and Thailand from those used in the United States—including using placebos in drug trials for fatal illnesses such as AIDS.

Infection and Inequity

Very expensive antiretroviral drugs against HIV disease were priced out of the reach of poor Africans even as their bodies provided the experimental fodder to test these medications' efficacy. Between 1995 and 1997, a U.S. research program tested "subclinical" doses of HIV medications such as zidovudine on pregnant women in Africa and the Dominican Republic. "Subclinical" means a dose of the medication lower than that known to work, so there was a real chance that the medications would offer no protection at all. Zidovudine, given orally during pregnancy, intravenously during labor, and orally to the baby after birth, was known to reduce by two-thirds the chance that an HIV-positive mother would transmit the virus to her baby. It was available in the United States and France for that purpose, but it was very expensive and researchers sought to discover whether lower doses could have the same protective effect, enabling them to market the treatment for less and to treat more people.

To address the question of whether lowered zidovudine doses are protective, the National Institutes of Health and the UN sponsored eighteen trials involving seventeen thousand women. The two studies in the United States administered the full-dose treatment, which is known to work. Women in fifteen African trials, however, were not given the full known effective dose, and many received placebos—no medication at all. African medical workers in Uganda and the Ivory Coast protested that they "do not feel comfortable with the use of placebo," to no avail. Moreover, a Harvard investigator in Thailand, Marc Lallemant, refused to give placebos despite considerable pressure to do so from the CDC.

The intent of these studies was not to discover a treatment for HIV-positive women in Africa: when the study ended, the researchers took the zidovudine with them and none of the women in the study could afford to buy it. The idea was to save money by determining how low a dose of these every expensive medicines would protect U.S. and Western women, whose governments, HMOs, or insurers could afford the treatment.

Principles governing international research with human subjects are articulated by the Declaration of Helsinki, which states, "In any medical study, every patient including those of a control group, if any, should be assured of the best proven diagnostic and therapeutic method." The best proven method cannot be a lower dose than that shown to work, and in the U.S. arm of the study, all women subjects received this best dose in apparent acknowledgment of this ethical principle. But many U.S. health-policy experts and even ethicists argued that "local" standards of treatment should apply in the developing world.

David Satcher, MD, who was then director of the Centers for Disease Control and had the ultimate say on the study's existence, has defended the research on the basis of its benefits, because the study found that lower doses of antiretrovirals did indeed protect the children of infected African and Thai women against HIV infection. This consequentialist defense ignores the heightened risk to which only Thai and African women were exposed, and from which Western women, who were given the full complement of the drug, were protected. Both Satcher and Harold Varmus, MD, then the director of the National Institutes of Health, went on to defend the research by pointing out that "no treatment," the standard offered by the placebo, *was* the standard of care in the health-care vacuum of the poor developing countries under study. Dr. Varmus and Dr. Satcher argued that the use of a placebo control is ethical because assignment to the placebo group would "not carry a risk beyond that associated with standard practice."[43] "Research does not create an entitlement," agreed Robert J. Levine of Yale University. These researchers contended that HIV trials conducted in the developing world among sick people with placebos—that is, without any effective medication—do not violate any human rights because treatment is practically unavailable in an impoverished place like Africa.[44]

Thus, in a variation on the "blame poverty, not patents" theme, they urged us to blame the health-care vacuum of the global South for less-than-scrupulous medical care, not the researchers who observe a double standard of research ethics between American and African control groups.

Drs. Peter Lurie and Sidney Wolfe of Public Citizen best summarized the arguments of those who disagreed. Babies' lives might have been saved by using an effective medication in the comparisons, they maintained. Other critics believe that some participants in the trials may not have been given informed consent. Wendy K. Mariner of Boston University pointed out that trials such as these can be ethical only if the protocol includes a plan from the beginning to make the tested treatment available to the local population should it prove effective. But there was not, and the successful treatment was withheld after the study's end. Yohana J. S. Mashalla, MD, vice president of the Medical Association of Tanzania, told *Scientific American* that the studies sought to demonstrate in developing countries the value of a therapy that was adopted only in developed ones, compounding their exploitative nature.[45]

Dr. Marcia Angell criticized the study's lack of equipoise, a term that refers to the fact that because it is unethical to give a research subject a treatment that is known to be inferior to the accepted standard of care, a researcher must have genuine uncertainty about whether the substance he is testing is better or worse than the standard of care that he is using in control groups. Obviously these investigators in the African and Thai arms of the study knew the subclinical doses were not better than the clinical standard.

The Declaration of Helsinki demands that "only when there is no known effective treatment is it ethical to compare a potential new treatment with a placebo. . . . Instead, subjects in the control group of the study must receive the best known treatment."

In an editorial, Angell pointedly observed that the "local" treatment standard for medical research "could result in widespread exploitation of vulnerable Third World populations for research programs that could not be carried out in the sponsoring country." She went on to compare the antiretroviral trials with the Tuskegee syphilis experiment, in which 399 black men with syphilis were tricked into a research study by being promised treatment for their "bad blood." But they were not treated and instead were studied for forty years in an attempt to characterize the disease more extensively. She wrote,

The fact remains that many studies are done in the Third
World that simply could not be done in the countries sponsoring the work. Clinical trials have become a big business, with
many of the same imperatives. To survive, it is necessary to
get the work done as quickly as possible, with a minimum of
obstacles. When these considerations prevail, it seems as if we
have not come very far from Tuskegee after all.[46]

Human-subjects research regulations are supposed to protect
research subjects abroad as well as those at home. Requiring evidence
that the drug being administered meets or exceeds the standard of medical care is de rigueur for Western trials, but university IRBs (and revised
international research agreements) now employ an ethical sleight of
hand to stipulate that the tested drug must meet or exceed the standard
of care *in the country where the study is being evaluated.* In impoverished,
medically underserved sub-Saharan African countries, that standard of
care has historically tended to be nothing at all.

Even this dilute standard is not always observed. Only 56 percent of
the 670 researchers in one study reported that their research in developing countries had been reviewed by a local IRB or health ministry.[47]
A 2004 study found that 90 percent of China's published clinical-trial
results did not report an ethical review of the protocol. Less than one in
five studies (18 percent) offered credible evidence of informed consent.[48]

Consent Optional

Informed consent has been inconsistently observed in the developing
world. Although Western scientists are supposed to seek the consent of
their developing-world subjects, this has never been a popular requirement, as the exasperated 1964 complaint of Francis D. Moore, MD, illustrates.

Several years ago an individual from this country went
to Nigeria to try out a new measles vaccine on a lot of small
children. Now how exactly are you going to explain to a black
African jungle mother the fact that measles vaccine occasionally produces encephalitis but that more important than that

it might sensitize the child for the rest of his life to some other protein in the vaccine? We now know that any sort of immune response excites cross reactions. For example, if a person develops a heightened immune reaction to some specific antigen such as typhoid he will be found to have other high titers against non specific antigens at the same time. In fact, there is a suspicions [*sic*] that some of the so-called auto-immune diseases are aroused by exposure of the reticuloendothelial system to completely different antigens. The possibility therefore arises that measles vaccines applied to thousands and thousands of children might excite in some of them such diseases as thyroiditis and ulcerative colitis. Can you imagine trying to explain that to a jungle mother? . . . One of the greatest assets of a good doctor is the ability to look a patient in the eye and have the patient go along with him on a hazardous course of treatment. . . . The same quality is exhibited by a medical experimenter when he looks at [a] patient and says that he thinks everything is all right.[49]

Moore avoided the troublesome task of individual disclosure and consent in the mid-twentieth century, and so do many contemporary researchers in poor venues who do not want to take the time to translate their proposal into the local language and culture.

They do not want to explain to hundreds or thousands of subjects such risks as iatrogenic encephalitis and sensitization—concepts that would have been as murky to a Connecticut homemaker in 1964 as they were to Moore's "jungle mother." Scientists like Moore do not want to risk having their potential subjects reject the experiment once they understand the possible health costs. Neither do they especially want to explain why they are testing a new therapeutic approach to HIV infection thousands of miles away from the millions of cases in their own country. Moore doesn't mention this sort of question in his tirade against informed consent, but I suspect that it is among the more difficult of the questions his jungle mother might put to him today. Such arguments recall the lament of Jeremy Bentham, father of utilitarianism, that "the plea of impossibility offers itself at every step, in justification of injustice in all its forms."

Today, many researchers claim that they dispense with informed consent because the very concept wars with the local culture. They explain that the local headman, for example, who typically is paid for his trouble, makes decisions for the entire community about whether to submit to medical research studies; so, out of respect for that community, the researcher elicits only *his* consent.

This is a very convenient—and rare—species of cultural sensitivity in the Western research milieu. One wonders how researchers who respond with such acute sensitivity to such counterintuitive wishes of subjects can bear to withhold medications after they are tested and approved. Surely the subjects prefer to continue to receive the lifesaving drugs that they have tested, so why are *these* wishes ignored when the subjects' ostensible wish to be compelled into research is slavishly complied with?

However, researchers' claim that informed consent wars with the local culture is belied by the statements, papers, and sometimes the laws promulgated by medical ethicists in the countries where U.S. and other scientists conduct their laissez-faire research. Uganda, for example, decried such sidestepping of informed consent by the West and compared it with the oppressive policies of Idi Amin. The nation's ethicists also pointed out that it violated their established laws that guaranteed informed consent to research subjects.

Moreover, such failures to provide informed consent are ethical abuses that are not tolerated in the United States, and so should not be tolerated abroad. If respect for individual health and rights motivates the researcher, nothing stops her from obtaining informed consent from the subject as well as a blanket consent from the headman, and enrolling only those persons who consent.

The researcher's claim that she dispenses with consent in deference to local custom is unconvincing and is likely based on cultural misunderstandings, or worse. Even in those societies where a headman or representative of the group makes some decisions for its members, an individual might be willing to adhere to the headman's will when a few chickens are involved, but may well desire to make his own decisions where lifesaving or life-threatening medical research is at stake.

One could wish that scientists and corporations would exhibit a similar level of respect for cultural indigenous precepts when they seize and patent plants and genes in the teeth of dramatic protests, opposition, and legal challenges from the same native peoples.

Compelling Patent Justice

The pomp of a governmental signing ceremony on May 4, 2007, in Brasília reached its climax when Brazilian President Luiz Inácio Lula da Silva rose and smiled broadly for television cameras. Around the nation, TV screens were eagerly scrutinized by native groups in villages, by healthcare workers, AIDS patients, and office workers who paused long enough to watch Lula make good on a decades-old threat. Amid applause, he signed with a flourish the decree that was taken as a declaration of war by U.S. pharmaceutical companies.

Brazil had just parted with Big Pharma in as dramatic and public a manner as possible. For the first time, it had signed a compulsory license that allows the nation to make or import a generic version of Merck's patented antiretroviral medication efavirenz. At least sixty-five thousand people in Brazil were receiving efavirenz free from the government, and although Merck had lowered its price from $580 to $400 annually, Brazil argued that it could obtain the generic version for $165. For years Brazil had been trying to negotiate a contract with Merck that would allow it to distribute the medication to its populace more cheaply, and it had repeatedly warned that if an affordable price was not offered, it would disregard the patent altogether to address the AIDS public-health emergency, as the TRIPS agreement allows. Now, using the compulsory license, Brazil stood to save $30 million a year, even after paying Merck the required royalty.

"Our decision today involves this one drug, but we can take the same steps with any other that we consider necessary," Lula announced. "It doesn't matter if it's a U.S., German, French, Brazilian or Argentine company." Pedro Chequer, of the Joint United Nations Programme on HIV/AIDS and the former director of Brazil's AIDS program, echoed Lula's euphoria: "I am really proud of this wonderful political decision."

A heartened Thailand quickly issued its own compulsory license for efavirenz as well as for two other expensive patented medications. "Many other countries will likely follow suit," predicted James Love, the economist behind Knowledge Ecology International, a Washington think tank.[50]

Merck warned that such acts would have a chilling effect on future drug design and pronounced itself "profoundly disappointed." So was the U.S. Chamber of Commerce, as Lieutenant General Daniel W. Christman (ret.), the chamber's senior vice president, wrote that "Just days after Brazil was recognized for improving its enforcement of intellectual property (IP) rights, its government has made a major step backward. Breaking off discussions with Merck and seizing its intellectual property sends a dangerous signal to the investment community. Merck researchers invested hundreds of millions of dollars to develop this ground-breaking medicine."[51]

The cost of such research investments is typically exaggerated, as discussed in Chapter 2. Therefore, we can view with skepticism claims that compulsory licenses will hamper research and development, especially in light of the knowledge that efavirenz, like more than 99 percent of medications, was developed and tested with the needs and markets of the West, not developing nations, in mind. "They were created for the European and U.S. markets, and that's where the incentive comes from to invest in developing them," contends Sean Flynn, an intellectual-property expert at American University in Washington, D.C.[52] "There must be a better way to support medical research than condemning 90 percent of people who need a drug to death, just to maintain high prices for the other 10 percent," adds Love.

Brazil was not the first nation to issue compulsory licenses, but developing countries' earlier forays into defying pharmaceutical houses dispensed with patents on older, first-generation drugs that were nearing expiry anyway. Now the game has changed because it involves expensive second-line AIDS drugs with a long patent life ahead of them. Drug firms also fear that compulsory licenses may extend far beyond AIDS drugs, to medications for other common ailments. "There's a big push in Thailand to do it for everything," Love told *Science* magazine.[53]

Challenges remain, especially for India, which leads the world in the production of cheap medications thanks to its expertise in reverse-engineering drugs and its manufacturing capabilities. India's patent system covers the processes by which medicines are made, not the medicine formulations themselves, so copying drugs allowed it to dominate the cheap markets and to provide copycat drugs to other nations too poor to afford Western prices. But once India signed the TRIPS agreement, it was forced to honor patents on drugs themselves. Those medications it manufactured before 1995 will always remain off-patent, but India may lose its ability to provide cheap versions of the others.[54]

For countries such as India, Brazil, Thailand, and sub-Saharan African nations, throwing off the yoke of Western patents is a matter of survival, not profits. More than 22.4 million people in Africa alone are living with HIV disease, and twelve million have already died of AIDS. Fully 90 percent of people with HIV live in developing nations and cannot afford the medications they need to keep them alive. Without patent markups, the average price tag on these medications would be cut by more than 90 percent—that means $1,000 a year instead of $10,000, and similar math applies to tuberculosis, malaria, and cancer drugs.[55]

The pharmaceutical industry, as we've seen, argues that poverty, not its patents, is the villain; that what Africa needs is a better health-care infrastructure, not cheaper drugs; that the industry's intellectual-property interests are being illicitly appropriated; and that compulsory licensing is little better than theft.

Yet, as James Love points out, talk of a lack of respect for intellectual property in certain developing countries gives way to a more respectful characterization of compulsory licensing when Western nations do it. Italy has granted compulsory licenses on a Merck antibiotic, a prostate-and-baldness drug, as well as a GSK migraine medication—with nary an outraged ripple in the press. Since 2006, U.S. courts have issued compulsory licenses on automatic transmission patents that benefited Toyota, on set-top box[56] patents that benefited DirecTV, on digital-rights management, or DRM, technology that helps owners restrict access to digital information such as movies, literature, music, or software. Johnson & Johnson financially benefited from a compulsory license on a medical device.[57] The United States decries the Brazilian compulsory license to get AIDS drugs to patients, but the U.S. Federal Trade Commission recently issued its own compulsory license on computer memory chips in the case of Rambus Corporation, a chip designer.[58]

Bernard Lemoine, director of France's National Pharmaceutical Industry Association, captured his industry's disturbing indifference to human life when he complained, "I don't see why special effort should be demanded from the pharmaceutical industry. Nobody asks Renault to give cars to people who haven't got one."[59]

Perhaps spurred by such sentiments, people of the developing world are no longer passively awaiting the trickle of largesse from the pharmaceutical industry. The Doha concession, which enables nations to set aside the patents that bar their access to medicines, is the beginning of a long-delayed chapter on pharmaceutical activism and self-determination.

And yet simply dispensing with patents is not the ultimate answer to the harms that flow in the wake of pharmaceutical greed. The answer—for patients, subjects, researchers, and patent holders alike—depends upon our ability to generate new, workable, and nonexploitative models of drug development. The answer also depends upon our ability to forge the sometimes surprising coalitions that can seek and enable universal access to essential medicines while ensuring viability (and profits, however muted) to the pharmaceutical industry.

Next, the epilogue explores this new horizon in drug development.

EPILOGUE

Back to the Future?

In formal logic a contradiction is the signal of a defeat, but in the evolution of real knowledge it marks the first step in progress toward a victory.

—ALFRED NORTH WHITEHEAD

What has this book's catalog of greed, imperiled health, failures, infuriating injustices, and inspiring visions taught us that can help us forge a better system of incentives and rewards for needed medical research and health care? How can we move forward toward fulfillment of our wishes for more and better medicines?

Perhaps we should first take a step back.

The monopolies enabled by the Bayh-Dole Act and related laws of the 1980s have successfully allied for-profit corporations and universities. This pharmaceutical-academic alliance through patents certainly did succeed by some measures. It provided a way to more quickly develop the university innovation that lay fallow by allowing academia to transfer patents and licenses to corporations. The number of these developed patents has soared beyond five thousand, and hundreds of biotechnology firms sprouted as technology-transfer offices proliferated and earned their institutions at least $45 billion. This innovation has been a huge financial success, making tens of billions in profits for both universities and corporations: until recently, pharmaceutical firms constituted the most profitable industry not only in the country, but on the planet.

But the relationship is asymmetrical: when corporations bought and licensed university patents and funded postpatent research and development, they also began to dictate the terms under which these patents were developed to generate income, giving for-profit corporations sway over the means, timing, and methods of U.S. medical research itself, to say nothing of their ability to determine what research would be carried out and what research directions would be ignored. In this manner they usurped the traditional role—and the traditional cultural values, directed at the public weal—of university medical research.

Failure to Launch

The system has failed for U.S. patients, who pay more for health care and receive less. Too often, they cannot afford the industry's very expensive medications. Moreover, the bodies and body parts of Americans have been appropriated for marketable tissues, and Icelanders' bodies have been mined for their genes. Recently, Americans have even been given over to nonconsensual research with a profound lack of transparency.

The system has proved equally problematic for researchers and other medical innovators who have largely lost their autonomy. As a result of their financial success, university medical research has been invested with the profit-seeking mentality of the corporation; but the corporation remains largely immune to the altruistic, profit-scorning, collaborative ideal that characterized pre-1980s medical-research culture.

In place of the collegial collaboration that marked pre-1980s research, today's investigators find silence imposed on them that strictly prohibits sharing data, theories, and findings at conferences, as Dr. William Catalona discovered to his chagrin. Data sharing, which was once the norm, is even criminalized, as Drs. Zhu and Kimbara discovered when they found themselves sitting in jail cells over an intellectual-property dispute after they left Harvard. Some researchers see their drug trials brought to an abrupt end by a drug maker's insistence that the drug be a financial blockbuster as well as a medical success. Others, such as investigators seeking better breast cancer, hepatitis C, and hemachromatosis treatments, are prevented by a patent from pursuing their chosen research direction.

Susan Molchan of the NIH saw decades of work to combat Alzheimer's disappear with the illicit sale of $6 million in government-subsidized tissue samples to Pfizer; Christopher Parish's life's work was cut short by

Polpharma when his promising liver cancer drug showed signs of falling short of blockbuster status; and William Catalona's research into prostate cancer was similarly ended when the University of Washington seized control over tissue samples from prostate cancer sufferers—over his objections and those of the "donors" who contributed them.

Today, profit-driven medical monopolies also present problems for physicians and hospitals, who are sometimes sued, as was Thunder Bay for treating patients in strict compliance with the law but against the monopolistic interests of patent holders such as Bayer Healthcare. Other physicians cite a fear of lawsuits as a deterrent to giving patients necessary tests, as Deepak Gill of the Children's Hospital at Westmead, Australia, did when the hospital strictly rationed tests of infants at risk for Dravet disease, a severe form of childhood epilepsy. "The patent system was established, I believe, to protect the lone inventor," mused Swedish-American engineer Ernst F. W. Alexanderson, the holder of 322 patents. "In this it has not succeeded. The patent system protects the institutions which favor invention."

Monopolistic medical research has not worked out for the poor in the developing world, either, because the system has neither pursued nor provided remedies for the diseases of poor people. Instead, it profits hugely from its ability to conduct cheap, rapid research with relatively poorly informed subjects who live amid a health-care vacuum that causes them to grasp desperately at any proffered medical straw, even a medical-research study without the usual Western protections of informed consent and without the provision of standard treatment to control subjects. They are asked to assume risks that are not required of Westerners.

Frankly, though, aside from the very limited focus on preserving colonial subjects' fitness for work, the medical needs of poor people in the developing world were never a priority of Western health care, even before 1980. However, the need to maximize patent profits has spurred pharmaceutical firms to offer a legitimizing discourse for this long-standing indifference. The industry now cites the need to protect its intellectual-property rights as an excuse for not developing and offering affordable drugs, blaming "poverty, not patents" for the medical misery of those for whom it chooses not to develop desperately needed drugs.

The current system's failures for all these groups should be quite enough to spur us to create a new paradigm, but there is one more group for whom the monopolistic system seems to be faltering: pharmaceutical companies, which have lost their fiscal primacy and fallen to the number-three spot in profitability among global industries. These companies still earn billions today, but may not do so tomorrow. Profits are falling despite their flouting of FDA laws and their perversion of the medical-publication process (such as the ghostwritten hormone-replacement-therapy articles by DesignWrite for Wyeth Laboratories, the faux medical journals penned for Merck by Elsevier, and the payola to drug evaluators and to prominent medical "thought leaders" such as psychiatrists Joseph Biederman of Harvard and Frederick K. Goodwin, lately of NPR). The artificial "clinical trials" aimed at selling pills in volume, the courting of consumers via direct-to-consumer advertisements, the churning out of cheap doppelgänger "me too" drugs, and other life-management strategies to extend the life of their patents by decades have not saved pharmaceutical companies from losing ground.

For years, the $1-billion-a-year blockbuster drugs have been drying up rapidly, falling off the "patent cliff" with little innovation in the pipeline to replace them. Pharmaceutical firms' widespread strategy of buying up biotechnology companies to supply the missing innovation is unproven, and, frankly, it smells of desperation. Whether most firms will admit it or not, this particular patent-based system is no longer working well enough for them, either.

Repeal Bayh-Dole

Progress is desirable, but the compulsion to avoid backsliding should not so blind us to the current system's failings that we are afraid to examine alternatives. These alternatives are legion, but to select the best of them we must include a return to selected past incentives and policies in order to recapture valuable aspects of the university's lost medical culture. We need not be trapped in the past, but we can choose to glean its advantages as we go forward. As a Ghanaian proverb reminds us, "It is not wrong to go back for that which you have forgotten."

What has been abandoned in the wake of Bayh-Dole is patient primacy and altruism. Researchers once derived their satisfaction from the prospect of becoming a famous benefactor by devising the means of healing many people. They also desired the intellectual challenge and the fame of achievement, and were motivated by such rewards instead of merely by money—and these rewards dovetailed with the medical needs of the populace. To return these intangible motivations to center stage, we should uncouple the conduct of medical research from the pressure to protect a monopoly at all costs that is exerted on researchers today by their institutions and sponsoring corporations.

So what will work to attain the dream of affordable medical innovation for all without rendering universities and pharmaceutical companies destitute and unable to function, and without sacrificing medical progress?

Repealing Bayh-Dole would be a good start. The transformation of U.S. medical research was born in the law, and revoking those laws is one approach to reversing their effects. I fully understand that this sounds like a radical response to many, and I am not sanguine about the likelihood that Bayh-Dole can be repealed anytime soon. In the decades since Bayh-Dole became law, there have been unsuccessful moves to amend the legislation, defeated by the desire of universities and companies to maintain the status quo.[1]

Those who maintain that repealing Bayh-Dole is impossible should remember, however, that the same thing was said about revoking gene patents. As we saw in Chapter 5, experts of all stripes expressed shock in March 2010 when Judge Robert W. Sweet of the Federal District Court in Manhattan ruled seven of Myriad Genetics' twenty-three patents on the breast and ovarian cancer genes BRCA1 and BRCA2 invalid. Although a panel of three Federal District Court judges restored most of these patents as this book went to press, they upheld the invalidation of patents that granted Myriad the exclusive right to compare the patient's gene sequence with its patented sequences. The other patent reinstatements will be appealed, likely in the Supreme Court. Just a month earlier, a very broad patent on Ariad Pharmaceutical's NF-κB gene, which determines how genes themselves are replicated and affects the production of many drugs, was also invalidated.[2]

The dissatisfaction with such patent monopolies is broad among laypersons and scientists alike, and if the decision against Myriad stands on appeal, it seems no less likely that Bayh-Dole could present the next, broader target once people understand the profound effect it has had on medical research and their ability to obtain health care.

There have long been signs that some in the nation's medical leadership are wearying of the current monopolistic system as well: in February 2005, the National Institutes of Health, which disburses $30 billion for medical-research money each year, recommended that "whenever possible, non-exclusive licensing should be pursued," a guideline that was immediately endorsed by the National Research Council, a preeminent adviser to the nation on research policy.[3]

Even if reversing Bayh-Dole proves not to be the best answer or an unattainable option, the answer must lie in the law, just as these dangerous monopolies originated in the law.

The laws must establish a balance between the needs of corporations and those of U.S. citizens because the corporate world, and in particular the pharmaceutical industry, has been unable to police itself and indeed has no incentive to do so: its interests have been served by the monopolistic policies that generated the problem.

Moreover, it is not the legal responsibility of the pharmaceutical industry to provide affordable medications for the ailments that are of most import to most of the world: its mission is to make money. The primacy of altruistic public-policy concerns that lead researchers to work on remedies not because they will sell but because they will heal was the purview of the university medical-research system, and that system has been elbowed out of existence. In the old system medical researchers championed altruism, free and open collaboration, and meticulously accurate publication. This all-but-vanished medical culture enshrined fame, not fortune, as the ultimate motivation because it distrusted patents and all but sneered at profit-making as it sought to serve the public weal.

This model was a necessary counterweight to the profit-driven system: we need it back. Who else but the independent university and researcher can be trusted consistently to put healing first without regard for the profit-making demands of a corporation?

Placing the welfare of patients first *is* the responsibility of the government that funds the initial research on which drug makers' patents rest. U.S. medical research is possible only because of the taxpayers' huge investment, so it is the business of the federal government to ensure that this investment goes into generating medications that Americans need—and can afford. We have a moral responsibility to the developing world to provide the same for them, especially because they supply the means to conduct research that produces our medications more cheaply and efficiently than we can do ourselves.

Another legal remedy we must explore is eliminating health-care lobbyists from all governmental discussions of medications and intellectual property. No one elects lobbyists, yet they have heavily influenced health-care legislation and most have loyalties to the pharmaceutical industry, not the American people. Were it not for their influence, for example, the Patient Protection and Affordable Care Act would have included badly needed drug-price controls. President Obama set an excellent precedent when he barred most lobbyists from working within the administration, but potential conflicts may have slipped under the radar: for example, the Centers for Medicare and Medicaid Office of Legislation is managed by Amy Hall, who is married to chief PhRMA lobbyist Bryant Hall. We are not able, or willing, to legislate marriages between lobbyists and government power brokers, but the prospect of their pillow talk makes me nervous.[4] Only completely removing lobbyists from health-care decisions will protect the best interests of the American people.

We should also restructure the manner in which pharmaceutical corporations contribute to the FDA budget. Corporations currently provide 40 percent of the costs to evaluate their own products, a conflict of interest that is rendered especially worrisome by the FDA's penchant for approving medications with serious issues over the protestations of its own evaluating physicians. Instead, the contribution of drug companies should be restructured, perhaps in the form of taxes, to minimize the possible conflict.

A law on the books currently provides a putative exemption for "noncommercial" patent prevention that universities hope would allow the conduct of necessary not-for-profit research into patented genes, viruses, and other entities without being sued for patent protection. We need this law to enable research on breast cancer genes, hepatitis C, and Dravet syndrome that has been stymied by legal threats or action.

But in a 2002 court case, *Madey v. Duke University*,[5] an appeals court interpreted the law so narrowly that it was rendered useless as protection for researchers. The court ruled that because universities compete for grants, faculty, and students, make money by licensing and selling their patents, and sue others for infringing on their patents, they are no different from other corporations (universities tend to be incorporated) and so cannot automatically enjoy the exemption. Many professed to be shocked by this turn of events, but it is unsurprising because universities cannot have it both ways. We need this exemption law to be modified or replaced by a new law that removes the handcuffs from those who are seeking needed cures, without fear of reprisals from patent holders. And we need universities to regain enough of their prior not-for-profit character that they can be distinguished from moneymaking corporations.[6]

The patent system itself could benefit from fine-tuning as a result of the thirty years of experience we have had since Bayh-Dole was enacted. One type of utility patent granted for the biological entities should concern us: the twenty years of unfettered profitability that can be extended by various strategies that are well known to the industry. But all patents are not of equal importance, and we should consider a tiered system that reflects this. A patent on a tool such as PCR, which enables the production of large amounts of DNA, might be granted for the entire twenty-year period, whereas a patent on a "me too" medication might be granted for only a five-year period and might not provide for exclusivity but instead allow the manufacture of generics under certain conditions. We can also learn from some refinements of European patent systems, which, for example, build in a six-month "comment period" during which anyone can criticize or applaud the awarding of the patent and make a case for its revocation or permanent adoption. Such systems also make patent revocation easier upon the production of new evidence that questions the eligibility of the patent. This might alleviate the million-dollar price on some patent suits, freeing these funds for drug research and development.

Because the U.S. government contributes so heavily to research, a law should be passed that allows it to exact some conditions when patents are sold or licensed to corporations. Chief among these conditions should be: (1) the right to exercise some measure of price controls; (2) establishing conditions under which it will automatically exercise its march-in powers and reassign the patent should the company balk at making it available or affordable; and (3) the right to stipulate that the medications pursued address important critical medical issues and not only trivial lifestyle conditions.

Finally, legislation should seek to establish some degree of equity in the conduct of offshore research between the West and the developing world to supplement the Declaration of Helsinki. Since, as Chapter 9 made clear, Third World research saves a great deal of money for U.S. corporations and results in medications that benefit U.S. patients, our laws should ensure that the foreign research subjects are treated with concern and respect and that they benefit, too. We can best do this by dictating that IRBs apply a single standard of research ethics, ensuring that patients benefit from the same informed consent that comparative groups enjoy here, and that they are provided with the U.S. standard of care, just as they would be on our shores. We should also guarantee the subjects, and preferably their entire communities, affordable access to the medication that is proven safe and effective after being tested on them.

Research is based on the careful collection and interpretation of data and its objective reporting in peer-reviewed medical journals. But as long as corporations are allowed to subvert the process for their own financial ends, we will never be able to produce reliably safe and effective medications.

To this end, pharmaceutical companies and medical investigators should be required to report *all* their data, not selectively cherry-pick positive findings. Medical journals must have access to all of a study's data before they can honestly pronounce their publications "peer reviewed." To minimize conflicts of interest, journals should be barred from paying medical reviewers anything other than nominal fees (on the order of a few hundred dollars). And as Tufts University professor Sheldon Krimsky has suggested, ghostwriting medical journal articles should be banned as a form of plagiarism, and researchers who have financial interests in drugs or medical devices should not be permitted to test those entities or those of their competitors in drug trials.

Legal remedies will not be enough, however. We also need to go back not only to reverse the ravages of three decades of monopolistic control of medical research, but also to retrieve the moral authority of noncommercial values in medical research. I am not suggesting that medical research should be unprofitable or that researchers should not be rewarded for their work. I am suggesting that something other than money should direct and control the direction and policies of medical research. By using patent monopolies in an imaginative and flexible manner, some have already proven that nonexploitative research can be fruitful *and* profitable. I give some examples here.

Pooling Resources

Remember the patent pool that saved the prewar airplane industry by combining the strengths of the Wright Brothers and the Curtiss Company?

In 2003, an unusual collaboration was forged among scientists, drug and medical-imaging industries, universities, and governmental groups such as the National Institutes of Health and the FDA. Rather than patenting their every discovery, the groups pledged to pool their Alzheimer's data, using a cornucopia of methods from PET scans to tests of spinal fluid. They made every bit of information available on the internet, instantaneously accessible to anyone in the world with access to the Web. This meant that no one could submit patent applications, although private companies could ultimately patent and profit from any drugs or imaging tests that were developed as a result of the effort.

This streamlined effort proved efficient, and the National Institutes of Health even managed to raise some money to further support it. But serious funds materialized only when private industry signed on. When Dr. Steven M. Paul left his position as scientific director at the National Institute of Mental Health to head neurological research at Eli Lilly, he encouraged Lilly and other companies to donate. Ultimately, the contributions totaled $94.4 million.

By 2010, the industry, philanthropic agencies, and the government were collaborating on one hundred studies to test drugs that might slow or stop the disease. Their work promises to make an early diagnosis and perhaps an effective treatment of Alzheimer's possible. "It's not science the way most of us have practiced it in our careers," enthused University of Pennsylvania researcher Dr. John Q. Trojanowski, "but we all realized that we would never get biomarkers unless all of us parked our egos and intellectual-property noses outside the door and agreed that all of our data would be public immediately."[7]

What's more, the Alzheimer's collaboration provided a model that has been adopted by the Michael J. Fox Foundation, which seeks better treatments for Parkinson's disease. Six hundred study subjects have been enrolled in trials in the United States and Europe as part of a $40 million project to better characterize Parkinson's disease.

Marketing Altruism

In seeking alternative roads to innovation, the pharmaceutical industry is gazing toward a market that it has traditionally shunned as unprofitable: the developing world, or at least that portion of it with strong intellectual-property protections, where drug makers think their patents will be respected. The sheer number of potential new consumers in medically underserved countries and their huge burden of disease mean that substantial profits are possible even at modest prices—if the correct marketing strategies are adopted.[8]

As the pharmaceutical companies cast about for a new model to shore up their flagging profits and dwindling innovation, researchers such as Christopher Parish, the inventor of the cancer drug Progen, seek new ways to get their drugs to the people who need them without hindrance from those who insist on the primacy of patent-driven profits. So do philanthropic health-care advocates such as Dr. Paul Farmer, whose Harvard-based Partners in Health brought effective medication regimens to Haiti and other parts of the developing world despite naysayers' insistence that providing expensive AIDS drugs was a fiscal impossibility. Similarly, the Bill and Melinda Gates Foundation, the world's largest medical charity, has undertaken the mission of enhancing health care and reducing poverty for the world's medically disadvantaged.

Can we provide incentives for the industry's new drug research while ensuring global access at low prices? Some insist that you cannot serve God and Mammon, and that in this binary scenario we must sacrifice either corporate profits or poor patients' health.

The Gates Foundation, however, *is* seeking to marry devotees of God and Mammon. It has already met with success in developing and distributing medications through the advance market commitment, or AMC, which is a contract, typically offered by a government, that is used to guarantee a viable market if a medicine is successfully developed.

In partnership with the World Health Organization and other philanthropic groups, the Gates Foundation has provided vast quantities of lifesaving medications to the poor, but it also realized that it needs new drugs and so must rely on the medical innovations of pharmaceutical companies. For example, vaccines against many Third World killers already exist, but those that work so well in the United States and Europe can be useless in the developing world, where health workers have little or no access to the refrigeration, clean water, sterile needles, and skilled caregivers to administer injections on which we in the West can rely.

This was brought home in 1996, when the West African dry season arrived and doctors in Africa's meningitis belt held their collective breath, fearing disaster as they always did when the land grew parched.[9] By late January, their worst fears had materialized, in the form of the largest plague of bacterial meningitis that had ever been recorded. It killed thousands at a time, many of them children, and persisted unabated until June, although new cases continued to appear for years. No one knows why the dry season sometimes brings meningitis to a wide swath of sub-Saharan Africa, and no one can explain why this epidemic was so deadly and so prolonged. But the sparsely distributed doctors knew they lacked enough weapons against it, even with the assistance of Doctors Without Borders, which flew in to help. But this was a temporary measure because, under the usual circumstances in that part of the world, antibiotics are far too expensive and too hard to distribute and administer: amid the continent's dearth of hospitals, clinics, and healers, who would give them?

In the West, meningitis is feared but rare, as the disease, caused by a virus, is not very contagious. In West Africa, however, it infiltrates communities easily, spreading through sneezing, coughing, kissing, and even sharing eating utensils or cigarettes. Just a few days after developing a fever, headache, and a stiff neck, its victims can be dead.

Rapid access to physicians, intensive-care units, and copious antibiotics keeps most victims in the West alive. Only seven of every two hundred people who contract meningitis in the United States die, and only 850 Americans died from it in 1999. But in Africa, where access to treatment is rare, at least one in ten victims dies, and one in five of those who survive does so at the price of lingering neurological damage, including mental retardation, deafness, epilepsy, and cerebral palsy.

By 1997 the epidemic had infected more than 250,000 Africans.

By contrast, only about 25,000 Americans contracted meningitis that year—but 25,000 was the number of Africans who died.

At $70 a dose, Western antibiotics are priced out of African patients' reach. The continent needed a vaccine, but one developed with the pricing, storage, and administration limitations of the region in mind. On February 9, 2007, the Bill and Melinda Gates Foundation announced that it had contracted with Canada, Italy, Norway, Russia, and the United Kingdom to launch the first advance market commitment to help speed the development and availability of a new vaccine against pneumococcal disease, a major cause of pneumonia and meningitis that kills 1.6 million people every year. The Gates Foundation committed $1.5 billion and expressed its hope to save the lives of 5.4 million children by 2030. By June 12, 2009, the coalition had joined with the World Bank, UNICEF, and the World Health Organization. The AMC projected that the long-term price for developing countries would be only $3.50: by contrast, similar Novartis and Sanofi Pasteur vaccines sell for $80 to $100 per dose.[10]

In 2009, tragedy struck once more as an equally deadly meningitis epidemic flared. But it may be the last one, because in December 2010 the Gates AMC announced success: a vaccine against the group A meningitis strain that causes more than four out of five African cases, which could be administered under conditions of privation. It had cost less than $100 million to develop and would sell for only $.50 a dose in ravaged countries like Burkina Faso. An ecstatic Bill Gates compared the development of this Africa-friendly vaccine with earlier ones against measles, smallpox, and polio. "All those things were created because rich people got sick. This is the first vaccine that went through the whole process where there was no rich world market, and it had to be optimized at a very low price."

This is only the most recent of several vaccines that could dramatically lower infant mortality in Africa. In 2009, the Meningitis Vaccine Project introduced the MenAfriVac vaccine developed by the Serum Institute of India, to several African countries, including Rwanda and Gambia, where eight hundred thousand children under five die annually of infectious disease. Mali and Niger are next.[11]

Many are skeptical that private philanthropy can address the global problem of medication access, but the altruism of Gates, who has promised to give away 90 percent of his roughly $50 billion for-tune, is proving infectious: he has induced at least forty of his fellow billionaires—including Warren Buffett, Larry Ellison, Michael Bloom-berg, George Lucas, and Barry Diller—to commit half of their wealth to philanthropy[12] as well via "The Giving Pledge."[13] Not all these donors will focus on supplying needed medicines, but some will, and Gates's efforts will have legs, especially if they also inspire many nonbillionaires to support drug development for the poor.

However, private philanthropy will not have to undertake this challenge alone. In addition to the Gates Foundation, the WHO, the Center for American Progress, and the governments of Burkina Faso and Mali, the profit-free AMC models now have support from an unex-pected source—some pharmaceutical companies, including Merck and Wyeth.[14] These companies have begun to join cooperative efforts seek-ing to offer wider access to their medicines rather than restricting access to those who can pay high prices.

In June 2011, major pharmaceutical firms shattered expectations when they announced that they were slashing prices on vaccines to save the lives of desperately poor children in countries such as Brazil, Nigeria, and rural India, who die in prodigious numbers each year from prevent-able ailments. Rotavirus, for example, is the chief cause of debilitating diarrheal disease that is the second largest killer of children under five worldwide. GlaxoSmithKline boasted that it will provide its Rotarix rotavirus vaccine at a 67-percent reduction, a mere $2.50 a dose. Merck's Rotateq vaccine will cost $5 a dose, which may fall to $3.50 after thirty million doses are sold.[15] Sanofi Pasteur's newly affordable rotavirus vac-cine is being developed by its Indian subsidiary Shantha, and the com-pany also promises deep cuts to the price of its yellow-fever vaccine. The Global Alliance for Vaccines and Immunisation (GAVI) estimates that these price reductions will save the lives of millions of children and may benefit as many as 250 million children by 2015.[16]

Not only the world's children will benefit. In a renaissance of old-fashioned research collaboration, countries that are devising pan-demic vaccines pledged in April 2011 to share virus samples with the WHO's network of laboratories in return for affordable access to the vaccines derived from them. Drug makers have promised to cover half of the $58 million annual cost of protecting the poorest nations.[17] Also,

Merck's Gardasil shot against some cancer-causing strains of the human papillomavirus (HPV) will be sold for $5 per dose, also a 67-percent reduction.[18]

News reports typically treated the announcement of the vaccine price-slashing as an utter surprise. To the astute observer, it is not, although it is true that the move reflects not one, but two 180-degree reversals in the attitudes of pharmaceutical companies toward the vaccine market—the tacit proscription against the development and testing of medicines for diseases of the developing world; and the seeming abandonment of research and development into new vaccines in favor of other, more profitable medications.

But vaccines' potential market is every child and many adults, so their sellers can make up in sheer volume what they lose in per-capita pricing. Quite alive to this economic fact, drug makers have revised their market vision to concentrate on large vaccine markets rather than shunning them.[19]

Unalloyed praise has greeted these companies' declarations of lowered pricing, as if they were driven purely by the industry's altruism. However, the price slashing was made possible only by the substantial monetary and technical contributions of not-for-profit bodies such as the WHO, GAVI, and the Bill and Melinda Gates Foundation, and by Western government subsidies. These bodies pay drug companies for needed vaccines, providing a guaranteed market for the low-cost medicines through the Advance Market Commitment (AMC) described earlier and via similar subsidy arrangements. The Gates Foundation alone has pledged to donate $1 billion to GAVI over the next five years;[20] and, in fact, GAVI announced that the $4.3 billion in funding from nonprofits has exceeded its expectations.[21] Some major Western governments were initially recalcitrant, but have now pledged their support as well.

Moreover, low vaccine prices are also subsidized by the efforts of the people of the developing world. As Chapter 9 richly details, the low-cost research innovation performed with populations in developing nations has significantly reduced the time and costs of the clinical trials that make new medicines possible. The people and industries of the Third World now provide a low-cost center for new vaccine development; and as wealth increases in these countries, their governments will bolster emerging health-care markets into which pharmaceutical companies can tap.[22]

Affordable vaccines fulfill the needs of the pharmaceutical industry as well,[23] which needs these new markets because it has been losing its blockbusters to patent cliffs; and, in the developing world, its profits are further threatened by governments like those of Thailand and Brazil that exercise march-in powers to bypass pharmaceutical patents altogether and license generic versions of needed drugs.[24] Pharmaceutical firms may calculate that reducing the prices is preferable to having their patents invalidated or utterly ignored. It is also preferable to being seen as responsible for the mass deaths of unvaccinated children, so providing affordable vaccines will burnish the industry's badly tarnished corporate image.

And rightly so. One of this book's oft-repeated themes has been the need to recognize and reward the actions of pharmaceutical companies when they put aside their own financial interests in order to provide needed medicines to those who cannot afford their inflated prices. Now, something even better seems to be in the offing—a market model that serves the needs of both patients and pharmaceutical companies. The sort of win-win model promoted by advanced directives and other coalitions for medicine design and distribution is the best hope for toppling the towering hurdles that separate the Third World poor from the medicines they need. The tiered-price scheme for vaccines reflects exactly the sort of flexibility needed in devising more workable and equitable ways of extracting profit from medication patents.

There is no question that the new courting of the developing world, with belated but very welcome attention to the killers that threaten it, augurs well for both the developing world and for pharmaceutical firms, which absolutely should be credited with doing the right thing.

But some question exists as to whether the children of the global South can depend upon the industry to keep its promises. Recall that in the case of African sleeping sickness, drug companies partnered with Doctors Without Borders to provide Ornidyl in 2001—but did so only for five years, leaving sixty to seventy million Africans[25] as vulnerable to the disease as they were before the drug was developed. The future of affordable vaccines in developing nations is threatened by the fact that GAVI today faces a struggle to pay the Western drug makers; there already yawns a $3.7 billion shortfall between the promises and the vaccines.

Will today's jubilation be short-lived? This will be a win-win scenario only as long as people in the developing world can depend upon the continued availability of affordable vaccines. If the slashed prices don't remain low, the model will again revert to exploitation, with the developing world providing the bodies and low-cost research, but unable to access the essential medicines that their risks make possible. National governments and health-advocacy partners must demand a long-term commitment to a stable source of affordable medicines.

Fiscal motives help drive this generosity, because these companies need new business models to shore up their faltering innovation, and developing nations represent a potentially enormous untapped market. Moreover, the corporate image of pharmaceutical makers benefits greatly from the goodwill created by their very public altruism. The motivations of Merck and Wyeth undoubtedly include a desire to promote human welfare, and if they sustain their contributions, human health and saved lives will certainly be their effect.

Global Pharmaceutical Vision

Heartened by this corporate altruism, some visionaries have embraced new models that use patent monopolies in a symbiotic manner to meet the needs of both patients and pharmaceutical firms. For example, Aidan Hollis, a professor of economics at the University of Calgary, and Thomas Pogge, a professor of international affairs at Yale, have developed an alternative model in which pharmaceutical companies continue to obtain patents on their products and are paid for the use of those patents and products. However, the size of the payments will directly reflect the extent to which their new drugs reduce the global burden of disease.

Pogge and Hollis suggest that all governments contribute to a Health Impact Fund that would compensate companies in proportion to their products' effect in ameliorating pressing health concerns and reducing disease. In their scheme, the pharmaceutical company (or other patent holder) must agree to supply its medications at cost around the world and to aid in the measurement of its medicines' health impact, which would typically be a direct assessment of how much the new drugs reduced deaths and disability every year, followed by an annual payout.[26]

Thus, instead of profiting from a patent whose exclusivity allows it to set high prices that can be met by a relative few, the company would charge low prices for the drug and receive a share of the fund for a decade as it distributes its drug much more widely than current high prices would allow.[27]

This system would provide an incentive to address the biggest killers worldwide, such as malaria and tuberculosis, rather than minor lifestyle ailments that only relatively affluent Westerners can afford to medicate. The Pogge-Hollis model would also establish global equity, in that every life will have an equal value: thus a company would receive the same financial reward for saving the lives of poor Indians and Africans as it does for saving Europeans and Americans.

Finally, this model brilliantly removes the disincentives for a drug maker to license cheap generic drugs during the life of its patent, because the more people can afford its medication, the greater the drug maker's payout from the fund.[28]

Conspiracy of Caring

Still other medical-research groups dispense with patent protections altogether, as did the CDC and the Human Genome Project when they sought to hasten innovation by placing their findings in the public domain. University of Toronto structural biologist Aled Edwards has organized an even more radical change than mere collaboration: open-access drug development, the antithesis of the patent system. In this throwback to pre–Bayh-Dole days, before patent concerns led firms to criminalize collaboration, Edwards proposes that industry and academia cooperate and put the results of their innovation in the public domain by posting their findings, free, on the internet. This publication will preclude patenting the information because it will no longer be novel. Instead, he insists that sharing expertise and results through such a partnership will save time and money by creating effective drugs much more quickly and efficiently.

Edwards's model is more than a vision. His Structural Genomics Consortium already exists as a nonprofit collaboration of the University of Toronto, Oxford University, and Sweden's Karolinska Institute, in collaboration with drug makers Merck, Novartis, and GlaxoSmithKline.[29]

The consortium hosts 250 scientists from more than one hundred laboratories in industry and academia that study the three-dimensional structure of medically important human proteins, which are critical preludes to drug discovery.

In just five years, consortium scientists have produced structures for one-fifth of all human proteins, all of which are freely available to any scientist. Edwards has predicted that new cancer drugs will be the first results to emerge from the open-access pipeline because so many are already working in that field. Should the Edwards model catch on, perhaps the next Christopher Parish, partnering with a similar consortium, will find his race for a cure unobstructed by a patent stumbling block.

Unfortunately, nearly all researchers and corporations still operate under the patent model, which limits access to necessary medications and tests. The sort of profit-based decisions that derailed PI-88, Ornidyl, and other lifesaving medications contradicts the argument that patent protection drives the best health outcomes. The primacy of the profit motive and the jealous defense of patents have led not to wider drug availability but to the withholding of many needed therapies.[30]

Drug companies are culpable for the abandonment of badly needed drugs, but they are not solely to blame. Although the pharmaceutical industry should be held to ethical standards that would shape their drug-development policies, its chief mission entails maximizing profits. The federal government's responsibility, on the other hand, includes protecting its investment of taxpayers' dollars to ensure that funds are not shunted away from research on badly needed new drugs. Accordingly, the government should impose limits on profitability and should exert pressure on pharmaceutical companies to address the pressing medical issues that stand between Americans and better health.

Federal agencies already offer carrots in the form of grants and tax credits, but it is now time to wield a stick, too, even if this means passing new measures or revising the laws that grant corporations access to government-subsidized university research.

In return for its fiscal support, the government should demand that a certain percentage of each company's research be directed to specified critical health issues. It could achieve this by curtailing a company's access to government-subsidized patents and to tax credits if a firm fails to devote enough resources to more meaningful drug innovation. Perhaps, too, the government should consider issuing compulsory licenses on a frankly punitive basis for companies that fail to venture beyond lifestyle illnesses.

Pharmaceutical companies will doubtless strenuously object to such limitations on their economic autonomy, and admittedly, the need to undertake such measures would seem unfortunate, though not as distasteful and disastrous as the industry's tendency to ignore critical global health challenges. It would be preferable if the industry itself adopted a standard for allocating resources to more serious medical issues. Instead, it often pursues profits to the exclusion of addressing serious disease. This state of affairs can no longer be tolerated—its costs in lives and moral inequity are far too high.

ACKNOWLEDGMENTS

In 1992, while on a fellowship for Advanced Studies in Public Health at the Harvard School of Public Health, I had the good fortune to meet Marcia Angell, MD, professor of social medicine at the Harvard Medical School and author of *The Truth About Drug Companies*, who documented her prescient concerns about the corrupting influence of corporations' financial contributions to—and sometimes their control of—medical research initiatives. Listening to her, I understood that until this problem is corrected, it will jeopardize research and treatment, a realization that set me on the path that has led to this work. I am very thankful to her for generously giving her attention to portions of this work, and for her brilliant ethical vision.

I owe a great debt to others at the school, notably Jay A. Winsten, PhD, director of the school's Center for Health Communication, and former Deputy Director Robert Meyers, now president of the Washington Journalism Center, as well as Lawrence O. Gostin, JD, and the late William J. Curran, JD, a professor of public health law, who provided unstinting advice over afternoon tea and an invaluable legal perspective over the years. Patricia Thomas, then editor of the *Harvard Health Letter* and now Knight chair in Health and Medical Journalism at the University of Georgia, remains a perceptive adviser and good friend.

As a 2002–5 research fellow in medical ethics at Harvard Medical School, I benefited greatly from the wisdom of faculty, especially Walter Robinson, MD; Allan M. Brandt, PhD, now dean of the Graduate School of Arts and Sciences; Millie Solomons, EdD, Robert Truog, MD, Paul Farmer, MD, Richard Cash, MD, Dan Wikler, MD, and Director Byron J. Good, PhD, who kindly extended my fellowship to facilitate the research upon which this book is based. The other ethics fellows remain a valuable source of advice and support, especially Eva Winkler, MD,

Russell Gruen, MD, and Khadija Pierce, PhD, all of whom responded very helpfully to my ethical arguments.

I am also deeply indebted to the largesse of Stanford University, which gave me a fellowship to its Professional Publishing Course in 1995 and a John S. Knight Fellowship for Professional Journalists in 1997, under the guidance of Directors James V. Risser, JD, and James R. Bettinger. Carl Djerassi, PhD, professor emeritus of chemistry and a prolific author, accepted me into his splendid writing course for scientists and further deepened my understanding of scientists' motivations, both noble and checkered.

I wish to thank the following institutions for inviting me to share portions of this work: the American Society for Bioethics and the Humanities; the Law and Society Association, which invited me to present at its annual meetings in Berlin and in Montreal; Dr. Barbara Prainsack of Kings College, London; and David Gurwitz of Tel Aviv University, who invited me to speak on DNA databases and corporate interests in "Private Fears in Public Places? Ethical and Regulatory Concerns Regarding Human Genomic Databases," at the 15th Annual International Conference on Intelligent Systems for Molecular Biology (ISMB) in Vienna. The Brocher Foundation included me in its "Genetic Data Collections and Individual Freedom" program in Geneva.

Michele Bratcher Goodwin, JD, Everett Fraser Professor of Law at the University of Minnesota, has been especially supportive, appointing me as a visiting fellow to DePaul University College of Law and to its Health Law Institute, and inviting me to speak about tissue appropriation as part of the seminal University of Minnesota 2010 International Congress on Human Trafficking.

Robert W. Blum, the William H. Gates Sr. Chair, Department of Population, Family and Reproductive Health at the Johns Hopkins Bloomberg School of Public Health, invited me as the inaugural speaker in its "Race and Research" series, where I discussed racial aspects of body appropriation.

Joanne Jones-Rizzi invited me to speak at the Science Museum of Minnesota, St. Paul, in conjunction with its Deadly Medicine exhibit; and Steve Feinstein, the beloved late director of the Center for Holocaust and Genocide Studies, invited me to the university to discuss parallels in the erosion of informed consent within the U.S. legal matrix and in Germany under National Socialism.

I especially thank patent-law experts Craig Nard, JD, and E. Richard Gold, JD, who have been remarkably generous with their time and advice on biotechnology patent law and policy. I am also grateful to the late Victor McKusick, MD, and to the late Jay Katz, MD, Elizabeth Dollard Professor Emeritus of Law, Medicine, and Psychiatry at Yale University, who was always generous with his time, insights, and warm, wry humor.

Others who have been open and generous with their expertise and advice include: Matthew Wynia, MD, of the American Medical Association Institute for Ethics; Columbia Law School professor Patricia Williams, JD; Eddie L. Hoover, MD, editor in chief of the *Journal of the National Medical Association*; Stephen Schondelmeyer, PharmD, PhD, of the University of Minnesota; Joel Lexchin, MD, of York University; John Abramson, MD, author of *Overdosed America*; and LaVera Crawley, MD, of Stanford University. So have Professor Thomas A. LaVeist of Johns Hopkins; Richard Smith, MD, chief executive of UnitedHealth; Lynn G. Dressler; DrPH; Sidney Wolfe, MD, MPH; Peter Lurie, MD; Adriane Fugh-Berman, MD; Andrew Bernard, MD; Simon Van Nieuwenhove, MD; James Bowman, MD; Myron Weisfeldt, MD; David Smith, MD; Carl Millcr, MD, of Weill Medical College of Cornell University; and Heather Logge, MD, of the University of California at San Francisco. So have Tufts professor Sheldon Krimsky, PhD; Heather Butts, JD, MPH, executive director of HEALTH for Youths; Philip Alcabes, PhD, professor of law and English; Karla F. C. Holloway; Alex Dajkovic of the Institut Curie in Paris; Leroy Baylor; Marcy Darnovsky; Debra Abell; Nancy King, JD; Daniel Nelson, PhD; Evan K. Thalenberg, JD; and Nicholas Szokoly, JD; Roger Hodge; Robert Wilson, editor of *The American Scholar*; Matt Potter of the *San Diego Reader*; and Tom Blackwell of the *National Post* have also spent time and effort in explaining fine points of their expertise and sometimes providing a sounding board for my evolving musings about the issues that are covered in this book.

All the talented, supportive scribes of the Invisible Institute have been trusted advisers and friends, especially its founders Annie Murphy Paul and Alissa Quart, as well as the inspiring Katherine Russell Rich, Susan Cain, Abby Ellin, Randi Hutter Epstein, MD, Deborah Siegel,

Catherine Orenstein, Paul Raeburn, Elizabeth DeVita-Raeburn, Tom Zoellner, Joshua Prager, Rebecca Skloot, author of the acclaimed *The Immortal Life of Henrietta Lacks,* and Sheri Fink, MD, PhD, author of *War Hospital,* who deployed her medical expertise to give me detailed feedback on an early outline of this book and provided outstanding encouragement and feedback as it progressed.

All the above persons and organizations helped me immensely, but this book could not have been written without the brave people who told their stories. Not all of them wish to be named, but they include: Martha Milete; Daniel, Debbie, and Joshua Greenberg; Genae Girard; David "Sonny" Lacks; the late David Lacks Sr.; "Heather," "David," and the Reverend Charles Williams, president of the National Council for Community Empowerment of Detroit.

The Alfred P. Sloan Foundation rendered financial support for early work on the proposal for this book, and the New York Public Library gave me coveted berths in the Wertheim Study and the Allen Room.

Finally, I am thrilled by the opportunity to thank my adept editor, Gerry Howard, who provided a treasure trove of organizational advice, and for the efficiency and warmth of Hannah Wood. I am also grateful to production editor Nora Reichard, who enhanced this book's clarity and conformation to style without compromising its voice. The keen judgment of my wonderful agent Lisa Bankoff and my brilliant, witty lawyer Zick Rubin have provided, as always, a constant source of support and guidance.

My deepest gratitude goes, as always, to my husband, Ron DeBose, whose stores of affection, patience, support, and good advice seem endless. I am blessed in my sisters and brothers Kathy, Eric, Theresa, and Pete, whom we miss more than words can say.

NOTES

INTRODUCTION: PATENTS, PROFITS, AND THE HIGH COST OF LIVING

1 Clifton Leaf, "The Law of Unintended Consequences," *Fortune*, September 19, 2005, http://money.cnn.com/magazines/fortune/fortune_archive/2005/09/19/8272884/index.htm(accessed September 3, 2008).
2 *Diamond v. Chakrabarty*, 447 U.S. 303 (1980). The *Pseudomonas* microorganism patented in *Chakrabarty* degraded or "ate" crude oil. Its creation promised a revolutionary ecological breakthrough in the methodology of cleaning up oil spills and anticipated important genetic engineering feats that usefully transformed microorganisms.
3 Sheldon Krimsky, *Science in the Private Interest: Has the Lure of Profits Corrupted Biomedical Research?* (New York: Rowman & Littlefield Publishers, Inc., 2004), passim.
4 *Fortune 500*, "Top Industries: Most Profitable," May 4, 2009, http://money.cnn.com/magazines/fortune/fortune500/2009/performers/industries/profits/.
5 "Landmark Study Reports Breakdown in Biotech Patent System," PhysOrg.com, September 9, 2008, http://www.physorg.com/news140178906.html (accessed May 24, 2011).
6. Jess Bravin, "In Reversal, Court Rules Human Gene Can Be Patented," *Wall Street Journal*, July 30, 2011 http://online.wsj.com/article/SB10001424053111903635604576476130562033622.html (accessed August 2, 2011).

CHAPTER 1: A NEW LEASE ON LIFE

1 Andrew Kimbrell, *The Human Body Shop: The Engineering and Marketing of Life* (New York: HarperCollins, 1993), 245.
2 Judith Ann Schiff, "An Unsung Hero of Medical Research: A Technique Invented Nearly 100 Years Ago by a Yale Scientist Led to a Revolution in Biology," *Yale Alumni Magazine* 64, no. 2 (February 2001), http://www.yalealumnimagazine.com/issues/02_02/old_yale.html (accessed November 21, 2010).

3 Bruce Alberts et al., eds., *The Molecular Biology of the Cell*, 4th ed. (New York: Garland Science, 2002).

4 United States Congress, U.S. Office of Technology Assessment, *Ownership of Human Tissues and Cells: New Developments in Biotechnology* (Washington, D.C.: U.S. Office of Technology Assessment, 2002).

5 "Update: U. Cal. and the Hagiwaras Settle Ownership Dispute," *Biotechnology Law Report* 2, no. 3–4 (1983): 43.

6 Marjorie Sun, "Scientists Settle Cell Line Dispute: But Question of Claiming Ownership Based on Family Ties to Cell Donor Is Sidestepped," *Science* 220, no. 4595 (April 1983): 393.

7 "Pair Charged with Theft of Trade Secrets from Harvard Medical School," U.S. Department of Justice press release (Washington, D.C., June 19, 2002), http://www.justice.gov/criminal/cybercrime/zhuCharges.html.

8 *United States v. Zhu*, 02-M-0421 (June 19, 2002).

9 Andrew Lawler, "Arrest of Ex-Harvard Postdocs Raises Questions of Ownership," *Science* 296, no. 5577 (June 28, 2002): 2310.

10 Adam M. Guren, "HMS Fellows Indicted for Alleged Lab Theft," *The Harvard Crimson*, June 27, 2005, http://www.thecrimson.com/article/2005/6/27/hms-fellows-indicted-for-alleged-lab/.

11 Andrew Lawler, "U.S. Asks for Delay in Science Theft Case," *Science* 297, no. 5581 (July 26, 2002): 496.

12 Charles Anthon, *A Classical Dictionary: Containing an Account of the Principal Proper Names Mentioned in Ancient Authors, and Intended to Elucidate All the Important Points Connected with the Geography, History, Biography, Mythology, and Fine Arts of the Greeks and Romans Together with an Account of Coins, Weights, and Measures, with Tabular Values of the Same* (New York: Harper & Bros., 1841), 1273.

13 M. Frumkin, "The Origin of Patents," *Journal of the Patent Office Society* 27, no. 3 (March 1945): 143.

14 Toshiko Takenaka, *Patent Law and Theory: A Handbook of Contemporary Research* (Northampton, MA: Edward Elgar Publishing, 2009), 101, 139, 359.

15 Devon Fanfair, Salil Desai, and Christopher Kelty, "Patent or Perish," in *Nanotechnology: Content and Context*, eds. Christopher Kelty and John Hutchinson (Houston: Rice University, May 2007), 59–71, http://cnx.org/content/m14509/1.1/.

16 Adam Mossoff, "Rethinking the Development of Patents: An Intellectual History, 1550–1800," *Hastings Law Journal* 52 (2001): 1255.

17 Krimsky, *Science in the Private Interest*, 58.

18 Benjamin Franklin, *The Autobiography of Benjamin Franklin*, p. 55, http://www.ushistory.org/franklin/autobiography/page55.htm (accessed May 20, 2011).

19 U.S. Constitution, Art. I, sec. 8, cl. 8.

20 Thomas O. Jewett, "Thomas Jefferson: Father of Invention," *The Early America Review* 3, no. 1 (Winter 2000), http://www.earlyamerica.com/review/winter2000/jefferson.html (accessed November 21, 2010).

21 Ibid.

22 Some accounts credit Jefferson with approximately sixty-four patent approvals: Ibid.

23 Kenneth W. Dobyns, *The Patent Office Pony: A History of the Early Patent Office*, http://www.myoutbox.net/popch25.htm (accessed November 22,

2010). Also available in print (Fredericksburg, VA: Sargeant Kirkland's Museum and Historical Society, 1994).

24 Abraham Lincoln, "Second Lecture on Discoveries and Inventions" (lecture, Jackson, IL, February 11, 1859), cited in *Abraham Lincoln Online*, http://showcase.netins.net/web/creative/lincoln/speeches/discoveries.htm.

25 Adam Mossoff, "Who Cares What Thomas Jefferson Thought About Patents? Reevaluating the Patent 'Privilege' in Historical Context," *Cornell Law Review* 92, no. 953 (2007): 1012.

26 *Atlantic Works v. Brady*, 1017 U.S. 192, 200 (1883).

27 *United States Supreme Court Reporter* (Rochester, NY: Lawyers' Cooperative Publishing Co.), 27:439, 440.

28 "On October 6th, U.S. President William Clinton is expected to join the U.S. Secretary of Agriculture Dan Glickman and other national leaders to honor one of America's greatest scientists," Tuskegee University press release (Tuskegee, AL, October 6, 2001). Only a few of Carver's inventions were patented, some reportedly to benefit the university.

29 Fanfair et al., "Patent or Perish."

30 David Holcberg, "Should Genes Be Patented?" *Capitalism Magazine*, April 13, 2002, http://www.capitalismmagazine.com/science/genetics/1534-should-genes-be-patented.html (accessed November 23, 2010).

31 Sinclair Lewis, *Arrowsmith* (New York: Modern Library, 1925), 72.

32 Krimsky, *Science in the Private Interest*, 77.

33 Merrill Goozner, *The $800 Million Pill: The Truth Behind the Cost of New Drugs* (Berkeley: University of California Press, 2004), 106, 212.

34 Jane Smith, *Patenting the Sun: Polio and the Salk Vaccine* (New York: William Morrow, 1990), 159.

35 Nelson Rees was codirector of the Cell Culture Laboratory at the Naval Biosciences Laboratory in Oakland, California. This laboratory was part of the University of California, Berkeley.

36 Michael A. Gold, *A Conspiracy of Cells: One Woman's Immortal Legacy and the Medical Scandal It Caused* (Albany, NY: SUNY Press, 1986), 7; Hannah Landecker, "Immortality, in Vitro: A History of the HeLa Cell Line," in *Biotechnology and Culture: Bodies, Anxieties, Ethics*, ed. Paul Brodwin (Bloomington: Indiana University Press, 2000), 53–74.

37 H. G. Dexler, W. G. Dirks, and R. A. Macleod, "False Human Hematopoietic Cell Lines: Cross-Contaminations and Misinterpretations," *Leukemia* 13, no. 10 (October 1999): 1601.

38 Harriet Washington, "Henrietta Lacks: An Unsung Hero," *Emerge Magazine* 6, no. 1 (October 1994): 29.

39 Harriet Washington, "Henrietta Lacks"; W. A. Nelson-Reses and R. R. Flandermeyer, "HeLa Cultures Defined," *Science* 191, no. 4222 (January 1976): 96. The abstract clearly notes the importance of the tissues gleaned from Lacks's children in establishing the identity of HeLa cells versus those derived from other cell lines. The abstract reads in part, "[g]enotype of the patient Henrietta Lacks from whose cervical carcinoma the HeLa cell was derived *was deduced from the phenotypes of her husband and children*, and from studies of the HeLa cell. Hemizygous expression of glucose & phosphate dehydrogenase in HeLa, together with the deduced heterozygosity of Mrs. Lacks, is consistent with clonal origin of her neoplasm" (italics mine).

40 Russell W. Brown and James Henderson, "The Mass Production and Distribution of HeLa Cells at Tuskgee Institute, 1953–1955," *Journal of the History of Medicine and Allied Sciences* (1983) 38(4): 415–31.

41 However, Gey had chosen to disseminate the pseudonyms only *after* Henrietta Lacks's name had been discovered by journalists, presumably to confuse them and to induce them to adopt a fictitious name as real.

42 Landecker, "Immortality, in Vitro: A History of the HeLa Cell Line," 53–74.

43 Harriet Washington, "Henrietta Lacks," 29.

44 William J. Curran Esq., Harvard School of Public Health, personal interviews with the author, October 10, 1991, and March 23, 1992; telephone interview with the author, June 10, 1994.

45 Joe Miller, "Patent Law: How Patents Grew over Time to Include Living Organisms," *Cooking Up a Story*, July 29, 2009, http://cookingupastory .com/patent-law-how-patents-grew-over-time-to-include-living-organisms (accessed November 22, 2010).

46 L. Hayflick and P. S. Moorhead, "The Serial Cultivation of Human Diploid Cell Strains," *Experimental Cell Research* 25 (1961): 585–621.

47 John Walsh, "Public Attitude Toward Science Is Yes, But—" *Science* 15, no. 4530 (January 1982): 270–72. The suit also claimed that Hayflick "had sold cells that had been accidentally contaminated with bacteria and cleaned up with antibiotics, without informing the appropriate authorities about the previous contamination."

48 Philip M. Boffey, "The Fall and Rise of Leonard Hayflick, Biologist Whose Fight with U.S. Seems Over," *New York Times*, January 19, 1982.

49 WI-38 was developed by Dr. Leonard Hayflick in 1962, by taking lung cells from an aborted female baby at approximately the end of the third month of pregnancy. His article in *Experimental Cell Research* states that "all embryos were obtained from surgical abortions and were of approximately three months' gestation."

50 A. M. Chakrabarty, "Patenting of Life-Form: From a Concept to Reality," in *Who Owns Life?*, eds. David Magnus, Arthur Caplan, and Glenn McGee (Amherst, NY: Prometheus Books, 2002), 25–39.

51 Ibid., 18.

52 *Diamond v. Chakrabarty*, 447 U.S. 303 (1980).

53 Donald S. Chisum, Craig A. Nard, Herbert E. Schwartz, Pauline Newman, and F. Scott Kieff, *Principles of Patent Law: Cases and Materials* (New York: Foundation Press, 1998), 783–88.

54 Council on Governmental Relations, "The Bayh-Dole Act: A Guide to the Law and Implementing Regulations," September 1999, http://www.ucop.edu/ ott/bayh.html.

55 *Patent Rights in Inventions Made with Federal Assistance*, U.S. Code 35 (February 2010), chap. 18.

56 United States Congress, Senate Committee on the Judiciary, *The University and Small Business Patent Procedures Act: Hearings Before the Committee on the Judiciary on S. 414*, 96th Cong., 1st sess., May 16 and June 6, 1979.

57 Birch Bayh, interview by Gene Quinn, *IP Watchdog*, December 15, 2010, http://ipwatchdog.com/2010/11/07/exclusive-interview-senator-birch-bayh -on-bayh-dole/id=13198/ (accessed December 24, 2010).

58 *Bayh-Dole Act of 1980*, U.S. Code 35 (February 2010), chap. 18, sec. 200
    (December 12, 1980). The text of the Bayh-Dole Act is available at www
    .cptech.org/ip/health/bd (accessed May, 2009).
59 Leaf, "The Law of Unintended Consequences."
60 Council on Governmental Relations, "The Bayh-Dole Act."
61 *Stevenson-Wydler Technology Innovation Act of 1980*, U.S. Code 15 (February
    2010), chap. 63, sec. 3701 (October 21, 1980).
62 *The Economic Recovery Tax Act of 1981*, Public Law 97-34, U.S. Statutes at
    Large 95 (1981): 172.
63 The Federal Technology Transfer Act of 1986 (Public Law 99-502) amended
    the Stevenson-Wydler Innovation Act by mandating technology transfer for
    federal and requiring that preference be given to U.S. corporate partners.
    Subsequently, the National Competitiveness Technology Transfer Act of 1989
    (Public Law 101-189) exhorted contractor laboratories (GOCO) to cooperate
    with corporations and universities.
64 Golde signed contracts with the Genetics Institute, Inc., Sandoz, Ltd., Sandoz
    United States, Inc., and Sandoz Pharmaceutical Corporation in 1981, 1982,
    and 1983.
65 His claim was dismissed in 1986, but a 1988 appeal acknowledged Moore's
    property ownership rights of his tissues and gave him a share of the patent.
    However, this decision was reversed in 1990 when the court held that Moore
    had no property rights in his own tissue, although Moore could sue Golde
    for a share on the basis that Golde had not fulfilled his "fiduciary duty" to tell
    Moore that his spleen was a potential gold mine. Defendants argued that they
    should have to disclose in part because the donor might object to taking part
    in research. Had the 1988 appellate decision been upheld, others who found
    themselves in the same position might have become at least partial owners of
    the lucrative cell lines established from their bodies—a biotechnology firm's
    nightmare, and a potential windfall for people such as the Lackses.
66 Jeremy Pearce, "Dr. David Golde, 63, Expert on Blood Disorders, Is Dead,"
    New York Times, August 14, 2004.
67 John Vidal and John Carvel, "Lambs to the Gene Market," *Guardian*,
    November 12, 1994.
68 Rick Weiss, "US Denies Patent for Part-Human Hybrid," *Washington Post*,
    February 13, 2005.
69 Ibid.
70 Gene Quinn, "PTO Hiring Freeze and Budget Problems," *IPWatchDog*,
    March 2, 2009, www.ipwatchdog.com/2009/03/02/pto-hiring-freeze-and
    -budget-problems/id=2099/ (accessed 14 August 2009).
71 In late 2008, a large number of patent examiners were hired, which is a step
    in the right direction. Before then, a mere two hundred PhDs were charged
    with evaluating the life-patent-related applications that flooded the office,
    including a backlog of nearly eight hundred thousand applications.
72 "In early 2000, the US Patent and Trademark Office received a patent
    application of 400,000 pages. Not much later, the European Patent Office
    received one of 500,000 pages. Since May of this year, USPTO has on
    its hands a patent application from Shell Oil bearing no less than 7,200
    individual claims": GRAIN, *One Global Patent System? WIPO's Substantive*

Patent Law Treaty (Barcelona, Spain, October 2003), http://www.grain.org/briefings/?id=159.

73 Gene Quinn, "Patent Examiners Told to Issue Patents," *IPWatchdog*, May 22, 2009, www.ipwatchdog.com/2009/05/22/patent-examiners-told-to-issue-patents/id=3671/Last (accessed June 22, 2009).

74 Leaf, "The Law of Unintended Consequences."

75 Ibid.

76 Ibid.

77 Ibid.

78 Samantha Stainburn, "Who Owns Your Great Idea?" *New York Times*, January 4, 2009, http://www.nytimes.com/2009/01/04/education/edlife/whoseidea-t.html.

79 Ibid.

80 James D. Watson, *The Double Helix: A Personal Account of the Discovery of the Structure of DNA* (New York: Atheneum, 1968; London: Weidenfeld and Nicolson, 1981), 16–19, 69–71, 166–70.

81 Krimsky, *Science in the Private Interest*.

82 Sheldon Krimsky, "Perils of University-Industry Collaboration," *Issues in Science and Technology* 16, no. 1 (September 22, 1999): 14.

CHAPTER 2: THE HIGH COST OF LIVING

1 "Heather" is not her real name, and some elements of her story have been changed to protect her privacy.

2 Elan Corporation, Plc., "2001 Annual Report and Form 20-F," July 3, 2005, http://en.wikipedia.org/wiki/Primidone-cite_ref-elanrationalise_41-0Élan Corporation (accessed July 4, 2008).

3 Eva C. Winkler, MD, and Russell L. Gruen, MD, PhD, "Principles for Ethical Decision-Making in Healthcare Organizations," unpublished manuscript.

4 Richard Pazdur, MD, "FDA Approval for Cetuximab," National Cancer Institute, Cancer Drug Information, http://www.cancer.gov/cancertopics/druginfo/fda-cetuximab

5 Robert Bazell, "Strange Medicine:Why Are the New Cancer Drugs So Expensive?" *Slate*, Wednesday, June 23, 2004, http://www.slate.com/id/2102844/.

6 Matthew Herper, "The World's Most Expensive Drugs," *Forbes.com*, February 22, 2010, http://www.forbes.com/2010/02/19/expensive-drugs-cost-business-healthcare-rare-diseases.html.

7 "Roche and Genentech Reach a Friendly Agreement to Combine the Two Organizations and Create a Leader in Healthcare Innovation," The Roche Group media release (Basel, Switzerland, March 12, 2009), http://www.roche.com/media/media_releases/med-cor-2009–03–12.htm.

8 The Pharmaceutical Research and Manufacturers of America, "Inside Innovation: The Drug Discovery Process," Innovation.org, http://www.innovation.org/index.cfm/InsideDrugDiscovery.

9 "Most Expensive Medicine—World Record Set by Soliris," World Records Academy, February 23, 2010, http://www.worldrecordsacademy.org/business/most_expensive_medicine_world_record_set_by_Soliris_101573.htm (accessed December 18, 2010).

10 Roger Collier, "Drug Development Cost Estimates Hard to Swallow," *Canadian Medical Association Journal* 180, no. 3 (2009): 279–80.

11 J. A. DiMasi, "The Price of Innovation: New Estimates of Drug Development Costs," *Journal of Health Economics* 22, no. 2 (March 2003): 151–85.

12 The 1987 cost, unadjusted for inflation, had been calculated at $231 million: Robert Pear, "Research Cost for New Drugs Said to Soar," *New York Times*, December 1, 2001.

13 James Love, "IRS Data Shows Drug Industry Cost Estimates Exaggerated," Knowledge Economy International news release (Washington, D.C, November 30, 2001), http://lists.essential.org/pipermail/ip-health/2001-November/002489.html.

14 George Foster, "Opposing Forces in a Revolution in International Patent Protection: the U.S. and India in the Uruguay Round and Its Aftermath," *UCLA Journal of International Law and Foreign Affairs* 3 (1998): 283.

15 "DiMasi's new study puts out-of-pocket clinical trial costs at $282 million, based on the NCEs [NMEs] in his study. His estimate is four times more than an estimate of clinical trial costs ($75 million) published by the Congressional Research Service in April 2001. Moreover, DiMasi's estimate of clinical trial costs greatly exceeds the drug industry's own data on the subject. PhRMA's own survey of 1999 R&D expenditures states that clinical trial costs account for 29 percent of all R&D costs. (See Table 6, 'Domestic U.S. R&D by Function' in 'Pharmaceutical Industry Profile 2001.') Yet DiMasi's study says clinical trials account for 70 percent of all R&D costs ($282 million out of $403 million total out-of-pocket expenditures for each drug).": "Critique of the DiMasi/Tufts Methodology and Other Key Prescription Drug R&D Issues," Public Citizen, http://www.citizen.org/congress/article _redirect.cfm?ID=6532 (accessed December 4, 2010).

16 The Pharmaceutical Research and Manufacturers of America, "Survey of 1999 R&D Expenditures: Table 6, Domestic U.S. R & D by function," *Pharmaceutical Industry Profile 2001*, cited in "Critique of the DiMasi/Tufts Methodology and Other Key Prescription Drug R&D Issues," Public Citizen.

17 Numbers of NMEs approved per year: 2009, twenty-six; 2008, twenty-five; 2007, eighteen; 2006, twenty-two; 2005, twenty-six; 2004, twenty-four; 2003, twenty-six; 2002, twenty-eight; 2001, twenty-three; 2000, twenty-six; 1999, thirty-three: "New Molecular Entity Approvals for 2010," United States Food and Drug Administration, February 17, 2011, http://www.fda.gov/Drugs/DevelopmentApprovalProcess/HowDrugsareDevelopedandApproved/DrugandBiologicApprovalReports/ucm242674.htm.

18 *The Economist*, "Economics A-Z: Opportunity Cost," http://www.economist .com/research/Economics/alphabetic.cfm?letter=O#opportunitycos (accessed December 4, 2010); George Stigler, "The Nature and Role of Originality in Scientific Progress," *Economica* 12 (November 1955).

19 "Tufts Drug Study Sample Is Skewed; True Figure of R&D Costs Likely Is 75 Percent Lower," Public Citizen press release (Washington, D.C., December 4, 2001), http://www.citizen.org/pressroom/pressroomredirect.cfm?ID=954.

20 "The Net Cost of Every Dollar Spent on R&D Must Be Reduced by the Amount of Tax Avoided by that Expenditure": United States Congress, U.S. Office of Technology Assessment, *Ownership of Human Tissues and Cells:*

New Developments in Biotechnology (Washington, D.C.: U.S. Office of Technology Assessment, 2002), 15.

21 A 2002 report by the General Accounting Office compared the average costs of noncommercial, government-funded clinical research to that conducted by the drug industry and found that drug makers' costs were significantly higher than that of comparable government-managed clinical trials.

22 Goozner, *The $800 Million Pill*, 239.

23 They do so by preventing the enzyme HMG-CoA reductase from allowing runaway cholesterol production by the liver.

24 Goozner, *The $800 Million Pill*, 238; Melody Peterson, "Madison Avenue Plays Growing Role in Drug Research," *New York Times*, November 22, 2002.

25 Frank Davidoff et al., "Sponsorship Authorship and Accountability," *New England Journal of Medicine* 286, no. 10 (September 2001): 825.

26 "Critique of the DiMasi/Tufts Methodology and Other Key Prescription Drug R&D Issues," Public Citizen.

27 Pear, "Research Cost for New Drugs Said to Soar."

28 By contrast, *therapeutic equivalence* is necessary to permit pharmacists to substitute a generic drug for a branded drug when filling a prescription. Therapeutic equivalence applies to those medications that have both bioequivalence and pharmaceutical equivalence (that they share the same active ingredient, strength, and manner of administration).

29 Pauline W. Chen, MD, "When Patients Don't Fill Their Prescriptions," *New York Times*, May 20, 2010.

30 Stephen Schondelmeyer and Leigh Purvis, "Trends in Retail Prices of Brand Name Prescription Drugs Widely Used by Medicare Beneficiaries, 2005 to 2009," *Rx Price Watch Report* (Washington, D.C.: AARP Public Policy Institute, August 2010), http://assets.aarp.org/rgcenter/ppi/health-care/rxpricewatch.pdf.

31 "Average Health Insurance Premiums and Worker Contributions for Family Coverage, 1999–2009," *Kaiser/HRET Survey of Employer-Sponsored Health Benefits, 1999–2009*, Henry J. Kaiser Family Foundation, September 15, 2009, http://slides.kff.org/chart.aspx?ch=1182.

32 CMS Data Compendium, Centers for Medicare & Medicare Services, U.S. Department of Health and Human Services, December 14, 2005, https://www.cms.gov/DataCompendium (accessed May 11, 2009).

33 Gay Men's Health Crisis, Inc., "First Wave of Cuts Hits New York's ADAP," *Treatment Issues*, ed. Bob Huff, December 2002, http://www.thebody.com/content/art13619.html.

34 Becky Allen, "September 2010 ADAP Update: The Sprinklers Are On, but the Water Pressure's Low," *The Body Pro*, September 23, 2010, http://www.thebodypro.com/content/art58596.html.

35 Laurie Felland and James Reschovsky, "More Non-Elderly Americans Face Problems Affording Prescription Drugs," *Center for Studying Health System Change Tracking Report No. 22* (Washington, D.C.: HSC, January 2009), www.hschange.org/CONTENT/1039/ (accessed February 11, 2010).

36 Roger H. Rumble and Kevin Morgan, "Longitudinal Trends in Prescribing for Elderly Patients: Two Surveys Four Years Apart," *British Journal of General Practice* 44 (1994): 571–75; James Wooten, PharmD, and Julie Galavis, RN, BSN, "Polypharmacy: Keeping the Elderly Safe," *Modern Medicine*, August 1,

2005, http://www.modernmedicine.com/modernmedicine/CE+Library/
Polypharmacy-Keeping-the-elderly-safe/ArticleStandard/Article/detail/
172920.

37 "Summary and Charts," *Survey: The Public on Prescription Drugs and
Pharmaceutical Companies*, USA Today/Kaiser Family Foundation/
Harvard School of Public Health, March 4, 2008, p. 3, http://www.kff.org/
kaiserpolls/7748.cfm.

38 "Putting Off Care Because of Cost," *Health Tracking Poll*, Henry J. Kaiser Family Foundation, July 14, 2009, http://www.kff.org/kaiserpolls/
upload/7944.pdf. This nationally representative, random sample survey of
1,695 adults ages eighteen years and older was conducted by telephone from
January 3 to January 23, 2008. The margin of sampling error for the survey is
plus or minus 3 percentage points for total respondents.

39 Paying lobbyists by individual pharmaceutical companies such as Pfizer and
Amgen constituted the bulk of the difference between PhRMA's expenditures and that for the category in toto: "Pharmaceuticals/Health Products
2010," Lobbying Spending Database, OpenSecrets.org/Center for Responsive
Politics, January 31, 2010, http://www.opensecrets.org/lobby/indusclient
.php?lname=H04&year=a (accessed March 27, 2010).

40 "Top Industries 2010," Lobbying Spending Database, Open Secrets.org/
Center for Responsive Politics, January 31, 2001, http://www.opensecrets.org/
lobby/top.php?showYear=2009&indexType=i (accessed March 27, 2010).

41 "Bristol-Myers Squibb: Summary," Heavy Hitters: Bristol-Myers Squibb,
Open Secrets.org Center for Responsive Politics, www.opensecrets.org/orgs/
summary.php?id=D000000149 (accessed August 21, 2009).

42 Gilbert Ross, "Why Drug 'Reimportation' Won't Die: The Drug Industry
Made a Foolish Bet in Supporting Health Reform," *Wall Street Journal*, January 7, 2010.

43 Roger Pilon, "Drug Reimportation: The Free Market Solution," *CATO Institute Policy Analysis* no. 521, August 4, 2004, http://www.cato.org/pub_display
.php?pub_id=2305 (accessed January 26, 2005).

44 Dan Eggen, "Drugmakers Fight Plan to Allow Drug Reimportation," *Washington Post*, December 15, 2009.

45 *Huffington Post*, "The Worst Drug Company Marketing Techniques,"
March 18, 2010, http://www.huffingtonpost.com/2009/11/11/the-worst-drug
-company-ma_n_353709.html.

46 Ben Hirschler, "Heart Expert Says Cost Cuts May Undermine Drug R&D,"
Reuters News Service, August 28, 2010, http://www.reuters.com/article/
idUSTRE67R0TI20100828 (accessed November 22, 2010).

47 "Scientists are also working to thwart the potential devastation of biological
warfare agents. Ten separate treatments for anthrax and three for smallpox
are in development. Although medical progress eradicated naturally occurring smallpox in humans worldwide by 1980, concerns remain that the virus
could be used as a bioterrorism weapon": "Nearly 400 Medicines and Vaccines
in Development to Fight Infectious Diseases," Pharmaceutical Research and
Manufacturers of America press release (Boston: September 10, 2010), http://
www.phrma.org/news/news/nearly_400_medicines_and_vaccines
_development_fight_infectious_diseases (accessed November 7, 2010).

48 Louis J. Currat, *10/90 Report on Health Research 2003–2004*, Global Forum for

Health Research, www.globalforumhealth.org (accessed June 28, 2010). Since the Commission on Health Research for Development identified this "10/90 gap," constant advocacy has resulted in improvements in funding, and the epidemiology of diseases has shifted substantially, so that even though a dramatic imbalance remains between the developing world's medical problems and the resources devoted to them, objective studies, when they are performed, may well show some improvement in these numbers.

49 *Fortune 500*, "Most Profitable Industries: Our Ranking of America's Largest Corporations, 2010," May 3, 2010, http://money.cnn.com/magazines/fortune/fortune500/2010/industries/21/index.html.

50 Public Citizen, *2002 Drug Industry Profits: Hefty Pharmaceutical Company Margins Dwarf Other Industries* (Washington, D.C.: Public Citizen's Congress Watch, June 2003), http://www.citizen.org/documents/Pharma_Report.pdf.

51 Federal Trade Commission, *Generic Drug Entry Prior to Patent Expiration: An FTC Study* (Washington, D.C.: Federal Trade Commission, July 2002), 57, http://www.ftc.gov/os/2002/07/genericdrugstudy.pdf.

52 Plavix is Sanofi's version of clopidogrel bisulfate, which was marketed by Bristol-Myers Squibb in the United States.

53 *Federal Trade Commission, et al. v. Watson Pharmaceuticals, Inc., et al.*, CV-09–00598 (January 27, 2009), FTC File No. 0710060.

54 *Federal Trade Commission, et al. v. Watson Pharmaceuticals, Inc., et al.* ("Generic Androgel"), CV-09–00598 (civil complaint filed in U.S. District Court for the Central District of California, January 27, 2009), FTC File No. 0710060.

55 Hoechst Marion Roussel, Inc./Carderm Capital L.P./Andrx Corp., 131 F.T.C. 927 (2001).

56 Federal Trade Commission, *Generic Drug Entry Prior to Patent Expiration: An FTC Study*, 24, http://www.ftc.gov/os/2002/07/genericdrugstudy.pdf.

57 Federal Trade Commission, Bureau of Competition, Health Care Division, *Overview of FTC Antitrust Actions in Pharmaceutical Services and Products* (Washington, D.C.: Federal Trade Commission, June 2010), http://www.ftc.gov/bc/0610rxupdate.pdf.

58 Safet Metjahhic, "Delaying Generic Drugs: The Legal Landscape Surrounding Reverse Payment Agreements to Protect Patent Holders," *New York Intellectual Property Law Association Bulletin* (February–March 2010): 10–11.

59 Martin A. Voet, *The Generic Challenge: Understanding Patents, FDA and Pharmaceutical Life-Cycle Management*, 2nd electronic ed. (Boca Raton, FL: Brown Walker Press, 2008), 12–19.

60 Kathleen Jaeger, president and CEO, Generic Pharmaceutical Association, "Proposed Free Trade Agreement with Malaysia," Testimony before the Office of the United States Trade Representative and the Interagency Trade Policy Staff Committee, Washington, D.C., May 3, 2006.

61 T. W. Solomons and Craig Fryhle, *Organic Chemistry*, 8th ed. (Hoboken, NJ: Wiley, 2003), 208, 214.

62 Goozner, *The $800 Million Dollar Pill*, 221, 246.

63 Dirk Van Duppern, "The Cost of the Newest Cancer Drugs," *The Lancet* 370, no. 9584 (July 2007): 317.

64 Gardiner Harris, "Prilosec's Maker Switches Users to Nexium, Thwarting Generics," *Wall Street Journal*, June 6, 2002.

65 Goozner, *The $800 Million Dollar Pill*, 214.

66 James Netterwald, PhD, "Recycling Existing Drugs," *Drug Discovery & Development*, January 1, 2008.

67 Sidney M. Wolfe, MD, Public Citizen's Health Research Group, "Congressional Testimony on FDA Deficiencies," Testimony before the Congressional Agriculture–FDA Appropriations Subcommittee Hearing on Drug Safety, February 27, 2008, http://www.citizen.org/hrg1835. Also, in a comment on the *Slashdot Blog* post "Patent Examiners Flee the USPTO," reader "Doctor-Phil" wrote that "Patent examiners are under continual pressure to approve patents. We all have quotas set by our payscale and by the area in which we work and failure to meet the quotas results in being fired": Doctor-Phil, Friday, July 29, 2005 (2:18 pm), comment on *Slashdot Blog*, "Patent Examiners Flee the USPTO," Friday, July 29, 2005, http://yro.slashdot.org/story/05/07/29/1230256/Patent-Examiners-Flee-USPTO.

68 Lynne Taylor, "EU Single Patent 'Breakthrough,'" *Pharma Times*, December 8, 2009, http://www.pharmatimes.com/Article/09-12-08/EU_single_patent_%E2%80%9Cbreakthrough%E2%80%9D.aspx.

69 Steve Connor, "Your Life in Their Patent," *The Independent*, December 1, 1994.

70 Jane Zhang, "Battle Erupts over Disclosure on Drug Prices," *Wall Street Journal*, August 19, 2006, p. A6, http://online.wsj.com/article/SB125064608529842021.html (accessed September 1, 2009).

71 Ibid.

72 Ibid.

73 "You have called for a war against cancer to find the cures that, in our lifetimes, will put an end to cancer, just as we once managed to put polio behind us": Billy Tauzin, "Conversation with the President," Annual Meeting of the Pharmaceutical Research and Manufacturers of America, San Antonio, TX, April 4, 2009, http://www.phrma.org/news_room/speeches/conversation_with_the_president (accessed November 17, 2010).

74 Frank R. Lichtenberg, *Why Has Longevity Increased More in Some States Than in Others? The Role of Medical Innovation and Other Factors*, Medical Progress Report no. 4 (New York: Manhattan Institute, July 2007), http://www.manhattan-institute.org/html/mpr_04.htm.

75 Dean Baker, PhD, and Adriane Fugh-Berman, MD, "Do New Drugs Increase Life Expectancy? A Critique of a Manhattan Institute Paper," *Journal of General Internal Medicine* 24, no. 5 (2009): 678–82.

76 Ibid.

77 ALLHAT Website, http://allhat.sph.uth.tmc.edu/.

78 ALLHAT Officers and Coordinators, "Diuretic Versus α-Blocker as First-Step Antihypertensive Therapy: Final Results from the Antihypertensive and Lipid-Lowering Treatment to Prevent Heart Attack Trial (ALLHAT)," *Hypertension* 42, no. 3 (2003): 239–46.

79 R. S. Keefe, R. M. Bilder, S. M. Davis, et al., "Neurocognitive Effects of Antipsychotic Medications in Patients with Chronic Schizophrenia in the CATIE Trial," *Archives of General Psychiatry* 64, no. 6 (2007): 633–47.

80 Joel Lexchin, "Are New Drugs as Good as They Claim to Be?" *Australian Prescriber* 27, no. 2 (2004): 3, http://www.australianprescriber.com/magazine/27/1/2/3/ (accessed March 22, 2011).

CHAPTER 3: HITTING THE BRAKES

1 "Progen's First U.S. Clinical Trial with PI-88 Begins," *Worldwide Biotech/Entrepreneur Magazine*, September 1, 2001, http://www.entrepreneur.com/tradejournals/article/77298877.html (accessed March 17, 2011).

2 J. A. Joyce et al., "A Functional Heparan Sulfate Mimetic Implicates Both Heparanase and Heparan Sulfate in Tumor Angiogenesis and Invasion in a Mouse Model of Multistage Cancer," *Oncogene* 24, no. 25 (June 2005): 4037–51.

3 "Progen Technology Switches on Cancer Fighting Genes and Inhibits Tumor Growth," Progen Pharmaceuticals Ltd., press release (Queensland, Australia, April 20, 2009), http://www.progen.com.au/Docs/prs/AACR_2009_announcement_v3.pdf (accessed April 21, 2009).

4 Ahmedin Jemal, DVM, PhD, Freddie Bray, PhD, Melissa M. Center, MPH, et al., "Global Cancer Statistics," *CA: A Cancer Journal for Clinicians* 61, no. 2 (February 4, 2011): 69–70, http://caonline.amcancersoc.org/cgi/content/full/caac.20107v1 (accessed March 17, 2011).

5 PI-88 has since been dubbed Muparfostat.

6 G. M. Keating and A. Santoro, "Sorafenib: A Review of Its Use in Advanced Hepatocellular Carcinoma," *Drugs* 69, no. 2 (2009): 223–40, http://adisonline.com/drugs/abstract/2009/69020/Sorafenib_A_Review_of_Its_Use_in_Advanced.6.aspx (accessed May 1, 2010).

7 BBC News, "Liver Drug Too Expensive," November 19, 2009, http://news.bbc.co.uk/2/hi/health/8367614.stm.

8 Nyssa Skilton, "Drug Companies 'Must Be Forced' to Help the Public," *Canberra Times*, December 16, 2008.

9 "Progen Pharmaceuticals Ltd signs Muparfostat (PI-88) non-binding Letter of Intent for License and Collaboration with Medigen Biotech Corp," Progen Pharmacueticals Ltd., press release (Queensland, Australia, April 30, 2010), http://www.progen.com.au/Docs/prs/LOI%20Medigen%20Biotech%20Corp.pdf (accessed March 17, 2011).

10 Nyssa Skilton, "Science of Stymied Research," *Canberra Times*, January 3, 2009.

11 Pharmaceutical Research and Manufacturers of America, "Inside Innovation: The Drug Discovery Process."

12 *Fortune 500*, "Global 500: Our Ranking of the World's Largest Corporations," July 21, 2008, http://money.cnn.com/magazines/fortune/global500/2008/index.html.

13 Tom Blackwell, "Ontario Hospital Sued by Bayer," *National Post*, August 16, 2007.

14 "Regional Named in Patent Infringement Lawsuit," *Chronicle-Journal*, August 25, 2007, http://www.chroniclejournal.com/content/news/local/2007/08/25/regional-named-patent-infringement-lawsuit.

15 According to research firm IMS Health Canada: Blackwell, "Ontario Hospital Sued by Bayer."

16 According to E. Richard Gold, director of McGill University's Centre for Intellectual Property Policy, telephone interview with the author, July 9, 2009.

17 *Bayer Healthcare AG et al. v. Thunder Bay Regional Health Sciences Centre,* 2009, Ottawa Docket Summary, Summary of T-1450-07 Patent Infringement, December 17, 2009.

18 The Roche Group, "Roche and Genentech Reach a Friendly Agreement."

19 "As of 21 February 2010, worldwide more than 213 countries and overseas territories or communities have reported laboratory confirmed cases of pandemic influenza H1N1 2009, including at least 16226 deaths": Global Alert and Response, World Health Organization, "Update 89," *Pandemic (H1N1) 2009,* February 26, 2010, http://www.who.int/csr/don/2010_02_26/en/index .htm (accessed February 27, 2010).

20 Paul Elias, "Race to Patent SARS Virus Renews Debate," *Associated Press Newsfeed,* May 5, 2003, http://cmbi.bjmu.edu.cn/news/0305/63.htm.

21 "How Many Genes Are in the Human Genome?" Human Genome Project Information, Biological and Environmental Research Information System, U.S. Department of Energy, September 19, 2008, http://www.ornl.gov/sci/ techresources/Human_Genome/faq/genenumber.shtml.

22 Jamie Shreeve, "The Blueprint of Life," *U.S. News & World Report,* October 1, 2005, http://www.usnews.com/usnews/news/articles/051031/31genome.htm (accessed March 16, 2011).

23 Faren Clum, "The Human Genome Project vs. Celera Genomics," *The Human Genome Project: A Brief History,* ed. Huntington Outreach Project for Education at Stanford, December 6, 2008, http://hopes.stanford.edu/n3439/ hd-genetics/human-genome-project.

24 Matthew Rimmer, "The Race to Patent the SARS Virus: The TRIPS Agreement and Access to Essential Medicines," *Melbourne Journal of International Law* 5, no. 2 (October 2004): 335–74.

25 World Health Organization, Media Center, "Fact Sheet No. 259: African Trypanosomiasis (Sleeping Sickness)," October 2010, http://www.who.int/ mediacentre/factsheets/fs259/en/.

26 "The Estimated Number of Actual Cases Was Between 50 000 and 70 000": Ibid.

27 African trypanosomiasis is confined mainly to tropical Africa between 15 degrees North and 20 degrees South latitude: Ibid.

28 Ibid.

29 Richard D. Pearson, MD, "African Trypanosomiasis (African Sleeping Sickness)," in *The Merck Manual* (Whitehouse Station, NJ: Merck & Co., Inc., December 2009), http://www.merckmanuals.com/professional/sec14/ch186/ ch186b.html (accessed March 16, 2011).

30 David C. Dugdale III, MD, Jatin M. Vyas, MD, PhD, and David Zieve, MD, MHA, "Sleeping Sickness," *Medline Plus,* ed. National Institutes of Health, U.S. National Library of Medicine, December 3, 2008, http://www.nlm.nih .gov/medlineplus/ency/article/001362.htm.

31 Ann G. Sjoerdsma, *Starting with Serotonin: How a High-Rolling Father of Drug Discovery Repeatedly Beat the Odds* (Alexandria, VA: Improbable Books, 2008).

32 Institute of Medicine, *Saving Lives, Buying Time: Economics of Malaria Drugs*

in an Age of Resistance, ed. Kenneth J. Arrow, Claire B. Panosian, and Hellen Gelband (Washington, D.C.: National Academies Press, 2004).

33 The quote is not verbatim. We know that Schechter gave his immediate assent but do not know with what words he agreed to provide eflornithine to Van Nieuwenhove: Sjoerdsma, *Starting with Serotonin*, chapter 26.

34 S. Van Nieuwenhove, P. J. Schechter, J. Declercq, et al., "Treatment of Gambiense Sleeping Sickness in the Sudan with Oral DFMO (DL-alfa-difluoromethylornithine), an Inhibitor of Ornithine Decarboxylase; First Field Trial," *Transactions of the Royal Society of Tropical Medicine and Hygiene* 79, no. 5 (1985): 692–98.

35 David Greenwood, *Antimicrobial Drugs: Chronicle of a Twentieth-Century Medical Triumph* (New York: Oxford University Press, 2008), 284.

36 "Supply of Sleeping Sickness Drugs Secured," Doctors Without Borders/ Médecins Sans Frontières press release (Geneva, May 3, 2001), http://www .doctorswithoutborders.org/press/release.cfm?id=677.

37 "It took years of international pressure to find a solution to restart the production of the life-saving drug. This coincided with the media attention around the launch of Bristol-Myers Squibb's (BMS) Vaniqa, an eflornithine-based product intended to remove women's facial hair": Ibid.

38 Duncan Mboyah, "Kenya to Be Declared Sleeping Sickness Free," *Coastweek .com*, February 25, 2011, http://www.coastweek.com/xin_250211_06.htm (accessed March 22, 2011).

39 "Skin Medica Pharmaceuticals," website, http://pharmaceuticals.skinmedica .com/vaniqa.

40 Ed Silverman, "Pfizer Buys Rights to Drug to Fix a Curved Penis," *Pharmalot*, December 18, 2008, www.pharmalot.com/2008/12/Pfizer-Buys-Rights-to-a -Drug (accessed January 3, 2009).

41 "Erectile dysfunction, or ED, can be a total inability to achieve erection, an inconsistent ability to do so, or a tendency to sustain only brief erections. These variations make defining ED and estimating its incidence difficult": "Erectile Dysfunction," National Kidney and Urologic Diseases Information Clearinghouse, National Institute of Diabetes and Digestive and Kidney Diseases (Washington, D.C.: NIH Publication No. 06-3923, December 2005).

42 Natasha Singer, "Sure, It's Treatable. But Is It a Disorder?" *New York Times*, December 12, 2009.

43 Avery Johnson, "J&J's Prozac Cousin Approved Overseas, but Not for Depression," *Health Blog/Wall Street Journal*, February 10, 2009, http://blogs .wsj.com/health/2009/02/10/jjs-prozac-cousin-approved-overseas-but-not -for-depression (accessed March 16, 2011).

44 Diana Samuels, "Bush's 'PEPFAR' AIDS Treatment Program Saved a Million Lives in Africa, Stanford Researchers Say," *San Jose Mercury News*, April 6, 2009, http://www.mercurynews.com/breakingnews/ci_12087859 (accessed April 7, 2009).

45 His name has been changed.

46 At least two drugs against hepatitis C, Vertex's drug telaprevir and Merck's boceprevir, are waiting in the wings, but they have yet to be tested in clinical trials or for FDA approval: Ewen Callaway, "Boost for Drugs Against Hepatitis C," *NatureNews*, August 13, 2010, http://www.nature.com/news/2010/ 100813/full/news.2010.408.html (accessed September 7, 2010).

47 Harriet A. Washington, *Living Healthy with Hepatitis C* (New York: Dell, 2000).

48 Chiron's pertinent European patents for hepatitis C virus (HCV) blood-screening assays are European patent No. 0 318 216; in the UK, the patent is GB 2,212,511: Daniel Raymond, "Chiron's Hepatitis C Patents," *The Hepatitis C Harm Reduction Project*, June 22, 2004, http://hepcproject .typepad.com/hep_c_project/2004/06/chirons_hepatit.html.

49 Murex's test costs 30p; Chiron's costs £2, more than six times as much.

50 Connor, "Your Life in Their Patent."

51 Denise Gellene, "Chiron Relaxes Patent Licenses: The Biotech Firm Acts amid Criticism that Its Upfront Fees Stifle Work on Drugs for Hepatitis C," *Los Angeles Times*, June 22, 2004, http://www.latimes.com/technology/ la-fi-chiron22jun22,1,7764351.story?coll=la-headlines-technology.

52 In an unusual departure from nomenclature conventions, the gene symbol (*HFE*, for *High Fe* [iron]) is not an abbreviation of the official disease name, hemochromatosis.

53 "Classic Hemochromatosis (HFE), an Autosomal Recessive Disorder, Is Most Often Caused by Mutation in a Gene Designated HFE on Chromosome 6p21.3": "HEMOCHROMATOSIS; HFE," *Online Mendelian Inheritance in Man,* ed. Ada Hamosh, MD (Baltimore: McKusick-Nathans Institute of Genetic Medicine, Johns Hopkins University School of Medicine, November 3, 2010), http://www.ncbi.nlm.nih.gov/omim/235200 (accessed August 23, 2009).

54 David Blumenthal et al., "Withholding Research Results in Academic Life Science: Evidence from a National Survey of Faculty," *Journal of the American Medical Association* 277, no. 15 (1997): 1224–28; Aaron S. Kesselheim, MD, JD, and Michelle M. Mello, JD, PhD, "Medical Process Patents Monopolizing the Delivery of Health Care," *New England Journal of Medicine* 355, no. 9 (2006): 2036–41.

55 "Genes: HFE," Genetics Home Reference: Understanding Genetic Conditions, The National Library of Medicine, http://ghr.nlm.nih.gov/gene/HFE (accessed March 22, 2011).

56 Jon F. Merz, Antigone G. Kriss, Debra G. B. Leonard, and Mildred K. Cho, "Diagnostic Testing Fails the Test," *Nature* 415 (February 7, 2002): 577–79.

57 M. E. Cogswell et al., "Screening for Hemochromatosis: A Public Health Perspective," *American Journal of Preventive Medicine* 16, no. 2 (February 1999): 134–40.

58 "Although the condition is genetic, it is usually not inherited: Only about 1 in 10 affected infants inherits the gene from his parents. The gene mutation usually arises during development in infants born to unaffected parents": "SCN1A Epilepsy Gene Test: Diagnostic Advances for Managing Patients with Seizures," Genetic Technologies Corporation Pty. Ltd., July 2005, www .gtmedical.com.au/resource/Clinician_Epilepsy_broch2.pdf (accessed November 18, 2010).

59 Julie Robotham, "Sick Babies Denied Treatment in DNA Row," *Sidney Morning Herald*, November 29, 2008.

60 Anne Zieger, "DNA Patent Threatens Infant Healthcare in Australia," *Sydney Morning Herald*, December 3, 2008.

61 W. F. Lloyd, *Two Lectures on the Checks to Population* (excerpt), in *Popula-*

tion, Evolution, and Birth Control, ed. G. Hardin (San Francisco: Freeman, 1964), 37.

62 Alfred North Whitehead, *Science and the Modern World* (New York: Free Press, 1997), 10–11.

63 Wesley M. Cohen and Steven Merrill, eds., *Patents in the Knowledge-Based Economy*, Committee on Intellectual Property Rights in the Knowledge-Based Economy, National Research Council (Washington, D.C.: National Academies Press, 2003), 287–88.

64 Daniel J. DeNoon, "Pharmacies Can Still Make Preterm Birth Drug: Generic Versions of Makena Will Not Be Banned, FDA Says," WcbMD Health News website, March 30, 2011.

65 "Preemie Outrage: Cost of Drug That Prevents Premature Birth to Rise from $10 to $1500," *Daily Mail Reporter*, March 9, 2011, 8.

66 Marc Iskowitz, "More Blockbusters Exit as Fosamax, Advair Go Off-Patent," *Medical Marketing and Media* 43, no. 5 (March 2008): 363.

67 Kathy Method, "Going Going Gone: Patents Set to Expire Soon on Many Brand-Name Drugs," *DrugTopics Supplements*, August 10, 2009, http://drugtopics.modernmedicine.com/drugtopics/article/articleDetail.jsp?id=617015&pageID=1&sk=&date.

68 Megan Ogilvie, "Secrecy Slowing Drug Research; Leading Scientist Urges Transparency to Deliver Drugs to Patients Sooner," *Toronto Star*, April 4, 2009.

69 Tom Ramstack, "Patent Bill Seen Hurting Little Guy," *Washington Times*, July 19, 2007.

70 Stephen Schondelmeyer, telephone interview with author, April 7, 2009.

71 Stephen W. Schondelmeyer, PharmD, PhD, "Patent Extensions of Pipeline Drugs: Impact on U.S. Health Care Expenditures" (Minneapolis: PRIME Institute, College of Pharmacy, University of Minnesota, July 1999).

72 Gina Chon, Damna Cimilluca, and Jeanne Whalen, "Sanofi Unveils Genzyme 'Bear Hug,'" *Wall Street Journal*, August 30, 2010.

73 Alex Roland, "A Laboratory and Licensing; Committees and Engines, 1915–1918," *SP-4103 Model Research*, vol. 1 (Washington, D.C.: Business, National Aeronautics and Space Administration Scientific and Technical Information Branch, 1985), http://history.nasa.gov/SP-4103/ch2.htm (accessed December 8, 2010).

74 Jeanne Clark, Joe Piccolo, Brian Stanton, and Karin Tyson, *Patent Pools: A Solution to the Problem of Access in Biotechnology Patents?* (Washington, D.C.: United States Patent and Trademark Office, December 5, 2000), http://www.uspto.gov/web/offices/pac/dapp/opla/patentpool.pdf (accessed September 2010).

75 Rebecca Eisenberg and Michael A. Heller, "Can Patents Deter Innovation? The Anticommons in Biomedical Research," *Science* 280, no. 5364 (1998): 698–701.

76 Mark Nance et al., "Patent Litigation: Is It Worth the Expense?" *Genetic Engineering & Biotechnology News* 26, No. 7 (2006), http://www.genengnews.com/gen-articles/patent-litigation-is-it-worth-the-expense/1454/ (accessed March 22, 2011).

77 Cohen and Merrill, *Patents in the Knowledge-Based Economy*.

CHAPTER 4: POISON PILLS

1 Gardiner Harris and Benedict Carey, "Researchers Fail to Reveal Full Drug Pay," *New York Times,* June 8, 2008, http://www.nytimes.com/2008/06/08/us/08conflict.html.

2 Rita Rubin, "FDA Panel to Vote on Antipsychotic Drugs for Kids," *USA Today,* June 9, 2009.

3 Martha Rosenberg, "Parents Fight Use of New Psych Meds for Kids," *San Francisco Chronicle,* September 13, 2009.

4 Duff Wilson, "Child's Ordeal Shows Risks of Psychosis Drugs for Young," *New York Times,* September 1, 2010.

5 Gardiner Harris, "Drug Maker Told Studies Would Aid It, Papers Say," *New York Times,* March 19, 2009.

6 "ADHD is a problem with inattentiveness, over-activity, impulsivity, or a combination. For these problems to be diagnosed as ADHD, they must be out of the normal range for the child's age and development": Brandon Keim, "Could Antidepressants Rewire Adolescent Brains?" Wired Science, *Wired,* May 30, 2009, http://www.wired.com/wiredscience/2007/05/could_antidepre/ (accessed August 4, 2009).

7 Gardiner Harris, "Research Center Tied to Drug Company," *New York Times,* November 24, 2008.

8 "The rationale of this center," Johnson & Johnson internal documents stated, "is to generate and disseminate data supporting the use of risperidone [Risperdal] in children and adolescents." Ibid.

9 Ibid.

10 The Best Pharmaceuticals for Children Act of 2002 (BPCA) renewed our authority to grant six months of additional marketing exclusivity to manufacturers who conduct and submit pediatric studies in response to our written requests. Best Pharmaceuticals for Children Act, January 4, 2002 (Public Law 107-109), http://www.fda.gov/Drugs/DevelopmentApprovalProcess/DevelopmentResources/ucm049876.htm.

11 Xi Yu, "Three Professors Face Sanctions Following Harvard Medical School Inquiry," *Harvard Crimson,* July 2, 2011.

12 "Letter from Joseph Biederman, Thomas J. Spencer, and Timothy E. Wilens," July 1, 2011.

13 *The Infinite Mind,* "The Bipolar Child," LCMedia original broadcast, September 20, 2005, http://www.lcmedia.com/mind133.htm.

14 Gardiner Harris, "Radio Host Has Drug Company Ties," *New York Times,* November 21, 2008.

15 Natalie Angier, "Disputed Meeting to Ask If Crime Has Genetic Roots," *New York Times,* September 19, 1995.

16 Warren E. Leary, "Struggle Continues Over Remarks by Mental Health Official," *New York Times,* March 8, 1992.

17 Certain tenets of the U.S. Code of Federal Regulations (CFR 21 50.23 and 50.24) allow research to be conducted in trauma emergencies or in some national-defense situations without the subjects' knowledge or permission.

18 Carl Elliott, *White Coat, Black Hat: Adventures on the Dark Side of Medicine* (Kindle version) (Boston: Beacon Press, 2010), 43.

19 National Academy of Science, Institute of Medicine, Board on Population Health, *The Future of Drug Safety: Promoting and Protecting the Health of the Public* (Washington, D.C.: The National Academies, September 22, 2006), http://www.iom.edu/Reports/2006/The-Future-of-Drug-Safety-Promoting -and-Protecting-the-Health-of-the-Public.aspx.

20 Ibid.; Diedtra Henderson, "Report: FDA Needs More Authority, Funds," *Boston Globe*, September 23, 2006.

21 Melody Peterson, *Our Daily Meds: How the Pharmaceutical Companies Transformed Themselves into Slick Marketing Machines and Hooked the Nation on Prescription Drugs* (New York: Farrar, Straus & Giroux, 2008).

22 "Testimony of David J. Graham, MD, MPH, November 18, 2004," to the United States Senate Committee on Finance, Thursday, November 18, 2004, 10:00 A.M., 216 Hart Senate Office Building.

23 Ben Goldacre, "The danger of drugs . . . and data," *Guardian*, May 9, 2009.

24 Matthew Herper, "The FDA Ignores Its Advisors a Quarter of the Time," The Medicine Show Blog, *Forbes*, October 12, 2010, http://blogs.forbes.com/ matthewherper/2010/10/12/the-fda-ignores-its-advisors-a-quarter-of-the -time/.

25 Peter Lurie, MD, MPH, and Sidney M. Wolfe, MD, "FDA Medical Officers Report Lower Standards Permit Dangerous Drug Approvals," Public Citizen, December 2, 1998, http://www.citizen.org/hrg1466; Wolfe, "Congressional Testimony on FDA Deficiences."

26 Ibid.

27 David Willman, "The Rise and Fall of the Killer Drug Rezulin," *Los Angeles Times*, June 4, 2000.

28 David Willman, "Strategy Developed to Get Latinos 'to Take the Risk,' " *Los Angeles Times*, June 30, 2002, http://articles.latimes.com/2002/jun/30/ nation/na-rezside30.

29 David Willman, "Diabetes Drug Rezulin Pulled Off the Market," *Los Angeles Times*, March 22, 2000.

30 S. E. Nissen and K. Wolski, "Effect of Rosiglitazone on the Risk of Myocardial Infarction and Death from Cardiovascular Causes," *New England Journal of Medicine* 356, no. 24 (2007): 2457–71; Bruce M. Psaty, MD, PhD, and Curt D. Furberg, MD, PhD, "Rosiglitazone and Cardiovascular Risk," *New England Journal of Medicine* 356, no. 24 (2007): 2522–24.

31 Brandon Keim, "Glaxo, Doctors Battle over Interpretation of New Avandia Study," Wired Science, *Wired*, June 6, 2007, http://www.wired.com/ wiredscience/2007/06/glaxo_doctors_b (accessed March 23, 2011).

32 Juhi Yajnik, "University Sues Pfizer over COX-2 Research," *The Scientist*, October 27, 2006, http://www.the-scientist.com/news/display/25408/ (accessed April 29, 2011).

33 W. L. Xie, J. G. Chipman, D. L. Robertson, R. L. Erikson, and D. L. Simmons, "Expression of a Mitogen-Responsive Gene Encoding Prostaglandin Synthase Is Regulated by mRNA Splicing," *Proceedings of the National Academy of Sciences* 88, no. 7 (April 1991): 12692–96.

34 Tom Harvey, "BYU Spices Up Celebrex Lawsuit Against Pfizer," *Salt Lake Tribune*, September 21, 2010, http://www.sltrib.com/sltrib/money/49883490-79/ byu-pfizer-simmons-celebrex.html.csp (accessed May 12, 2011).

35 Although children under eighteen are discouraged from taking aspirin to avoid the very rare Reye's syndrome that can attack the liver and brain in the wake of the flu or other viral illness, and although high doses of ibuprofen have been linked to higher stroke risks for the elderly, most people can find an over-the-counter NSAID that offers them effective, safe pain relief.

36 A 100-pill bottle of Walgreens generic aspirin, for example, can be bought for $1, or $.01 a pill. Vioxx costs $396 for 50 pills, or $7.92 a pill: 792 times the price of the aspirin. Insurance coverage hides the true costs of prescription medications from most of us.

37 J. M. Wright, "The Double-Edged Sword of COX-2 Selective NSAIDs," *Canadian Medical Association Journal* 167, no. 10 (2002): 1131–37.

38 "CELEBREX® (Celecoxib) Capsules, G. D. Searle & Co.," *Physicians' Desk Reference* (Montvale, NJ: PDR Network, LLC, 2010), http://www.pdr.net/drugpages/productlabeling.aspx?mpcode=76000300 (accessed November 20, 2010).

39 Barry Meier, Gina Kolata, and Andrew Pollack, "Medicine Fueled by Marketing Intensified Trouble for Pain Pills," *New York Times*, December 19, 2004.

40 Drew Griffin and Andy Segal, "Feds Found Pfizer Too Big to Nail," CNN .com Health, *CNN*, April 02, 2010, http://articles.cnn.com/2010-04-02/health/pfizer.bextra_1_bextra-pfizer-and-pharmacia-generic-drugs?_s =PM:HEALTH.

41 This is an abbreviation for *qui tam pro domino rege quam pro se ipso in hac parte sequitur*, which means "one who sues in this matter for the king as well as on behalf of himself."

42 Bill Berkrot, "Pfizer Whistleblower's Ordeal Reaps Big Rewards," *Reuters*, September 3, 2009, www.reuters.com/article/businessNews/idUSN021592920090903 (accessed September 7, 2009).

43 "Justice Department Announces Largest Health Care Fraud Settlement in Its History," Department of Health and Human Services, press release (Washington, D.C., September 2, 2009), http://www.hhs.gov/news/press/2009pres/09/20090902a.html.

44 Gardiner Harris, "Pfizer Pays $2.3 Billion to Settle Marketing Case," *New York Times*, September 3, 2009.

45 Carrie Johnson, "In Settlement, a Warning to Drugmakers: Pfizer to Pay Record Penalty in Improper-Marketing Case," *Washington Post*, September 3, 2009.

46 F. E. Silverstein, G. Faich, J. L. Goldstein, et al., "Gastrointestinal Toxicity with Celecoxib vs Nonsteroidal Anti-Inflammatory Drugs for Osteoarthritis and Rheumatoid Arthritis: The CLASS Study: A Randomized Controlled Trial. Celecoxib Long-Term Arthritis Safety Study," *Journal of the American Medical Association* 284, no. 10 (September 2000): 1247–55; C. Bombardier, L. Laine, A. Reicin, et al., "Comparison of Upper Gastrointestinal Toxicity of Rofecoxib and Naproxen in Patients with Rheumatoid Arthritis. VIGOR Study Group," *New England Journal of Medicine* 343, no. 21 (November 2000): 1520–28.

47 Richard Knox, "Merck Pulls Arthritis Drug Vioxx from Market," *All Things Considered*, September 30, 2004, http://www.npr.org/templates/story/story .php?storyId=4054991 (accessed November 20, 2010).

48 Ben Goldacre, "The Dangers of Drugs . . . and Data."

49 Senator Charles Grassley, letter to Pfizer via electronic transmission, March 3, 2009, http://graphics8.nytimes.com/packages/pdf/business/2009_03_03 _Pfizer_letter.pdf.

50 They are Drs. Thomas Fleming (University of Washington), Curt Furberg (Wake Forest University), Steven Nissen (the Cleveland Clinic), and Alastair Wood (Vanderbilt University).

51 John McKenzie, "Medical Journal Changes Independent Policy," abcnews .com, June 12, 2002, http://abcnews.go.com/WNT/story?id=130296&page=1.

52 Peter Gorner, "New England Journal of Medicine Eases Conflict-of-Interest Policy for Authors," *Chicago Tribune*, June 13, 2002.

53 Adriane J. Fugh-Berman, "The Haunting of Medical Journals: How Ghost- writing Sold 'HRT,' " *PLoS Medicine* 7, no. 9 (September 2010): e1000335, http://www.plosmedicine.org/article/info%3Adoi%2F10.1371%2Fjournal .pmed.1000335 (accessed November 20, 2010).

54 The Drug Industry Document Archive, a searchable database of drug-company documents, is available at http://dida.library.ucsf.edu.

55 Andrew P. Lea, DesignWrite, Inc., "RE: Premarin/TMG publication plan proposal," email, May 20, 2003, http://dida.library.ucsf.edu/tid/duc37b10 (accessed November 21, 2010).

56 B. Janas, DesignWrite, Inc., "updated outline," email, April 13, 2010, http:// dida.library.ucsf.edu/pdf/boc37b10 (accessed August 21, 2009).

57 "Proposal for Jeff Solomon—Medical Education and Communication Plan for the Premarin Product Line," DesignWrite, Inc., August 12, 1996, http:// dida.library.ucsf.edu/pdf/jrb37b10 (accessed August 21, 2009).

58 "Bylined articles will allow us to fold Lexapro messages into articles on depression, anxiety and comorbidity developed by (or ghostwritten for) thought leaders": Ibid.

59 Matthew Perrone, "Glaxo Used Ghostwriting Program to Promote Paxil," Associated Press/*Boston Globe*, August 20, 2009.

60 Alicia Mundy, *Dispensing with the Truth: The Victims, the Drug Companies, and the Dramatic Story behind the Battle over Fen-Phen* (New York: St. Mar- tin's Press, 2001), 162–67.

61 C. Seth Landefeld and Michael A. Steinman, MD, "The Neurontin Legacy—Marketing through Misinformation and Manipulation," *New England Journal of Medicine* 360, no. 2 (2009): 103–6.

62 David Healy, MD, FRCPsych, and Dinah Cattell, "Interface between Author- ship, Industry and Science in the Domain of Therapeutics," *British Journal of Psychiatry* 183 (2003): 22–27.

63 Joseph S. Ross, MD, MHS, Kevin P. Hill, MD, MHS, et al., "Guest Author- ship and Ghostwriting in Publications Related to Rofecoxib: A Case Study of Industry Documents from Rofecoxib Litigation," *Journal of the American Medical Association* 299, no. 15 (2008): 1800–12.

64 "Randomised trial of intravenous streptokinase, oral aspirin, both, or neither among 17,187 cases of suspected acute myocardial infarction: ISIS-2. ISIS-2 (Second International Study of Infarct Survival) Collaborative Group," *Lan- cet* 2, no. 8607 (1988): 349–60.

65 Peter Sleight, "Debate: Subgroup Analyses in Clinical Trials: Fun to Look

At—but Don't Believe Them!" *Current Control Trials in Cardiovascular Medicine* 1, no. 1 (2000): 25–27.

66 Jonathan D. Kahn, "How a Drug Becomes 'Ethnic': Law, Commerce, and the Production of Racial Categories in Medicine," *Yale Journal of Health Policy, Law, and Ethics* 4, no. 1 (Winter 2004): 1–46.

67 "Although blacks and whites suffer the same rate of death from congestive heart failure, blacks tend to die earlier, which is unsurprising considering their well-documented lesser access to heart disease technology and other cardiac care and differences in diet, exercise and stress exposure": Ibid.

68 Keith J. Winstein, "NAACP Presses US on Heart Drug," *Wall Street Journal*, January 25, 2007.

69 "NitroMed was criticized for the drug's high cost, which at $1.80 a pill (or $5.40 a day) equaled 4 to 7 times the price of generic isosorbide plus hydralazine": Martha Lincoln, "Because You Want More Life to Live: BiDil, a Heart Failure Prescription for Self-Identified Blacks," *Corporations and Health Watch*, May 1, 2008, http://www.corporationsandhealth.org/news/61/59/Because-You-Want-More-Life-to-Live-BiDil-a-Heart-Failure-Prescription-for-Self-Identified-Blacks (accessed December 20, 2010).

70 Jonathan Kahn, JD, PhD, "How a Drug Becomes 'Ethnic': Law, Commerce, and the Production of Racial Categories in Medicine," *Yale Journal of Health Policy, Law, and Ethics* 4, no. 1 (2004); also see Kahn, "Getting the Numbers Right: Statistical Mischief and Racial Profiling in Heart Failure Research," *Perspectives in Biology and Medicine* 46, no. 4 (Autumn 2003): 473–83.

71 Mary Ann Moon, "Industry Funded CV Trials—Biased to Positives?" *Internal Medicine News*, June 15, 2006, http://www.internalmedicinenews.com/index.php?id=2049&type=98&tx_ttnews[tt_news]=9824&cHash=da03e20e36 (accessed March 22, 2011).

72 Paul M. Ridker, MD, and Jose Torres, BA, "Reported Outcomes in Major Cardiovascular Clinical Trials Funded by For-Profit and Not-for-Profit Organizations: 2000–2005," *Journal of the American Medical Association* 295, no. 19 (2006): 2270–74.

73 Cara Bouwer, "Sponsored Research Tends to Show Bias," *Business Day*, June 13, 2007, 5.

74 Mark Henderson, "Drug Trials 'Give Best Results to Sponsors,'" *Sunday Times* (London), June 5, 2007, http://www.timesonline.co.uk/tol/news/science/article1884627.ece.

75 David J. Sackett and Andrew D. Oxman, "HARLOT plc: An Amalgamation of the World's Two Oldest Professions," *British Medical Journal* 327, no. 7429 (2003): 1442–45.

76 Thoma M. Burton, "Despite Heart Attack Deaths, Polyheme Still Being Tested on Trauma Patients," *Wall Street Journal*, February 22, 2006.

77 Merck & Co. sponsored ADVANTAGE (Assessment of Differences between Vioxx and Naproxen to Ascertain Gastrointestinal Tolerability and Effectiveness). Kevin P. Hill, MD, MHS; Joseph S. Ross, MD, MHS; David S. Egilman, MD, MPH; and Harlan M. Krumholz, MD, SM, "The ADVANTAGE Seeding Trial: A Review of Internal Documents," *Annals of Internal Medicine* 149, no. 4 (August 19, 2008): 251–58, http://www.annals.org/content/149/4/251.full.

78 Harold C. Sox and Drummond Rennie, "Seeding Trials: Just Say 'No,'" *Annals of Internal Medicine* 149, no. 4 (August 2008): 279–80.

79 Richard Smith, "Medical Journals and Pharmaceutical Companies: Uneasy Bedfellows," *British Medical Journal* 326 (2003): 1202.

80 Harriet A. Washington, "Flacking for Pharma: Big Pharmaceutical Companies Don't Just Compromise Doctors; They Also Undermine the Top Medical Journals and Skew the Findings of Medical Research," *The American Scholar* (Summer 2011): 2–14

81 Bob Grant, "Merck Published Fake Journal," *The Scientist*, April 30, 2009, http://www.the-scientist.com/blog/display/55671/.

82 Ben Goldacre, "The Danger of Drugs . . . and Data."

83 "Progressive Librarians Guild Calls for Elsevier to End Corrupt Publishing Practices and for Library Associations to Take Advocacy Role on Behalf of Scientific Integrity," Progressive Librarians Guild news release (Lawrenceville, NJ, May 12, 2009), http://libr.org/plg/elsevier.php; Bob Grant, "Elsevier Published 6 Fake Journals," *The Scientist*, May 7, 2009, http://www.the-scientist.com/blog/display/55679/.

84 Ben Goldacre, "The Danger of Drugs . . . and Data."

85 Margaret Hunt, Virology, Chapter Thirteen: Influenza Virus (Orthomyxovirus), Microbiology and Immunology Online, http://pathmicro.med.sc.edu/mhunt/flu.htm.

86 D. J. Sencer and J. D. Millar, "Reflections on the 1976 Swine Flu Vaccination Program," *Emerging Infectious Diseases* 12, no. 1 (January 2006), http://www.cdc.gov/ncidod/EID/vol12no01/05–1007.htm (accessed June 1, 2011).

87 Ibid.

88 Ibid.

89 Helen Epstein, "Flu Warning: Beware the Drug Companies!" *New York Review of Books*, May 12, 2011.

90 Helen Epstein, "Beware Tamiflu," *New York Review of Books*, May 26, 2011.

91 Helen Epstein, "Flu Warning: Beware the Drug Companies!"

92 Ibid.

93 S. Vallet, A. Palumbo, N. Raje, et al., "Thalidomide and Lenalidomide: Mechanism-Based Potential Drug Combinations," *Leukemia & Lymphoma* 49, no. 7 (2008): 1238–45.

94 AdisInsight, Wolters Kluwer Pharma Solutions, "Thalidomide" (800004827), March 15, 1995, http://bi.adisinsight.com/rdi/viewdocument.aspx?render=view&mode=remote&adnm=800004827&PushValidation=121745 (retrieved September 17, 2010).

95 "Thalidomide," Center for the Evaluation of Risks to Human Reproduction, National Toxicology Program, Department of Health and Human Services, http://cerhr.niehs.nih.gov/common/thalidomide.html (accessed September 17, 2010).

96 "Against Leprosy," Thalidomide, Föreningen för de Neurosedynskadad/The Swedish Thalidomide Society, http://www.thalidomide.org/web/against-leprosy/ (accessed September 17, 2010).

97 F. J. Paumgarten and I. Chahoud, "Thalidomide Embryopathy Cases in Brazil after 1965," *Reproductive Toxicology* 22, no. 1 (2006): 1–2; "Thalidomide Scares Again/Talidomida volta a assustar," Brazilian Department of Health

press release (Rio de Janeiro, November 1, 2006), http://www.saude.df.gov
.br/003/00301009.asp?ttCD_CHAVE=31041.

98 Seth W. Glickman, MD, MBA, et al., "Ethical and Scientific Implications of
the Globalization of Clinical Research," *New England Journal of Medicine*
360, no. 8 (February 2009): 816.

99 Michael Kremer, "Pharmaceuticals and the Developing World," *Journal of
Economic Perspectives* 16, no. 4 (2002): 67–90.

100 Phillip Knightley et al., *Suffer the Children: The Story of Thalidomide* (New
York: Viking, 1979), 40–41.

CHAPTER 5: GENE PATENTS

1 "Pigs Fly: Federal Court Invalidates Myriad's Patent Claims," posted by
John Conley and Dan Vorhaus, *Genomics Law Report*, March 30, 2010, www
.genomicslawreport.com/index.php/2010/03/30/pigs-fly-federal-court
-invalidates-myriads-patent-claims/, accessed April 2, 2010.

2 Sharon Begley, "In Surprise Ruling, Court Declares Two Gene Patents
Invalid," *Newsweek*, March 29, 2010.

3 The BRCA genes, like other patented genes, are products of nature, but an
artificial gene was first reported synthesized on June 2, 1970, by MIT professor Har Gobind Khorana, who was then a chemist at the University of Wisconsin (www.super70s.com/Super70s/Timeline/1970/ and www.answers
.com/topic/har-gobind-khorana).

4 Atomic mass units, or daltons: this is a conventional, infinitesimal measure
of matter on the atomic scale. 1 amu = 1.66×10^{-24} grams.

5 Under thirty-five years of age.

6 Esther John, Alexander Miron, Gail Gong, Amanda I. Phipps, Anna Felberg,
Frederick P. Li, Dee W. West, and Alice S. Whittemore, "Prevalence of Patho-
genic *BRCA1* Mutation Carriers in 5 US Racial/Ethnic Groups," *Journal of the
American Medical Association* 298, no. 24 (October 2007): 2869–76.

7 Steve Benowitz, "French Challenge to BRCA1 Patent Underlies European
Discontent," *Journal of the National Cancer Institute* 94, no. 2 (January 2002):
80–81.

8 "Genetics," Breastcancer.org, February 15, 2011, http://www.breastcancer.org/
risk/factors/genetics.jsp, accessed March 9, 2011.

9 *Association of Molecular Pathology et al. v. United States Patent and Trademark Office*; Myriad Genetics et al. in United States District Court Southern
District of New York, 26.

10 Myriad Genetics et al., 27–28.

11 American Intellectual Property Law Association, *Report of Economic Survey*
(Arlington, VA: AIPLA, 1999), table 22.

12 Benowitz, "French Challenge to BRCA1."

13 Karen van Kampen, "Owning the Code," *National Post Business Magazine*,
September 1, 2005, 56.

14 John Schwartz, "Cancer Patients Challenge the Patenting of a Gene," *New
York Times*, May 13, 2009.

15 NF-κB stands for *nuclear factor kappa-light-chain-enhancer of activated B
cells*, a proteinaceous complex found in all nearly animal cells that governs

the regulation of DNA transcription: A. R. Braiser, "The NF-κB regulatory network," *Cardiovascular Toxicology* 6, no. 2 (2006): 111–30.

16 Charlotte Harrington, "News and Analysis: Patent Watch," *Nature Reviews Drug Discovery* 9 (2010): 352–53, http://www.nature.com/nrd/journal/v9/n9/full/nrd3273.html (accessed March 9, 2011).

17 Sharon Begley, "In Surprise Ruling, Court Declares Two Gene Patents Invalid," *Newsweek,* March 29, 2010, http://www.newsweek.com/blogs/the-human-condition/2010/03/29/in-surprise-ruling-court-declares-two-gene-patents-invalid.html (accessed June 23, 2011).

18 American Civil Liberties Union, "BRCA: Genes and Patents," May 27, 2009, http://www.aclu.org/free-speech/brca--genes--and--patents (accessed May 2010).

19 Van Kampen, "Owning the Code," 57.

20 Jeffery P. Struewing, Dvorah Abeliovich, Tamar Peretz, Naaman Avishai, Michael M. Kaback, Francis S. Collins, and Lawrence C. Brody, "The carrier frequency of the *BRCA1* 185delAG mutation is approximately 1 percent in Ashkenazi Jewish individuals," *Nature Genetics* 11 (1995): 198–200.

21 "Against the monopoly of Myriad Genetics on tests of susceptibility to breast and ovarian cancer: role reversal of situation in the European patent office," Institut Curie press release (Paris, November 20, 2008), http://www.curie.fr/sites/default/files/decision-OEB-Myriad-Genetics-predisposition-sein.pdf.

22 The organization is also known as the Committee for Prevention of Genetic Diseases, and has offices in Brooklyn and Israel.

23 Arthur Allen, "Who owns your DNA? Genetic research that can save lives is often stymied by biotech companies' greedy patent claims," *Salon*, March 7, 2000, http://www.salon.com/health/feature/2000/03/07/genetic_test/index.html (accessed November 1, 2010).

24 Greenberg, 264 F. Supp. 2d at 1069-70.

25 Radhika Rao, "Genes and Spleens: Property, Contract, or Privacy Rights in the Human Body?" *Journal of Law Medicine Ethics* 35, no. 3 (2007): 371–82.

26 Allen, "Who Owns Your DNA?"

27 "A survey of laboratories revealed a possible price premium for ASPA [Canavan's] testing, with per-unit costs higher than for other genetic tests in the Secretary's Advisory Committee on Genetics, Health, and Society Case Studies": Alessandra Colaianni, Subhashini Chandrasekharan, and Robert Cook-Deegan, MD, "Impact of Gene Patents and Licensing Practices on Access to Genetic Testing and Carrier Screening for Tay-Sachs and Canavan Disease," *Genetics in Medicine* 12, no. 4 (April 2010): S5-S14, http://journals.lww.com/geneticsinmedicine/Fulltext/2010/0400 (accessed July 19, 2010).

28 Ibid.

29 E. G. Campbell, B. R. Clarridge, M. Gokhale, L. Birembaum, S. Hilgartner, N. A. Holtzman, and D. Blumenthal, "Data Withholding in Academic Genetics: Evidence from a National Survey," *Journal of the American Medical Association* 287, no. 4 (January 2002): 473–80.

30 Vida Foubister, "Gene Patents Raise Concerns for Researchers, Clinicians," *American Medical News*, February 21, 2000, http://www.ama-assn.org/amednews/2000/02/21/prsb0221.htm (accessed March 23, 2011).

31 Julian Borger, "Gene Patents Hit Research," *Guardian*, December 15, 1999.

32 Daniel Kevles, *In the Name of Eugenics: Genetics and the Uses of Human Heredity* (Cambridge, MA: Harvard University Press, 1998).

33 Finn Bowring, *Science, Seeds, and Cyborgs: Biotechnology and the Appropriation of Life* (London: Verso, 2003).

34 James Bowman, MD, personal interview on May 15, 2006; written communication, July 11, 2005, and September 14, 2007.

35 Kevles, *In the Name of Eugenics.*

36 Ibid.

37 The erroneous characterization of sickle-cell carriers or heterozygotes as "sick" is ironic because heterozygotes actually enjoy the medical advantage of increased resistance to malaria. Thus, heterozygotes are actually healthier than either homozygotes, who have sickle-cell disease, or people with two normal copies of the gene, who have no additional protection against malaria. In fact, in malarious areas such as West Africa, sickle-cell heterozygotes are 15 percent more likely than people without the HBB "sickle-cell gene" to survive and reproduce: this is called the "heterozygote advantage."

38 Harriet A. Washington, *Medical Apartheid: The Dark History of Medical Experimentation on Black Americans from Colonial Times to the Present* (New York: Doubleday, 2007), 310.

39 *2007 Course Catalog*, School of Aerospace Medicine, United States Air Force, 16, http://afspp.afms.mil/idc/groups/public/documents/afms/ctb_073557 .pdf (accessed May 19, 2010).

40 Sharon F. Terry, "Learning Genetics," *Health Affairs* 22, no. 5 (2003): 166–71.

41 Ibid., 171.

42 Justin Gillis, "Gene Research Success Spurs Profit Debate," *Washington Post*, December 30, 2000.

CHAPTER 6: LIQUID ASSETS, LETHAL RISKS

1 Milete was given not blood but PolyHeme, which is red and resembles blood.

2 Jay Katz, MD, and Jos V. M. Welie, "Blurring the Lines: Research, Therapy, and IRBs (New FDA Regulations on Informed Consent and Emergency Research in Life-Threatening Situations)," *Hastings Center Report* 27, no. 1 (January–February 1997): 9–12.

3 G. L. Kierman, "Scientific and Ethical Considerations in the Use of Placebo Controls in Clinical Trials in Psychopharmacology," *Psychopharmacology Bulletin* 22, no. 1 (1986): 25–29.

4 It "permits drug-by-drug waiver approval on the basis that consent is 'not feasible' in a specific military operation involving combat or the immediate threat of combat": George J. Annas, "Protecting Soldiers from Friendly Fire: The Consent Requirement for Using Investigational Drugs and Vaccines in Combat," *American Journal of Law & Medicine* 24, nos. 2–3 (1998): 245–60.

5 Chris Adams, "FDA Clears BioPort to Resume Shipments of Anthrax Vaccine," *Wall Street Journal*, January 31, 2002. "In various follow-up visits by FDA inspectors, BioPort was cited for deficiencies in record-keeping, sterility precautions and manufacturing deviations."

6 "*Feres v. United States*, 340 U.S. 135 (1950), is a case in which the Supreme Court of the United States ruled that the United States is not liable under

the Federal Tort Claims Act for injuries to members of the armed forces sustained while on active duty and not on furlough and resulting from the negligence of others in the armed forces. The opinion is an extension of the English common-law concept of sovereign immunity": Jennifer L'Hommedieu Stankus, JD, MS-4, "Understanding Medical Liability in Military Medicine," *American College of Emergency Physicians (ACEP)/ACEP News,* February 2009, http://www.acep.org/content.aspx?id=43974.

7 *Feres v. United States,* 340 U.S. 135 (1950).

8 Preliminary Injunction, *Doe v. Rumsfeld,* Civil Action No. 03-707 (EGS), December 22, 2003, http://www.cbsnews.com/htdocs/pdf/anthraxdocument .pdf.

9 *Doe v. Rumsfeld,* 341 F. Supp. 2d 1, 6 (D.D.C. 2004); "Anthrax Vaccinations Halted Again," United Press International, Military.com, October 28, 2004, http://www.military.com/NewsContent/0,13319,FL_anthrax_102804,00.html.

10 *Doe v. Rumsfeld.*

11 Marie McCullough, "Technical Difficulties Put Anthrax Vaccine out of Reach; Some Experts Said That May Be a Good Thing, in Part Because of Questions About Its Maker and the Inoculation Itself," *Philadelphia Inquirer,* October 30, 2001, A10.

12 Stephen Kinzer, "A Nation Challenged: The Biological Threat; Military's Sole Supplier of Anthrax Vaccine Still Can't Make It," *New York Times,* October 6, 2001, 1B.

13 Keith Epstein and Bill Sloat, "Drug Trials: Do People Know the Truth About Experiments?" *Cleveland Plain Dealer,* December 15, 1996.

14 Michelle H. Biros, MD, *Annals of Emergency Medicine* 42, no. 4 (October 2003): 550–64.

15 46 percent.

16 Hon. George M. Marovich, United States District Court, Northern District of Illinois Eastern Division. Memorandum Opinion and Order, in *Re Northfield Laboratories, Inc.* No. 06 C 1493 Securities Litigation, 2.

17 Charles Natanson, MD, Steven J. Kern, BS, Peter Lurie, MD, MPH, et al., "Cell-Free Hemoglobin-Based Blood Substitutes and the Risk of Myocardial Infarction and Death," *Journal of the American Medical Association* 299, no. 19 (April 2008): 2304–12.

18 Northfield Laboratories, "PolyHeme Q&A," in PolyHeme® Clinical Trial PowerPoint presentation, Wishard Health Services, January 21, 2004.

19 ABC-TV, "US Medical Experiments Without Consent?" *World News with Charles Gibson,* May 27, 2007, http://abcnews.go.com/WNT/Video/playerIndex?id=3217758 (accessed February 25, 2010).

20 www.Im4justice.com. This site seems to have been taken down in early 2010.

21 Matt Potter, "Bad Blood?" *San Diego Reader,* Thursday, July 28, 2005.

22 Eleven of the thirty-two original testing sites, or 34.4 percent.

23 All sixteen were subjects, but they were not all infused with PolyHeme; six were infused with saline, as controls.

24 "Study Patient Characteristics," in PolyHeme® Trauma Trial PowerPoint presentation, slide 15, Methodist Hospital & Wishard Health Services.

25 The FDA also noted that "the safety data of all controlled studies reveal that the administration of PolyHeme places the patients at a higher risk

of significant adverse events," and stated that "therefore, in the absence of clinical benefit, the risk:benefit assessment of the product in trauma is unfavorable."

26 Rob Stein, "Critical Care Without Consent: Ethicists Disagree on Experimenting During Crises," *Washington Post*, May 27, 2007.

27 "Researchers Overwhelmed by 'Opt Outs' from No-Consent Medical Studies," *Seattle Times*, June 7, 2007.

28 Myron Weisfeldt, MD, telephone interview with author, June 18, 2009.

29 Glenn McGee, PhD, "The Wonders of PolyHeme . . . by Press Release," blog .bioethics.net, *American Journal of Bioethics*, January 9, 2009, http://blog .bioethics.net/2009/01/the-wonders-of-polyhemeby-press-release/.

30 When contacted through the JHU press office, Dr. Norris refused to speak with me.

31 Thomas M. Burton, "Amid Alarm Bells, a Blood Substitute Keeps Pumping," *Wall Street Journal*, February 22, 2006.

32 Carl Elliott, "Not-So-Public Relations: How the Drug Industry Is Branding Itself with Bioethics," *Slate*, December 15, 2003, http://www.slate.com/ id/2092442 (accessed March 28, 2009).

CHAPTER 7: A TRAFFIC IN TISSUES

1 "Ardais Corporation Announces Agreement with AstraZeneca for Access to Clinical Samples," Ardais Corp. press release, PRNewswire, Lexington, MA, February 4, 2003.

2 Ibid.

3 Dan Holtzclaw, DDS, MS, Nicholas Toscano, DDS, MS, Lisa Eisenlohr, PhD, et al., "The Safety of Bone Allografts Used in Dentistry: A Review," *Journal of the American Dental Association* 139, no. 9 (2008): 1192–99.

4 David Hinckley, "Boss of Notorious Body Snatching Ring Gets 54 Years for Harvesting," *New York Daily News*, March 19, 2008.

5 BBC News, "Plea Deal in US Body Parts Case," January 16, 2008, http://news .bbc.co.uk/2/hi/americas/7192462.stm.

6 Genomics is a relatively new scientific discipline whose ambition is to identify pathogenic genes and then improve life and health by creating drugs that will target and nullify the effects of these troublemaking genes.

7 Deborah Josefson, "US Hospitals to Ask Patients for Right to Sell Their Tissue," *British Medical Journal* 321, no. 7262 (2000): 658.

8 *Moore v. Regents of University of California*, 51 Cal. 3d 120; 271 Cal. Rptr. 146; 793 P.2d 479 (1990).

9 Josefson, "US Hospitals to Ask Patients for Right to Sell Their Tissue."

10 Anne Paxton, "Brisk Trade in Tissue for Proteomics and Genomics Research," *CAP Today*, March 2003, http://www.cap.org/apps/cap.portal?_nfpb=true& cntvwrPtlt_actionOverride=%2Fportlets%2FcontentViewer%2Fshow& _windowLabel=cntvwrPtlt&cntvwrPtlt{actionForm.contentReference} =cap_today%2Ffeature_stories%2Fbiorepositories.html&_state=maximized &_pageLabel=cntvwr (accessed March 6, 2009).

11 Ibid.

12 *Doris Jackson, in Her Own Right and as Administratrix of the Estate of Thomas*

Seaborn, Deceased v. City of Philadelphia and Hospital of the University of Pennsylvania, 26 Phila. Co. Rptr. 545, 551–52 (Pa. Com. Pl. 1993).

13 Michele Goodwin, *Black Markets: The Supply and Demand of Body Parts* (New York: Cambridge University Press, 2006), 120.

14 Ibid., 177.

15 Thomas Hargrove and Lee Bowman, "Autopsy Rates Differ by Race, Age, Sex, Education," Scripps Howard News Service, August 12, 2009, www .scrippsnews.com/content/autopsy-rates-differ-race-age-sex-education.

16 "Cornea Donation & Transplantation Statistics," Eye Bank Association of America, Washington, D.C., http://www.restoresight.org/donation/statistics.

17 *Brotherton v. Cleveland* Nos. 94-3465; 96-3034, 96-3085, United States Court of Appeals for the Sixth Circuit 173 F.3d 552; 1999; 923 F.2d 482 (6th Cir. 1990).

18 Ibid.

19 *Florida v. Powell*, Fla., 497 So.2d 1188 (1986).

20 Leigh Hopper, "Heat Wave Heralds a Deadly Season," *Houston Chronicle*, June 1, 2003.

21 Personal verbal communication with Joyce Carter, MD, 2000 and 2004.

22 Michele Goodwin, "Feds Should Monitor Body Parts Sales," *Los Angeles Times*, March 13, 2004.

23 Amanda Euringer, "Foreskin Face Cream," *The Tyee*, January 30, 2007, http:// thetyee.ca/Views/2007/01/30/Foreskin/.

24 John Schwartz and Steve Vogel, "Amid German Uproar, U.S. Auto Researchers Defend Use of Corpses," *Washington Post*, November 25, 1993.

25 Jonathan Leake and Charles Masters, "Renault Used Child Corpses to Improve Car Safety Seats," *Sunday Times* (London), April 19, 1998.

26 This set of trauma-research protocols is under way at eleven U.S. and Canadian sites and will not conclude until 2012.

27 C. O. Callender and P. V. Miles, "Minority Organ Donation: The Power of an Educated Community," *Journal of the American College of Surgeons* 210, no. 5 (2010): 708–15, 715–17.

28 Thomas Hargrove and Lee Bowman Scripps, "Autopsy Rates Differ by Race, Age, Sex, Education," Howard News Service, August 12, 2009, http://www .scrippsnews.com/category/author/-thomas-hargrove-and-lee-bowman -scripps-howard-news-service (accessed July 11, 2011). "When looking at all 4.9 million deaths, whites were autopsied less than 6 percent of the time compared to 11 percent for blacks, 14 percent for Hispanics, 8 percent for Asians and 13 percent for American Indians."

29 Janice Frink Brown, "D.C. Gift Act Allows Hospitals to Remove Organs of Crime Victims," *Washington Afro-American*, June 17, 1995.

30 Harriet A. Washington, "Vital Signs: Harvesting Organs from Silence," *Emerge Magazine*, January 31, 1995.

31 www.drcatalona.com/litigation.asp (accessed September 20, 2009).

32 The OHRP later determined that this language was indeed exculpatory in violation of 45 C.F.R. § 46.116.

33 William Catalona, MD, "Dr. Catalona's Response to Public Statements Posted by Washington University Regarding His Dispute with WU over Who Has Jurisdiction of Prostate Tissue and Blood Samples," www.drcatalona .com/qanda.html.

34 Order in *Washington University v. Catalona*, No. 4:03CV1065 (E. Dist. Mo. April 14, 2006), on appeal Nos. 06-2286 & 06-2301 (8th Cir.); *Washington University v. Catalona*, 437 F. Supp. 2d 985 (E.D. Mo. 2006), affirmed by 490 F.3d 667 (8th Cir. 2007).

35 See also: Eric G. Campbell, PhD, Brian R. Clarridge, PhD, Manjusha Gokhale, MA, et al., "Data Withholding in Academic Genetics: Evidence from a National Survey," *Journal of the American Medical Association* 287, no. 4 (2002): 473–80.

36 Arthur Caplan, "The Sale of Tissue Samples from NIH to Pfizer," blog .bioethics.net, *American Journal of Bioethics*, June 1, 2006, http://blog .bioethics.net/2006/06/sale-of-tissue-samples-from-nih-to.html.

37 David Wildman, "Case Study: Dr. P. Trey Sunderland III; $508,050 from Pfizer, but No 'Outside Positions to Note,'" *Los Angeles Times*, December 22, 2004.

38 Richard A. Epstein, "Mad Scientists: Go Away, Ethics Police. Leave the NIH Alone," *Slate*, Tuesday, February 15, 2005, http://www.slate.com/id/2113520/ (accessed May 21, 2008).

39 Baruch S. Blumberg, Irving Millman, W. Thomas London, et al., "Ted Slavin's Blood and the Development of HBV Vaccine," letter to the editor, *New England Journal of Medicine* 312, no. 3 (1985): 189.

40 Richard M. Titmuss, *The Gift Relationship: From Human Blood to Social Policy* (New York: Pantheon Books, 1971).

41 Ibid.

CHAPTER 8: BIOCOLONIALISM

1 Emily Marden, "The Neem Tree Patent: International Conflict over the Commodification of Life," *Boston College International and Comparative Law Review* 22, nos. 2–3 (1999): 279.

2 Scott Holwick, "Note, Developing Nations and the Agreement on Trade-Related Aspects of Intellectual Property Rights," *Y.B. Colo. Journal of International Environmental Law and Policy* 49 (2000): 57–58.

3 Naomi Roht-Ariaza, "Of Seeds and Shamans: The Appropriation of the Scientific and Technical Knowledge of Indigenous and Local Communities," *Michigan Journal of International Law* 919, no. 938 (1996): 926–27.

4 Institute of Biodiversity Conservation, "Conservation, Sustainable Use, Access and Benefit Sharing," http://www.ibc-et.org/ (accessed May 22, 2008).

5 Diarmuid Jeffreys, *Aspirin: The Remarkable Story of a Wonder Drug* (New York: Bloomsbury Publishing, 2005). See also: Camilla Dickson and James Dickson, *Plants and People in Ancient Scotland* (Mount Pleasant, SC: Arcadia Publishing/NPI Media Group 2000).

6 Biotechnology for Sustainable Development in Africa, "African Medicinal Plants, a Resource to Develop and Protect—the Plant of the Month: Catharanthus roseus," http://www.bdafoundation.org/en/content/african -medicinal-plants (accessed January 3, 2010).

7 Carolina Bruun, "Intellectual Property Rights Reach Indigenous Communities in the Amazon," *Mongabay.com*, March 21, 2007, http://news.mongabay .com/2007/0321-galvani.html (accessed March 17, 2010).

8 Ibid.

9 Andrew J. Pollack, "Biological Products Raise Genetic Ownership Issues: Governments Are Demanding Share of Profits," *New York Times*, November 26, 1999; see also *Diamond v. Chakrabarty*, 447 U.S. 303, 309 (1980).

10 William S. Burroughs and Allen Ginsberg, *The Yage Letters* (San Francisco: City Lights Publishers, 1991).

11 Martin A. Lee, "Vision Quest: Shamanism vs. Capitalism: The Politics of Ayahuasca," *Ayahuasca Spirit Quest*, March 1, 2003, www.biopark.org/peru/vision-quest-metzner.html (accessed May 31, 2009).

12 Pablo Amaringo and Luis Eduardo Luna, *Ayahuasca Visions: The Religious Iconography of a Peruvian Shaman* (New York: North Atlantic Books, 1999).

13 Richard Spruce and A. R. Wallace, *Notes of a Botanist on the Amazon and Andes* (New York: Johnson Reprint Corp., 1970).

14 By some accounts, the year was 1981.

15 According to the TRIPS Agreement, developing countries were supposed to implement the agreement by 2000, while the least-developed countries are not required to implement the intellectual-property provisions relating to pharmaceuticals before 2015. (This is a result of the Doha Declaration on TRIPS Agreement and Public Health, 2001.)

16 Vandana Shiva, *Biopiracy: The Plunder of Nature and Knowledge* (Cambridge, MA: South End Press, 1999).

17 James Nurton, "TRIPs Council to Review Doha Declaration," *Managing Intellectual Property*, June 16, 2010, http://www.managingip.com/Article/2601610/TRIPs-Council-to-review-Doha-Declaration.html (accessed June 29, 2010); World Health Organization, *The Doha Declaration on TRIPS Agreement and Public Health*, http://www.who.int/medicines/areas/policy/doha_declaration/en/index.html (accessed June 29, 2010).

18 TRIPS also permits the patenting of animals, but it does not force the recognition of these patents in the same manner: "Agreement on Trade-Related Aspects of Intellectual Property Rights," April 15, 1994, *Marrakesh Agreement Establishing the World Trade Organization, Annex 1C, Legal Instruments—Results of the Uruguay Round*, vol. 31, 33 I.L.M. 81 (1994).

19 Doctors Without Borders/Médecins Sans Frontières, "Sell-Out at WTO on DOHA Declaration?" press release, Geneva, February 12, 2003, http://www.doctorswithoutborders.org/press/release.cfm?id=382&cat=press-release (accessed May 21, 2009).

20 According to Ciel's website (www.ciel.org), these included the Coordination Body of Indigenous Organizations of the Amazon Basin and the Coalition for Amazonian Peoples and the Environment.

21 Alan L. Durham, *Patent Law Essentials: A Concise Guide* (Westport, CT: Quorum Books, 1999).

22 "Conditions for patentability; novelty and loss of right to patent," U.S. Code 35, Sec. 102.

23 Ibid.

24 Lee, "Shamanism vs. Capitalism."

25 BBC News, "India Wins Landmark Patent Battle," March 9, 2005, http://news.bbc.co.uk/1/low/sci/tech/4333627.stm (accessed October 7, 2010).

26 R. L. Mahunnah and K. E. Mshigeni, "Tanzania's Policy on Biodiversity

Prospecting and Drug Discovery Programs," *Journal of Ethnopharmacology* 51, nos. 1–3 (April 1996): 221–28.

27 Muhimbili University of Health and Allied Sciences, "MUHAS Cooperative Research Agreement IPR Form II/06," Dar es Salaam, Tanzania, 2006, http://bit.ly/eZsGxb (accessed January 17, 2011).

28 www.monsanto.com/features/helping_haitian_farmers.asp?wt.svl=2 (accessed May 2, 2010).

29 Jonathan M. Katz, "Monsanto Gives Haiti $4 Million in Hybrid Seeds," *Bloomberg Business Week*, May 14, 2010, http://www.businessweek.com/ap/financialnews/D9FMUQN80.htm (accessed June 1, 2010).

30 Monsanto Africa Corporate Website, http://www.monsantoafrica.com/.

31 Sara Novak, "Haitian Farmers Refuse Monsanto's Seeds and Instead Commit to Burning Them," *TreeHugger*, May 30, 2010, www.treehugger.com/files/2010/05/haitian_farmers_refuse_monsantos_seeds_and_instead _commit_to_burning_them.php (accessed May 30, 2010).

32 Thiram is an ethylene bisdithiocarbamate.

33 Pesticide Management Information Project, Cooperative Extension Office, Cornell University. "Thiram," *EXTOXNET*, http://pmep.cce.cornell.edu/profiles/extoxnet/pyrethrins-ziram/thiram-ext.html (accessed April 16, 2010).

34 Elizabeth Vancil, Monsanto's Development Partnership director, email communication to Emmanuel Prophete, director of seeds at the Haitian Ministry of Agriculture, and others, released by the Haitian Ministry of Agriculture, date unavailable.

35 Ibid.

36 Center for Food Safety, *Monsanto vs. US Farmers* (Washington, D.C.: Center for Food Safety, 2005), http://www.centerforfoodsafety.org/pubs/lowresCFSMonsantovsFarmersReport1.13.2005.pdf; Center for Food Safety, "*Monsanto vs. US Farmers*, November 2007 Update" (Washington, D.C.: Center for Food Safety, 2007), http://www.centerforfoodsafety.org/pubs/Monsanto%20November%202007%20update.pdf.

37 Ibid.

38 The Monsanto Co., "Seed Piracy: Updates and Summaries," company newsletter, September/October 2009, http://www.cban.ca/Resources/Topics/Monsanto/Monsanto-s-Seed-Piracy-Newsletter (accessed June 9, 2010).

39 The Canadian Biotechnology Action Network, *Monsanto*, http://www.cban.ca/Resources/Topics/Monsanto.

40 La Vía Campesina/International Peasant Movement, "La Vía Campesina Carries Out Global Day Of Action Against Monsanto," press release, October, 16, 2009, http://viacampesina.org/en/index.php?option=com _content&view=article&id=797:peasants-worldwide-rise-up-against -monsanto-gmos&catid=49:stop-transnational-corporations&itemid=76 (accessed June 13, 2010).

41 Nathan B. Batalion, "Introduction," *50 Harmful Effects of Genetically Modified Foods* (Oneonta, NY: Americans for Safe Food, 2000), http://www .raw-wisdom.com/50harmful.

42 William Neuman and Andrew Pollack, "U.S. Farmers Cope with Roundup-Resistant Weeds," *New York Times*, May 3, 2010, http://www

.nytimes.com/2010/05/04/business/energy-environment/04weed.html?_r=1; Neuman and Pollack, "Where Weedkiller Won't Work," *New York Times*, May 3, 2010, http://www.nytimes.com/interactive/2010/05/03/business/weeds-graphic.html?ref=energy-environment.

43 Michael Pollan, "We Knew It Was Coming," *New York Times*, June 1, 2010, http://roomfordebate.blogs.nytimes.com/2010/05/06/invasion-of-the-superweeds/?ref=energy-environment (accessed June 1, 2010).

44 Masaharu Kawata, GMO Information Service, "Monsanto Failed Halfway in Developing Herbicide Tolerant Rice in Japan," December 5, 2002, http://www.mindfully.org/GE/GE4/Monsanto-Rice-Failed-Japan5dec02.htm (accessed June 24, 2010).

45 Lucia Graves, "Roundup: Birth Defects Caused by World's Top-Selling Weedkiller, Scientists Say," *Huffington Post*, June 24, 2011, http://www.huffingtonpost.com/2011/06/24/roundup-scientists-birth-defects_n_883578.html (accessed June 28, 2011).

46 According to a study by the Sakal Newspapers Limited of the two districts, Amravati and Yavatmal.

47 Amy Waldman, "Debts and Drought Drive India's Farmers to Despair," *New York Times*, June 6, 2004, http://www.nytimes.com/2004/06/06/world/debts-and-drought-drive-india-s-farmers-to-despair.html (accessed February 3, 2011).

48 Raj Patel, *Stuffed and Starved: The Hidden Battle for the World Food System* (London: Portobello Books, 2007).

49 Tamil Nadu, "Spate of Farmers' Suicides in India Worrying WHO," *The Hindu*, October 15, 2006, http://www.hindu.com/2006/10/15/stories/2006101514820800.htm.

50 P. Sainath, "17,368 Farm Suicides in 2009," *The Hindu*, December 27, 2010, http://www.thehindu.com/opinion/columns/sainath/article995824.ece?homepage=true (accessed January 4, 2011).

51 Ibid.

52 Sonia Faleiro, "A Death of a Son, Grandson, and All of Life's Dreams," September 2, 2006, http://soniafaleiro.blogspot.com/2006/09/death-of-son-grandson-and-all-of-lifes.html (accessed May 13, 2010).

53 K. Samu, Human Rights Documentation, Indian Social Institute, "Agriculture & Farmers' Suicide—2006." Report, New Delhi, 2006, p. 43. http://www.isidelhi.org.in/hrnews/HR_THEMATIC_ISSUES/Agriculture/Agriculture-2006.pdf.

54 Indian agriculture department statistics.

55 PBS, "Seeds of Suicide: India's Desperate Farmers," *Frontline*, July 26, 2005, http://www.pbs.org/frontlineworld/rough/2005/07/seeds_of_suicid.html#.

56 The Editors, "Do Seed Companies Control GM Crop Research?" *Scientific American*, August 13, 2009, http://www.scientificamerican.com/article.cfm?id=do-seed-companies-control-gm-crop-research (accessed June 17, 2010).

57 Toni McNulty, "A New Earthquake Hits Haiti—Monsanto," *Wired: Haiti Rewired*, May 12, 2010, http://haitirewired.wired.com/profiles/blogs/a-new-earthquake-hits-haiti (accessed May 12, 2010).

58 "Linda J. Fisher: Director, Covanta Holding Corporation," *Forbes.com*, http://people.forbes.com/profile/linda-j-fisher/23695 (accessed February 16, 2009).

59 Kim Griggs, "'Human' Cow Milk an MS Aid?" *Wired*, August 2, 2000, http://www.wired.com/science/discoveries/news/2000/08/37921 (accessed February 15, 2011).

60 "Paul Reynolds provides a detailed account of the opposition by the Ngati Wairere sub-tribe (hapu) in the central North Island of Aotearoa to AgResearch, a government research agency, which attempted to place copies of human genes into cows to produce a human-cow hybrid. The opposition was based on the concern about lack of consultation with local communities and the impact this type of research will have on whakapapa (genealogy). The case provided a platform for future consciousness raising on biotechnology amongst Maori": from *Pacific Genes and Life Patents, Pacific Experiences & Analysis of the Commodification & Ownership of Life*, eds. Aroha Mead and Dr. Steven Ratuva (Japan: Call of the Earth/Llamado de la Tierra, the United Nations University Institute of Advanced Studies, 2007).

61 Alok Jha, "First British Human-Animal Hybrid Embryos Created by Scientists," *Guardian*, April 2, 2008, http://www.guardian.co.uk/science/2008/apr/02/medicalresearch.ethicsofscience.

62 "Phyllomedusa Bicolour," http://species.wikimedia.org/wiki/Phyllomedusa _bicolor (accessed April 25, 2010).

63 Donald W. Hansen Jr. et al., "Systemic Analgesic Activity and ∂-Opiod Selectivity in [2,6-Dimetyl-Ty^{1}r,D-Pen^2,D-Pen^5]enkephalin," *Journal of Medicinal Chemistry* 35, no. 4 (1992): 684–87.

64 *The Tristan da Cunha Website*, http://www.tristandc.com/ (accessed April 24, 2009).

65 Noé Zamel, "In Search of the Genes of Asthma on the Island of Tristan da Cunha," *Canadian Respiratory Journal* 2, no. 1(1995): 18–22.

66 "Tristan da Cunha," Wikipedia, http://en.wikipedia.org/wiki/Tristan_da _Cunha (accessed April 24, 2009).

67 Sequana Therapeutics, Inc., "Sequana Discovers Asthma Gene," press release, *BusinessWire*, May 21, 1997, http://www.allbusiness.com/medicine-health/diseases-disorders-respiratory/6985305–1.html (accessed April 24, 2010).

68 Axys Pharmaceuticals, "Arris and Sequana Merge to Form New Company, Axys Pharmaceuticals; Deal Valued at $166 Million," November 3, 1997, http://www.secinfo.com/dr6nd.84Ea.c.htm.

69 Randall Mayes, "In Defense of Patenting DNA: A Pragmatic Libertarian Perspective," *Ethical Technology*/ The Institute for Ethics & Emerging Technologies, July 26, 2009, http://ieet.org/index.php/IEET/more/mayes20090726/ (accessed May 29, 2008).

70 Sequana press release dated October 28, 1997.

71 GENSET Corp., "Research Milestone in Prostate Cancer Alliance," press release, *PR Newswire*, December 17, 1996, http://www.prnewswire.co.uk/cgi/news/release?id=58604 (accessed February 17, 2011).

72 GENSET Corp., "GenSet and the Chinese Academy of Medical Sciences to enter joint venture for Genomics Research," press release, November 4, 1996.

73 Mayes, "In Defense of Patenting DNA."

74 Havasupai, www.havasupaitribe.com (accessed May 3, 2007).

75 Heather M. Butts, JD, MPH, and Ruth L. Fischbach, PhD, MPE, "What Should IRBs Consider When Reviewing a Protocol in Which Race Will Be

Identified?" (Lecture, EGIR Conference, May 19, 2006, presentation slides 24–27).

76 The 1778 advent of Captain Cook is generally acknowledged as the beginning of Hawaiian–Western interactions.

77 Cheryl Ernst, "Making the Most of the Hawaiian Genome," *Health: University of Hawai'i System Newsletter*, March 3, 2003, http://www.hawaii.edu/ur/newsatuh/archives/030303/health.htm (accessed February 17, 2011).

78 Pei Koay, "Icelandic (Ad)ventures: New Research? New Subjects? New Ethics?" in *Twentieth-Century Ethics of Human Subjects Research: Historical Perspectives on Values, Practices, and Regulations*, eds. Volker Roelke and Giovanni Maio (Stuttgart, Germany: Franz Steiner Verlag, 2004).

79 It is widely believed that presumed consent is used to harvest organs in many European countries as well, but this is a misconception. Most of these countries never claim to presume that their citizens would consent to obtain organs, an important distinction in that there is no assumption of the dead person or his family's having ownership in the body, and no mechanism for opting out: Robert Veatch and Jonathan Pitt, "The Myth of Presumed Consent: Ethical Problems in New Organ Procurement Strategies," *Transplantation Ethics*, ed. Robert M. Veatch (Washington, D.C.: Georgetown University Press, 2001), 167.

80 Michael Specter, "Decoding Iceland," *The New Yorker*, January 18, 1999, 40–51.

81 Kevin Davies, *Cracking the Genome: Inside the Race to Unlock Human DNA* (New York: The Free Press), 134.

82 Jocelyn Kaiser, "deCODE Genetics Rises from the Ashes," *ScienceInsider*, January 21, 2010, http://news.sciencemag.org/scienceinsider/2010/01/decode -genetics-1.html.

CHAPTER 9: THE LABORATORY OF THE WEST

1 The case *Abdullahi et al v. Pfizer* is available at http://www.pdf-searcher.com/Abdullahi-et-al-v.-Pfizer-Decision.html# (accessed November 22, 2010).

2 Joe Stephens, "The Body Hunters: As Drug Testing Spreads, Profits and Lives Hang in Balance," *Washington Post*, December 17, 2000, http://www.washingtonpost.com/wp-dyn/world/issues/bodyhunters/.

3 IPS-Inter Press Service/Global Information Network, "Nigeria: Lawsuit Revived Against U.S. Company over Testing," October 14, 2003; Muyiwa Adeyemi, "Niger Suspends Boycott," *Guardian*, February 28, 2004; see also George J. Annas, "Faith (Healing), Hope and Charity at the FDA: The Politics of AIDS Drug Trials," *Villanova Law Review* 34 (1989): 771, 772.

4 Joe Stephens, "The Body Hunters: As Drug Testing Spreads, Profits and Lives Hang in Balance," *Washington Post*, December 17, 2000, http://washingtonpost.com/wp-dyn/articles/A11939-2000Dec15.html.

5 Duff Wilson, "A Secret Cable Discusses Pfizer's Actions in Nigeria Case," *New York Times*, December 10, 2010, http://www.nytimes.com/2010/12/11/business/11pfizer.html (accessed March 22, 2011).

6 Yvonne Ndege, "Nigerian Pfizer Victims' Compensation Fears—26-06-2011," Al Jazeera, http://tvjin.net/2011/06/27/nigerian-pfizer-victims-compensation -fears-26-06-2011/ (accessed June 24, 2011).

7 "Trovan: Pfizer Commences Screening of Victims," April 9, 2011, *Channels*, http://www.channelstv.com/global/news_details.php?nid=26633&cat =Health (accessed June 9, 2011).

8 Ndege, "Nigerian Pfizer Victims' Compensation Fears."

9 Office of U.S. Global AIDS Coordinator, Bureau of Public Affairs, U.S. Department of State, *The United States President's Plan for Emergency AIDS Relief*, http://www.pepfar.gov/about/index.htm.

10 Ibid.

11 Pari Shah and Ann Juergens-Behr, "Vaccine Programs in Developing Countries" (Course Presentation, Bio 160, Brown University), http://www.brown .edu/Courses/Bio_160/Projects2000/VaccineIssues/Vaccines.html.

12 Michael Kremer, "Pharmaceuticals and the Developing World," *Journal of Economic Perspectives* 16, no. 4 (Fall 2002): 68, 71, 79, 90.

13 Brook K. Baker, "The Eight Deadly Lies of Big Pharma," *The Nation* (Thailand), April 21, 2007, http://www.nationmultimedia.com/2007/04/21/ opinion/opinion_30.

14 Kremer, "Pharmaceuticals and the Developing World."

15 GlaxoSmithKline plc., "Our Commitment to Fighting Malaria," http://www .gsk.com/media/malaria.htm (accessed April 25, 2010).

16 Amir Attaran, DPhil, LLB, and Lee Gillespie-White, LLB, "Do Patents for Antiretroviral Drugs Constrain Access to AIDS Treatments in Africa?" *Journal of the American Medical Association* 286, no. 15 (2001): 1886–92.

17 Donald G. McNeil Jr., "Patents or Poverty? New Debate over Lack of AIDS Care in Africa," *New York Times*, November 5, 2001.

18 Amir Attaran, "Do Patents Prevent Access to Drugs for HIV in Developing Countries?" *Journal of the American Medical Association* 287, no. 7 (February 20, 2002).

19 Amir Attaran, DPhil, LLB, "How Do Patents and Economic Policies Affect Access to Essential Medicines in Developing Countries?" *Journal of Health Affairs* 23, no. 3 (2004): 155–56, http://content.healthaffairs.org/content/23/3/ 155.full.pdf (accessed February 21, 2009).

20 James Shikwati, "Poverty, Not Patents, Is to Blame," *Business Day* (Johannesburg), June 7, 2004, http://allafrica.com/stories/200406010952.html.

21 Amir Attaran, DPhil, LLB, "How Do Patents and Economic Policies Affect Access to Essential Medicines in Developing Countries?" *Journal of Health Affairs* 23, no. 3 (2004): 155–56, http://content.healthaffairs.org/content/23/3/ 155.full.pdf (accessed February 21, 2009).

22 Franklin Cudjoe, "Poverty and Sickness Won't Be Cured by Fighting Patents," *New Times, Rwanda's First Daily*, January 3, 2011, http://www.newtimes .co.rw/index.php?issue=13572&article=7362.

23 McNeil Jr., "Patents or Poverty?"

24 Nurton, "TRIPS Council to Review Doha Declaration"; WHO, "The Doha Declaration on TRIPS Agreement and Public Health."

25 Kremer, "Pharmaceuticals and the Developing World."

26 "The Burden of Different Diseases Can Be Compared Across Countries Using the Concept of Disability Adjusted Life Years. DALYs Take into Account Not Only the Lives Lost Through Disease, but Also the Number of Years of Disability Caused": Ibid.

27 Kremer, "Pharmaceuticals and the Developing World."

28 Ibid., 70.

29 World Health Organization, *High Level Forum on the Health MDGs. Addressing Africa's Health Workforce Crisis: An Avenue for Action*, 2004, www .hlfhealthmdgs.org/Documents/AfricasWorkforce-Final.pdf; see also Nullis-Kapp, "Health Worker Shortage Could Derail Development Goals (News)."

30 Central Bureau of Health Intelligence, Directorate General of Health Services, Ministry of Health and Family Welfare, *Health Information of India 2000 and 2001* (New Delhi: Government of India, 2003), http://cbhidghs.nic .in/Hii2000–01/content.htm.

31 World Health Organization, *The World Health Report 2003* (Geneva: World Health Organization, 2003).

32 Harriet A. Washington, "Why Africa Fears Western Medicine," *New York Times*, July 31, 2007, http://www.nytimes.com/2007/07/31/opinion/ 31washington.html.

33 John Murphy, "Distrust of U.S. Foils Effort to Stop Crippling Disease," *Baltimore Sun*, January 4, 2004, http://www.baltimoresun.com/news/bal-polio0104 ,1,1640318.story.

34 Washington, "Why Africa Fears Western Medicine."

35 Seth W. Glickman, MD, MBA, et al., "Ethical and Scientific Implications of the Globalization of Clinical Research," *New England Journal of Medicine* 360, no. 8 (February 2009): 816.

36 Ibid.

37 Kenneth A. Getz, "Global Clinical Trials Activity in the Details," *Applied Clinical Trials*, September 1, 2007, http://appliedclinicaltrialsonline .findpharma.com/appliedclinicaltrials/article/articleDetail.jsp?id=453243 (accessed January 30, 2009).

38 Washington Office on Haiti and the National Vaccine Information Center, "More Than 2000 Children in the Port-au-Prince Slum *Cite Soleil* Were Inoculated with High Doses of Edmonston-Zagreb (*EZ*)," April 1999.

39 J. P. Garnier, "Rebuilding the R&D Engine in Big Pharma," *Harvard Business Review* 68 (2008): 68–76.

40 World Health Organization, "Making the Most of Existing Health Workers," *Working Together for Health: The World Health Report 2006* (Geneva: World Health Organization, 2006), 66–95, http://www.who.int/whr/2006/chapter4/ en/index.html (accessed January 30, 2009).

41 Office of Inspector General, Department of Health and Human Services, *The Globalization of Clinical Trials: A Growing Challenge in Protecting Human Subjects* (Washington, D.C.: Department of Health and Human Services, 2001) (DHHS publication no. OEI-01–00–00190), http://oig.hhs.gov/oei/ reports/oei-01-00-00190.pdf.

42 Jim Edwards, "Pfizer Case over Test That Killed 11 Kids Could Blow the Lid Off Foreign Drug Trials," *The CBS Interactive Business Network*, June 30, 2010 http://industry.bnet.com/pharma/10008781/pfizer-that_killed_ 11_kids _ could_ blow_ the_ lid_ off_foreign_drug_ trials_case-over-test.com.

43 Amanda Silverio, "HIV Research in Africa: A Series of Paradoxes," *Stanford Journal of International Relations*, http://www.stanford.edu/group/sjir/3.2.05 _silverio.html.

44 Harold Varmus, MD, and David Satcher, MD, PhD, "Ethical Complexities of Conducting Research in Developing Countries," *New England Journal of Medicine* 337, no. 14 (October 1997): 1003–05.

45 Tim Beardsley, "Coping with HIV's Ethical Dilemmas," *Scientific American* 279, no. 1 (July 1998): 86, http://www.genethik.de/aids/aids09.htm.

46 Marcia Angell, "The Ethics of Clinical Research in the Third World," *New England Journal of Medicine* 337, no. 12 (September 1997): 847–49.

47 A. A. Hyder, S. A. Wali, A. N. Khan, et al., "Ethical Review of Research: A Perspective from Developing Country Researchers," *Journal of Medical Ethics* 30, no. 1 (2004): 68–72.

48 D. Zhang, et al., "An Assessment of the Quality of Randomized Controlled Trials Conducted in China," *Trials* 9 (2008): 22.

49 Francis Moore, "Letter to Jay Katz, September 2, 1964," reprinted in *Experimentation with Human Beings: The Authority of the Investigator, Subject Professions, and State in the Human Experimentation Process*, ed. Jay Katz, MD (New York: Russell Sage Foundation, 1972), 663.

50 Jon Cohen, "Brazil, Thailand Override Big Pharma Patents," *Science* 316, no. 5826 (2007): 816.

51 United States Chamber of Commerce, "Brazil Takes Major Step Backward on Intellectual Property Rights, Says US Chamber," press release, May 4, 2007, http://www.uschamber.com/press/releases/2007/may/brazil-takes-major -step-backward-intellectual-property-rights-says-us-chamber.

52 Cohen, "Brazil, Thailand Override Big Pharma Patents."

53 Ibid.

54 Editorial, "India's Choice," *International Herald Tribune*, January 18, 2005, http://www.nytimes.com/2005/01/18/opinion/18tues2.html.

55 "Pharmaceutical Patents and Developing Countries," AIDS.org, http://www .aids.org/atn/a-330-08.html (accessed July 13, 2009).

56 A set-top box or set-top unit connects a television with the external source of its signal.

57 James Love, "Brazil Puts Patients Before Patents," *Huffington Post*, May 4, 2007, http://www.huffingtonpost.com/james-love/brazil-puts-patients-befo _b_47651.html (accessed June 13, 2009).

58 *Patents and Technological Progress in a Globalized World: Liber Amicorum Joseph Straus*, eds. Wolrad Prinz zu Waldeck und Pyrmont, Martin J. Adelman, Robert Brauneis, and Josef Drexl (Berlin and Heidelberg: Springer, 2009), 153.

59 Sarah Joseph, "Pharmaceutical Corporations, Access to Drugs, and Human Rights," http://www.law.monash.edu.au/castancentre/conference2001/ papers/joseph.html, note 87 (accessed November 25, 2009).

EPILOGUE: BACK TO THE FUTURE?

1 Sara Boettiger and Alan B. Bennet, "Bayh-Dole: If We Knew Then What We Know Now," *Nature Biotechnology* 24 (2006): 320–23.

2 "NF-κB stands for *nuclear factor kappa-light-chain-enhancer of activated B cells*, a proteinaceous complex found in nearly all animal cells that governs the regulation of DNA transcription": A. R. Brasier, "The NF-κB Regulatory Network," *Cardiovascular Toxicology* 6, no. 2 (2006): 111–30.

3 "Bayhing for Blood or Doling Out Cash?" *The Economist*, December 20, 2005, http://www.economist.com/node/5327661 (accessed March 10, 2010).

4 Chris Frates, "Love Is Never Having to Say You Lobby," *Politico*, March 18, 2009, http://www.politico.com/news/stories/0309/20153.html (accessed January 13, 2011).

5 *Madey v. Duke University*, 307 F.3d 1351.

6 "Bayhing for Blood or Doling Out Cash?" *The Economist*.

7 Gina Kolata, "Sharing of Data Leads to Progress on Alzheimer's," *New York Times*, August 12, 2010, http://www.nytimes.com/2010/08/13/health/research/13alzheimer.html (accessed August 12, 2010).

8 The Stanford Bernstein Report concludes that the industry's best hope for survival lies in innovation, its traditional strength. But, it is important to note that R&D is not as productive as it used to be. The global industry saw 24 new drugs approved by the US Food and Drug Administration in 1998 with $27 billion R&D investment. In 2006, only 13 new drugs were approved, but investments in R&D rose to $64 billion. As a result the business model of a vertically integrated approach to developing, manufacturing and selling drugs has changed in favor of outsourcing. This new model favors developing countries that are able to attract investments, i.e., those with strong IP systems.

9 The African meningitis belt includes all or parts of Gambia, Senegal, Mali, Burkina Faso, Ghana, Niger, Nigeria, Cameroon, Chad, the Central African Republic, Sudan, Uganda, Kenya, Ethiopia, and Eritrea, according to http://www.lycos.com/info/meningitis--meningitis-belt.html (accessed November 2, 2010).

10 GAVI Alliance, Advanced Market Commitments for Vaccines, http://www.vaccineamc.org/index.html (accessed August 7, 2010).

11 "Our Mission: Eliminating Epidemic Meningitis in Sub-Saharan Africa," PATH, Meningitis Vaccine Project, http://www.meningvax.org/mission.php.

12 Kat Hannaford, "Bill Gates Convinces 40 Billionaires to Give Away Half Their Fortunes," *Gizmodo*, August 4, 2010, http://gizmodo.com/#!5604368/bill-gates-convinces-40-billionaires-to-give-away-half-their-fortunes.

13 The Giving Pledge, http://givingpledge.org/#enter (accessed December 1, 2010).

14 "Supporters," Advance Market Commitment for Vaccines, http://www.vaccineamc.org/progress_supporters.html.

15 Kate Kelland, "Drug Makers Cut Vaccine Prices for Poorer Nations," Reuters News Service, Monday, June 6, 2011, http://www.reuters.com/article/2011/06/06/us-vaccines-prices-gavi-idUSTRE7550UH20110606 (accessed June 6, 2011).

16 Gamal Fahnbulleh, "Billions Pledged to Vaccinate World's Poor," Sky News, June 13, 2011, http://uk.news.yahoo.com/pm-makes-promise-vaccinate-worlds-poor-001508370.html (accessed June 14, 2011).

17 Stephanie Nebehay, "Pharma Industry Pledges Pandemic Vaccines and Know-How in Landmark Deal," March 18, 2011, Reuters Health, http://www.reuters.com/article/2011/04/16/us-pandemic-vaccines-idUSTRE73F0HO20110416 (accessed June 17, 2011).

18 Kelland, "Drug Makers Cut Vaccine Prices."

19 Henry Grabowski, "Encouraging the Development of New Vaccines," *Health Affairs* 24, 3 (2005): 697–700, http://content.healthaffairs.org/content/24/3/697.full (accessed June 16, 2011).

20 Fahnbulleh, "Billions Pledged to Vaccinate."

21 Ibid.

22 Carroll, "Big Pharma Maps Out a Global Vaccine Strategy."

23 "Cheap Vaccines Make Business Sense," *Micah Challenge* antipoverty blog, http://www.micahchallenge.org/component/content/article/81-amanda-advocates/404-cheap-vaccines-make-business-sense (accessed June 25, 2011).

24 Ibid.

25 World Health Organization, "Fact Sheet No. 259: African Trypanosomiasis (Sleeping Sickness)," October 2010, http://www.who.int/mediacentre/factsheets/fs259/en/ index.html (accessed July 3, 2011).

26 Aidan Hollis and Thomas Pogge, *The Health Impact Fund: Making Medicines Available for All* (New Haven, CT: Incentives for Global Health, 2008), chapter 2.

27 Ibid., 3–4.

28 Ibid. See also Peter Singer, "Tuberculosis or Hair Loss? Refocusing Medical Research," *National Post*, September 15, 2008, http://www.project-syndicate.org/commentary/singer40/English (accessed May 24, 2011).

29 The Structural Genomics Consortium, http://thesgc.org.

30 Ogilvie, "Secrecy Slowing Drug Research."

BIBLIOGRAPHY

BOOKS

Abramson, John. *Overdosed America: The Broken Promise of American Medicine*, 3rd edition. New York: Harper Perennial, 2008.

Alberts, Bruce, et al., eds. *The Molecular Biology of the Cell*, 4th ed. New York: Garland Science, 2002.

Amaringo, Pablo, and Luis Eduardo Luna. *Ayahuasca Visions: The Religious Iconography of a Peruvian Shaman*. New York: North Atlantic Books, 1999.

Angell, Marcia. *The Truth About the Drug Companies: How They Deceive Us and What to Do About It*. New York: Random House, 2005.

Anthon, Charles. *A Classical Dictionary: Containing An Account of the Principal Proper Names Mentioned in Ancient Authors, and Intended To Elucidate All the Important Points Connected with the Geography, History, Biography, Mythology, and Fine Arts of the Greeks and Romans Together with an Account of Coins, Weights, and Measures, with Tabular Values of the Same*. New York: Harper & Bros., 1841.

Bowman, J., M.D., and Robert F. Murray Jr., M.D., M.S. *Genetic Variation and Disorders in People of African Origin*. Baltimore: Johns Hopkins University Press, 1990.

Bowring, Finn. *Science, Seeds, and Cyborgs: Biotechnology and the Appropriation of Life*, London: Verso, 2003.

Burroughs, William, and Allen Ginsberg. *The Yage Letters*. San Francisco: City Lights Publishers, 1991.

Chakrabarty, A. M. "Patenting of Life-Form: From a Concept to Reality." In *Who Owns Life?*, edited by David Magnus, Arthur Caplan, and Glenn McGee, 17–25. Amherst, NY: Prometheus Books, 2002.

Chisum, Donald S., Craig A. Nard, Herbert E. Schwartz, Pauline Newman, and F. Scott Kieff. *Principles of Patent Law: Cases and Materials*. New York: Foundation Press, 1998.

Cohen, Wesley M., and Steven Merrill, eds., *Patents in the Knowledge-Based Economy*. Committee on Intellectual Property Rights in the Knowledge-Based Economy. Washington, D.C.: National Research Council, 2003.

Davies, Kevin. *Cracking the Genome: Inside the Race to Unlock Human DNA.* New York: Free Press, 2001.

Dickson, Camilla, and James Dickson. *Plants and People in Ancient Scotland.* Mount Pleasant, SC: Arcadia Publishing/NPI Media Group, 2000.

Dobyns, Kenneth W. *The Patent Office Pony: A History of the Early Patent Office.* Fredericksburg, VA: Sargeant Kirkland's Museum and Historical Society, 1994.

Durham, Alan L. *Patent Law Essentials: A Concise Guide.* Westport, CT: Quorum Books, 1999.

Fanfair, Devon Salil Desai, and Christopher Kelty. "Patent or Perish." In *Nanotechnology: Content and Context*, edited by Christopher Kelty and John Hutchinson. Houston, TX: Rice University, May 2007. http://cnx.org/content/m14509/1.1/.

Franklin, Benjamin. *The Autobiography of Benjamin Franklin*, p. 55. http://www.ushistory.org/franklin/autobiography/page55.htm (accessed May 20, 2011).

Gold, Michael A. *A Conspiracy of Cells: One Woman's Immortal Legacy and the Medical Scandal It Caused.* Albany, NY: SUNY Press, 1986.

Goodwin, Michele Bratcher. *Black Markets: The Supply and Demand of Body Parts.* New York: Cambridge University Press, 2006.

Goozner, Merrill. *The $800 Million Pill: The Truth Behind the Cost of New Drugs.* Berkeley: University of California Press, 2004.

Hollis, Aidan, and Thomas Pogge. *The Health Impact Fund: Making Medicines Available for All.* New Haven, CT: Incentives for Global Health, 2008.

Jeffreys, Diarmuid. *Aspirin: The Remarkable Story of a Wonder Drug.* New York: Bloomsbury Publishing, 2005.

Katz, J., M.D. *Experimentation with Human Beings: The Authority of the Investigator, Subject Professions, and State in the Human Experimentation Process.* New York: Russell Sage Foundation, 1972.

Kevles, Daniel. *In the Name of Eugenics: Genetics and the Uses of Human Heredity.* Cambridge, MA: Harvard University Press, 1998.

Kimbrell, Andrew. *The Human Body Shop: The Engineering and Marketing of Life.* New York: HarperCollins, 1993.

Knightley, Phillip. *Suffer the Children: The Story of Thalidomide.* New York: Viking Adult, 1979.

Koay, Pei. "An Icelandic (Ad)venture: New Research? New Subjects? New Ethics?" In *Twentieth-Century Ethics of Human Subjects Research: Historical Perspectives on Values, Practices, and Regulations*, edited by Volker Roelke and Giovanni Maio, 335–349. Stuttgart, Germany: Franz Steiner Verlag, 2004.

Kremer, Michael, and Rachel Glennerster. *Strong Medicine: Creating Incentives for Pharmaceutical Research on Neglected Diseases.* Princeton, NJ: Princeton University Press, 2004.

Krimsky, Sheldon. *Science in the Private Interest: Has the Lure of Profits Corrupted Biomedical Research?* New York: Rowman & Littlefield Publishers, 2004.

Landecker, Hannah. "Immortality, In Vitro: A History of the HeLa Cell Line." In *Biotechnology and Culture: Bodies, Anxieties, Ethics*, edited by Paul Brodwin, 53–74. Bloomington: Indiana University Press, 2000.

Lewis, Sinclair. *Arrowsmith.* New York: Modern Library, 1925.

Lincoln, Abraham, "Second Lecture on Discoveries and Inventions." Lecture,

Jackson, IL, February 11, 1859. Cited in *Abraham Lincoln Online*, http://
showcase.netins.net/web/creative/lincoln/speeches/discoveries.htm.

Lloyd, W. F. "Two Lectures on the Checks to Population" (excerpt). In *Population, Evolution, and Birth Control*, edited by G. Hardin. San Francisco: Freeman, 1964.

Mead, Aroha, and Dr. Steven Ratuva, eds. *Call of the Earth/Llamado de la Tierra; Pacific Genes and Life Patents, Pacific Experiences & Analysis of the Commodification & Ownership of Life*. Tokyo: United Nations University Institute of Advanced Studies, 2007.

Moore, Francis. "Letter to Jay Katz, September 2, 1964." Reprinted in *Experimentation with Human Beings: The Authority of the Investigator, Subject Professions, and State in the Human Experimentation Process*, edited by Jay Katz, MD. New York: Russell Sage Foundation, 1972.

Mundy, Alicia. *Dispensing with the Truth: The Victims, the Drug Companies, and the Dramatic Story Behind the Battle over Fen-Phen*. New York: St. Martin's Press, 2001.

National Academy of Science, Institute of Medicine, Board on Population Health. *The Future of Drug Safety: Promoting and Protecting the Health of the Public*. Washington, D.C.: The National Academies, September 22, 2006. http://www.iom.edu/Reports/2006/The-Future-of-Drug-Safety-Promoting-and-Protecting-the-Health-of-the-Public.aspx.

Peterson, Melody. *Our Daily Meds: How the Pharmaceutical Companies Transformed Themselves into Slick Marketing Machines and Hooked the Nation on Prescription Drugs*. New York: Farrar, Straus & Giroux, 2008.

Prinz zu Waldeck und Pyrmont, Wolrad, Martin J. Adelman, Robert Brauneis, and Josef Drexl, eds. *Patents and Technological Progress in a Globalized World: Liber Amicorum Joseph Straus*. Berlin and Heidelberg: Springer, 2009.

Reynolds, P. Preston. "The Nuremberg Code, 1946–1949." In *Trials of War Criminals Before the Nürnberg Military Tribunals Under Control Council No. 10*. Washington D.C.: Government Printing Office, 1949–1953.

School of Aerospace Medicine, United States Air Force. *2007 Course Catalog*, 16, http://afspp.afms.mil/idc/groups/public/documents/ afms/ctb_073557 .pdf.

Shiva, Vandana. *Biopiracy: The Plunder of Nature and Knowledge*. Cambridge, MA: South End Press, 1999.

Smith, Jane. *Patenting the Sun: Polio and the Salk Vaccine*. New York: William Morrow, 1990.

Solomons, T. W., and Craig Fryhle. *Organic Chemistry*, 8th ed. Hoboken, NJ: Wiley, 2003.

Spruce, Richard, and A. R. Wallace. *Notes of a Botanist on the Amazon and Andes*. New York: Johnson Reprint Corp., 1970.

Takenaka, Toshiko. *Patent Law and Theory: A Handbook of Contemporary Research*. Northampton, MA: Edward Elgar Publishing, 2009.

Titmuss, Richard M. *The Gift Relationship: From Human Blood to Social Policy*. New York: Pantheon Books, 1971.

U.S. Congress, U.S. Office of Technology Assessment. *Ownership of Human Tissues and Cells: New Developments in Biotechnology*. Washington, D.C.: Books for Business, 2002.

Voet, Martin A. *The Generic Challenge: Understanding Patents, FDA and Pharmaceutical Life-Cycle Management*, 2nd electronic ed. Boca Raton, FL: Brown Walker Press, 2008.

Waldby, Catherine, and Robert Mitchell. *Tissue Economies: Blood, Organs, and Cell Lines in Late Capitalism*. Durham, NC: Duke University Press, 2006.

Washington, Harriet A. *Living Healthy with Hepatitis C*. New York: Dell, 2000.

————. *Medical Apartheid: The Dark History of Medical Experimentation on Black Americans from Colonial Times to the Present*. New York: Doubleday, 2007.

Watson, James D. *The Double Helix: A Personal Account of the Discovery of the Structure of DNA*. New York: Atheneum, 1968.

Whitehead, Alfred North. *Science and the Modern World*. New York: Free Press 1997.

ARTICLES/PAPERS/REPORTS

Allen, Arthur. "Who Owns Your DNA? Genetic Research That Can Save Lives Is Often Stymied by Biotech Companies' Greedy Patent Claims." *Salon*, March 7, 2000. Accessed November 1, 2010. http://www.salon.com/health/feature/2000/03/07/genetic_test/index.html.

Allen, Becky. "September 2010 ADAP Update: The Sprinklers Are On, but the Water Pressure's Low." *The Body Pro*, September 23, 2010, http://www.thebodypro.com/content/art58596.html.

Angell, Marcia. "The Ethics of Clinical Research in the Third World." *New England Journal of Medicine* 337, no. 12 (September 1997): 847–49.

Annas, George J. "Protecting Soldiers from Friendly Fire: The Consent Requirement for Using Investigational Drugs and Vaccines in Combat." *American Journal of Law & Medicine* 24, nos. 2–3 (1998): 245–60.

"Ardais Corporation Announces Agreement with AstraZeneca for Access to Clinical Samples." Ardais Corp. press release, PRNewswire. Lexington, MA. February 4, 2003.

Attaran, Amir, DPhil, LLB. "Do Patents Prevent Access to Drugs for HIV in Developing Countries?" *JAMA* 287, no 7 (February 20, 2002).

————. "How Do Patents and Economic Policies Affect Access to Essential Medicines in Developing Countries?" *Journal of Health Affairs* 23, no. 3 (2004): 155–56. Accessed November 1, 2010. http://content.healthaffairs.org/content/23/3/155.full.pdf.

Attaran, Amir, DPhil, LLB, and Lee Gillespie-White, LLB. "Do Patents for Antiretroviral Drugs Constrain Access to AIDS Treatments in Africa?" *Journal of the American Medical Association* 286, no. 15 (2001): 1886–92.

"Aventis to Donate Sleeping-Sickness Drugs." Reuters News Service. May 3, 2001.

Baker, Dean, PhD, and Adriane Fugh-Berman, MD. "Do New Drugs Increase Life Expectancy? A Critique of a Manhattan Institute Paper." Washington, D.C.: Center for Economic and Policy Research/Washington, D.C.: Department of Physiology and Biophysics, Georgetown University Medical Center.

Begley, Sharon. "In Surprise Ruling, Court Declares Two Gene Patents Invalid." *Newsweek*. March 29, 2010.

Benowitz, Steve. "French Challenge to BRCA1 Patent Underlies European Discontent." *Journal of the National Cancer Institute* 94, no. 2 (January 2002): 80–81.

Berkrot, Bill. "Pfizer Whistleblower's Ordeal Reaps Big Rewards." Reuters. September 3, 2009. Accessed September 7, 2009. http://www.reuters.com/article/businessNews/idUSN021592920090903.

Blackwell, Tom. "Ontario Hospital Sued by Bayer; Company Says Action Needed to Protect Patent." *National Post*, A1.

Blumberg, Baruch S., Irving Millman, W. Thomas London, et al. "Ted Slavin's Blood and the Development of HBV Vaccine." Letter to the Editor. *New England Journal of Medicine* 312, no. 3 (1985): 189.

Boffey, Philip M. "The Fall and Rise of Leonard Hayflick, Biologist Whose Fight with U.S. Seems Over." *New York Times*. January 19, 1982.

Bombardier, C., L. Laine, A. Reicin, et al. "Comparison of Upper Gastrointestinal Toxicity of Rofecoxib and Naproxen in Patients with Rheumatoid Arthritis. VIGOR Study Group." *New England Journal of Medicine* 343, no. 21 (November 2000): 1520–28.

Bouwer, Cara. "Sponsored Research Tends to Show Bias." *Business Day*. June 13, 2007, 5.

Braiser, A. R. "The NF-κB Regulatory Network." *Cardiovascular Toxicology* 6, no. 2 (2006): 111–30.

Brazilian Department of Health. "Thalidomide Scares Again/*Talidomida volta a assustar*." Press release, November 1, 2006. http://www.saude.df.gov.br/003/00301009.asp?ttCD_CHAVE=31041.

Brown, Russell W., and James Henderson. "The Mass Production and Distribution of HeLa Cells at Tuskgee Institute, 1953–1955." *Journal of the History of Medicine and Allied Sciences* 38, no. 4 (1983): 415–31.

Burton, Thomas M. "Amid Alarm Bells, A Blood Substitute Keeps Pumping." *Wall Street Journal*. February 22, 2006.

————. "Despite Heart Attack Deaths, PolyHeme Still Being Tested on Trauma Patients." *Wall Street Journal*. February 22, 2006.

Butts, Heather, JD, MPH, and Ruth L. Fischbach, PhD, MPE. "What Should IRBs Consider When Reviewing a Protocol in Which Race Will Be Identified?" Lecture, EGIR Conference. May 19, 2006.

Callender, C. O., and P. V. Miles. "Minority Organ Donation: The Power of an Educated Community." *Journal of the American College of Surgeons* 210, no. 5 (2010): 708–15, 715–17.

Campbell, E. G., B. R. Clarridge, M. Gokhale, L. Birembaum, S. Hilgartner, N.A. Holtzman, D. Blumenthal. "Data Withholding in Academic Genetics: Evidence from a National Survey," *JAMA* 287, no. 4 (Jan. 23–30, 2002): 473–80.

Caplan, Arthur. "The Sale of Tissue Samples from NIH to Pfizer." Blog.bioethics.net. *American Journal of Bioethics*. June 1, 2006. http://blog.bioethics.net/2006/06/sale-of-tissue-samples-from-nih-to.html.

"CELEBREX® (Celecoxib) Capsules, G. D. Searle & Co." *Physicians' Desk Reference*. Montvale, NJ: PDR Network, 2010. Accessed November 20, 2010. http://www.pdr.net/drugpages/productlabeling.aspx?mpcode=76000300.

Cohen, Jon. "Brazil, Thailand Override Big Pharma Patents." *Science* 316, no. 5826 (2007): 816.

Colaianni, Alessandra, Subhashini Chandrasekharan, and Robert Cook-Deegan, MD. "Impact of Gene Patents and Licensing Practices on Access to Genetic

Testing and Carrier Screening for Tay-Sachs and Canavan Disease." *Genetics in Medicine* 12, no. 4 (April 2010): S5–S14. Accessed July 19, 2010. http://journals.lww.com/geneticsinmedicine/Fulltext/2010/0400.

Conley, John, and Dan Vorhaus. "Pigs Fly: Federal Court Invalidates Myriad's Patent Claims." *Genomics Law Report*. March 30, 2010. Accessed April 2, 2010. www.genomicslawreport.com/index.php/2010/03/30/pigs-fly-federal-court -invalidates-myriads-patent-claims/.

Connor, Steve. "Your Life in Their Patent." *The Independent*. December 1, 1994. Accessed September 5, 2007.

Cudjoe, Franklin. "Poverty and Sickness Won't Be Cured by Fighting Patents." *New Times, Rwanda's First Daily*. January 3, 2011. http://www.newtimes .co.rw/index.php?issue=13572&article=7362.

Davidoff, Frank, et al. "Sponsorship Authorship and Accountability." *The New England Journal of Medicine*, 286, no. 10 (September 2001): 825.

Dexler, H., G. W. G. Dirks, and R. A. Macleod. "False Human Hematopoietic Cell Lines: Cross-Contaminations and Misinterpretations." *Leukemia* 13, no. 10 (October 1999): 1601.

DiMasi, J. A. "The Price of Innovation: New Estimates of Drug Development Costs." *Journal of Health Economics* 22, no. 2 (March 2003).

Doctors Without Borders/Médecins Sans Frontières. "Sell-Out at WTO on DOHA Declaration?" Press release. Geneva, February 12, 2003. Accessed May 21, 2009. http://www.doctorswithoutborders.org/press/release.cfm?id=382&cat =press-release.

Editors, The. "Do Seed Companies Control GM Crop Research?" *Scientific American*. August 13, 2009. Accessed June 17, 2010. http://www.scientificamerican .com/article.cfm?id=do-seed-companies-control-gm-crop-research.

Edwards, Jim. "Pfizer Case over Test That Killed 11 Kids Could Blow the Lid Off Foreign Drug Trials." *The CBS Interactive Business Network*. June 30, 2010. http://industry.bnet.com/pharma/10008781/pfizer-that_killed_11_kids _ could_ blow_ the_ lid_ off_foreign_drug_ trials_case-over-test.com.

Eisenberg, Rebecca, and Michael A. Heller. "Can Patents Deter Innovation? The Anticommons in Biomedical Research." *Science* 280, no. 5364 (1998): 698–701.

Elliott, Carl. "Not-So-Public Relations: How the Drug Industry Is Branding Itself with Bioethics." *Slate*. December 15, 2003. Accessed March 28, 2009. http:// www.slate.com/id/2092442.

Epstein, Keith, and Bill Sloat. "Drug Trials: Do People Know the Truth About Experiments?" *Cleveland Plain Dealer*. December 15, 1996.

Epstein, Richard A. "Mad Scientists: Go Away, Ethics Police. Leave the NIH Alone." *Slate*. February 15, 2005. Accessed May 21, 2008. http://www.slate .com/id/2113520/.

Ernst, Cheryl. "Making the Most of the Hawaiian Genome." *Health: University of Hawai'i System Newsletter*, March 3, 2003. Accessed February 17, 2011. http:// www.hawaii.edu/ur/newsatuh/archives/030303/health.htm.

Euringer, Amanda. "Foreskin Face Cream." *The Tyee*. January 30, 2007. http:// thetyee.ca/Views/2007/01/30/Foreskin/.

Faleiro, Sonia. "A Death of a Son, Grandson, and All of Life's Dreams." September 2, 2006. Accessed May 13, 2010. http://soniafaleiro.blogspot.com/2006/ 09/death-of-son-grandson-and-all-of-lifes.html.

Felland, Laurie, and James Reschovsky. "More Non-Elderly Americans Face Problems Affording Prescription Drugs." *Center for Studying Health System Change Tracking Report No. 22*. Washington, D.C.: HSC, January 2009. Accessed February 11, 2010. www.hschange.org/CONTENT/1039/.

Foubister, Vida. "Gene Patents Raise Concerns for Researchers, Clinicians." *American Medical News*. February 21, 2000. Accessed March 23, 2011. http://www.ama-assn.org/amednews/2000/02/21/prsb0221.htm.

Frumkin, M. "The Origin of Patents." *Journal of the Patent Office Society* 27, no. 3 (March 1945): 143.

Fugh-Berman, Adriane J. "The Haunting of Medical Journals: How Ghostwriting Sold 'HRT.'" *PLoS Medicine* 7, no. 9 (September 2010): e1000335. Accessed November 20, 2010. http://www.plosmedicine.org/article/info%3Adoi%2F10.1371%2Fjournal.pmed.1000335.

Gates, William H. "Humane Research." *Wall Street Journal*. January 27, 2003, 16A.

Gatty, Bob. "Bill Seeks to Overturn Medical Patents." *Physician's Management* 35 (1995): 27.

Glickman, Seth W., MD, MBA, et al. "Ethical and Scientific Implications of the Globalization of Clinical Research." *New England Journal of Medicine* 360, no. 8 (February 2009): 816.

Goldacre, Ben. "The Danger of Drugs . . . and Data." *Guardian*. May 9, 2009.

Goodwin, Michele. "Feds Should Monitor Body Parts Sales." *Los Angeles Times*. March 13, 2004.

Gorner, Peter. "*New England Journal of Medicine* Eases Conflict-of-Interest Policy for Authors." *Chicago Tribune*. June 13, 2002.

Grant, Bob. "Elsevier Published 6 Fake Journals." *The Scientist*. May 7, 2009. http://www.the-scientist.com/blog/display/55679/.

———. "Merck Published Fake Journal." *The Scientist*. April 30, 2009. http://www.the-scientist.com/blog/display/55671/.

Grassley, The Hon. Charles. Letter to Pfizer via electronic transmission. March 3, 2009. http://graphics8.nytimes.com/packages/pdf/business/2009_03_03_Pfizer_letter.pdf.

Griffin, Drew, and Andy Segal. "Feds Found Pfizer Too Big to Nail." CNN.com Health. April 02, 2010. http://articles.cnn.com/2010-04-02/health/pfizer.bextra_1_bextra-pfizer-and-pharmacia-generic-drugs?_s=PM:HEALTH.

Griggs, Kim. "'Human' Cow Milk an MS Aid?" *Wired*. August 2, 2000. Accessed February 15, 2011. http://www.wired.com/science/discoveries/news/2000/08/37921.

Guren, Adam M. "HMS Fellows Indicted for Alleged Lab Theft." *The Harvard Crimson*. June 27, 2005. http://www.thecrimson.com/article/2005/6/27/hms-fellows-indicted-for-alleged-lab/#.

Hannaford, Kat. "Bill Gates Convinces 40 Billionaires to Give Away Half Their Fortunes." *Gizmodo*. August 4, 2010. http://gizmodo.com/#!5604368/bill-gates-convinces-40-billionaires-to-give-away-half-their-fortunes.

Hargrove, Thomas, and Lee Bowman. "Autopsy Rates Differ by Race, Age, Sex, Education." Scripps Howard News Service. August 12, 2009. http://www.scrippsnews.com/content/autopsy-rates-differ-race-age-sex-education.

Harris, Gardiner. "Pfizer Pays $2.3 Billion to Settle Marketing Case," *New York Times*, September 3, 2009.

―――. "Prilosec's Maker Switches Users to Nexium, Thwarting Generics." *Wall Street Journal.* June 6, 2002. Accessed September 29, 2010. http://www.chelationtherapyonline.com/technical/p36.htm.

Harris, Gardiner, and Benedict Carey. "Researchers Fail to Reveal Full Drug Pay." *New York Times.* June 8, 2008.

Harvey, Tom. "BYU Spices Up Celebrex Lawsuit Against Pfizer." *Salt Lake Tribune.* September 21, 2010. Accessed May 12, 2011. http://www.sltrib.com/sltrib/money/49883490-79/byu-pfizer-simmons-celebrex.html.csp.

Hayflick, L., and P. S. Moorhead. "The Serial Cultivation of Human Diploid Cell Strains." *Experimental Cell Research* 25 (1961): 585–621.

Henderson, Diedtra. "Report: FDA Needs More Authority, Funds." *Boston Globe.* September 23, 2006.

Henderson, Mark. "Drug Trials 'Give Best Results to Sponsors.'" *Sunday Times* (London). June 5, 2007. http://www.timesonline.co.uk/tol/news/science/article1884627.ece.

Henry J. Kaiser Family Foundation. "Average Health Insurance Premiums and Worker Contributions for Family Coverage, 1999–2009." *Kaiser/HRET Survey of Employer-Sponsored Health Benefits, 1999–2009.* September 15, 2009. http://slides.kff.org/chart.aspx?ch=1182.

―――. "Putting Off Care Because of Cost." *Health Tracking Poll.* July 14, 2009. Accessed July 18, 2009. http://www.kff.org.

Herper, Matthew. "The World's Most Expensive Drugs." Forbes.com. February 22, 2010. http://www.forbes.com/2010/02/19/expensive-drugs-cost-business-healthcare-rare-diseases.html.

―――. "The FDA Ignores Its Advisors a Quarter of the Time." The Medicine Show Blog, *Forbes.* October 12, 2010. http://blogs.forbes.com/matthewherper/2010/10/12/the-fda-ignores-its-advisors-a-quarter-of-the-time/.

Hill, Kevin P., MD, MHS, Joseph S. Ross, MD, MHS, David S. Egilman, MD, MPH, and Harlan M. Krumholz, MD, SM. "The ADVANTAGE Seeding Trial: A Review of Internal Documents." *Annals of Internal Medicine* 149, no. 4 (August 19, 2008): 251–58. http://www.annals.org/content/149/4/251.full.

Holcberg, David. "Should Genes Be Patented?" *Capitalism Magazine.* April 13, 2002. Accessed November 23, 2010. http://www.capitalismmagazine.com/science/genetics/1534-should-genes-be-patented.html.

Huff, Bob. "First Wave of Cuts Hits New York's ADAP." *Treatment Issues.* December 2002. http://www.thebody.com/content/art13619.html.

Hyder, A. A., S. A. Wali, A. N. Khan, et al. "Ethical Review of Research: A Perspective from Developing Country Researchers." *Journal of Medical Ethics* 30, no. 1 (2004): 68–72.

Institut Curie. "Against the Monopoly of Myriad Genetics on Tests of Susceptibility to Breast and Ovarian Cancer: Role Reversal of Situation in the European Patent Office." Press release. Paris, November 20, 2008. http://www.curie.fr/sites/default/files/decision-OEB-Myriad-Genetics-predisposition-sein.pdf.

Institute of Medicine Board on Population Health and Public Health Practice. "The Future of Drug Safety: Promoting and Protecting the Health of the Public." September 22, 2006. http://www.iom.edu/Reports/2006/The-Future-of-Drug-Safety-Promoting-and-Protecting-the-Health-of-the-Public.aspx.

Jaeger, Kathleen. "Proposed Free Trade Agreement with Malaysia." Testimony Before the Office of the United States Trade Representative and the Inter-agency Trade Policy Staff Committee. May 3, 2006.

Janas, B. DesignWrite, Inc. "Updated Outline," e-mail. April 13, 2010. Accessed August 21, 2009. http://dida.library.ucsf.edu/pdf/boc37b10.

Jewett, Thomas O. "Thomas Jefferson: Father of Invention," *The Early America Review* 3, no. 1 (Winter 2000). Accessed November 21, 2010. http://www .earlyamerica.com/review/winter2000/jefferson.html.

Jha, Alok. "First British Human-Animal Hybrid Embryos Created by Scientists." *Guardian.* April 2, 2008. http://www.guardian.co.uk/science/2008/apr/02/ medicalresearch.ethicsofscience.

John, Esther, Alexander Miron, Gail Gong, Amanda I. Phipps, Anna Felberg, Frederick P. Li, Dee W. West, and Alice S. Whittemore. "Prevalence of Patho-genic *BRCA1* Mutation Carriers in 5 US Racial/Ethnic Groups." *Journal of the American Medical Association* 298, no. 24 (2007): 2869–76.

Josefson, Deborah. "US Hospitals to Ask Patients for Right to Sell Their Tissue." *British Medical Journal* 321, no. 7262 (2000): 658.

Joyce, J.A., et. al. "A Functional Heparan Sulfate Mimetic Implicates Both Hepa-ranase and Heparan Sulfate in Tumor Angiogenesis and Invasion in a Mouse Model of Multistage Cancer." *Oncogene* 24, no. 25 (June 2005): 4037–51.

"Justice Department Announces Largest Health Care Fraud Settlement in Its His-tory." Press release. Washington, D.C.: Department of Health and Human Services, September 2, 2009.

Kahn, Jonathan, JD, PhD. "How a Drug Becomes 'Ethnic': Law, Commerce, and the Production of Racial Categories in Medicine." *Yale Journal of Health Policy, Law, and Ethics* 4, no. 1 (2004): 1–46.

Katz, Jay, MD, and Jos V. M. Welie. "Blurring the Lines: Research, Therapy, and IRBs (New FDA Regulations on Informed Consent and Emergency Research in Life-Threatening Situations)." *Hastings Center Report* 27, no. 1 (January– February 1997): 9–12.

Katz, Jonathan M. "Monsanto Gives Haiti $4 Million in Hybrid Seeds." *Bloom-berg Business Week.* May 14, 2010, 25–29. Accessed June 1, 2010. http://www .businessweek.com/ap/financialnews/D9FMUQN80.htm.

Keim, Brandon. "Could Antidepressants Rewire Adolescent Brains?" *Wired.* May 30, 2009. Accessed August 4, 2009. http://www.wired.com/wiredscience/ 2007/05/could_antidepre/.

———. "Glaxo, Doctors Battle over Interpretation of New Avandia Study." *Wired.* June 6, 2007. Accessed March 23, 2011. http://www.wired.com/wiredscience/ 2007/06/glaxo_doctors_b.

Kierman, G. L. "Scientific and Ethical Considerations in the Use of Placebo Con-trols in Clinical Trials in Psychopharmacology." *Psychopharmacology Bulletin* 22, no. 1 (1986).

Knox, Richard. "Merck Pulls Arthritis Drug Vioxx from Market." *All Things Con-sidered.* September 30, 2004. Accessed November 20, 2010. http://www .npr.org/templates/story/story.php?storyId=4054991.

Kolata, Gina. "Sharing of Data Leads to Progress on Alzheimer's." *New York Times.* August 12, 2010. http://www.nytimes.com/2010/08/13/health/ research/13alzheimer.html.

————. "Sharing of Data Leads to Progress on Alzheimer's," *New York Times.* August 12, 2010. Accessed August 12, 2010. http://www.nytimes.com/2010/08/13/health/research/13alzheimer.html.

Kremer, Michael. "Pharmaceuticals and the Developing World." *Journal of Economic Perspectives* 16, no. 4 (2002): 67–90.

Krimsky, Sheldon. "Perils of University-Industry Collaboration." *Issues in Science and Technology* 16, no. 1 (September 22, 1999): 14.

Landefeld, C. Seth, and Michael A. Steinman, MD. "The Neurontin Legacy—Marketing Through Misinformation and Manipulation." *New England Journal of Medicine* 360, no. 2 (2009): 103–06.

Lawler, Andrew. "Arrest of Ex-Harvard Postdocs Raises Questions of Ownership." *Science* 296, no. 5577 (June 28, 2002): 2310.

————. "U.S. Asks for Delay in Science Theft Case." *Science* 297, no. 5581 (July 26, 2002): 496.

Lea, Andrew P. "RE: Premarin/TMG Publication Plan Proposal." DesignWrite, Inc. e-mail. May 20, 2003. Accessed November 21, 2010. http://dida.library.ucsf.edu/tid/duc37b10.

Leaf, Clifton. "The Law of Unintended Consequences." *Fortune.* September 19, 2005. Accessed September 3, 2008. http://money.cnn.com/magazines/fortune/fortune_archive/2005/09/19/8272884/index.htm.

Leake, Jonathan, and Charles Masters. "Renault Used Child Corpses to Improve Car Safety Seats." *Sunday Times* (London). April 19, 1998.

L'Hommedieu Stankus, Jennifer, JD, MS-4. "Understanding Medical Liability in Military Medicine." *American College of Emergency Physicians (ACEP)/ACEP News.* February 2009. http://www.acep.org/content.aspx?id=43974.

Lichtenberg, Frank R. "Why Has Longevity Increased More in Some States Than in Others? The Role of Medical Innovation and Other Factors," *Medical Progress Report.* The Manhattan Institute, No. 4, July 2007.

Lincoln, Martha. "Because You Want More Life to Live: BiDil, a Heart Failure Prescription for Self-Identified Blacks." *Corporations and Health Watch.* May 1, 2008. Accessed December 20, 2010. http://www.corporationsandhealth.org/news/61/59/Because-You-Want-More-Life-to-Live-BiDil-a-Heart-Failure-Prescription-for-Self-Identified-Blacks.

Love, James. "Brazil Puts Patients Before Patents." *Huffington Post.* May 4, 2007. Accessed June 13, 2009. http://www.huffingtonpost.com/james-love/brazil-puts-patients-befo_b_47651.html.

————. "IRS Data Shows Drug Industry Cost Estimates Exaggerated." News release. November 30, 2001. Accessed November 1, 2010. http://lists.essential.org/pipermail/ip-health/2001-November/002489.html.

Lovgren, Stefan. "One-Fifth of Human Genes Have Been Patented, Study Reveals." *National Geographic News.* October 13, 2005. http://news.nationalgeographic.com/news/2005/10/1013_051013_gene_patent.html.

Lurie, Peter, MD, MPH, and Sidney M. Wolfe, MD. "FDA Medical Officers Report Lower Standards Permit Dangerous Drug Approvals." *Public Citizen.* December 2, 1998. http://www.citizen.org/hrg1466.

McGee, Glenn, PhD. "The Wonders of PolyHeme . . . by Press Release." Blog.bioethics.net. *American Journal of Bioethics.* January 9, 2009. http://blog.bioethics.net/2009/01/the-wonders-of-polyhemeby-press-release/.

McNeil, Donald G. Jr. "Patents or Poverty? New Debate over Lack of AIDS Care in Africa." *New York Times.* November 5, 2001.

McNulty, Toni. "A New Earthquake Hits Haiti—Monsanto," *Wired: Haiti Rewired.* May 12, 2010. Accessed May 12, 2010. http://haitirewired.wired.com/profiles/blogs/a-new-earthquake-hits-haiti.

Mahunnah, R. L., and K. E. Mshigeni. "Tanzania's Policy on Biodiversity Prospecting and Drug Discovery Programs." *Journal of Ethnopharmacology* 51, nos. 1–3 (April 1996): 221–28.

Marden, Emily. "The Neem Tree Patent: International Conflict over the Commodification of Life." *Boston College International and Comparative Law Review* 22, nos. 2–3 (1999): 279.

Meier, Barry, Gina Kolata, and Andrew Pollack. "Medicine Fueled by Marketing Intensified Trouble for Pain Pills." *New York Times.* December 19, 2004, 1A.

Meier, Markus H. Overview of FTC "Antitrust Actions in Pharmaceutical Services and Products." Washington, D.C.: Health Care Division, Bureau of Competition, Federal Trade Commission. June 2010.

Merz, Jon F., Antigone G. Kriss, Debra G. B. Leonard, and Mildred K. Cho. "Diagnostic Testing Fails the Test." *Nature* 4, no. 15 (February 7, 2002): 577–79.

Method, Kathy. "Going Going Gone: Patents Set to Expire Soon on Many Brand-Name Drugs." *Modern Medicine.* August 10, 2009.

Miller, Joe. "Patent Law: How Patents Grew over Time to Include Living Organisms." *Cooking Up a Story.* July 29, 2009. Accessed November 22, 2010. http://cookingupastory.com/patent-law-how-patents-grew-over-time-to-include-living-organisms.

Monsanto Co., The. "Seed Piracy: Updates and Summaries." Company newsletter. September/October 2009. Accessed June 9, 2010. http://www.cban.ca/Resources/Topics/Monsanto/Monsanto-s-Seed-Piracy-Newsletter.

Mossoff, Adam "Rethinking the Development of Patents: An Intellectual History, 1550–1800." *Hastings Law Journal* 52 (2001): 1255.

———. "Who Cares What Thomas Jefferson Thought About Patents? Reevaluating the Patent 'Privilege' in Historical Context." *Cornell Law Review* 92, no. 953 (2007): 1012.

Muhimbili University of Health and Allied Sciences. "MUHAS Cooperative Research Agreement IPR Form II/06." Dar es Salaam, Tanzania, 2006. Accessed January 17, 2011. http://bit.ly/eZsGxb.

Nadu, Tamil. "Spate of Farmers' Suicides in India Worrying WHO." *The Hindu.* October 15, 2006. http://www.hindu.com/2006/10/15/stories/2006101514820800.htm.

Nance, Mark, et al. "Patent Litigation: Is It Worth the Expense?" *Genetic Engineering & Biotechnology News* 26, no. 7 (2006). Accessed March 22, 2011. http://www.genengnews.com/gen-articles/patent-litigation-is-it-worth-the-expense/1454/.

Natanson, Charles, MD, Steven J. Kern, BS, Peter Lurie, MD, MPH, et al. "Cell-Free Hemoglobin-Based Blood Substitutes and the Risk of Myocardial Infarction and Death." *Journal of the American Medical Association* 299, no. 19 (April 2008): 2304–12.

Nelson-Rees, W. A., and R. R. Flandermeyer. "HeLa Cultures Defined." *Science* 191, no. 4222 (January 1976): 96.

Neuman, William, and Andrew Pollack. "U.S. Farmers Cope with Roundup-Resistant Weeds." *New York Times.* May 3, 2010.

Nissen, S. E., and K. Wolski, "Effect of Rosiglitazone on the Risk of Myocardial Infarction and Death from Cardiovascular Causes." *New England Journal of Medicine* 356, no. 24 (2007): 2457–71.

Novak, Sara. "Haitian Farmers Refuse Monsanto's Seeds and Instead Commit to Burning Them." *TreeHugger.* May 30, 2010. Accessed May 30, 2010. www.treehugger.com/files/2010/05/haitian_farmers_refuse_monsantos_seeds_and_instead_commit_to_burning_them.php.

Office of Inspector General, Department of Health and Human Services. *The Globalization of Clinical Trials: A Growing Challenge in Protecting Human Subjects.* Washington, D.C.: Department of Health and Human Services, 2001. http://oig.hhs.gov/oei/reports/oei-01-00-00190.pdf.

Paumgarten, F. J., and I. Chahoud. "Thalidomide Embryopathy Cases in Brazil After 1965." *Reproductive Toxicology* 22, no. 1 (2006): 1–2.

Paxton, Anne. "Brisk Trade in Tissue for Proteomics and Genomics Research." *CAP Today.* March 2003.

Perrone, Matthew. "Glaxo Used Ghostwriting Program to Promote Paxil." Associated Press/*Boston Globe.* August 20, 2009.

Pollack, Andrew J. "Biological Products Raise Genetic Ownership Issues: Governments Are Demanding Share of Profits." *New York Times.* November 26, 1999.

Pollan, Michael. "We Knew It Was Coming." *New York Times.* June 1, 2010. Accessed June 1, 2010. http://roomfordebate.blogs.nytimes.com/2010/05/06/invasion-of-the-superweeds/?ref=energy-environment.

Potter, Matt. "Bad Blood?" *San Diego Reader.* July 28, 2005.

Progen Pharmaceuticals Ltd. "Progen Technology Switches on Cancer Fighting Genes and Inhibits Tumor Growth." Company press release. April 20, 2009. Accessed April 21, 2009. http://www.progen.com.au/Docs/prs/AACR_2009_announcement_v3.pdf.

Progressive Librarians Guild. "Progressive Librarians Guild Calls for Elsevier to End Corrupt Publishing Practices and for Library Associations to Take Advocacy Role on Behalf of Scientific Integrity." News release. May 12, 2009. http://libr.org/plg/elsevier.php.

"Proposal for Jeff Solomon—Medical Education and Communication Plan for the Premarin Product Line." DesignWrite Inc. August 12, 1996. Accessed August 21, 2009. http://dida.library.ucsf.edu/pdf/jrb37b10.

Psaty, Bruce M., MD, PhD, and Curt D. Furberg, MD, PhD. "Rosiglitazone and Cardiovascular Risk." *New England Journal of Medicine* 356, no. 24 (2007): 2522–24.

Public Citizen Congress Watch. "Drug Industry Profits: Hefty Pharmaceutical Company Margins Dwarf Other Industries." *Congress Watch 2003.* June 2003. http://www.citizen.org/documents/Pharma_Report.pdf.

"Randomised Trial of Intravenous Streptokinase, Oral Aspirin, Both, or Neither Among 17,187 Cases of Suspected Acute Myocardial Infarction: ISIS-2. ISIS-2 (Second International Study of Infarct Survival) Collaborative Group." *Lancet* 2, no. 8607 (1988).

Rao, Radhika. "Genes and Spleens: Property, Contract, or Privacy Rights in the Human Body?" *Journal of Law Medicine Ethics* 35, no. 3 (2007): 371–82.

Ridker, Paul M., MD, and Jose Torres, BA. "Reported Outcomes in Major Cardio-vascular Clinical Trials Funded by For-Profit and Not-for-Profit Organizations: 2000–2005." *Journal of the American Medical Association* 295, no. 19 (2006): 2270–74.

Robotham, Julie. "Sick Babies Denied Treatment in DNA Row." *Sidney Morning Herald.* November 29, 2008. Accessed October 5, 2010. http://www.smh .com.au/news/national/sick-babies-denied-treatment-in-row/2008/11/28/ 1227491827171.html.

Rosenberg, Martha. "Parents Fight Use of New Psych Meds for Kids." *San Francisco Chronicle.* September 13, 2009.

Ross, Gilbert. "Why Drug 'Reimportation' Won't Die: The Drug Industry Made a Foolish Bet in Supporting Health Reform." *Wall Street Journal.* January 7, 2010.

Ross, Joseph S., MD, MHS, Kevin P. Hill, MD, MHS, et al., "Guest Authorship and Ghostwriting in Publications Related to Rofecoxib: A Case Study of Industry Documents from Rofecoxib Litigation." *Journal of the American Medical Association* 299, no. 15 (2008): 1800–12.

Rubin, Rita. "FDA Panel to Vote on Antipsychotic Drugs for Kids." *USA Today,* June 9, 2009.

Sackett, David J., and Andrew D. Oxman. "HARLOT plc: An Amalgamation of the World's Two Oldest Professions." *British Medical Journal* 327, no. 7429 (2003): 1442–45.

Sainath, P. "17,368 Farm Suicides in 2009." *The Hindu.* December 27, 2010. Accessed January 4, 2011. http://www.thehindu.com/opinion/columns/ sainath/article995824.ece?homepage=true.

Schiff, Judith Ann. "An Unsung Hero of Medical Research: A Technique Invented Nearly 100 Years Ago by a Yale Scientist Led to a Revolution in Biology." *Yale Alumni Magazine* 64, no. 2 (February 2001). Accessed November 21, 2010. http://www.yalealumnimagazine.com/issues/02_02/old_yale .html.

Schondelmeyer, Stephen. "Patent Extension of Pipeline Drugs: Impact on U.S. Health Care Expenditures." PRIME Institute, College of Pharmacy. July 28, 1999.

Schondelmeyer, Stephen, and Leigh Purvis. AARP Public Policy Insitute. "Trends in Retail Prices of Brand Name Prescription Drugs Widely Used by Medicare Beneficiaries, 2005 to 2009." *Rx Price Watch Report.* August 2010. http:// assets.aarp.org/rgcenter/ppi/health-care/rxpricewatch.pdf.

———. "Trends in Retail Prices of Brand Name Prescription Drugs Widely Used by Medicare Beneficiaries, 2005 to 2009." *Rx Price Watch Report.* Washington, D.C.: AARP Public Policy Institute. August 2010. http://assets.aarp.org/ rgcenter/ppi/health-care/rxpricewatch.pdf.

Schwartz, John, and Steve Vogel. "Amid German Uproar, U.S. Auto Researchers Defend Use of Corpses." *Washington Post.* November 25, 1993.

Silverstein, F. E., G. Faich, J. L. Goldstein, et al. "Gastrointestinal Toxicity with Celecoxib Vs Nonsteroidal Anti-Inflammatory Drugs for Osteoarthritis and Rheumatoid Arthritis: The CLASS Study: A Randomized Controlled Trial: Celecoxib Long-Term Arthritis Safety Study." *Journal of the American Medical Association* 284, no. 10 (September 2000): 1247–55.

Singer, Peter. "Tuberculosis or Hair Loss? Refocusing Medical Research." *National Post* (fka *The Financial Post*). September 18, 2008, A17.

Skilton, Nyssa. "Science of Stymied Research." *Canberra Times*, January 3, 2009.

Sleight, Peter. "Debate: Subgroup Analyses in Clinical Trials: Fun to Look At—But Don't Believe Them!" *Current Control Trials in Cardiovascular Medicine* 1, no. 1 (2000): 25–27.

Smith, Richard. "Medical Journals and Pharmaceutical Companies: Uneasy Bedfellows." *British Medical Journal* 326 (2003): 1202.

Sox, Harold C., and Drummond Rennie. "Seeding Trials: Just Say 'No.'" *Annals of Internal Medicine* 149, no. 4 (August 2008): 279–80.

Specter, Michael. "Decoding Iceland." *The New Yorker*. January 18, 1999, 40–51.

Stein, Rob. "Critical Care Without Consent: Ethicists Disagree on Experimenting During Crises." *Washington Post*. May 27, 2007.

Stephens, Joe. "The Body Hunters: As Drug Testing Spreads, Profits and Lives Hang in Balance." *Washington Post*. December 17, 2000; A01. http://washingtonpost.com/wp-dyn/articles/A11939–2000Dec15.html.

Struewing, Jeffery P., Dvorah Abeliovich, Tamar Peretz, Naaman Avishai, Michael M. Kaback, Francis S. Collins, Lawrence C. Brody. "The Carrier Frequency of the *BRCA1* 185delAG Mutation Is Approximately 1 Percent in Ashkenazi Jewish Individuals." *Nature Genetics* 11 (1995): 198–200.

Sun, Marjorie. "Scientists Settle Cell Line Dispute: But Question of Claiming Ownership Based on Family Ties to Cell Donor Is Sidestepped." *Science* 220, no. 4595 (April 1983): 393.

Terry, Sharon F. "Learning Genetics." *Health Affairs* 22, no. 5 (2003): 166–71.

"Update: U. Cal. and the Hagiwaras Settle Ownership Dispute." *Biotechnology Law Report* 2, no. 3–4 (1983): 43.

U.S. Congress, U.S. Office of Technology Assessment. *Ownership of Human Tissues and Cells: New Developments in Biotechnology.* Washington, D.C.: U.S. Office of Technology Assessment, 2002.

U.S. Department of Justice. "Pair Charged with Theft of Trade Secrets from Harvard Medical School." Press release. June 19, 2002. http://www.usjoj.gov/criminal/cybercrime/zhuCharges.html.

Vallet, S., A. Palumbo, N. Raje, et al. "Thalidomide and Lenalidomide: Mechanism-Based Potential Drug Combinations." *Leukemia & Lymphoma* 49, no. 7 (2008): 1238–45.

Van Duppern, Dirk. "The Cost of the Newest Cancer Drugs." *The Lancet* 370, no. 9584 (July 2007): 317.

Varmus, Harold, MD, and David Satcher, MD, PhD. "Ethical Complexities of Conducting Research in Developing Countries." *New England Journal of Medicine* 337, no. 14 (October 1997): 1003–05.

Waldman, Amy. "Debts and Drought Drive India's Farmers to Despair." *New York Times*. June 6, 2004. Accessed February 3, 2011. http://www.nytimes.com/2004/06/06/world/debts-and-drought-drive-india-s-farmers-to-despair.html.

Walsh, John. "Public Attitude Toward Science Is Yes, But—." *Science* 15, no. 4530 (January 1982): 270–72.

Washington, Harriet A. "Flacking for Pharma: Big Pharmaceutical Companies Don't Just Compromise Doctors; They Also Undermine the Top Medical

Journals and Skew the Findings of Medical Research." *American Scholar* (Summer 2011): 2–14.

———. "Henrietta Lacks: An Unsung Hero." *Emerge Magazine* 6, no. 1 (October 1994): 29.

———. "Harvesting Organs from Silence." Vital Signs column. *Emerge Magazine.* January 31, 1995.

———. "Why Africa Fears Western Medicine." *New York Times.* July 31, 2007. http://www.nytimes.com/2007/07/31/opinion/31washington.html.

Weisfeldt, Myron, MD. Telephone interview with author. June 18, 2009.

Willman, David. "Case Study: Dr. P. Trey Sunderland III; $508,050 from Pfizer, But No 'Outside Positions to Note.'" *Los Angeles Times.* December 22, 2004.

———. "Physician Who Opposes Rezulin Is Threatened by FDA with Dismissal." *Los Angles Times.* March 17, 2000.

———. "The Rise and Fall of the Killer Drug Rezulin." *Los Angeles Times.* June 4, 2000.

———. "Strategy Developed to Get Latinos 'to Take the Risk.'" *Los Angeles Times.* June 30, 2002. http://articles.latimes.com/2002/jun/30/nation/na-rezside30.

———. "Diabetes Drug Rezulin Pulled Off the Market." *Los Angles Times.* March 22, 2000.

Wilson, Duff. "A Secret Cable Discusses Pfizer's Actions in Nigeria Case." *New York Times.* December 10, 2010. Accessed March 22, 2011. http://www.nytimes .com/2010/12/11/business/11pfizer.html.

———. "Child's Ordeal Shows Risks of Psychosis Drugs for Young." *New York Times.* September 1, 2010.

Winstein, Keith J. "NAACP Presses US on Heart Drug." *Wall Street Journal.* January 25, 2007.

Wolfe, Sidney M., MD. "Congressional Testimony on FDA Deficiences."

———. Public Citizen's Health Research Group. Survey cited in "Testimony Before the Congressional Agriculture—FDA Appropriations Subcommittee Hearing on Drug Safety (HRG Publication #1835)." February 27, 2008. http:// www.citizen.org/Page.aspx?pid=2339.

World Health Organization. "Making the Most of Existing Health Workers." *Working Together for Health: The World Health Report 2006.* Geneva: World Health Organization, 2006, 66–95.

Wright, J. M. "The Double-Edged Sword of COX-2 Selective NSAIDs." *Canadian Medical Association Journal* 167, no. 10 (2002): 1131–37.

Xie, W. L., J. G. Chipman, D. L. Robertson, R. L. Erikson, and D. L. Simmons. "Expression of a Mitogen-Responsive Gene Encoding Prostaglandin Synthase Is Regulated by mRNA Splicing." *Proceedings of the National Academy of Sciences* 88, no. 7 (April 1991): 12692–2696.

Yajnik, Juhi "University Sues Pfizer over COX-2 Research." *The Scientist.* October 27, 2006. Accessed April 29, 2011. http://www.the-scientist.com/news/ display/25408/.

Zamel, Noé. "In Search of the Genes of Asthma on the Island of Tristan da Cunha." *Canadian Respiratory Journal* 2, no. 1 (1995): 18–22.

Zhang, Jane. "Battle Erupts over Disclosure on Drug Prices." *Wall Street Journal.* August 19, 2006. Accessed September 1, 2009. http://online.wsj.com/article/ SB125064608529842021.html.

WEB SITES

"Against Leprosy." Thalidomide, Föreningen för de Neurosedynskadad/The Swedish Thalidomide Society. Accessed September 17, 2010. http://www .thalidomide.org/web/against-leprosy/.

Center for the Evaluation of Risks to Human Reproduction, National Toxicology Program, Department of Health and Human Services. "Thalidomide." Accessed September 17, 2010. http://cerhr.niehs.nih.gov/common/ thalidomide.html.

"Dr. Catalona's Response to Public Statements Posted by Washington University Regarding His Dispute with WU over Who Has Jurisdiction of Prostate Tissue and Blood Samples." William Catalona, MD. http://www.drcatalona .com/qanda.html.

Drug Industry Document Archive. http://dida.library.ucsf.edu.

GAVI Alliance. Advanced Market Commitments for Vaccines. Accessed August 7, 2010. http://www.vaccineamc.org/index.html.

GlaxoSmithKline plc. "Our Commitment to Fighting Malaria." Accessed April 25, 2010. http://www.gsk.com/media/malaria.htm.

Office of U.S. Global AIDS Coordinator, Bureau of Public Affairs, U.S. Department of State. The United States President's Plan for Emergency Aids Relief. http://www.pepfar.gov/about/index.htm.

"Skin Medica Pharmaceuticals." http://pharmaceuticals.skinmedica.com/vaniqa.

"Top Industries 2010," Lobbying Spending Database. Open Secrets.org/. Center for Responsive Politics. January 31, 2001. Accessed March 27, 2010. http://www .opensecrets.org/lobby/top.php?showYear=2009&indexType=i.

"Tristan da Cunha Website." Accessed April 24, 2009. http://www.tristandc.com/.

COURT CASES/STATUTES

Abdullahi et al v. Pfizer is available at http://www.pdf-searcher.com/Abdullahi-et -al-v.-Pfizer-Decision.html#. Accessed November 22, 2010.

"Anthrax Vaccinations Halted Again." United Press International, Military.com. October 28, 2004. http://www.military.com/NewsContent/0,13319,FL _anthrax_102804,00.html.

Association of Molecular Pathology et al. v. United States Patent and Trademark Office; Myriad Genetics et al. in United States District Court Southern District of New York, 26.

Atlantic Works v. Brady, 1017 U.S. 192, 200 (1883).

Bayer Healthcare AG et al. v. Thunder Bay Regional Health Sciences Centre, 2009. Ottawa Docket Summary, Summary of T-1450–07 Patent Infringement. December 17, 2009.

Bayh-Dole Act of 1980, U.S. Code 35 (February 2010), chap. 18, sec. 200 (December 12, 1980). The text of the Bayh-Dole Act is available at www.cptech.org/ip/ health/bd. Accessed May 2009.

Best Pharmaceuticals for Children Act, January 4, 2002 (Public Law No. 107-109). http://www.fda.gov/Drugs/DevelopmentApprovalProcess/Development Resources/ucm049876.htm.

Brotherton v. Cleveland. Nos. 94-3465; 96-3034, 96-3085, United States Court of Appeals for the Sixth Circuit 173 F.3d 552; 1999; 923 F.2d 482 (6th Cir. 1990).

Diamond v. Chakrabarty, 447 U.S. 303 (1980).

Doe v. Rumsfeld, 341 F. Supp. 2d 1, 6 (D.D.C. 2004). Preliminary Injunction, Civil Action No. 03–707 (EGS). December 22, 2003, http://www.cbsnews.com/htdocs/pdf/anthraxdocument.pdf.

Doris Jackson, in Her Own Right and as Administratrix of the Estate of Thomas Seaborn, Deceased v. City of Philadelphia and Hospital of the University of Pennsylvania, 26 Phila. Co. Rptr. 545, 551–52 (Pa. Com. Pl. 1993).

Economic Recovery Tax Act of 1981, Public Law 97–34, *U.S. Statues at Large* 95 (1981): 172.

Federal Technology Transfer Act of 1986 (Public Law 99–502).

Federal Trade Commission, et al. v. Watson Pharmaceuticals, Inc., et al. ("Generic Androgel"), CV-09–00598 (civil complaint filed in U.S. District Court for the Central District of California, January 27, 2009), FTC File No. 0710060.

Feres v. United States, 340 U.S. 135 (1950).

Florida v. Powell, Fla., 497 So.2d 1188 (1986).

Hon. George M. Marovich, United States District Court, Northern District of Illinois Eastern Division. Memorandum Opinion and Order, in *Re Northfield Laboratories, Inc.* No. 06 C 1493 Securities Litigation, 2.

Moore v. Regents of University of California, 51 Cal. 3d 120; 271 Cal. Rptr. 146; 793 P.2d 479 (1990).

Stevenson-Wydler Technology Innovation Act of 1980, U.S. Code 15 (February 2010), chap. 63, sec. 3701 (October 21, 1980).

United States v. Zhu, Case No. 02-M-0421 (June 19, 2002).

United States Supreme Court Reporter (Rochester, NY: Lawyers' Cooperative Publishing Co.), 27:439, 440.

U.S. Code of Federal Regulations (CFR 21 50.23 and 50.24).

Order in *Washington University v. Catalona*, No. 4:03CV1065 (E. Dist. Mo. April 14, 2006), on appeal Nos. 06–2286 & 06–2301 (8th Cir.); *Washington University v. Catalona*, 437 F. Supp. 2d 985 No Mo. 2006), affirmed by 490 F.3d 667 (8th Cir. 2007).

FILMS/BROADCASTS

The Infinite Mind: The Bipolar Child. LCMedia original broadcast. September 20, 2005. http://www.lcmedia.com/mind133.htm.

Seeds of Suicide: India's Desperate Farmers. Frontline, PBS, July 26, 2005. http://www.pbs.org/frontlineworld/rough/2005/07/seeds_of_suicid.html#.

US Medical Experiments Without Consent? ABC World News with Charles Gibson. May 27, 2007. http://abcnews.go.com/WNT/Video/playerIndex?id=3217758. Accessed February 25, 2010.

PERMISSIONS ACKNOWLEDGMENTS

Grateful acknowledgment is made to the following for permission to reprint previously published material:

Pages 105, 305: American Economic Association and Michael Kremer: Two figures from "Pharmaceuticals and the Developing World" by Michael Kremer from *Journal of Economic Perspectives*, 16:4, Fall 2002. Reprinted by permission of the American Economic Association and the author.

Page 87: Atlantic Information Services, Inc.: "Top 50 PBMs and Market Share by Annual Rx Volume" from *Drug Benefit News*, Volume 11, Issue 8, April 16, 2010, copyright © 2010 by Atlantic Information Services, Inc. Reprinted by permission of Atlantic Information Services, Inc.

Page 311: Aidan Hollis and Thomas Pogge: "World Pharmaceutical Market by Region in 2005" from *The Health Impact Fund: Making New Medicines Accessible for All* by Aidan Hollis and Thomas Pogge (Oslo, Norway, and New Haven, CT: Incentives for Global Health, 2008). Reprinted by permission of the authors.

Page 272: International Monetary Fund: "Table 2: Earlier Adoption" from the *Finance & Development* compilation, *Health and Development: Why Investing in Health Is Critical for Achieving Economic Development Goals*, copyright © 2004 by International Monetary Fund. Reprinted by permission of the International Monetary Fund.

Pages 71, 72, 76, 80, 112 The Kaiser Family Foundation: "Kaiser/HRET Survey of Employer-Sponsored Health Benefits, 2005–2010," Kaiser Slides, The Henry J. Kaiser Family Foundation & HRET, September 2010; "Percentage of Covered Workers Enrolled in a Plan with a General Annual Deductible of $1,000 or More for Single Coverage, by Firm Size, 2006–2010," Kaiser Slides, The Henry J. Kaiser Family Foundation &

HRET, September 2010; "Half Put Off Care Due to Cost," Kaiser Slides, The Henry J. Kaiser Family Foundation, March 2011; "Profitability of Pharmaceutical Manufacturers, 1995–2009," Kaiser Slides, The Henry J. Kaiser Family Foundation, September 2010; "U.S. Global Health Initiative (GHI) as a Share of the Federal Budget, FY 2012," Kaiser Slides, The Henry J. Kaiser Family Foundation, February 2011. Reprinted by permission of the Henry J. Kaiser Foundation.

INDEX